Financial Systems, Banking and Monetary Policy

Financial Systems, Banking and Monetary Policy

Ameila Fletcher

CLANRYE INTERNATIONAL
www.clanryeinternational.com

Clanrye International,
750 Third Avenue, 9th Floor,
New York, NY 10017, USA

ISBN: 978-1-64726-636-3

Cataloging-in-Publication Data

Financial systems, banking and monetary policy / Ameila Fletcher.
p. cm.
Includes bibliographical references and index.
ISBN 978-1-64726-636-3
1. Financial institutions. 2. Banks and banking. 3. Monetary policy. 4. Finance. I. Fletcher, Ameila.
HG1601 .F56 2023
332.1--dc23

For information on all Clanrye International publications
visit our website at www.clanryeinternational.com

CLANRYE INTERNATIONAL

Contents

Preface

A financial system refers to a complex and highly interlinked group of institutions, such as banks, NBFCs, insurance companies and stock exchanges that allow the exchange of funds. Lenders, borrowers and investors are the three primary participants in a financial system. These systems exist at local, national, and global levels. Banking is an industry that is made up of a large network of banks that provide various financial and non-financial services to individuals and businesses. Banks handle cash, credit and other financial transactions. They also issue loans on rates higher than the rate at which they accept deposits and thereby make a profit. Banks provide advances and loans in various forms such as cash credit, overdraft facility, call money and bill discounting. The central banks of different countries use the macroeconomic policy tool named monetary policy to influence the cost and availability of money supply in an economy. This book includes some of the vital pieces of work being conducted across the world, on various topics related to financial systems, banking and the monetary policy. Those in search of information to further their knowledge will be greatly assisted by it.

The information shared in this book is based on empirical researches made by veterans in this field of study. The elaborative information provided in this book will help the readers further their scope of knowledge leading to advancements in this field.

Finally, I would like to thank my fellow researchers who gave constructive feedback and my family members who supported me at every step of my research.

Ameila Fletcher

1

Understanding Money and Debt

Money, as the saying goes, makes the world go round. Everybody uses it; our modern societies would not function without it. Credit is just as crucial, as borrowing allows businesses to invest and consumers to buy goods and services today against their income tomorrow. But although money and debt are central in our societies and to our welfare, how they actually function is not easily understood.

The financial crisis of 2007–2009 and its social, economic and political consequences have led to debates in many countries about fundamental reform of the financial-monetary system. Citizens' initiatives – such as Positive Money in the United Kingdom – have pushed for a debate on a fundamentally different monetary system, called the sovereign money system. Along the same lines, Martin Wolf, one of the best-known columnists at the Financial Times, has called for an alternative monetary system. Economists at the International Monetary Fund (IMF) and the Bank of England (the UK central bank) are conducting research in this area. The Icelandic parliament has drawn up a proposal on this subject and in Switzerland a referendum was held in June 2018 on the similar Vollgeld initiative, in which 24% of voters supported it and 76% were opposed.[1]

In the Netherlands, the citizens' initiative *Ons Geld* ('Our Money') has placed monetary reform squarely on the public and political agenda. In 2015, the initiative – inspired by a popular theatre play that portrayed a financial system ridden by greed, elitism, instability and injustice – proposed placing money creation exclusively in public hands and gathered more than 120,000 signatures. In the ensuing Parliamentary debate in March 2016, a motion was adopted requesting the government to seek advice from the Netherlands Scientific Council for Government Policy (WRR) on the advantages and disadvantages of different monetary systems (see Box 1.1). The

The turnout was 33.8%, of which 24% supported the initiative and 76% opposed it.

WRR published this report (in Dutch) in January 2019. This book is the translation of this report.

Box 1.1 Motion Concerning a Request for Advice[2]

"The House

having heard the deliberations,

noting that a deeper investigation into the role and functions of banks in money creation and other functions is necessary;

considering that there is a need for a banking system with fewer risks for savers and the taxpayer;

requests the government to seek an advice from the Netherlands Scientific Council for Government Policy (WRR) on the operation of the monetary system and all forms of money creation by banks and to include in any event the advantages and disadvantages of alternative systems of money creation and the extent of seigniorage,

and returns to the day's agenda.

Omtzigt

Merkies"

The proposal for an alternative system casts light on a fact that will surprise many people, including many bank employees: most of our money is not created by governments or central banks, but by commercial banks. Banks create new money when they grant loans; while money is destroyed when loans are repaid (we explain this in Chap. 2). This means that the creation of money in our current system is inextricably linked to the creation of debt. Money and debt are in many ways two sides of the same coin. That means strong growth in debt – of concern to many international institutions and economists – cannot be seen in isolation from growth in the money supply.[3]

Before the financial crisis, many analysts paid scant attention to money and debt. Although by some measures the size of the financial sector had come to overshadow that of the real economy, many persisted to see money and debt as an insignificant 'veil' over economic activity, one without notable effects on the real economy. The financial sector generally did not feature in the macroeconomic models used for policy analyses (for example by the CPB, the Netherlands Bureau for Economic Policy Analysis). Economic models disregarding financial risks dominated education and policy discussions, while fundamental macroeconomic research devoted scant attention to the role of money and debt.[4]

---

[2]Parliamentary Papers (*Kamerstukken*) II, 2015–2016, 34346, no. 19. Our translation.

[3]In our current system, the creation of money is almost always tied to the creation of debt. However, the creation of debt is not necessarily tied to the creation of money.

[4]Bezemer (2018).

Citizens' initiatives are rightfully calling for greater attention to the role of money and debt in our societies which, as pillars of the financial system, have far-reaching effects. In what follows, we briefly introduce money and debt (Sects. 1.1 and 1.2) before discussing the role of trust (Sect. 1.3) and dynamism in the financial monetary system (Sect. 1.4). The introduction ends with an overview of the report (Sect. 1.5).

1.1 What Is Money?

There is no denying that views on money are as difficult to describe as shifting clouds (Schumpeter[5])

What is money? Is it 'the thing that makes the world go round' or 'the root of all evil'? Although money pervades our daily lives, it is much harder to define than we might expect. Even economists have difficulty identifying how and why money functions in capitalist economies.[6]

Money is first and foremost an (implicit) agreement between people and therefore a social construct.[7] An asset can only serve as money when people are confident that others will accept it as such.[8] The value of money is ultimately based not on the material of which it is made but on the confidence that it will be accepted by others.[9] Over the course of history, money has therefore taken many different forms: coins, shells, salt, coral, banknotes, and strings of ones and zeros in computer systems.

We take trust in money for granted to such an extent that we do not question where this trust comes from. Although largely a question of habit, trust in money does not appear out of thin air; it must be generated and maintained.[10] The mechanisms to do so depend on the system. In systems where money is made of materials that have value independent of their use as money – for example coins made of precious metals – these will include the verification of precious metal content, markings on coins attesting that they are genuine, and legal and statutory frameworks that for example criminalize counterfeiting. Such institutional frameworks are vital in systems such as ours where the material from which money is made has no value. For bank deposits, trust is generated by factors such as the deposit guarantee system, banking supervision and the availability of liquidity support for banks.

[5]Cited in Ingham (1996: 502).

[6]King (2016: 52). Part of the explanation for why economics continues to struggle with money may lie in the decades-long dominance of microeconomics in the discipline, which studies individual actors (people, businesses, households) making decisions about the allocation of scarce goods. Social relationships – where money gains significance – are secondary in microeconomics.

[7]Van Dalen & Klamer (2015: 14).

[8]Carruthers (2010).

[9]Boonstra (2018: 54).

[10]Giannini (2011: 14–15).

There are various theories on the origins of money.[11] The leading explanation is that money originated as a response to the inefficiencies of barter trade.[12] But as persuasive as this argument sounds, it is not backed by historical evidence.[13] Others argue that money has its origins in debt relationships when promissory notes became dissociated from the issuer and recipient and began circulating as a means of payment for goods and services.[14] Yet others emphasize the role of the state and religious authorities, with money originating from the taxes (or offerings) collected by these institutions.[15]

These historical accounts offer different perspectives on money, each with consequences for how money is understood. Those who see money as a response to the inefficiencies of bartering emphasize its spontaneous emergence; Carl Menger emphatically argued that '*no one invented money*'.[16] When the emergence of money is attributed to debt, the emphasis falls on social relationships, particularly between creditors and debtors.[17] Accounts that focus on the role of the state and religious authorities emphasize the role of these institutions in how money functions.

In economics, it is common to focus on the *functions* of money: as a means of payment, as a store of value, and as an accounting unit.[18] Money is, first and foremost, what society accepts as a general *means of payment*. It can be used to purchase products and services, pay wages, settle debts, buy financial instruments such as shares, and to pay tax. Money is thus (undifferentiated) purchasing power. As a means of payment, it is crucial that money can be transferred from one person to the next without affecting its utility; that it is divisible and can be used to pay different amounts; and that its value is sufficiently stable. People will accept a means of payment only if it can be used later to purchase something of comparable value.

Value stability gives rise to money's second function: as a means of saving (store of value). Since an asset can only serve as money if it largely retains its value over time, people may decide to keep money for a longer period. This in turn imposes

---

[11]Many authors have written incisively about the history of money. Adam Smith devoted a chapter of *Wealth of Nations* (1776) to the subject. Jevons treated the history of money in his 1875 *Money and the Mechanism of Exchange*, as did Carl Menger in 'On the origins of money' in 1892. Knapp wrote an alternative history of money in 1905 with *The State Theory of Money*, as did Mitchell-Innes in two articles in *The Banking Law Journal* in 1913 and 1914. Keynes considered the history of money in his 1930 *A Treatise on Money*. More recent publications include Ingham's 2004 *The Nature of Money*, Ferguson's 2008 *The Ascent of Money: A Financial History of the World*, and Graeber's 2011 *Debt: The First 5000 Years*. Detailed discussion of the various theories on the origins of money is beyond the scope of this report.

[12]Jones (1976); Van Dixhoorn (2013b; Goodhart & Jensen (2015: 3).

[13]Bezemer (2012); Humphrey (1985); Ryan-Collins (2015).

[14]Mitchell-Innes (1913); Wray (2004); Graeber (2011).

[15]Van Dixhoorn (2013b).

[16]Menger (1892).

[17]Wray (2004).

[18]Van Dalen & Klamer (2015); Van Dixhoorn (2013b); Burgess & Janssen (2007); Boonstra (2015).

another requirement on money: it must not be easily debased. While shares, bonds, jewellery or real estate can all serve as a means of saving, money is unique in that it can be used almost immediately as a means of payment. In the jargon, money is a highly 'liquid' means of saving, whereas jewellery is not. Saving by means of money also means more certainty – or at least running different risks – than by, for example, owning shares.

Third, money serves as a measuring or accounting unit, allowing comparisons between things that are completely different. Although a loaf of bread and an IPhone have little in common, their price can easily be compared. It also allows comparisons at the macro level, for example between countries' gross domestic product. This is again associated with money's first function: as a general means of payment, it is essential that services, products, property, financial instruments and taxes can be expressed in the same units.[19]

In this report, we consider money to be what is generally accepted as a means of payment.[20] On the basis of this definition, money today mainly consists of cash (notes and coins) and the instantly available funds in bank payment and savings accounts. There are also forms of quasi-money (such as deposits fixed for longer periods) which may or may not count as money. Even more broadly, certain short-term debts sometimes count as money.

The statistics we refer to in this report are based on three different monetary aggregates.[21] M1 is the narrowest definition of the money supply: it includes all cash and demand deposits at banks. M2 and M3 are wider definitions that include savings and for example shares in money market funds (see Table 1.1). These broader definitions include financial instruments that are, strictly speaking, not a means of payment but which can be easily turned into a means of payment with no or hardly any loss in value.

The current broad monetary aggregate (M3) comprises 7% cash, 39% bank deposits that can be used to make payments (deposits in payment accounts) and 51% deposits with a maturity of less than two years or a notice period of less than three months (savings deposits). Other financial resources make up 3% of M3 (see Fig. 1.1).

These official definitions of the money supply can differ from what actually functions as money. Innovations in the financial world can lead to new products that function as money or which can easily be converted into money. The boundaries

[19]A currency other than the one used for payment can function as an accounting unit. In the early 1990s, many products in Moscow supermarkets were priced in Deutschmarks. At the till, customers had to pay in roubles at the exchange rate of the day.

[20]This boundary can be murky. We cannot unequivocally answer whether a local Rotterdam currency such as the 'Dam' should be seen as money. Some places accept it, many others do not.

[21]Statisticians also have a fourth definition of the money supply: M0. Unlike M1, it comprises total cash and central bank reserves, designated collectively as the basic money supply. In our current system, central bank reserves do not count as money but as deposits held by commercial banks. We return to this in Chap. 2.

Table 1.1 Monetary aggregates

	M1	M2	M3
Cash	•	•	•
Bank deposits which can be used immediately to make payments	•	•	•
Deposits with a maturity of less than two years		•	•
Deposits with a notice period of less than three months		•	•
Repos[a]			•
Shares/units in money market funds			•
Debt securities with a maturity of up to two years			•

Repo stands for repurchase agreement. In a repo, a party sells a financial asset (such as a government bond) to another party with a promise to buy it back at a later time. The seller gains access to cash for a specified period, while the purchaser holds the financial instrument. For institutional investors, it is a way to 'park' their money relatively securely. Since the deposit guarantee system does not cover pension funds, a repo is a way to put aside large sums for a certain time against collateral

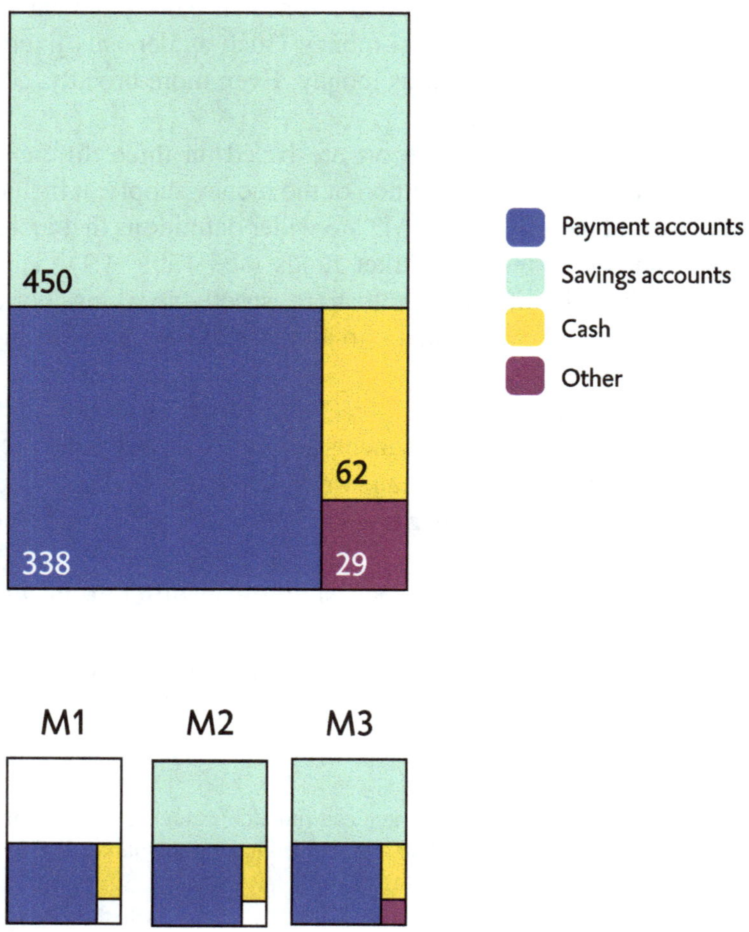

Fig. 1.1 Composition of the money supply
September 2018, € billions
Source: DNB table 5.4

around what constitutes money are thus fluid and far from clear-cut, as we see in the emergence of cryptocurrencies such as Bitcoin (see Box 1.2)

Box 1.2 Is Bitcoin Money?

So-called 'cryptocurrencies' – digital currencies generated by cryptography, the writing of computer codes – have recently attracted a great deal of attention. The best-known among them, Bitcoin, was launched in October 2008 just after the fall of Lehman Brothers. Bitcoin's developers hoped it would become an alternative to dominant forms of money that depend on governments, central banks and commercial banks. Trust in Bitcoin would not depend on trust in these institutions but (so it was claimed) on objective, rational, incorruptible mathematical calculations in a decentralized, shared and publicly accessible accounting system.

Is Bitcoin money? As things stand now, it does not fulfil money's three functions as outlined above. The ability to use Bitcoin as a means of payment remains extremely limited[22]; its value is volatile, having risen to over $20,000 in December 2017 before plunging to around $6,000 in the summer of 2018. This volatility makes Bitcoin unsuitable as a means of saving, although not as a means of speculation.[23] Finally, it has limited use as an accounting unit as only a handful of products and services quote their prices in Bitcoins. Anyone who wants to use Bitcoins needs a real-time app to see how much they are worth in dollars or euros.

Cryptocurrencies remain in their infancy; we do not know what the future has in store. Nevertheless, the Bitcoin example reveals the difficulties of creating a stable currency. The limited number of Bitcoins that can enter into circulation and decentralized verification techniques do not guarantee a stable and reliable currency. Mathematical methods for generating trust currently have clear limits. Trust in a currency is largely based on its stability. The euro, the dollar and many other currencies are backed by institutions whose explicit purpose is to provide guarantees and maintain stability. The question is whether a cryptocurrency without such institutional backing can ever become an alternative to these forms of money.

1.2 What Is Debt?

Although the role of debt in the economy is frequently discussed, the precise meaning of the term is often far from clear. Discussions often become confused as debt is framed not only in economic but in moral terms.[24] This applies particularly to

[22]Betlem (2017).

[23]Richter (2017); DNB (2018).

[24]Graeber (2011: 4).

Dutch and German, where the word *schuld* is used both for an obligation to another party (debt) and for responsibility for culpable acts (guilt). Many religions view debt as pernicious for both lenders and borrowers. The Bible states: "Let love be your only debt" (Romans 13:8) and "The borrower is servant to the lender" (Proverbs 22:7). Islam prohibits interest, which in some interpretations is equated with usury.[25] In Europe, interest was considered pernicious for many centuries.

At the same time, investments facilitated by debt are crucial for economic development. According to Ferguson, credit and debt rival all other technological innovations in fuelling the development of our civilization.[26] Debt enables the borrower to anticipate future income from employment, goods or capital and to invest it or spend it on consumption. Someone can buy an ice-maker with the earnings he expects to generate in the future from selling ice creams. A farmer can borrow on the strength of a future harvest to buy fertilizer and pay wages. A loan can be used to pay for training to improve one's employment prospects.

Debt is essentially a non-simultaneous exchange between two parties. Graeber describes debt as an exchange that has not been brought to completion.[27] It can be a social exchange, for example when you help someone to move house and expect that person to help you move house later. In a financial exchange, you borrow money that you will repay later, or buy a product that you will pay for later. Since one side of the exchange (granting the loan) takes place at a different time than the other side (repaying the loan), debt always runs the risk that something happens in the intervening period that prevents it from being repaid. The granting and drawing of a loan therefore require mutual trust and confidence in the future, captured by the word 'creditor' and its German equivalent *Gläubiger*.

> *The old saying holds. Owe your banker £1,000 and you are at his mercy; owe him £1 million and the position is reversed* (Keynes[28])

Although debt is generally entered into voluntarily, there are exceptions. A debt to the tax office, for example, does not emerge from a voluntary agreement between two parties. But even when the debt is incurred voluntarily, the two parties often have unequal positions. Laws therefore protect households from usury; governments prescribe maximum interest rates. Such safeguards have been in place for centuries and remain in place today.[29]

In principle, all debts must be repaid. But there are social, economic and practical reasons to place limits on this obligation. Although infamous debtors' prisons such as Marshalsea in London, the setting for Charles Dickens' Little Dorrit, no longer

[25]Visser (2009: 174).

[26]Ferguson (2008: 2).

[27]Graeber (2011).

[28]Quoted in Moggridge (1992: 756).

[29]The current maximum rate is equivalent to the statutory interest rate plus 12% on an annual basis. See: https://www.afm.nl/nl-nl/consumenten/themas/producten/lenen/max-rente.

exist, debtors can still be temporarily detained if they fail to repay.[30] The Netherlands was the first country in Europe to decriminalize bankruptcy and to introduce a more or less orderly procedure for it. A *Desolate Boedelkamer* (office of the commissioners for bankruptcies) where bankruptcies could be settled – and debtors could make a fresh start – was created in Amsterdam City Hall in 1627.[31] This is how Rembrandt was able to start painting again, rather than landing in prison or seeking sanctuary in the free town of Vianen. There is thus a socially recognised limit to the repayability of debts, as the lender accepts some degree of risk.[32]

The Dutch word for debt, *schuld*, has multiple meanings, which sometimes causes confusion. The meanings range from a moral debt or an abstract obligation to a specific debt and a contract enforceable by law. The many different forms that debt can take also explain the confusion as to whether money is always debt (see Box 1.3).

Box 1.3 Is Money Always Debt?

A question that often arises when discussing alternative money creation systems is whether money is always debt. In the current system, money is created when a loan is granted. The bulk of our money (bank deposits) is actually debt owed by the bank to account holders. Money is therefore inseparably linked to debt. But although some authors have claimed that 'all money is debt'[33], this is not necessarily the case. Our cash – coins and banknotes – does not constitute debt; one cannot exchange this money at the central bank for gold or anything else.[34] Although central banks record cash in their accounts as debt, it is to a certain extent an arbitrary choice to record money as debt and not as equity, which also appears on the liabilities side of the balance sheet.

Debt can serve as money if it is sufficiently divisible and transferable. But not all debt serves as money and not all forms of money are debt. This does not alter the fact that money is always a claim on current and future production. As newly generated money increases this claim, the unlimited creation of money is not without consequences (due to the risk of higher inflation).

---

[30]In 2013 there were around 22,000 cases of detention (involving around 7,000 unique individuals). In 2014 there were approximately 41,000 cases (WRR 2017: 155).

[31]Frederik (2012).

[32]Graeber (2011: 3).

[33]Van Dixhoorn (2013a); Bjerg (2015); Wray (2014); Boonstra (2015).

[34]Until 1971 there was an indirect link to gold. Guilders could be exchanged for dollars and dollars could in theory be exchanged for gold. See Chap. 3 for a detailed description.

1.3 The Importance of Trust

We have already alluded to trust a number of times. Trust is crucial for the functioning of money and for the contracting of loans. The financial crisis, however, has shaken this trust.[35] *Ons Geld* – the widely supported Dutch citizens' initiative advocating for an alternative system – can be read as an expression of mistrust in the current system, as can the popularity of cryptocurrencies.

Dutch citizens have less trust in the banking system than in the country's other institutions. Strikingly, highly educated people have less trust in the banking system than their less educated peers. This is unusual; the opposite generally applies to trust in institutions (see Fig. 1.2).

In a similar vein, a survey by the Dutch central bank (DNB) found that economists have less trust than the public at large in the stability of the financial system (see Fig. 1.3). Trust was correlated with the degree to which respondents believed regulations have been sufficiently tightened: respondents with less trust in the stability of the system were also more sceptical about the tightening of the rules.[36]

There has recently been much discussion about trust in the financial sector. The Dutch Banking Association (NVB) has launched a Banking Confidence Monitor,[37] universities have organized debates, and the finance minister has written a Letter to Parliament on trust in the financial sector.[38]

Trust in the financial monetary system involves many interlinked forms of trust: trust in policymakers (politics, central bank), trust in banks and other financial

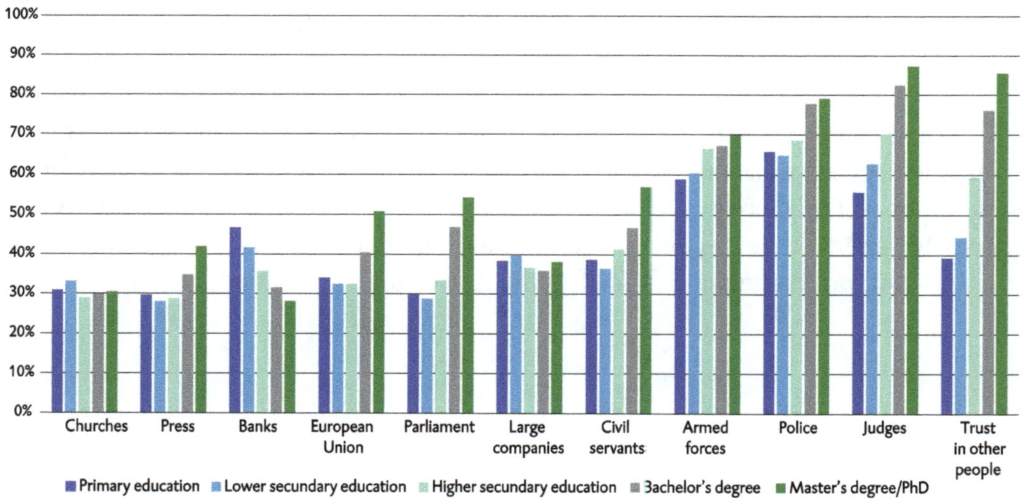

Fig. 1.2 Trust in institutions
Source: CBS (2017)

[35]See for example DNB (2015).

[36]DNB (2016).

[37]See for example NVB (2016).

[38]Letter to Parliament from the Minister of Finance, 21 June 2016.

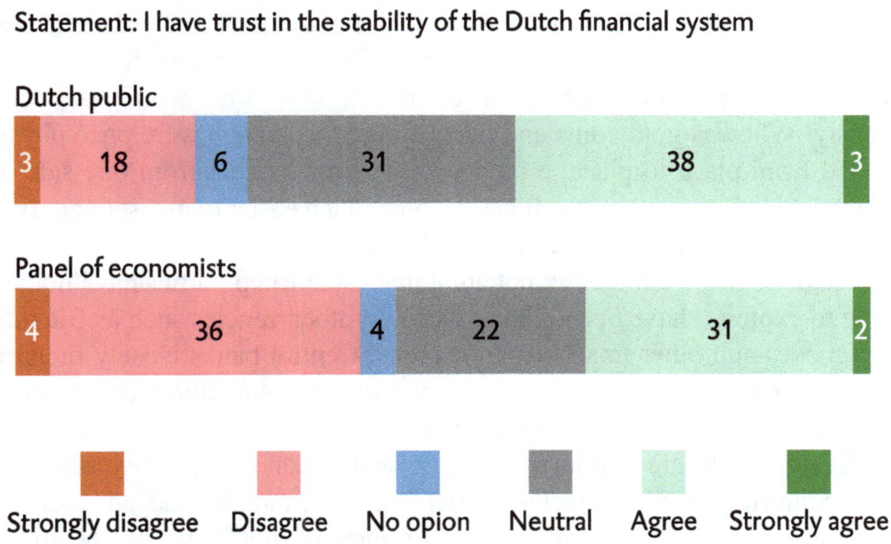

Fig. 1.3 Trust in the stability of the Dutch financial system
Source: DNB (2016)

institutions, trust in bankers, money and the future, and interpersonal trust. Trust in money crucially depends on institutions such as the central bank and the deposit guarantee system, and thus trust in these institutions. Financial crises not only reduce trust in financial institutions but are associated with the decline of interpersonal trust more generally.[39]

Trust cannot be enforced; it must ultimately be given. Trust must be earned through proven reliability, by meeting justified expectations. Trust also depends on the ability to express and discuss dissatisfaction.[40] This report will consider these two aspects of trust, gauging the reliability of the system in terms of its economic contribution, stability and fairness. Influence and legitimacy are further factors to consider when addressing dissatisfaction.

1.4 The Dynamism of the Financial Monetary System

Money and debt are part of a larger and changing financial monetary system comprised of banks, the central bank, but also public authorities, pension funds, insurance companies and shadow banks[41] play a role in it. Just as the assets used as money change over time, the financial monetary system does not stand still.

---

[39]Cruijsen et al. (2013).

[40]Nooteboom (2017).

[41]Shadow banks are institutions outside the regular banking system that undertake banking activities such as lending based on short term debt (WRR 2016: 84), but they cannot create deposit money.

Industrialization and globalization have had major consequences for the operation of our current system (we describe this in Chap. 3), as have technological developments. The speed at which money can be moved around the world has increased enormously. Whereas gold coins and paper bills of exchange were once physically transported from place to place, a payment can now be sent from one side of the world to the other in milliseconds. It has become much easier to invest not only in the local bakery but also in businesses in Brazil or South Africa.

New technologies – containing potential that established parties have not always been able to exploit – have opened the way to cryptocurrencies such as Bitcoin (see Box 1.2 above) and other financial innovations. Central banks closely monitor the development of new technologies, which may support innovation and better financial services but also pose risks to public interests such as the stability of the financial system. Central banks are also interested in how they can harness new technologies; in many countries, they conduct research on, for example, the advantages and disadvantages of a central bank digital currency (CBDC). While the monetary system will continue to change, precisely how is impossible to predict (see Box 1.4). "*The issue is shaping up to be every bit as vexed as those of robots and jobs,*" says Andrew Haldane, Chief Economist of the Bank of England.[42] "*Passions around cashless societies run high. If nothing else, this tells us that money is, always has been and always will be much more than a cryptographic code; it is a social convention.*"

Box 1.4 Fintech as a Revolution?

There is a lot of talk about "fintech", but what exactly is it? The then Managing Director of the IMF, Christine Lagarde, described it as "*the collection of new technologies whose applications may affect financial services, including artificial intelligence, big data, biometrics, and distributed ledger technologies such as blockchains*".[43] In the discussion about fintech, two questions are central: (1) what will fintech mean for financial *services*? and (2) what will it mean for financial *service providers*? Although these questions are related, the discussion will be clearer if they are discussed separately.

Payments, savings, finance and insurance are seen as the four classic functions of the financial sector. IMF researchers have added a fifth: advice on these four functions. In all five areas, there are new initiatives and applications of new technologies.[44] Debates often cite the power of distributed ledger technologies (blockchain) which can be used, for example, to create more decentralized payment architectures. Other developments include the use of machine learning and algorithms to automate trade in financial products

(continued)

[42]Foreword to Birch (2017).

[43]Lagarde (2017).

[44]He et al. (2017).

Box 1.4 (continued)

(high-frequency trading) and enable insurers to assess claims. It remains difficult to gauge the role of fintech and the potential of these new services.[45]

What will these innovations mean for existing financial institutions? Small fintech players do not currently pose real threats to large banks, which enjoy strong market positions due to their banking licences, size, expertise, skills and implicit and explicit guarantees. But when they are acquired by large banks, fintech players can spur innovation by their new owners. The question is what will happen when 'bigtech' companies such as Amazon, Apple, Facebook and Google begin offering financial services.[46] While Amazon has launched *Amazon Cash* and Google offers *Google Pay* in many countries, these developments will not necessarily intensify competition. Existing banks may choose, for example, to set up partnerships with these major entrants into the financial market.[47]

But the fact remains that today's large banks cannot take their future relevance for granted. Will there be a transition to greater diversity and reduced scale, a consolidation of the existing giants, or their absorption into bigtech companies such as Facebook, Amazon and Apple?[48] In any case, developments will be driven by a wide range of factors, including laws and regulations. Continuous political oversight is therefore essential.

Current developments and uncertainties are not all due to fintech; we are in unfamiliar terrain in other ways too. Debt as a percentage of GDP has never been higher.[49] Monetary policy is in uncharted waters. The European Central Bank's policy interest rate has been close to zero for many years and it has bought up unprecedented amounts of government and corporate bonds. How we would extricate ourselves from this unconventional monetary policy remains unclear – or, indeed, whether the current situation is the new normal which we have yet to grasp. Some companies and governments (including the Dutch government) can now issue bonds with negative interest rates. This means that the government and some companies actually *receive* interest from their lenders, illustrating in stark terms the uncertainty and uniqueness of the current situation. The current coronavirus crisis – which erupted after publication of the Dutch report and is therefore not discussed in this translation – only reinforces these uncertainties. In our complex and turbulent times, it is questionable whether existing solutions will work.

[45]Bijlsma and Van Veldhuizen (2016).

[46]In July 2019 (after the Dutch version of this report was published in the Netherlands) Facebook announced the development of a new cryptocurrency: Libra.

[47]Boot (2018).

[48]Bijlsma and Van Veldhuizen (2016).

[49]A further factor in the Netherlands is the pile of pension assets. These assets cannot be accessed directly in a crisis.

1.5 Overview of the Report

The Dutch government requested the WRR to issue an opinion on "the operation of the monetary system and all forms of money creation by banks and to include in any event the advantages and disadvantages of alternative systems of money creation and the extent of seigniorage". The present report is the response to this request.

In our current system, money is inextricably linked to debt and the operation of banks. This means changes affecting the monetary system will also inevitably lead to changes in credit and the financial landscape. The concerns that underpin the citizens' initiative *Ons Geld* ('Our Money') go further than simply safeguarding money and payments; they also concern the role of debt and banks in society. This report on money therefore also devotes attention to debt and the broader operations of the financial monetary system.

We first consider the mechanics of the current monetary system (Chap. 2), discussing how money is created and the main driving forces and constraints in money creation. While banks play an important role in our monetary system by creating new money when they lend, they do not do so in a vacuum: banks are influenced by the demand for loans, assessments of risks, financial regulation and monetary policy. In Chap. 3, we trace the development of the monetary system since the 19th century, examining the different forms money has taken over time and illustrating a constant dilemma between the need to maintain currency stability and the need for monetary flexibility.

In order to gauge the advantages and disadvantages of an alternative system of money creation, Chap. 4 focuses on key problems in the *current* system as they bear on four goals: economic contribution, stability, fairness and legitimacy. Chapter 5 then discusses an *alternative* monetary system which we refer to as the *sovereign money system.* This essentially involves a system in which money is directly or indirectly in public hands. Although more radical alternatives – such as abolishing national currencies or systems in which money is once again linked to a precious metal – have been proposed, these have remained largely undeveloped and insignificant in current debates. We thus focus on the sovereign money system and its variants. The potential advantages and disadvantages of this alternative system are analysed in Chap. 6.

The final part of the report focuses on avenues to address underlying problems, beginning with a discussion of the lessons drawn from the crisis and the main policy reforms in the current system (Chap. 7). The report ends with conclusions and recommendations (Chap. 8).

Bibliography

Betlem, R. (2017, July 14). Bitcoin? Is dat een nieuwe betaalkaart? *Het Financieele Dagblad.* https://fd.nl/weekend/1209813/bitcoin-is-dat-een-nieuwe-betaalkaart

Bezemer, D. (2012). Lessen uit de crisis: Waarom we opnieuw moeten nadenken over geld. *TPEdigitaal, 6*(3/4), 63–73.

Bezemer, D. (2018, March 21). Tien jaar later. *De Groene.*https://www.groene.nl/artikel/tien-jaar-later-2018-03-21

Bijlsma, M., & van Veldhuizen, S. (2016). Verandert fintech de financiële sector. *ESB.*

Birch, D. (2017). *Before babylon, beyond bitcoin. From money that we understand to money that understands us.* London: London Publishing Partnership.

Bjerg, O. (2015). How is bitcoin money? *Theory, Culture & Society, 33*(1), 53–72.

Boonstra, W. W. (2015). *Hoe werkt geldschepping?* Utrecht: Rabobank.

Boonstra, W. W. (2018). *Geld; Wat is het, wat doet het, waar komt het vandaag?* Amsterdam: VU University Press.

Boot, A. (2018). Bancaire strategie in tijden van fintech. *ESB, 4766*, 39–43.

Burgess, S., & Janssen, N. (2007). Proposals to modify the measurement of broad money in the United Kingdom: A user consultation. *Bank of England Quarterly Bulletin Q3.*

Carruthers, B. G. (2010). The sociology of money and credit. In *The handbook of economic sociology* (pp. 355–378). Princeton: Princeton University Press.

CBS. (2017). *Vertrouwen in mensen en in organisaties.* The Hague: CBS.

DNB. (2015). *Staat van het toezicht 2015.* Amsterdam: De Nederlandsche Bank.

DNB. (2016). *DNBulletin: Achterblijvend vertrouwen onderstreept noodzaak macroprudentieel beleid.* https://www.dnb.nl/nieuws/nieuwsoverzicht-en-archief/dnbulletin-2016/dnb346228.jsp#

DNB. (2018). *Jaarverslag 2017.* Amsterdam: DNB.

Ferguson, N. (2008). *The ascent of money: A financial history of the world.* New York: Penguin Putnam.

Frederik, J. (2012). *De geschiedenis van het 'banqueroet'.* Follow the Money, https://www.ftm.nl/artikelen/de-geschiedenis-van-het-banqueroet?share=1

Giannini, C. (2011). *The age of central banks.* Cheltenham/Northampton: Edward Elgar.

Graeber. (2011). *Debt: The first 5000 years.* Brooklyn: Melville House Publishing.

He, D., Leckow, R., Haksar, V. et al. (2017). *Fintech and financial services: Initial considerations* (IMF Staff Discussion Note SDN/17/05).

Humphrey, C. (1985). Barter and economic disintegration. *Man, 20*, 48–72.

Ingham, G. (1996). Money is a social relation. *Review of Social Economy, 54*(4), 507–529.

Ingham, G. (2004). *The nature of money.* Cambridge: Polity Press.

Jones, R. A. (1976). The origin and development of media of exchange. *Journal of Political Economy, 84*(4, Part 1), 757–775.

King, M. (2016). *The end of alchemy: Money, banking and the future of the global economy.* New York: W.W. Norton & Company.

Lagarde, C. (2017). *Fintech: Capturing the benefits.* Avoiding the Risks, https://blogs.imf.org/2017/06/20/fintech-capturing-the-benefits-avoiding-the-risks/

Menger, C. (1892). *The origins of money.* Auburn: Ludwig von Mises Institute.

Mitchell-Innes, A. (1913, May). What is Money? *The Banking Law Journal*, 377–408.

Moggridge, D. (1992). *Maynard Keynes. An economist's biography.* Abingdon: Routledge.

Nooteboom, B. (2017). *Vertrouwen. Opening naar een veranderende wereld.* Utrecht: Klement.

NVB. (2016). *Banking confidence monitor.* Available at: www.nvb.nl.

Richter, W. (2017, July 11). *Cryptocurrencies collapsed.* http://wolfstreet.com/2017/07/11/what-is-going-on-with-crypto-currencies-collapse/

Ryan-Collins, J. (2015). *Is monetary financing inflationary? A case study of the Canadian economy, 1935–75* (Levy Institute Working Paper, No. 84).

van Dalen, H., & Klamer, A. (2015). *Geld.* Amsterdam: Amsterdam University Press.

van Dixhoorn, C. (2013a). *Full Reserve Banking: An analysis of four monetary reform plans.* Utrecht: Sustainable Finance Lab.

van Dixhoorn, C. (2013b). *The 'Nature' of money: Does our current money system hinder sustainable development?* Master thesis Utrecht University.

van der Cruijsen, C., de Haan, J., & Jansen, D.-J. (2013). Trust and financial crisis experiences. *SSRN Electronic Journal.*

Visser, H. (2009). *Islamitisch bankieren: financieren met hindernissen.* Available at: http://www.verenigingrimo.nl/wp/wp-content/uploads/Recht-van-de-Islam-23_11-Visser.pdf

Wray, L. R. (2004). *The credit money and state money approaches* (CFEPS Working Paper, no. 32). Kansas City: CFEPS.

Wray, L. R. (2014). *From the state theory of money to modern money theory: An alternative to economic orthodoxy* (Working Paper, Levy Economics Institute, No. 792).

WRR. (2016). *Samenleving en financiële sector in evenwicht*, WRR report nr. 96, Den Haag: Sdu Uitgevers.

WRR. (2017). *Weten is nog geen doen. Een realistisch perspectief op redzaamheid*, WRR report nr. 97. Amsterdam: Amsterdam University Press.

2

Banks, Monetary Policy and Money Creation

This chapter describes how money is created. Many people mistakenly believe that money can only be created by governments or central banks.[1] But this is not the case: money today is mostly – but not exclusively – created by commercial banks. Section 2.1 describes the ways in which this is done. Section 2.2 outlines the forces that drive and constrain this means of money creation. Section 2.3 discusses the role of monetary policy. Section 2.4 closes the chapter with a brief conclusion.

2.1 Banks and Money Creation

The bulk of today's money supply consists of bank deposits (money in payment and savings accounts); only a small proportion consists of cash.[2] Understanding how money is created thus entails focusing on the creation of bank deposits. To understand how this works, we first examine the concept of the bank balance sheet (Box 2.1).

---

[1]In a survey conducted by Motivaction on behalf of Sustainable Finance Lab, 23,000 respondents in 20 countries were asked who they thought creates the bulk (over 95%) of our money. 20% of respondents thought it was banks. A much larger proportion believed money was created by the central bank or the government (27% and 22% respectively). The remainder responded 'Don't know'. Dutch respondents were divided as follows: banks 12%; central bank 22%; government 23%; don't know 43%.

[2]Cash consists of banknotes and coins. Banknotes are produced on behalf of the ECB and printed at various sites in Europe. Coins are struck on behalf of national governments. The creation of banknotes and coins does not alter the size of the money supply since this money only enters the economy when people convert their bank deposits into cash.

Fig. 2.1 A simplified bank balance sheet

Box 2.1 The Bank Balance Sheet

A bank's operations are best illustrated through its balance sheet. To keep it simple, imagine the balance sheet as a balanced pair of scales. On the left side are the bank's assets; on the right are its liabilities (see Fig. 2.1). The assets generate income for the bank and are funded by its liabilities. The simplified balance sheet below shows only the bank's main assets and liabilities.

On the left side are the bank's assets. These consist of loans granted by the bank including mortgages and corporate loans. These loans are an important source of income but may also lead to losses. The bank also holds marketable financial assets such as government bonds. These assets usually generate less income than loans but are easier to sell to other parties. Finally, the bank holds central bank reserves, used as a means of payment between banks and between banks and the central bank. This includes cash, which for a bank is interchangeable with central bank reserves.

On the right side of the balance sheet are the bank's liabilities, consisting of debts and equity. The debts include the balances of customers' payment and savings accounts. Banks are thus indebted to their account holders. Although savings accounts are similar to payment accounts, there are some differences.

(continued)

Box 2.1 (continued)
In normal times, the bank pays higher interest on savings accounts, but balances on these accounts cannot be used to make direct payments.[3] The bank also has debts to other banks and the central bank and issues bonds.

Finally, there is the bank's equity. Equity can be calculated by subtracting debts from assets. It is the money that the shareholders have invested in the bank, plus retained profits and minus any losses. Equity is important because it can absorb losses.

The two sides of the balance sheet are by definition always equal. If someone sells a €100 government bond to the bank, the bank's financial assets increase by €100 on the left side of the balance sheet and the seller's payment account balance rises by €100 on the right side. If a financial asset held by the bank (such as a government bond) falls in value and all other things remain equal, the bank's equity decreases by the same amount. If a bank suffers losses on its assets (left side) to the extent that equity disappears (right side), it is technically bankrupt.

So how is money created? While many people believe banks first raise money and then lend it to others, this is not how it works in the current system.[4] When a borrower obtains a loan from a bank, the bank simultaneously grants the loan and creates a bank deposit (the money). Banks thus create new money when granting loans.

We can explain this by using a simplified bank balance sheet (see Fig. 2.2) and an example. Suppose Anne wants to borrow €5,000 from the bank to buy a car. Before the bank grants a loan, it first checks her creditworthiness. If the bank grants the loan, it increases Anne's payment account balance by €5,000, thereby creating money. This new money is a debt that the bank owes Anne. At the same time, Anne incurs a debt of the same amount to the bank. This debt is added to the bank's assets on the left side of the balance sheet, while the amount on the payment account is added to the liabilities on the right side. The balance sheet remains in balance, but both sides are now longer. We say that the bank's balance sheet has increased.

In this type of money creation, new deposit money and a new loan are always created at the same time. Conversely, deposit money is destroyed when someone repays a debt to the bank. When Anne repays €500 to the bank, her bank deposit decreases by €500 (right side) and the bank's asset (the loan) also decreases by €500. Once again the balance sheet remains in balance (see Fig. 2.3). The repayment decreases the balance sheet.

---

[3]Although with online banking the practical difference in the case of some savings accounts is only a few seconds.

[4]At any rate, not in the case of banks licensed as monetary institutions. Banks that are not authorized to offer payment accounts must raise money first.

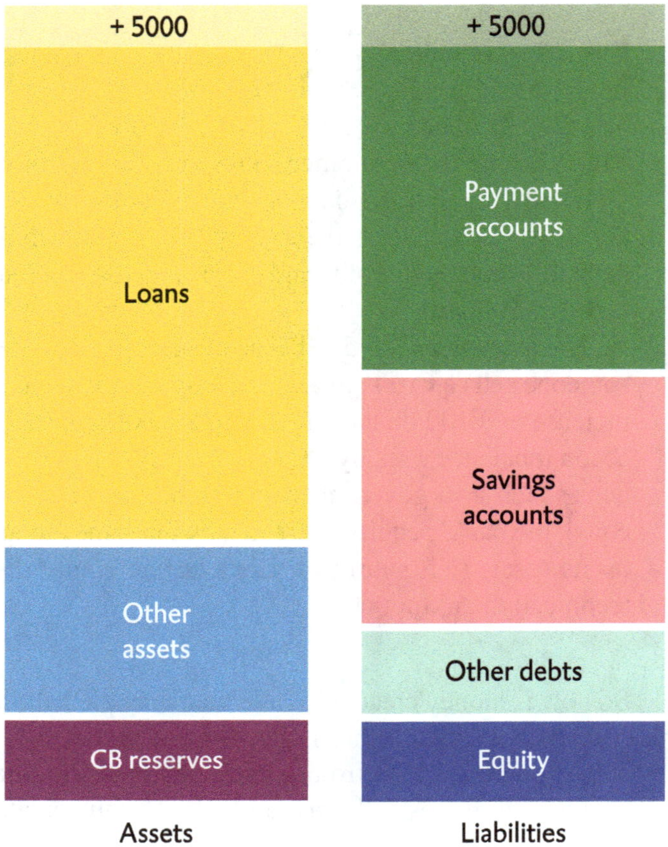

Fig. 2.2 Creation of deposit money by bank lending (This is a simplified bank balance sheet. It contains the same elements as the balance sheet in Fig. 2.1).

In addition to this form of money creation, money is also created or destroyed when banks buy or sell financial assets – for example government bonds, corporate bonds or shares – to or from non-banks. When Thomas sells the bank a government bond, the bank credits his payment account. The bank now has a new asset on the left side (the government bond) and a new liability on the right side (Thomas's higher bank balance). This increases the money supply. In the reverse case – when Thomas buys a government bond from the bank – a sum is debited from his account and an amount of deposit money is destroyed. But this way in which money is created and destroyed accounts for much less than the granting and repayment of loans.[5]

2.1.1 Electronic Payments and Cash Withdrawals

To understand how money is created, we also need to examine payments between account holders of different banks. In our example, Anne borrowed €5,000 from

[5]McLeay et al. (2014). A bank also creates money when it buys products or services and when employees are paid. These payments are made from income and are therefore a charge against profits. This affects equity on the balance sheet.

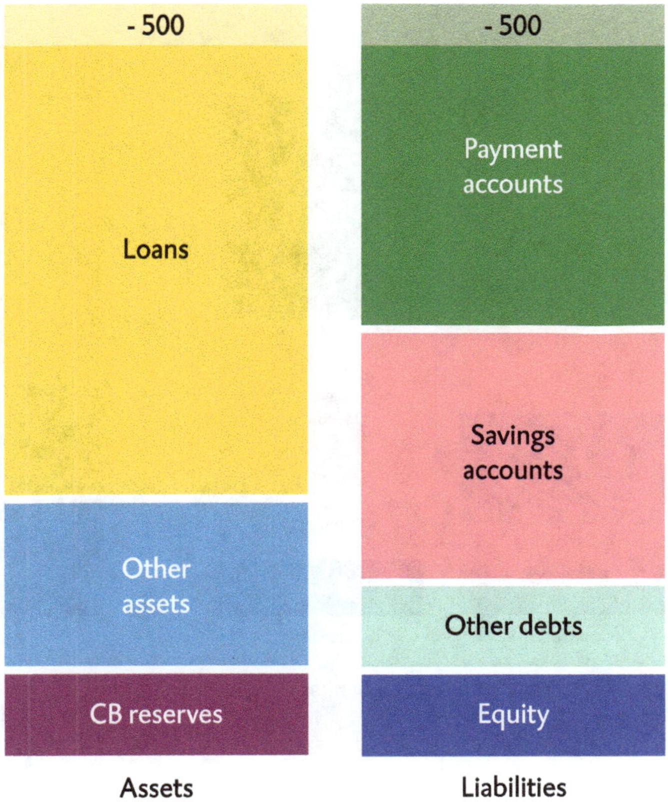

Fig. 2.3 Destruction of deposit money by debt repayment

Bank A to buy a car. When she buys this car and pays for it using a debit card, she instructs her bank to debit €5,000 from her payment account and credit €5,000 to the car dealer's payment account. But suppose the car dealer's account is at Bank B. How is this transaction processed?

The reserves that a bank holds with the central bank play a key role in the processing of transactions. These reserves serve as interbank money. They are not accessible to consumers and businesses and do not form part of the money supply. When deposits are transferred between banks, banks use these reserves to pay each other. In the example, Bank A reduces Anne's balance by €5,000 and asks Bank B to increase the car dealer's balance by €5,000. This means that Bank A's debt to Anne (the bank deposit) decreases by €5,000, while Bank B's debt to the car dealer increases by €5,000. Bank B will not want to assume this debt without having assets transferred to it by Bank A. Bank A therefore transfers €5,000 of its central bank reserves to Bank B. Both banks' balance sheets are now back in balance. The result is that Bank A has both lower liabilities (Anne's balance has declined by €5,000) and lower assets (its central bank reserves have also declined by €5,000). Precisely the opposite happens for Bank B (see Fig. 2.4).

Millions of transactions take place between customers of different banks each day, the net result of which is settled by banks using their central bank reserves. When a bank's central bank reserves fall below the required level, it must supplement them by borrowing reserves from other banks through an interbank loan or

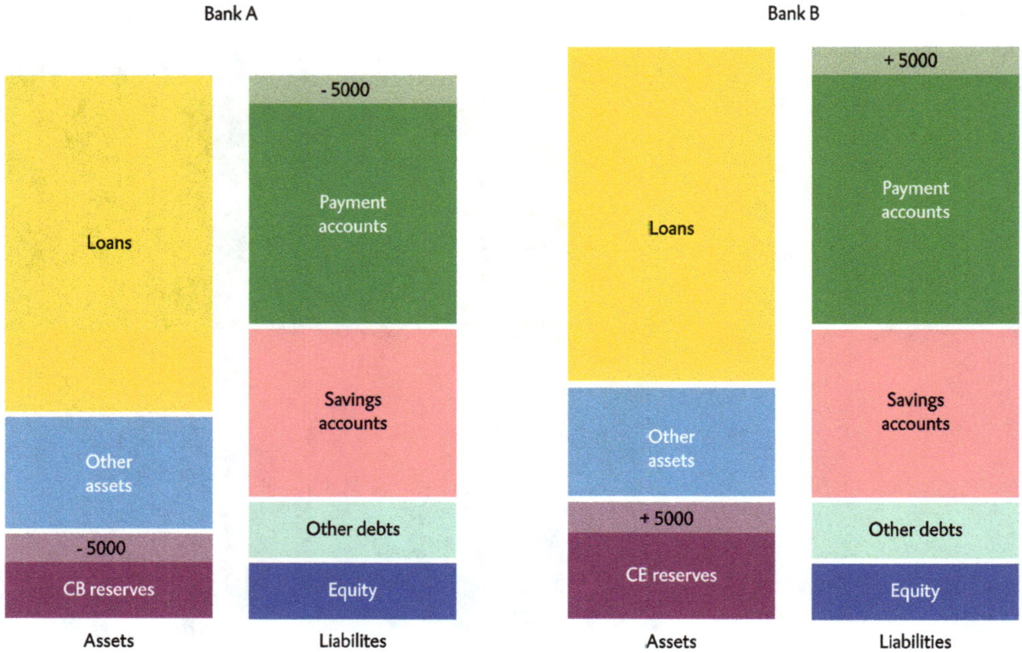

Fig. 2.4 Transfers between banks

from the central bank. Such a loan increases the bank's liabilities (debt owed to other banks or to the central bank) and assets (central bank reserves). Since banks must normally pay higher interest on such loans than on payment accounts, banks seek to retain customers (account holders) and limit high outflows from payment accounts. In short, banks need to keep their finances in order, attracting payment and savings account deposits and maintaining appropriate mixes of funding. But as the description above makes clear, banks do not have to raise money before they can grant new loans.

When a customer withdraws cash from a bank, deposit money is converted into cash. This changes the *composition* but not the *size* of the money supply. If Anne, in our example, had withdrawn the money she borrowed in cash from an ATM, we would again see changes on both sides of the bank's balance sheet: both the bank's central bank reserves (which include cash) and Anne's payment account balance would have decreased. When someone converts cash into deposit money, this does not affect the size of the total money supply.[6]

[6]Boonstra (2018: 114). This applies at the micro level. But when people exchange deposit money for cash *en masse*, this does affect the money supply because it triggers bank runs or limits the banks' ability to create money.

2.1.2 *Free Money?*

Banks create money through simple administrative acts when granting loans. This tends to cause confusion, because it suggests that banks can just create money and spend it; put differently, that banks get free money. That is not the case. The created money is a debt owed by the bank to the customer (the bank deposit) and is the customer's money. But the customer has also incurred a debt to the bank. The creation of deposit money thus involves the simultaneous creation of a debt owed by the customer to the bank and a debt owed by the bank to the customer, a phenomenon known as 'mutual debt acceptance'.[7]

Although 'mutual debt acceptance' may suggest that the two debts mirror one another, the debts have different characteristics. The customer's debt to the bank, for example a mortgage, often has a longer maturity and must be repaid (with interest, the bank's income) at regular intervals. The bank's debt to the customer (the payment account balance) has no fixed repayment term – it may in fact never be repaid. It serves as money: it can be used to make payments and can be withdrawn at any time. The customer can convert it into cash or transfer it to another bank.

A point of discussion is whether banks earn 'seigniorage' profits – profits generated through the creation of money. Traditionally, seigniorage represents the difference between the cost of producing money and its purchasing power. If the government mints a euro coin incurring material and production costs of 10 cents and then spends this euro, the government realizes 90 cents of seigniorage.[8] But because banks cannot spend the new money they create, they do not earn this type of seigniorage. Rather, bank profits largely derive from the difference between the interest received on loans and the interest paid on bank deposits, known as the interest margin. This does not mean that banks do not financially benefit from their ability to create new money. That they can create bank deposits when granting loans gives them a funding advantage over 'ordinary' businesses, although they do have to bear the costs of maintaining the payments system (seigniorage and bank profits are discussed in more detail in Box 4.3).

2.2 Driving and Constraining Forces

Although commercial banks today create the bulk of the money supply when they grant loans, this does not mean that there are no constraints on creating money. The financial sector, households, businesses and governments all play driving or constraining roles, with the central bank occupying a pivotal position.[9] The creation

[7]See Boonstra (2015: 16); Boonstra (2018: 115).

[8]In many countries (including in the EU) governments are not allowed to print money and spend it. This means that governments do not incur this form of seigniorage.

[9]See Tobin (1963); McLeay et al. (2014).

of money is influenced by three key factors: the behaviour of households and businesses; banks' balance sheet risks and associated regulations; and the influence of monetary policy and the role of the central bank. These factors are interrelated and influence one another. The first two are discussed in this section. Monetary policy is discussed in Sect. 2.3.

2.2.1 The Role of Households and Businesses

Banks create money when they grant loans. This highlights an important prerequisite: there must be demand for credit. In the creation of money as elsewhere, it takes two to tango.

Demand for credit largely depends on the plans, wishes and expectations of borrowers. Moreover, not all lending requires the bank's explicit consent. Take for example businesses making use of credit lines. The bank gives businesses a margin within which they can borrow money; the bank cannot determine precisely how much will be lent (and therefore how much money will be created). The number of transactions is so vast that it is impossible to control or approve every transaction in which money is created. Overdrafts usually occur on the initiative of the borrower.

Another factor is what borrowers do with their payment account balances. Suppose Peter borrows money to buy a house from William, who moves into a rented apartment. Since William still has a mortgage, he uses the proceeds from the sale to repay it. The newly created money is then (at least in part) destroyed. Creating money can also lead to increased spending on goods and services. If William has already repaid his mortgage, he can use his newly obtained money for other purposes. The money may thereby find its way to businesses that use it to finance expenditures, etc. In that way the newly created money facilitates more spending in the economy. If the money is used to *import* goods, deposit money will flow abroad (to the exporter's bank account) and the money supply shrinks. In short, the behaviour of borrowers and account holders affects the size of the money supply.

Whether there is net money creation at the national level therefore largely depends on people's willingness to incur debt, their desire to repay debt, and the extent to which they wish to hold funds in payment or savings accounts at domestic banks. All of this in turn largely depends on people's beliefs about what the future has in store for their incomes and assets. Uncertainty about the future is a major source of instability. In good times, with rising house prices, people may become overly optimistic and take on high levels of debt. This is encouraged by banks, which in good times are usually generous in granting credit (encouraged by the rising value of collateral, e.g. housing prices). Overall, this leads to strong credit growth and money creation. But when future prospects appear ominous, parties often hit the brakes at the same time: businesses and households become reluctant to take on more debt and focus on repaying existing debts. Banks cut credit lines because collateral values collapse and the future appears dire. Contractions in credit and the money supply then go hand in hand.

Banks themselves of course play a role in shaping the demand for bank credit. They pursue particular credit policies, deciding who they will or will not lend to, and on what terms (interest rates, fees, repayment periods, amount of collateral, etc.). Because banks earn income from lending, they seek to attract borrowers; they monitor their competitors, basing their loan conditions and interest rates partly on what other banks are offering. Future prospects, assessments of risk, and the central bank interest rate – which affects funding costs for banks – all heavily influence their actions. All this in turn affects the demand for loans.

2.2.2 Banks' Balance Sheet Risks

The second major factor that influences contemporary money creation concerns balance sheet risks for banks. When banks create money by granting loans, they must consider two types of risk. First, there is the risk that the bank's equity will be unable to absorb falling asset values (outstanding loans and other financial products). This is known as 'solvency risk'. Second, there is the risk that the bank will be unable to meet cash withdrawals and transfers to other banks, or that short-term funding will dry up. This is called 'liquidity risk'. Since bank failures generally have far-reaching social consequences, governments have introduced legal requirements for bank solvency and liquidity.

2.2.2.1 Absorbing Losses – Leverage and Capital Ratios

Like other businesses, banks fund themselves through a combination of debt and equity (the money invested by shareholders, plus retained profits, less losses) (see Fig. 2.5).

Banks are unique in that much of their debt consists of account holders' deposits – debts that are used as money in society. As explained earlier, the bank creates these debts when it grants loans, but it must ensure that these do not rise excessively relative to equity. After all, it is the equity that absorbs the bank's losses when assets fall in value. Sufficient equity ensures that the bank's debts can be repaid and that losses or declining asset values do not lead to bank failure. Bank failures can threaten the stability of the financial system, with far-reaching consequences for society as a whole.

At the same time, the bank's shareholders prefer the bank to fund itself largely through debt, which is generally cheaper than funding through equity. Like other businesses, banks' interest expenses are tax-deductible. Furthermore, the bank's debts largely consist of bank deposits. As customers use bank deposits to make payments, they are prepared to accept lower remuneration than other creditors. This means that while the bank's shareholders have an interest in ensuring that the bank can absorb losses, they also prefer a high proportion of debt so as to increase return

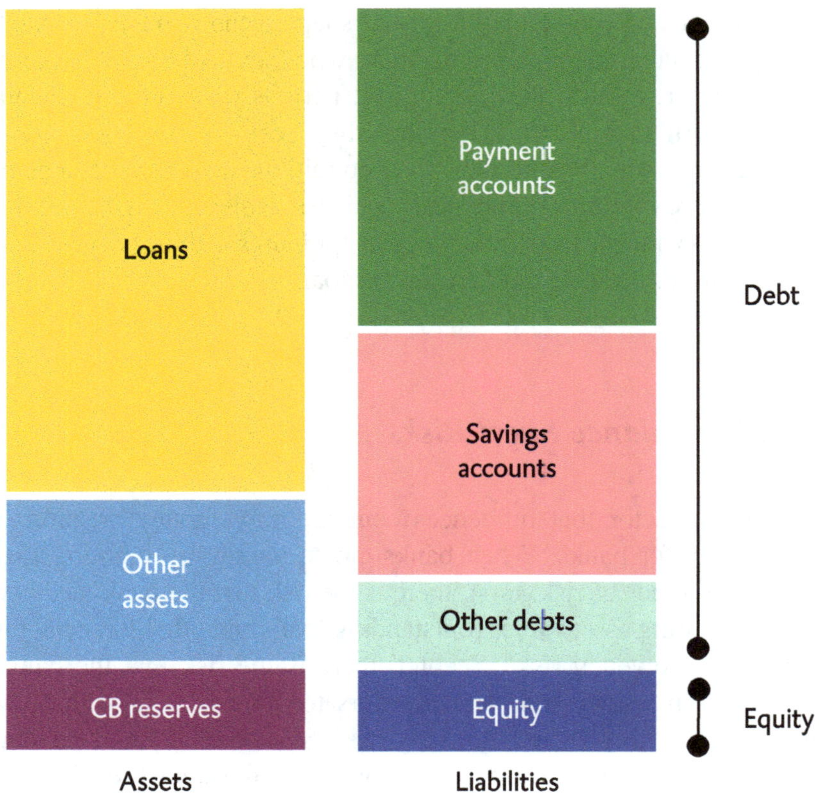

Fig. 2.5 Bank equity and debt

on equity.[10] Banks therefore need to strike the right balance between debt and equity; the right balance will not necessarily be the same for all stakeholders.

The ratio of equity to total assets is also referred to as the 'leverage ratio' – an important metric for banks, shareholders and regulators. Consider two banks, both with a balance sheet of €100 million (see Fig. 2.6). The difference is that Bank A has a leverage ratio of 4% (€4 million of equity) and Bank B has a leverage ratio of 20% (€20 million of equity). If the value of these banks' assets rises by 4% (€4 million), the value of the equity also rises by €4 million. For the shareholders of Bank A, this means the value of the equity doubles (from €4 million to €8 million). For the shareholders of Bank B, it means the value rises by only 20% (from €20 million to €24 million). With the same increase in the value of a bank's assets, the equity of Bank A has risen relatively more than that of Bank B. This is the leverage effect: a relatively small rise in the value of assets generates a large rise in the value of the bank to its shareholders. But this cuts both ways. If the value of the bank's assets falls by 4%, Bank A's equity evaporates and the bank is on the verge of bankruptcy, whereas Bank B faces no problems.

[10] Admati and Hellwig (2013).

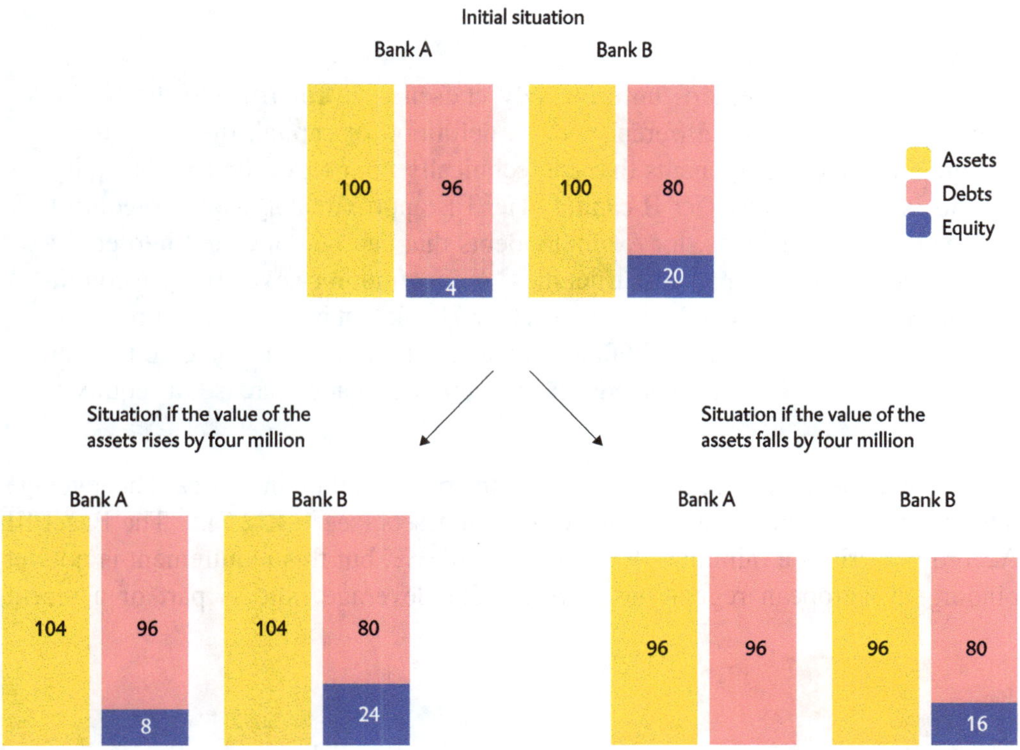

Fig. 2.6 How leverage works

When banks have little equity, a minor shock can cause immediate problems, for them and for the financial sector as a whole.[11] This is why there are legal requirements governing banks' equity levels. In technical terms, this is called capital regulation (see Box 2.2). Since the 1980s, policy in this area has been developed by the *Basel Committee on Banking Supervision* (BCBS).

Box 2.2 Equity and Capital

Equity consists of the money shareholders have invested in a firm. Over time, equity grows through retained profits (profits that have not been distributed to shareholders or other capital providers) and shrinks through any losses. When discussing banks, we often use the terms 'capital' or 'capital buffers' instead of equity. Particularly the term 'buffers' generates confusion as it suggests money held by a bank in a physical or virtual safe. A bank's capital is also sometimes confused with the reserves that a bank holds at the central bank. But central bank reserves are assets of the bank, on the left side of its balance sheet. Capital is the means by which the bank is financed (on the right side of the balance sheet).

(continued)

[11]DNB (2010); Wolf (2014)

Box 2.2 (continued)

Capital is the perhaps unfortunately chosen term referring to the bank's equity. But there is a difference. In its definition of capital, the Basel Committee includes components that are technically not part of the bank's equity. This is referred to as Tier II capital (Tier I is approximately equal to equity). Tier II capital includes, for example, debts that can be converted into equity when a bank faces financial difficulties. A contemporary example is a contingent convertible (CoCo) bond – a loan to the bank that is converted into a share (equity) if the bank's capital falls below a certain minimum. The creditor then becomes a shareholder. This reduces the bank's debt and increases its equity.[12]

If a bank's leverage becomes excessive, the risk of failure increases. The leverage ratio expresses equity as a percentage of total assets (see Fig. 2.7).[13] The Basel III Accord prescribes a minimum leverage ratio of 3%, but this requirement is not yet binding in European regulations.[14] A binding leverage ratio is part of a recent

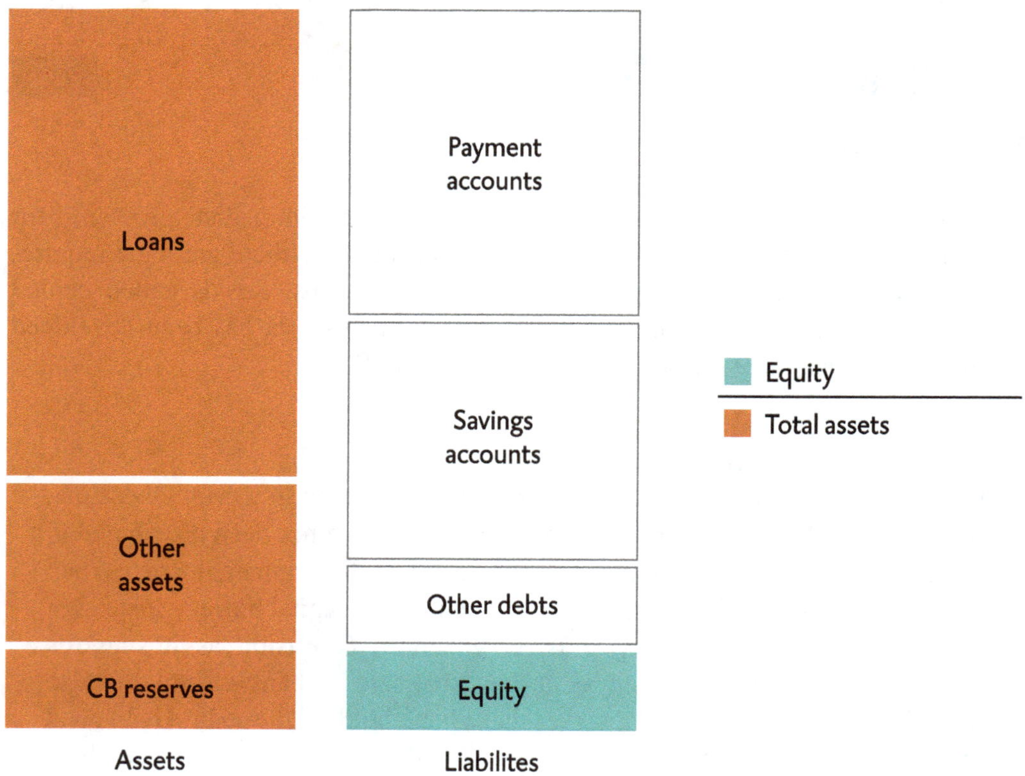

Fig. 2.7 The leverage ratio

[12]Ministry of Finance (2016).

[13]To be precise, this is Tier I capital, which is broadly equal to equity.

[14]BCBS (2010).

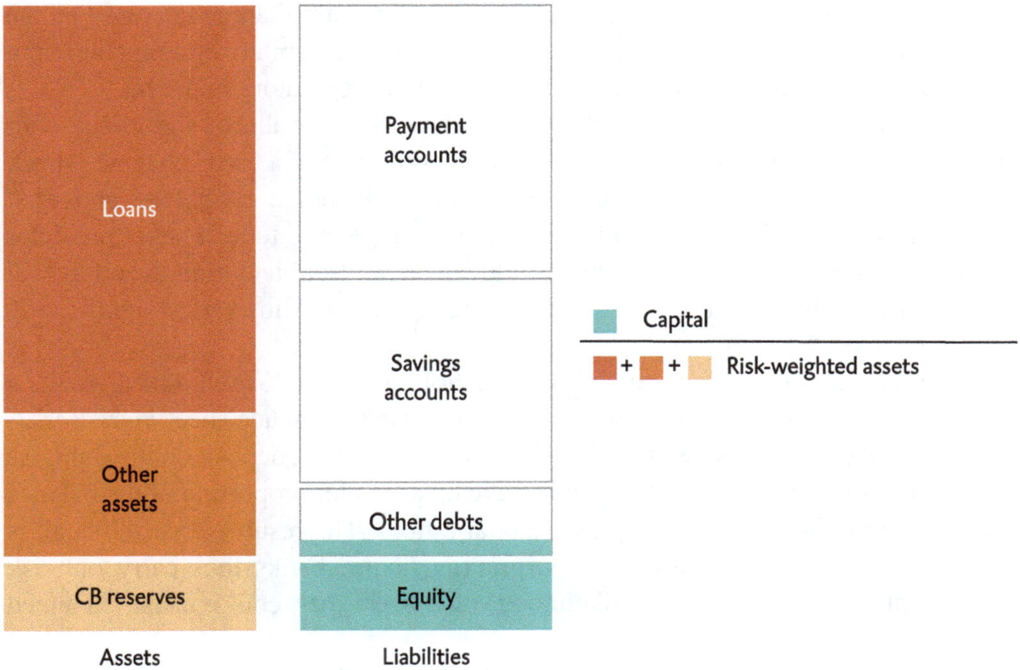

Fig. 2.8 The capital ratio

package of measures recently adopted in EU legislation.[15] Anticipating these agreements, Dutch policymakers have specified that from 2018 Dutch systemic banks must meet the minimum requirement of 4%.[16] The current government plans to abolish this requirement when the new European capital ratio rules (see below) come into force.[17]

Regulators believe that a leverage ratio (that only expresses equity as a proportion of total assets) encourages banks to hold riskier, higher-yielding assets with the same amount of equity. Regulations and supervision therefore focus primarily on the ratio by which assets are risk-weighted, known as the capital ratio. The capital ratio expresses capital as a percentage of a bank's total *risk-weighted* assets (see Fig. 2.8). This means that a bank must hold more capital to cover risky assets than to cover safe assets. If a bank invests primarily in safe government bonds, it does not need as much equity as a bank that grants risky loans.

Banks must maintain a minimum capital ratio of 8%, although in practice additional requirements lead to higher buffers. Capital requirements have changed over time, both above the line (items that count as capital) and below the line (the weighting of asset risks). Since the Basel II Accord, the major banks enjoy a great deal of freedom in calculating their risks.[18] Banks can use a standardized approach

---

[15]European Commission (2016a, b)

[16]Ministry of Finance (2016)

[17]Ministry of Finance (2018)

[18]BCBS (2004).

(used by smaller banks) or the so-called 'internal rating based' approach (used by the major banks). In this latter approach, banks calculate their capital requirements using their own risk-models, although these models require regulatory approval.[19]

This risk-based approach has drawn criticism in the wake of the crisis, with experts calling for requirements that also consider the size of a bank's balance sheet. The Basel III Accord thus included a minimum leverage ratio (see above).[20] Research by the Bank of England revealed the leverage ratio to be a better predictor (than the capital ratio) of which banks would encounter trouble during the crisis.[21] It was also found that risk assessments for similar asset portfolios varied significantly between banks.[22]

What does all this have to do with the creation of money? When a bank grants a loan and thereby creates a new bank deposit, the bank's balance sheet *increases*. A loan is added on the left side of the balance sheet, and a bank deposit on the right. As a bank grants more loans, its equity will make up a smaller proportion of the balance sheet, lowering both the leverage and capital ratio.[23] The result is that the bank is now less able to absorb losses. When granting loans, banks thus carry out risk assessments to determine the likelihood of losses that could cause financial difficulty.

If the bank's equity is too low relative to total assets, lending may be constrained. The bank may decide to grant fewer loans or to strengthen its equity by retaining earnings or, if possible, by attracting new equity. How a bank's equity position will affect its lending is based on a combination of its own risk assessments and legal requirements, i.e. the minimum capital and leverage requirements. The amount of equity can thus limit a bank's ability to create money.

To what extent does a bank's equity position limit the creation of money? Risk-weighted capital requirements do not constitute an absolute limit. Asset risks are often underestimated in good times and overestimated in bad. In good times, a relatively low level of equity is deemed sufficient, allowing for more lending. In bad times, assets are considered much riskier and the balance sheet must be shortened. Risk weighting can therefore have procyclical effects. Furthermore, balance sheet *ratios* are never an absolute brake on lending and money creation, for so long as a bank can maintain its level of equity by retaining profits or attracting new equity, it can continue to grow without any decline in its ratios.

Another reason why capital requirements are not an absolute limit on money creation and lending is that banks have found innovative ways to remove assets from the balance sheet. The mortgage packages that were so popular in the years preceding the crisis were largely motivated by the desire of banks to shorten their balance

---

[19]WRR (2016).

[20]BCBS (2010).

[21]Aikman et al. (2014); King (2016: 139).

[22]BIS (2016).

[23]Conversely, when a loan is repaid, the bank balance sheet decreases and the leverage and capital ratios rise.

sheets so that they could continue to meet statutory capital requirements. Banks set up special institutions (part of the 'shadow banking system', further discussed in Chap. 4) to buy up bundles of mortgages which they financed by issuing special bonds (mortgage-backed securities), which proved popular among pension funds and insurance companies. The mortgages were no longer on the banks' balance sheets and the banks had scope to grant new loans.

2.2.2.2 Meeting Withdrawals: Liquidity Ratios and Reserve Requirements

The second risk a bank must consider is liquidity risk. If a large number of households and firms simultaneously wish to turn their deposits into cash or transfer money to other banks, a bank can only meet their requests if it has sufficient cash or central bank reserves.[24] If it does not, it must have assets such as government bonds that can be readily sold and converted into cash or central bank reserves, i.e. liquid assets.

The most familiar type of liquidity problem is the bank run of the kind that hit the British bank Northern Rock in 2007, when account holders queued *en masse* to withdraw their balances in cash. Although this is the classic image, most bank runs today are electronic and thus less visible. Nevertheless, when many account holders transfer their deposits electronically to other banks, such bank runs are just as problematic for individual banks.[25] Another potential cause of liquidity problems is banks' reliance on short-term debt funding. Although these loans are readily rolled over in good times, this can stop suddenly when lenders begin to doubt the bank's creditworthiness. In the 2007–2008 financial crisis, it was this type of bank run that caused the biggest problems.[26]

Liquidity problems are inherent to banking due to the differences in maturity between a bank's assets and liabilities. On average, a bank's assets have longer maturities than its liabilities: mortgages, for example, may have a maturity of 30 years and corporate loans of five years, whereas bank deposits can be withdrawn on a daily basis. If deposit money is withdrawn in cash, the same amount is deducted from both sides of the bank's balance sheet, with reductions on the left side in cash (the bank's asset) and right side in account holders' deposits (the bank's liability). If deposit money is transferred to another bank, the balance sheet also contracts on both sides: central bank reserves on the left and bank deposits on the right. If the bank lacks sufficient central bank reserves, it can sell liquid assets (such as highly rated government bonds) to other banks in order to supplement its central bank reserves. A bank can also borrow reserves from other banks, thereby adding new liabilities to the

[24] A bank can easily convert central bank reserves into cash and vice versa. For banks, cash and central bank reserves are interchangeable.

[25] Boonstra (2018: 134–135).

[26] Liikanen Report (2012).

right side of the balance sheet.[27] Finally, a bank can borrow reserves from the central bank, against specified collateral. In the event of a liquidity crunch, the central bank may decide to provide emergency funding, unless it considers the bank no longer viable.

It is therefore crucial for banks to have sufficient stable funding (right side of the balance sheet) to prevent liquidity problems. They must also have sufficient central bank reserves and readily saleable assets (left side of the balance sheet) to cope with spiking withdrawals or when loans to the bank are not rolled over.

The 2007–2009 financial crisis revealed liquidity risks to be much more severe than previously thought. Banks had assumed that they would be able to sell assets such as mortgage-backed securities under all circumstances. They also expected that in case of difficulty, they would always have access to short-term funding from other financial institutions. Both assumptions proved incorrect. In response, the Basel Committee on Banking Supervision introduced liquidity rules in the new Basel III Accord.[28] The Accord specifies two ratios that banks must adhere to: (1) the liquidity coverage ratio (LCR); and (2) the net stable funding ratio (NSFR). The LCR has already been implemented in the European Union. The NSFR has only been recently adopted, and will only enter into force in 2021.[29]

The liquidity coverage ratio requires banks to have sufficient liquid assets to survive a period of liquidity stress lasting 30 days. The bank is required to hold a stock of high-quality liquid assets at least as large as the total expected net outflows during the stress period (see Fig. 2.9).

If a bank expects €100 million to flow out over a period of 30 days, it must have at least €100 million of high-quality liquid assets (see Box 2.3 for the definition of liquid assets). The liquidity coverage ratio is designed to ensure that problems in the financial sector do not disrupt payments in the real economy.[30]

Box 2.3 High-Quality Liquid Assets

A crucial question when assessing a bank's liquidity is what can be considered a high-quality liquid asset. The *Bank for International Settlements* states that the criteria are, first, the fundamental characteristics of the financial asset: its riskiness, ease of valuation, correlation with other risky assets, and whether the asset is listed on a developed and recognized exchange. Second, regulators

(continued)

[27]It is possible, however, that the drying up of funding will put the bank under such pressure that it is forced to sell less liquid assets. This will often result in losses for the bank as other market participants will only buy them at cut prices. Liquidity problems can therefore also represent solvency risks for banks.

[28]BCBS (2010).

[29]Central banks can also impose reserve requirements, although these are currently used in the service of monetary policy, not to regulate banks' liquidity. This is explained in section 2.3.

[30]BIS (2016)

Box 2.3 (continued)
look at market-related characteristics. An asset is deemed liquid when there is a sizable, active market for it, with limited volatility in its trading price, and when investors consider it a 'safe haven' in times of crisis. It is particularly important that the asset meets these criteria in times of crisis, when liquidity in many markets dries up.[31]

Supervisors use these criteria to calculate banks' liquidity coverage ratio. Assets that are considered liquid in almost all circumstances, such as highly rated government bonds, count as 100% in this calculation. Assets that are likely to be harder to sell without a loss during a crisis are given a 'haircut' and are only partially included in the LCR. Individual corporate loans or mortgages do not count as they are barely marketable.

Since the liquidity of assets largely depends on market conditions, there is a degree of circularity in its regulation: liquidity rules affect those very conditions – and hence the liquidity of assets. This can lead to unintended consequences. The very fact of designating certain assets as 'liquid' increases their liquidity, while other assets become less liquid. Imposing minimum liquidity requirements can also make banks less willing to sell their liquid assets in emergencies, as they fear breaching the requirements. Paradoxically, this can make the assets less liquid, because in bad times everyone wants to adhere to the requirements. To limit this problem, the Basel standard includes an explicit provision allowing banks to (temporarily) breach the minimum requirement in an emergency. Whether they will dare to do so in practice – also given the associated reputational risks – remains to be seen.[32]

The second standard for liquidity is the net stable funding ratio (NSFR) which aims to ensure that banks rely on sufficiently stable sources of funding. The NSFR requires longer-term loans to be funded by long-term liabilities (see Fig. 2.10). The stability of both the assets and liabilities is weighted. The weighted stability of liabilities, or 'available stable funding', must exceed that of assets ('required stable funding'). The NSFR is designed to ensure balance between the maturity of a bank's assets and its sources of funding, known as maturity matching.[33]

On the assets side, all loans outstanding for longer than one year fall into a category requiring 100% stable funding. Many other assets require less stable funding and are therefore weighted (between 5% and 85%). Only cash, central bank reserves, claims on the central bank with residual maturities of less than six months, and so-called "trade date" receivables arising from sales of financial instruments, foreign currencies and commodities require 0% stable funding. On the other side of the balance sheet, different types of funding variously count as stable forms

[31]BIS (2013: 13–22).

[32]Stellinga and Mügge (2017).

[33]BIS (2014).

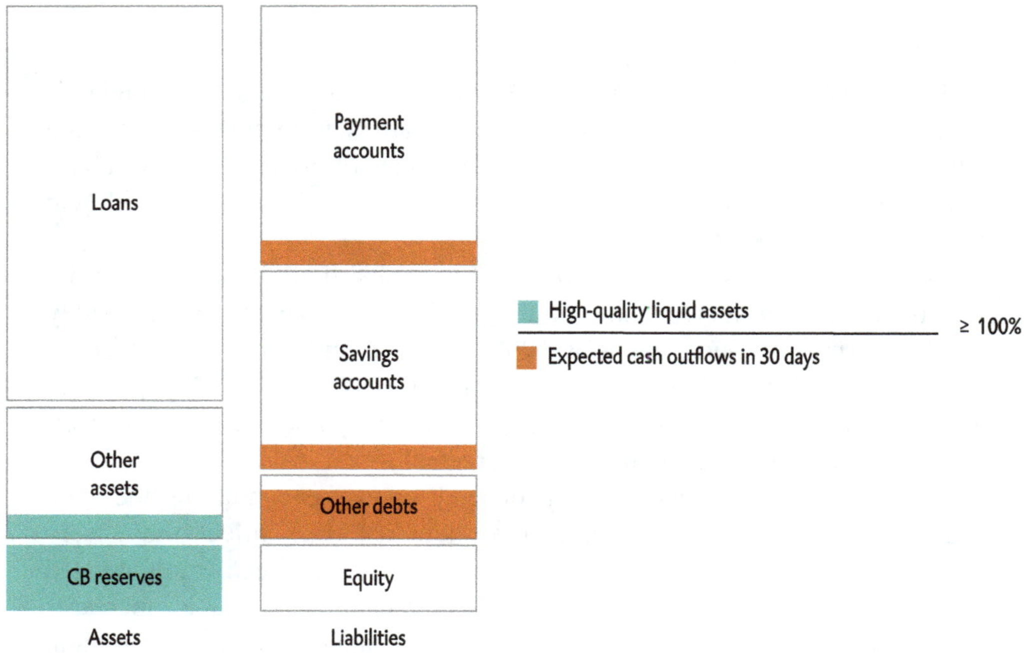

Fig. 2.9 Liquidity coverage ratio (LCR)

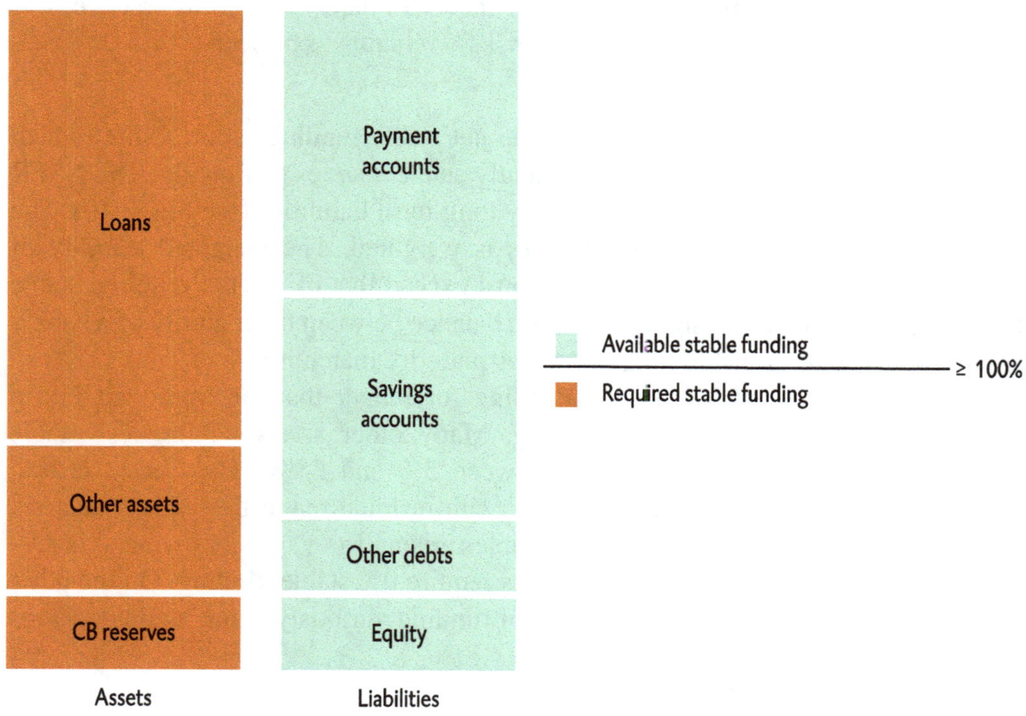

Fig. 2.10 Net Stable Funding Ratio

of funding. Equity capital and bank deposits, for example, are considered 90–100% stable; other forms of funding are considered less stable.[34]

How do liquidity ratios affect the creation of money? If a bank grants a five-year loan to Farid, his debt to the bank has a maturity of five years whereas he can withdraw the newly created deposit at any time. Since the created asset and liability have different maturities, every new loan results in an additional maturity difference on the bank's balance sheet, thereby in principle increasing liquidity risks. But in practice, bank deposits are considered a very stable source of funding. For the net stable funding ratio, consumers' and small businesses' bank deposits are deemed 90–95% stable.[35] Although customers do transfer money between banks, the overall volume of bank deposits, in the short run, remains roughly the same. It is only when borrowers withdraw deposits *en masse* in cash, or transfer them to other banks or abroad, that individual banks face liquidity problems.

In addition to these liquidity requirements there are also other policies for limiting or absorbing banks' liquidity risks. We have already mentioned the possibility for banks to borrow from the central bank. Deposit insurance also plays a role: as customers know that deposits up to certain amount (in the EU: €100,000) are guaranteed, they are less likely to withdraw their money if they suspect problems at their bank. The deposit insurance scheme does not apply to professional financial market participants; other providers of bank funding (such as bondholders or providers of short-term loans) also have no repayment guarantee if a bank fails. Liquidity problems are therefore more likely to come from this side. Liquidity is moreover affected by market sentiment. When optimism prevails, assets have higher valuations and appear highly liquid, while constraints on credit and money creation arising from liquidity requirements are less effective. But optimism can evaporate in a crisis: "*[when] liquidity dries up, it disappears altogether rather than being re-allocated elsewhere*".[36]

Alongside requirements for liquidity, central banks also impose minimum reserve requirements. These include maintaining a certain minimum percentage of reserves relative to bank deposits at the central bank (see Fig. 2.11). Reserve requirements, however, currently play a limited role in many developed countries and are not used to control bank liquidity. The United Kingdom, for example, has no requirements at all. In the euro area, the requirements are fairly lenient: central bank reserves must average at least 1% of total payment and savings account deposits, debt securities issued with a maturity of up to two years and money market funding.[37]

Confusion surrounds minimum reserve requirements because they can serve three different objectives.[38] They may have a prudential aim, ensuring that banks have sufficient liquid assets to meet any sudden outflows of funds. The central bank can

[34]Note that these are only estimates. Bank deposits can be withdrawn on a large scale despite their high stability weighting.

[35]BIS (2014).

[36]Brunnermeier et al. (2009: 23).

[37]ECB (2011, 2016).

[38]Gray (2011).

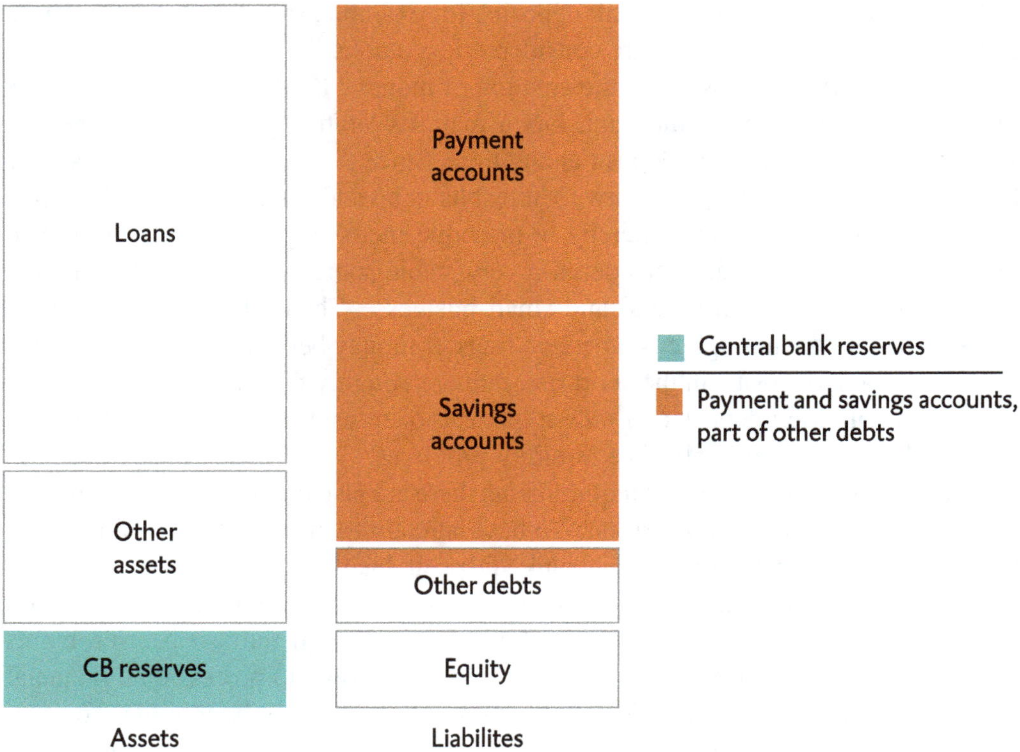

Fig. 2.11 Minimum reserve requirements

also use reserve requirements to directly influence the money supply: if it strictly limits available reserves, lending is constrained. Finally, the central bank can use reserve requirements to facilitate interest rate policy; the mandatory holding of reserves means banks must accept the interest rate that the central bank sets for these reserves. In developed economies reserve requirements are currently used solely for this last objective.

To what extent do reserve requirements constrain the creation of money? In our current monetary policy framework, there is no cap on central bank reserves: commercial banks are free to borrow reserves from the central bank so long as they can provide high-quality collateral. This means that reserve requirements do not directly constrain the creation of money. Although central banks in developed economies no longer apply reserve requirements to constrain or cap credit growth as they did in the past, reserves continue to function as an indirect brake on money creation through central bank interest rates.

2.3 Monetary Policy

A final important factor that affects money creation is monetary policy. We have outlined how the interest charged on loans and the interest paid on payment and savings accounts impacts money creation. These interest rates are influenced by the central bank's monetary policy. In this section we first discuss the objectives and instruments of monetary policy (Sect. 2.3.1), followed by the effects of monetary policy (Sect. 2.3.2) and quantitative easing (Sect. 2.3.3).

2.3.1 *Objectives and Instruments*

The goals, focus and instruments of monetary policy have changed over time, as has the line between monetary policy and other policy domains. While the currency's internal and external stability has always been a core aim, the means of achieving this have changed over time. Moreover, central banks have also had other objectives such as contributing to economic development, employment and financial stability.[39] Particularly since the 1980s, however, keeping inflation in check has been the holy grail in many countries. The principal aim of current European monetary policy is price stability (Article 127(1) TFEU). The ECB defines this as low and stable inflation below, but close to, 2% (see Box 2.4).

Box 2.4 The 2 Percent Target

The centrality of the objective of price stability is set out in the Treaty on the Functioning of the European Union (Article 127(1) TFEU). In 1998 the ECB's Governing Council defined price stability as "a year-on-year increase in the Harmonized Index of Consumer Prices (HICP) for the euro area of below 2%. Price stability must be maintained over the medium term." In 2003 the Governing Council specified that the aim was to achieve inflation close to, but below, 2%.

Price stability was thus operationalized in several ways. The aim is not absolute currency stability but low inflation (close to, but below, 2%). The ECB gives a number of reasons for this.[40] Low inflation provides scope to tackle the risks of deflation (decreasing prices). Since interest rates cannot fall far below zero, it is easier for the central bank to combat inflation than it is to combat deflation. The ECB also wants a margin to deal with differences in inflation across euro area countries, thereby insulating some countries from the effects of very low inflation or even deflation.[41] The margin also allows for the possibility that the method for inflation measurement (HICP) overstates actual inflation.

(continued)

---

[39]Capie et al. (1994).

[40]ECB (2018).

[41]Deflation can cause problems due to wage rigidity and by increasing debt in real terms.

Box 2.4 (continued)

The definition further clarifies that inflation is measured by the rise in consumer prices, the Harmonized Index of Consumer Prices. 'Harmonized' means that all countries in the European Union use the same methodology to measure inflation.[42] Importantly, this measurement approach excludes price rises in other areas, particularly real estate, shares and other financial assets.

Finally, the definition makes clear that the ECB focuses on the medium term, accepting short term deviations from its target. In case of a deviation the ECB aims to achieve a predictable and gradual return to the desired level.

The ECB aims to ensure price stability by influencing the interest rates at which financial institutions do business with each other (money market rates). The main monetary policy instruments are: (1) standing facilities; (2) open market transactions; and (3) reserve requirements.[43] In the past central banks also used more direct instruments to limit credit growth (see Chap. 3); instruments that are nowadays generally labelled as 'macroprudential' policy tools.

Standing facilities allow banks to borrow central bank reserves overnight against accepted collateral (the marginal lending facility) or deposit their reserves with the central bank (the deposit facility). The interest rates that banks pay or receive are usually the upper and lower limits of money market interest rates.[44]

The second central bank instrument consists of the open market transactions. In contrast to standing facilities, these transactions take place at the central bank's initiative. These are generally one-week loans (against accepted collateral) for which banks can 'bid'. The aim is to bring the money market interest rates to the desired level. The central bank can purchase financial instruments using central bank reserves – a particular form of open market transaction now used as part of 'quantitative easing' (see below).

The third instrument comprises minimum reserve requirements (discussed above). This is the average amount of central bank reserves commercial banks are required to hold, currently set at 1% of total payment and savings account deposits, debt securities with a maturity of up to two years, and money market funding. As stated above, in the current system reserve requirements are not used to directly limit the creation of money and debt. This is because the ECB is always prepared to create new central bank reserves and lend these to banks (against collateral and at specified interest rates).

[42]ECB (2018).

[43]ECB (2004, 2011); DNB (2018).

[44]In the money market, market participants create and trade short-term financial assets.

2.3.2 How Monetary Policy Works in Practice

Price stability – or actually stable inflation – is the main aim of monetary policy. Here the central bank wields three important instruments. But how does this work in practice?

Figure 2.1 showed that banks hold reserves at the central bank. These reserves are part of a bank's assets and thus enter on the left side of the balance sheet. Banks need these reserves when customers transfer money from Bank A to Bank B (Bank A must transfer an equivalent amount of central bank reserves to Bank B) and when customers withdraw cash. The central bank sets the interest rate at which banks can deposit their excess reserves and the rate at which banks can borrow additional reserves (these rates serve as the floor and ceiling of the so-called interest rate corridor). These interest rates influence the rates that banks charge each other (money market interest rates) and ultimately also other interest rates.

It is important to note that a *credible* central bank generally has to do little to influence these rates; it often suffices to express a particular preference. Banks after all know that the central bank will ultimately intervene to enforce the desired interest rate. For example, in the ECB's early years it could announce a specific target while waiting several days before taking specific actions to bring it about. But in the intervening period, interest rates had already moved in the desired direction. Market participants' knowledge and expectations of central bank objectives are often just as important as the central bank's actions to achieve its objectives.[45]

Particularly since the introduction of unconventional monetary policies, central banks have followed a strategy known as forward guidance, whereby they deliberately influence future expectations by communicating their longer term aims. The central bank discloses not only what it is doing now, but also what it expects to do in the future. But for this mechanism to work, central banks must back their words with action. In the UK, forward guidance has become less effective, as the Bank of England has on multiple occasions backtracked on earlier promises in the face of unexpected economic developments.[46]

The central bank's ultimate objective is price stability, and it uses its influence on the money market interest rate to achieve this. The ways in which the money market interest rate is translated into price stability is known as the 'transmission mechanism'. It is less mechanical than the word suggests and by no means clear-cut as inflation is influenced by numerous factors. A great deal also depends on market participants' *expectations* about the future. As the ECB states: "*central banks typically see themselves confronted with long, variable and uncertain lags in the conduct of monetary policy.*"[47]

---

[45] Disyatat (2008).

[46] Wallace (2017).

[47] ECB (2011: 58). The ECB was not the first to observe this. Friedman (1961), for example, described the uncertainties and the time lag before monetary policy actions take effect.

A full account of all aspects of this transmission mechanism is beyond the scope of this report.[48] One crucial element, however, bears directly on money creation. Suppose the central bank expects inflation to exceed the target over the medium term. It then aims for a higher money market interest rate and uses its own instruments to achieve this. If the interest rate for borrowing central bank reserves and interbank loans rises, this influences banks' behaviour. To maintain profitability, banks will raise the interest charged on loans. If every bank does so, the demand for credit will fall. On the liabilities side, banks will try to be less dependent on the more expensive money market and increase the share of saving deposits in their funding. Competition then causes interest rates on savings accounts to rise as well. Households and businesses will then find saving more attractive and spend less of their income. Both have the same overall effect: businesses will invest less and households will spend less on products and services. The idea is that this will help keep inflation under control over the medium to long term.[49]

This highly simplified description of how monetary policy works differs from how many introductory economics textbooks continue to describe it. Textbooks often suggest that central banks focus on the *amount* of central bank reserves as increasing or reducing them would – by means of a 'money multiplier' – lead to a higher or lower money supply. Although some countries followed this policy in the past, it is not how monetary policy works today. As the ECB states, this is an example in which "*academic economists developed theories detached from reality, without resenting or even admitting this detachment*".[50] Indeed, the mechanism operates in reverse. Instead of the 'monetary base' being created at the *initiative* of the central bank and being translated by banks into the total money supply, the central bank sets the interest rate and supplies the appropriate central bank reserves.[51] We consider this issue further in Box 2.5.

Box 2.5 The Money Multiplier

The term 'money multiplier' suggests that central banks increase central bank reserves and that banks then automatically grant more credit, thereby multiplying the central bank's money. But numerous factors influence bank lending and money creation, including the demand for loans, whether banks expect these loans to be repaid, bank liquidity and equity, what other banks are doing, etc. We thus cannot assume that banks will automatically increase their balance sheets when central banks issue more reserves. The relationship is actually the *reverse*: the dynamics of private money creation lead to changes in payment and savings account balances at banks, which affect banks' *demand* for central bank reserves and the amount of central bank reserves. Rather than

(continued)

[48]See ECB (2011: 58–62) for more information.

[49]ECB (2011).

[50]ECB (2004). See also McLeay et al. (2014); Disyatat (2008); Goodhart (2011).

[51]McLeay et al. (2014); Disyatat (2008).

Box 2.5 (continued)
a 'money multiplier', it would be more accurate to speak of a 'money divisor'.[52]

The amount of reserves is not fixed in our current system. Central banks seek to control inflation through the interest rate charged on central bank reserves. Since this interest rate is set by the central bank, the amount of central bank reserves must then adapt to commercial banks' demand for these reserves.

Central bank reserves play a key role in influencing this interest rate. Banks can borrow central bank reserves (or deposit excess reserves) at interest rates set by the ECB. If central bank reserves were fixed and central banks provided no facilities, they would be unable to influence the interest rate in this way, as it would lead to wild fluctuations in the money market interest rate. After all, individual banks cannot easily predict what will happen to these reserves on a day-to-day basis and how much reserves they will need. It largely depends on the extent to which account holders need cash or transfer money to other banks.

It is therefore not the case that the central bank first determines the amount of reserves and that this – by means of a fixed multiplier – leads to a certain volume of money being created by banks. Nevertheless, the volume of central bank reserves can indirectly affect bank lending. Banks generally try to hold an amount of reserves that is stable relative to their balance sheets. The amount of reserves can also influence money market interest rates, particularly when the central bank does not intervene.[53]

2.3.3 *Quantitative Easing*

Since the 1970s, the dominant objective of monetary policymakers has been to curb inflation. But the latest financial crisis revealed another danger: deflation. This was due to the *debt hangover* from the 2007–2009 crisis. Households and businesses took a much gloomier view of the future and repaid debt rather than taking out new loans. Banks' balance sheet problems and their pessimism about the future also led to more restrained credit policy. To absorb this shock, central banks cut interest rates sharply in the hope that (through different transmission channels) this would contribute to price stability.[54] The policy interest rate, however, rapidly approached the

[52]Goodhart (2011).

[53]See Disyatat (2008: 6).

[54]Central bankers pursued numerous operations to support the financial system, precisely because financial stability and price stability had become inextricably linked in the crisis. As Lastra and Goodhart (2015) put it: "*in practice the primary objective of central banking has become financial stability (also for the ECB)*".

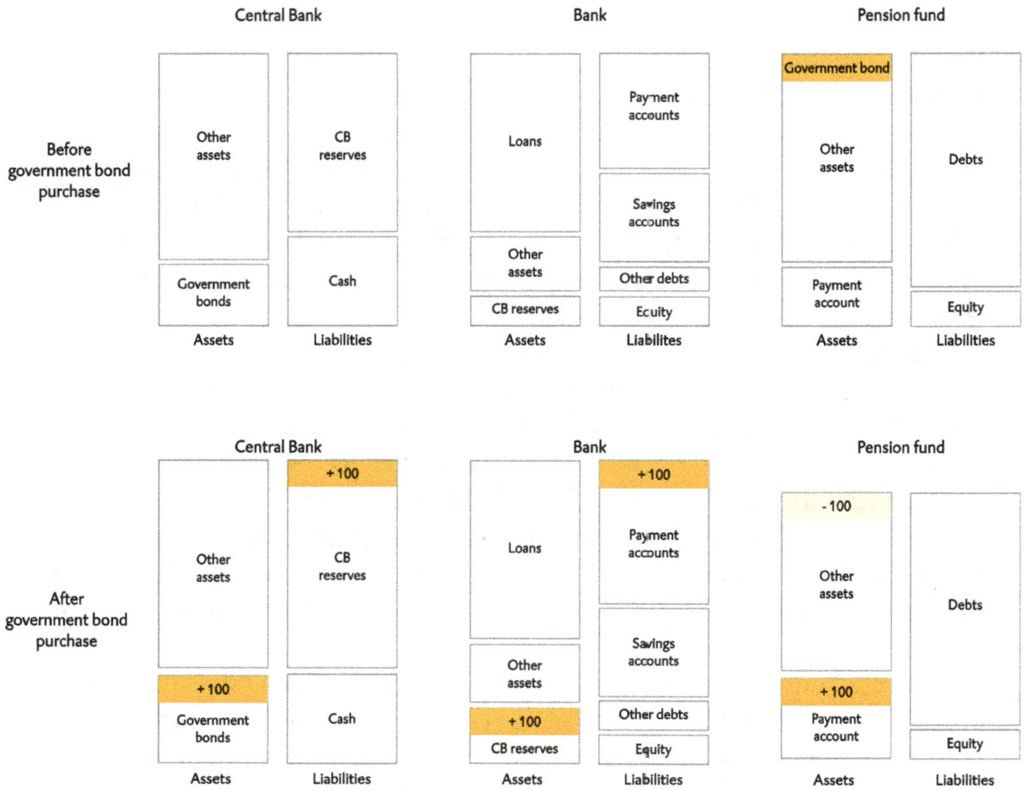

Fig. 2.12 Schematic representation of quantitative easing

lower limit of 0%. This is known as the zero lower bound problem.[55] Credit was extremely cheap but money creation and inflation fell short of the target. The interest rate policy could not provide a solution.

In response, many central banks – including the US Federal Reserve, the Bank of England and in 2014 the ECB – switched to a policy known as quantitative easing, with the aim of influencing long-term interest rates. Quantitative easing means that the central bank purchases financial assets (such as government and corporate bonds) from pension funds, banks or large companies. When the central bank buys a government bond from a pension fund, money is credited to the pension fund's payment account at a commercial bank. The commercial bank's new liability to the pension fund (the bank deposit) is offset by the simultaneous increase in the commercial bank's central bank reserves. The bank balance sheet thus remains balanced. The purchase of a government bond from the pension fund thus increases the money supply (see Fig. 2.12). But when the central bank buys bonds from a commercial bank, the money supply does not increase directly, although central

[55]With an interest rate of 0%, central banks have little scope to lower interest rates to influence the market. If interest rates turn sharply negative, banks will at some point have to start charging negative interest on bank deposits to remain profitable. People may then withdraw money as they would otherwise face punitive interest on their bank deposits, potentially causing funding problems for banks.

bank reserves do. This only changes the left side of the bank balance sheet (assets): bonds decrease and central bank reserves increase.

The intended transmission mechanism involves influencing interest rates in order to reduce funding costs for households, businesses and governments and to increase spending in order to achieve the 2% inflation target. The idea is that as a result of selling their bonds to the central bank, pension funds will have higher payment account balances than they want. Payment accounts yield little or no interest while pension funds risk losing their money if banks get into financial difficulties. Central banks expect that pension funds will use these newly created bank deposits to purchase financial instruments that generate higher returns, such as corporate bonds and shares. Greater demand for these financial instruments will drive up their value and reduce funding costs for businesses (because interest rates move in the opposite direction to the bond price). Central banks hope that this will stimulate businesses to increase spending, which should ultimately result in inflation of around 2%.[56] The rising value of financial assets could also make owners feel wealthier and encourage them to spend more.

Another possible effect is that increased central bank reserves give banks additional scope to grant loans. Whether monetary policymakers saw this as an important part of the transmission mechanism is not entirely clear.[57] The Bank of England explicitly states that this is not an important part of the intended transmission mechanism.[58]

2.4 Conclusion

This chapter showed that money creation works rather differently than is commonly assumed. Normally it is not the central bank but commercial banks that create the bulk of the money supply. They do so mainly by granting loans, which consists of the simultaneous creation of an asset (the loan) and a debt for the bank (deposit money on the borrower's account). When the borrower repays the loan, the money is destroyed.

The new money does not belong to the bank but to the borrower. Bank deposits function as money and can be exchanged for cash. By far the largest part of our current money supply (over 90%) consists of bank deposits. Banknotes are printed on behalf of the ECB and coins are struck on behalf of national governments, but because they are put into circulation against bank deposits, this does not increase the total money supply.

The fact that banks can create deposit money when granting loans does not mean there are no constraints on money creation. The growth and contraction of the money

[56]McLeay et al. (2014).

[57]See Goodhart (2013).

[58]McLeay et al. (2014).

supply are influenced by the interaction of many factors.[59] This chapter discussed the three most important ones: the behaviour of households and businesses, banks' balance sheet risks, and monetary policy. We have seen how monetary policy operates primarily through interest rates, and why this policy is difficult to pursue when interest rates approach zero. Money creation and monetary policy have not always operated in this way. The next chapter discusses how our monetary system has evolved over time.

Bibliography

Admati, A. R., & Hellwig, M. (2013). *The bankers' new clothes: What's wrong with banking and what to do about it.* Princeton: Princeton University Press.

Aikman, D., Galesic, M., Gigerenzer, G., Kapadia, S., Katsikopoulos, K. V., Kothiyal, A., Murphy, E., & Neumann, T. (2014). Taking uncertainty seriously: Simplicity versus complexity in financial regulation. *Bank of England Financial Stability Paper, 28.* https://doi.org/10.2139/ssrn.2432137.

BCBS. (2004). *Basel II: International convergence of capital measurement and capital standards a revised framework.* Basel: BIS.

BCBS. (2010, December). *Basel III: A global regulatory framework for more resilient banks and banking systems.* Basel: BIS.

BIS. (2013). *Basel III: The liquidity coverage ratio and liquidity risk monitoring tools.* Basel: Bank for International Settlements.

BIS. (2014). *Basel III: The net stable funding ratio.* Basel: Bank for International Settlements.

BIS. (2016). *Reducing variation in credit risk-weighted assets – Constraints on the use of internal model approaches.* Basel: Bank for International Settlements.

Boonstra, W. W. (2015). *Hoe werkt geldschepping?* Utrecht: Rabobank.

Boonstra, W. W. (2018). *Geld; Wat is het, wat doet het, waar komt het vandaag?* Amsterdam: VU University Press.

Brunnermeier, M. K., Crocket, A., Goodhart, C., Persaud, A. D., & Shin, H. S. (2009). *The fundamental principles of financial regulation.* Geneva: International Center for Monetary and Banking Studies (ICMB) and Centre for Economic Policy Research (CEPR).

Capie, F., Goodhart, C., & Schnadt, N. (1994). The development of central banking. In S. Fischer, C. Goodhart, & N. Schnadt (Eds.), *The future of central banking: The tercentenary symposium of the Bank of England* (pp. 1–261). Cambridge: Cambridge University Press.

Disyatat, P. (2008). *Monetary policy implementation: Misconceptions and their consequences* (BIS working paper 269). Basel: Bank for International Settlements.

DNB. (2010, June). *Een eeuw financiële leverage van Nederlandse banken* (DNB Quarterly Report, 2010).

DNB. (2018). *Beleidsinstrumenten.* Available at: www.dnb.nl

ECB. (2004). *The operational target of monetary policy and the rise and fall of reserve position doctrine.* Frankfurt am Main: ECB.

ECB. (2011). *The monetary policy of the ECB.* Available at: www.ecb.europa.eu

ECB. (2016). *Wat zijn minimumreserveverplichtingen?* Available at: ecb.europa.eu

ECB. (2018). *The definition of price stability.* Available at: https://www.ecb.europa.eu

European Commission (2016a) Proposal for a directive of the European Parliament and of the Council amending Directive 2013/36/EU as regards exempted entities, financial holding

[59]Lavoie (2003).

companies, mixed financial holding companies, remuneration, supervisory measures and powers and capital conservation measures, Brussels: EC.

European Commission (2016b) Proposal for a regulation of the European Parliament and of the Council amending Regulation (EU) No 575/2013 as regards the leverage ratio, the net stable funding ratio, requirements for own funds and eligible liabilities, counterparty credit risk, market risk, exposures to central counterparties, exposures to collective investment undertakings, large exposures, reporting and disclosure requirements and amending Regulation (EU) No 648/2012, Brussels: EC.

Friedman, M. (1961). The lag in effect of monetary policy. *Journal of Political Economy, 69*(5), 447–466.

Goodhart, C. A. E. (2011). Money, credit and bank behaviour: Need for a new approach. *National Institute Economic Review, 214*(1), F73–F82.

Goodhart, C. A. E. (2013). *Goodhart's Law, Le Libellio d' AEGIS*. Vol. 9, n° 4 – Hiver 2013.

Gray, S. (2011). *Central bank balances and reserve requirements* (IMF Working Paper).

King, M. (2016). *The end of alchemy: Money, banking and the future of the global economy*. New York: W.W. Norton & Company.

Lastra, R. M., & Goodhart, C. (2015, September 23). Interaction between monetary policy and bank regulation. In: European Parliament – Directorate General for internal policies – Policy Department A: Economic and scientific policy (ed.), *Interaction between monetary policy and bank regulation* (pp. 37–54). Monetary Dialogue, Brussels: European Parliament.

Lavoie, M. (2003). A fully coherent post Keynesian model of the euro zone. In P. Arestis, M. Baddeley, & J. McCombie (Eds.), *Globalisation, regionalism and economic activity* (pp. 98–126). Cheltenham: Edward Elgar.

Liikanen Report. (2012). *High-level expert group on reforming the structure of the EU banking sector*. Brussels: European Commission.

McLeay, M., Radia, A., & Thomas, R. (2014). Money creation in the modern economy. *Bank of England Quarterly Bulletin, Q1*, 14–27.

Ministry of Finance. (2016). *Kamerbrief overzicht verschillende kapitaaleisen*, Kamerstukken II, 32013, no. 119.

Ministry of Finance. (2018). *Kamerbrief over update akkoord Bazelse Comité*, Kamerstukken II, 2017–2018, 32013, no. 169.

Stellinga, B., & Mügge, D. (2017). The regulator's conundrum. How market reflexivity limits fundamental financial reform. *Review of International Political Economy, 24*(3), 393–423.

Tobin, J. (1963). *Commercial banks as creators of 'Money'* (Cowles Foundation Discussion Papers 159). Yale University.

Wallace, T. (2017, September 14). Is the Bank of England running out of rhetorical firepower on interest rates? *The Telegraph*.

Wolf, M. (2014, April 24). Strip private banks of their power to create money. *Financial Times*.

WRR. (2016). *Samenleving en financiële sector in evenwicht*, WRR report nr. 96, Den Haag: Sdu Uitgevers.

3

Money and its Creation: A Historical Overview

The previous chapter described how money creation works in our current system. We saw that the lion's share of money today consists of bank deposits – numbers on the balance sheets of commercial banks – while a much smaller proportion consists of cash (banknotes and coins). The dominance of deposit money means commercial banks play a leading role in money creation. This chapter puts this situation in a historical context. The functioning of our financial monetary system and the role of banks have changed fundamentally over time. The chapter reveals that what we take for granted today was often far from self-evident yesterday. Today we consider banknotes to be as secure as coins. But well into the nineteenth century, the Dutch were wary of banknotes issued by the central bank.

The historical perspective also illustrates the path-dependency of the financial monetary system. There was never an opportunity to redesign the system from scratch: reforms and innovations required public and private actors to work within historically given constraints and often came with unintended and unforeseen consequences. We also see the recurrence – albeit in different guises – of fundamental issues and debates about the financial monetary system. The current debate on private money creation, for example, echoes nineteenth-century discussions in the United Kingdom and the United States on whether banks should be allowed to issue their own banknotes. A historical perspective challenges what we now take for granted and allows us to draw lessons from the past. This may help us to better understand contemporary challenges.

We focus on the period from the early nineteenth century. This was when governments advanced explicit strategies to govern their national financial monetary systems and banks began to play greater roles in facilitating economic development. We discuss four periods in turn: (1) the 'long nineteenth century' up to the First World War, with an emphasis on the 1870–1914 period, (2) the interwar period (1918–1939), (3) the Bretton Woods period (1944–1973) and (4) the decades leading up to the latest crisis (1973–2008).

Although our focus is on the Netherlands, we mention developments in other countries as well as global trends that have left their mark on this country. For each period, we discuss the importance of various forms of money (coins, banknotes and bank deposits), what they were used for, and how they were created. We also discuss developments in the financial sector, given its close connection to money. Finally, we discuss how policymakers in each period tried to influence the design and developments of the financial monetary system.

3.1 Money and Finance in the Nineteenth Century

The Netherlands was in dire economic straits in the early nineteenth century. Industrial production in the preceding 150 years had hovered between stagnation and contraction, while trade was mostly limited to colonial products and agricultural exports. International conflicts and French rule had left the government in severe debt. Banking remained relatively underdeveloped, partly due to the existence of alternative financing channels. A bewildering variety of Dutch and foreign coins were in circulation. Against this chaotic background, the government sought to rationalize and modernize the financial monetary system. This section recounts the main developments of this period.

3.1.1 Money and Payments

People in the nineteenth century paid mainly with coins. When the Netherlands regained independence from France in 1813, the coins in circulation included guilders, stuivers, duiten and daalders (national currency) as well as numerous provincial and foreign coins. The currency stock was furthermore of dubious quality. King Willem I set out to end the confusion by establishing the decimal guilder (based on the example of the *franc germinal*) as the national currency. Unification with the southern provinces (what later would become Belgium) also made this reform essential.

In the wake of the Coinage Act of 1816, the National Mint in Utrecht obtained the exclusive right to mint coins. Although other coins were not immediately prohibited, they were declared invalid and withdrawn from circulation in several steps. This process accelerated in the 1840s, when the government embarked on a comprehensive conversion of the coin stock. A complete prohibition of all foreign coins only came with the passing of the 1901 Coinage Act.[1]

The nominal value of money was directly linked to that of precious metal – be it silver, gold or a combination thereof. People could exchange banknotes for cash or metal at the central bank. The bulk of Dutch 'standard' coins (rijksdaalder, guilder and half guilder) contained an officially specified amount of silver (see Box 3.1).

[1]Van Renselaar and Stokman (2001); DNB (2001); Jonker (1997)

Box 3.1 Minting of Standard and Token Coins
The Netherlands in the nineteenth century had both 'standard coins' and 'token coins' in circulation. The former refers to coins whose face value corresponds with their precious metal content; the latter to coins whose metal value is lower than their face value. A silver guilder struck in 1850, for example, was a standard coin: it contained 9.45 grams of silver – the legally specified amount. In contrast, the silver quarter contained only 0.64 grams of silver and was therefore a token coin. Everyone was free to exchange standard coins struck by the National Mint for precious metal. Token coins, however, could only be struck on behalf of the government as these involved seigniorage, meaning that their free minting would have distorting effects.[2]

Paper money (banknotes) was used primarily for payments between large and medium-sized businesses, between financial institutions and for government spending.[3] Initially there were two types of paper money: banknotes issued by the Dutch central bank (De Nederlandsche Bank; DNB) and banknotes and tender paper known as *kassierspapier*.[4] DNB at the time was a private institution, founded in 1814 by Willem I as a circulation bank (a bank that issues paper money) to boost economic development. DNB banknotes entered into circulation when people brought coins or precious metals to DNB to exchange them, and when DNB lent to a business or a bank. The latter involved the creation of money, with DNB increasing the money supply as it granted credit.

The Dutch trading community remained wary of DNB banknotes until long after the founding of the bank in 1814, mainly due its relationship with King Willem I, who imposed compulsory financing through DNB on a number of occasions during his reign. Recipients of DNB banknotes sought to swiftly exchange them for coins at the DNB office in Amsterdam. Outside of the capital, people had no trust in DNB banknotes whatsoever. The circulation of paper money in the Netherlands thus got off to a rocky start.[5] Moreover, there was a trusted alternative in the form of the *kassierspapier* – tender paper issued by the *kassier* (treasurer) as proof of deposit of coinage or securities. This tender paper served as a means of payment within the trading communities of Amsterdam and Rotterdam. Since the reliability of these banknotes was tied to the reliability of the *kassier*, they were mainly used as a local means of payment. There was only a limited degree of money creation: *kassiers* generally held a large part of the entrusted funds in cash.[6]

---

[2]National Bank of Belgium (1957); Kymmell (1992)

[3]Kymmell (1992: 32–33); DNB (2001)

[4]The Dutch government also occasionally issued paper money ('coin notes') when withdrawing obsolete coins from circulation. People received coin notes as proof of deposit and could use them to obtain newly minted coins.

[5]Uittenbogaard (2014)

[6]Jonker (1997)

Over time DNB banknotes began to replace *kassierspapier*, particularly after the currency reform of the late 1840s.[7] They first achieved prominence in Amsterdam, and gradually gained ground elsewhere in the country as DNB opened branches outside of the capital. Nevertheless, it was still many years until the Coinage Act of 1901 when DNB banknotes were officially recognized as legal tender. Their high denominations (between 25 and 1000 guilders) meant that their use was largely confined to companies and financial institutions. In those days, most of the Dutch population would never have held a banknote.[8]

What role did bank deposits play? Although the Netherlands was a pioneer in the seventeenth century (i.e. during the Dutch Republic, 1588–1795), deposit money scarcely played a role following the demise of the Amsterdamse Wisselbank (see Box 3.2). The absence of a well-developed banking system was a key factor in this; as we will see, financing needs were largely met by merchants and through the stock market – a situation that continued until the turn of the twentieth century. The proportion of deposit money within the total money supply then doubled from 20% in 1890 to 40% on the eve of the First World War.[9] Like banknotes, however, this type of money was used primarily by traders, entrepreneurs and companies.[10]

Box 3.2 Amsterdamse Wisselbank

The Netherlands was a pioneer in the use of deposit money in the seventeenth century. Traders could open an account by depositing cash at the Amsterdamse Wisselbank (1609–1820). The Wisselbank had a sound reputation as it held practically all of its money in cash (an example of a full reserve bank comparable to what is sought by proponents of a sovereign money system, discussed in Chap. 5). A bank run in the 'disaster year' of 1672 did not lead to its bankruptcy, a fate that befell many similar institutions. The Wisselbank emerged as a lynchpin of international trade, with traders doing business by transferring balances to each other. The accounting unit – the bank guilder – played a role comparable to that of the pound sterling in the nineteenth century and the dollar after 1945. But with the Republic's economic decline and unsecured lending to the Dutch East India Company and the city of Amsterdam (the Wisselbank was a municipal institution), the Wisselbank had squandered its reputation by the end of the eighteenth century. After continuing as a local bank, it finally went bust in 1820.

[7]Jonker (1997); Uittenbogaard (2014). After independence was restored in 1813, a large number of coins with different values and denominations were in circulation. The currency reform withdrew many old coins and replaced them with paper money ('paper coins'). Although meant to be temporary, this paper money led to a permanent increase in the money supply.

[8]Kymmell (1992: 32); Van Renselaar and Stokman (2001)

[9]DNB (2001)

[10]Van Renselaar and Stokman (2001)

In other countries, for example the United Kingdom, the United States and Switzerland, paper money developed along a different trajectory. In these countries, commercial banks were the first to issue banknotes; their issuance was nationalized only later. Given the parallels with the debate on a sovereign money system, we discuss an example in Box 3.3.[11]

Box 3.3 Dynamics in Money Creation: The Case of the United Kingdom

The United Kingdom pioneered developments in the financial monetary system, with banknotes issued by the Bank of England and merchant banks playing key roles from as early as the seventeenth century. Regional banks (country banks) granted loans in the form of private banknotes: debt certificates issued in fixed denominations which could be used for payment, a case of private money creation. But trust in banknotes issued by merchant banks had a downside: aggregate lending could reach irresponsible levels and lead to financial instability. The UK's suspension of the gold standard between 1797 and 1825 to finance the Napoleonic Wars led to heated debate on the principles underpinning the financial monetary system.

The 1844 Bank Charter Act introduced by Robert Peel's government granted the Bank of England the exclusive right to issue banknotes, which had to be fully backed by gold or government debt.[12] As the government sought to centralize and stabilize the creation of money with the Bank of England, commercial banks had to cease being money-creating institutions. Here we see clear parallels with current plans to nationalize money creation (going back to the Chicago Plan of the 1930s, discussed below).

The fixed limits imposed on the Bank of England, however, limited its ability to support banks in distress. There was, after all, a limit on the amount of money (banknotes) that the Bank of England could lend to institutions in difficulty. This restriction was ill-suited to the rapidly industrializing economy and the pivotal role of the London market in facilitating global trade. The Bank Charter Act had to be suspended three times between 1844 and 1866 as the fixed limit on money creation proved problematic during crises. The idea that central banks should be able to act as a lender of last resort – formulated by Henry Thornton (1802) and Walter Bagehot (1873), among others – gained traction.

(continued)

[11]There is an important difference between private banknotes and bank deposit money. If an account holder at bank A makes a payment with deposit money and the recipient has a payment account with another bank (bank B), bank A must transfer assets to bank B, directly affecting banks A's balance sheet. But if bank A issues banknotes, these can circulate without directly affecting its balance sheet. There is thus greater risk of excessive money creation through the issuance of private banknotes than by issuing deposits (Boonstra 2018).

[12]Exceptions applied to a number of Scottish and Northern Irish banks. These banks are still permitted to issue their own banknotes, but they do so under the control of the Bank of England.

Box 3.3 (continued)

Further challenges to centralised money creation came from developments in the banking sector. After 1844, banks soon discovered an alternative to self-issued banknotes: bank deposits. As bank deposits rapidly grew in popularity, banks continued to play key roles in the creation of money. Around 1913, the proportion of deposit money in the UK's total money supply reached an unprecedented 96%.[13] Other countries where the issuance of banknotes was nationalized (such as Switzerland and the United States) witnessed a similar rapid growth in bank deposit money.

3.1.2 Financing

Well into the nineteenth century, the Dutch economy was based largely on agriculture, small-scale industry, services and international trade. Lending mostly served to facilitate domestic and foreign trade. Companies purchasing goods did not always have cash, but received the goods on credit from the supplier. In exchange, the supplier received a written promise (*promesse*) that he would be paid later. It could also be the case that the supplier resided in another city or country, making it risky and difficult to send cash. A 'bill of exchange' (*wissel*) was used instead, where the customer instructed a financial institution (usually a bank) to pay the supplier. Such transactions usually involved two banks: the supplier's bank and the customer's bank, which then conducted the transactions between themselves. Much of this era's international trade passed through London, which served as a clearing house and the world's financial hub. On the eve of the First World War, over half of all international transactions were settled in pound sterling.[14]

Apart from trade credit, Dutch entrepreneurs could turn to short-term loans backed by collateral in the form of securities (usually Dutch or foreign government bonds). Many entrepreneurs invested their surplus cash and profits in such interest-bearing securities. If an entrepreneur needed short-term finance to cope with unforeseen circumstances, he could use these securities to borrow money on the *prolongatiemarkt* where one- or three-month loans with fixed interest rates were provided by commission agents, bankers and a number of *kassiers*. These loans were often extended ('prolonged') automatically, against the interest rate prevailing on the extension date.

The efficiency of the *prolongatiemarkt* and lacklustre economic development meant that the Dutch banking system remained comparatively small and underdeveloped until the late nineteenth century. Entrepreneurs could finance investments with their own income, savings or money acquired from their social networks. Few

[13]Murau (2017); Knafo (2006); Van Zanden (1997b); Capie et al. (1994)

[14]Williams (1968); Kymmell (1992: 40–48)

large banks existed to grant long- or short-term credit. Among the banks, DNB was by far the most important lender.[15]

The growth of domestic industry as well as international trade after 1860 fuelled the demand for credit, thereby triggering changes in the Dutch banking system.[16] Many of the banks established in this period – Credietvereeniging Amsterdam (1853), Commandietkas te Rotterdam (1861), Rotterdamsche Bank (1863), Twentsche Bank (1861) and Amsterdamsche Bank (1872) – sought to become 'modern banks', raising money specifically to provide long-term finance. Operating on the basis of 'fractional reserves', the deposits on their books exceeded the amount of cash they held. Dutch banks saw British banking and DNB as sources of inspiration. As the board of the Kas-Vereeniging, formed in 1865, put it: "The DNB example shows that a bank can also be sound even if not all its debts are covered by hard cash; after all, it is highly unlikely and indeed almost inconceivable that all banknotes will be presented at the same time".[17] The money supply thus grew as bank deposits could serve as, or be immediately converted into, a means of payment.[18]

The application of these modern ideas to Dutch banking did not proceed smoothly at first. Banks continued to focus on trade credit and were hampered by their unfamiliarity with the risks of long-term financing, companies' scepticism about relying on banks and the sustained popularity of the *prolongatiemarkt*. But by the beginning of the twentieth century developments over the preceding decades began to bear fruit. The banking system now grew rapidly (in total assets, loans and deposits) as banks began to finance large companies, making riskier long-term investments in industry and abandoning their preference for more secure short-term lending. The real breakthrough, however, had to await the First World War, when the *prolongatiemarkt* was closed for an extended period (see Sect. 3.2).[19]

3.1.3 Policy and Regulation

The stability of the national currency is an overarching concern for governments. There are two aspects: the currency's *external* value (in terms of foreign currency) and its *internal* value (in terms of purchasing power or precious metal).[20] In the nineteenth century, most governments tied their currencies to silver, gold or both (the 'bimetal standard'). Since most countries did this, the *internal* link also ensured

[15]Kymmell (1992: 19); Jonker (1997)

[16]Van Goor (2001: 74–79); cf. Van Riel (2016)

[17]Quoted in Kymmell (1996: 200). Our translation.

[18]Van Goor (2001); Jonker (1997)

[19]Van Goor (2001: 124); Jonker (1997: 118)

[20]Capie et al. (1994)

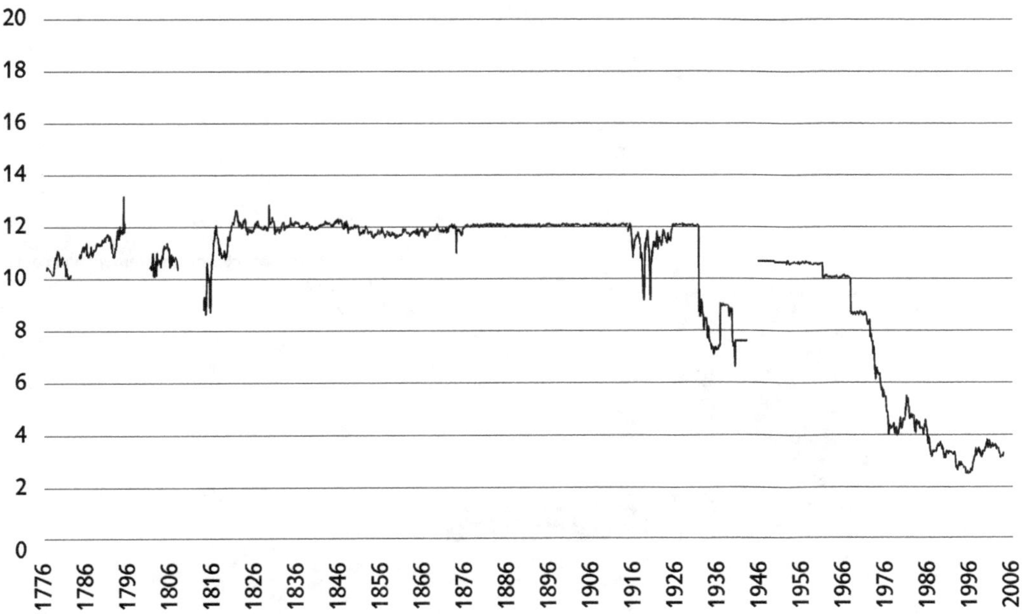

Fig. 3.1 Exchange rate of British pound and Dutch guilder
Guilders per pound
Source: Posthumus/Korthals Altes/Own analysis

an *external* link, with exchange rates between currencies being more or less fixed.[21] Figure 3.1 shows the exchange rate between the British pound and the Dutch guilder and its striking stability over the nineteenth century.

The direct link between currencies and precious metals exposed countries to supply and demand forces. The Netherlands, for example, felt compelled to leave the bimetallic standard when large gold deposits were discovered in California in 1847. The declining international price of gold meant that people in the Netherlands could import gold cheaply and have it struck into gold coins with higher face value, which over time would be unsustainable. Something similar happened in 1875 when the Netherlands switched from silver to gold.[22] Following the Franco-Prussian War of 1871, the new German Empire, like the United States, switched from the bimetallic or silver standard to gold. Many other countries followed suit. It was expected that a glut of silver would lead to inflation in countries that pegged their currencies to silver. Although tying a currency to a precious metal suggests stability, it makes the currency vulnerable to unpredictable factors, as seen in the international dynamics influencing Dutch policy choices.[23]

Linking currencies to precious metals had macroeconomic implications. The global adoption of the gold standard led to a worldwide shortage of gold, leading

[21]Eichengreen (1992)

[22]People spoke of a 'limping standard' because silver coins, although they could not be freely minted, were not withdrawn from circulation.

[23]Van Zwet (2001); Van Riel (2018)

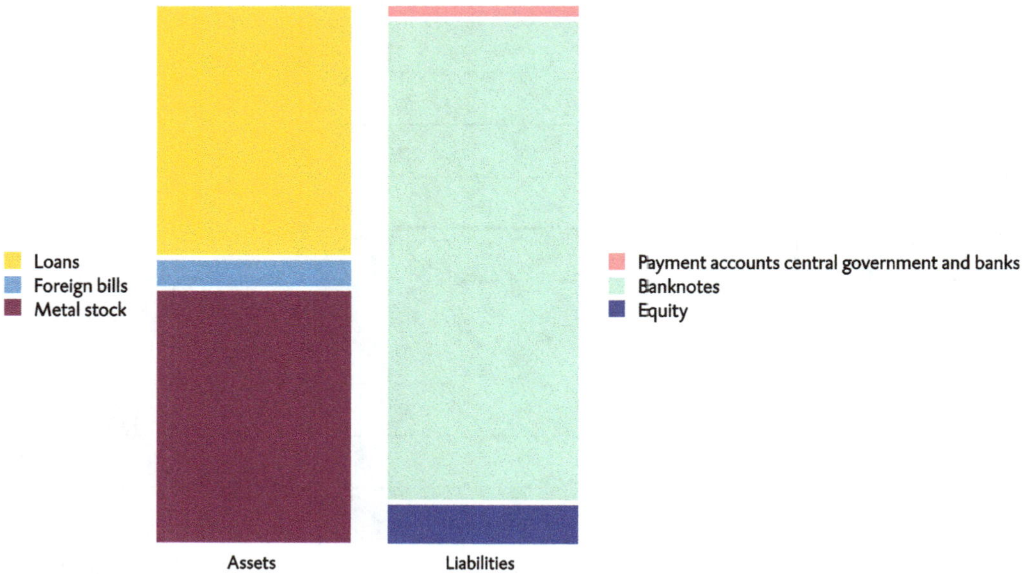

Fig. 3.2 DNB balance sheet in 1914
Source: Kymmell (1996: 65)

to systematic deflation. Between 1880 and the mid-1890s, manufacturing and consumer prices fell by roughly a quarter in the Netherlands.[24] Declining prices were not only tied to the limited availability of gold but also to a surge of cheap agricultural exports from the US and the UK, rapid industrialization and lower transport costs. It was only in the 1890s that deflation halted. This was aided by many governments easing their gold reserve requirements, central banks beginning to hold foreign currency reserves, and merchant banks expanding the money supply through the creation of deposit money.[25]

In the Netherlands DNB was responsible for safeguarding the metallic standard. In practice this meant it had to hold sufficient reserves of precious metal and coins to ensure that DNB banknotes could always be exchanged for silver and, later, gold. In its first 50 years, DNB was thus severely limited in the number of banknotes it could issue, although requirements were eased on a number of occasions. In the Banking Act of 1863, these requirements were replaced by a rule requiring DNB to cover at least 40% of the value of its outstanding banknotes with its stock of metal. From 1888 onwards claims on other central banks also counted as a cover. Figure 3.2 shows DNB's balance sheet in 1914. The coverage ratio (metal plus foreign bills of exchange divided by banknotes) was 57%.

Like many other central banks of the day, DNB had no explicit responsibility for guaranteeing financial stability. But by the end of the nineteenth century it was common for central banks to act as lenders of last resort, supporting banks in distress

[24] Van Zanden and Van Riel (2004)

[25] Van Riel (2018)

by lending reserves (banknotes, coins or metal) – a role also embraced by DNB.[26] DNB had already been presenting itself as the 'bankers' bank' for some time: in 1860 half of all bills of exchange issued by *kassiers* and bankers were owned by DNB. As such, DNB had supported a number of financial actors during the international credit crisis of 1857.[27]

The fixed relationship between currency and precious metals implied potential conflict between monetary policy and financial stability policy. When banks encountered liquidity problems, the central bank as the lender of last resort had to assist them. But this would deteriorate the central bank's position, increasing its balance sheet (more loans on the left side, more issued banknotes on the right side) and lowering its coverage ratio, potentially raising doubts about the exchangeability of banknotes.[28] While DNB did not encounter such problems in this period, acute problems arose in the UK in 1890–1891 with Baring Brothers & Co. incurring such large losses on Argentinian government bonds that the Bank of England had to step in. But the Bank of England lacked sufficient gold and could therefore only grant emergency aid by drawing loans from other central banks.[29]

3.1.4 Summary: Money Creation in the Nineteenth Century

In the nineteenth century people in the Netherlands mainly used coins. Coins were public money: the conditions for their production were set by the government, which specified the metal content of standard coins and had exclusive authority to mint token coins. It was not until midway through the century that the coin stock was standardized.

Up until the Banking Act of 1863 and the opening of branches outside of Amsterdam, DNB banknotes were used primarily to finance trade. Money creation by means of banknotes thus depended on developments in trade. As DNB was then a private, for-profit organization its banknotes were a hybrid public-private form of money. The creation of deposit money (i.e. by banks) was primarily linked to short-term trade credit and only gradually to long-term credit. The structural rise in the share of bank deposits in the total money supply only took place in the early twentieth century.

In this period the main constraint on money creation was the (policy-based) link to precious metal. It applied first and foremost to coins made partly or entirely of precious metals, but also to DNB's creation of money through banknotes linked to its metal stocks. At the same time, growing international trade and the industrialization of key economic sectors required an expansion of the money supply,

[26]Capie et al. (1994).

[27]Kymmell (1992: 71)

[28]Uittenbogaard (2014: 138–9)

[29]Eichengreen (1992)

rendering the link to metal an inflexible constraint. This inflexibility was most keenly felt during financial crises as it undermined the ability of the central bank to act as a lender of last resort. The creation of deposit money and the loosening of the link between metal and banknotes provided a solution to this problem.

Striking the right balance between anchoring the currency and ensuring sufficient flexibility was for many countries a perennial challenge. An overly rigid system led to problems in facilitating economic growth and solving crises. Although the Netherlands was less affected by this problem than the UK, national and international developments compelled the Dutch government to frequently adapt its poli-cies. Beginning in the 1850s, the coverage ratio of DNB banknotes was eased in stages. The guilder's link to metal was also adapted several times under international influence to avoid further problems.

3.2 The Interwar Period and the Great Depression (1918–1939)

The First World War marked the end of the 'first wave of globalisation' which began around 1870, facilitated by the liberalisation of international trade, the structural decline of transport costs and the widespread adoption of the gold standard. The war and its financing rendered the gold standard unsustainable. As international payments were frozen, investors lost income and access to their assets. While the extent to which countries sought refuge in debt or higher taxes varied, several switched to monetary financing (printing more money for government spending) which generally led to rising inflation. The war was followed by a difficult period of adjustment, with the accumulated debt in countries with weak political institutions ultimately leading to hyperinflation. The problem was most extreme in Germany, which was in a state of economic collapse due to untenably high war debt, the Versailles obligations and the occupation of the Ruhr by France and Belgium in 1923. Excessive money creation and rising prices reinforced each other, and it was not until 1924 that the situation stabilized. In response to this chaotic period, governments sought to return to the pre-war 'golden days'.

The Dutch financial monetary system continued to evolve in this period. The foundations were laid for deposit money to spread to 'ordinary people' with the establishment of a national giro institution (the Postcheque- en Girodienst; PCGD) and municipal giro institutions. Cash (coins) nevertheless remained the norm for most people. The financial sector also evolved rapidly as banks began to focus even more on facilitating industrialization; the creation of deposit money was thereby linked to long-term corporate financing. But this development quickly led to a crisis. Between 1921 and 1924 many banks encountered difficulties; some had to be rescued by DNB (backed by the government).

3.2.1 *Money and Payments*

In the interwar period, coins remained the usual means of payment for most individuals and small businesses; non-cash payments were still in their infancy. Deposit money was used primarily for payments by large companies. These were often payments between customers of the same bank. Transfers to other banks' customers were too difficult and expensive, although from 1937 attempts were made to develop a cheaper and faster alternative by means of a bank giro system for cheque payments.[30] But at a time when there were still 25 clearing banks, the time and cost benefits were minimal. DNB banknotes were therefore preferred to non-cash payments for larger transactions.

Merchant banks catered to companies and wealthy individuals; deposits and payments made through them were primarily for business purposes. Small businesses in particular fell through the cracks: they often had to make payments over greater distances, but the facilities to do so (drawing bills of exchange or sending banknotes by post) were expensive and cumbersome. To allow a wider public to access non-cash payments, the Dutch government established the Postcheque- en Girodienst (PCGD) in 1918, which grew from 33,000 account holders in 1920 to 113,000 in 1925.[31] Paralleling this national initiative, innovation also took place at the municipal level, with the municipality of Amsterdam setting up the municipal giro system to make payments for municipal services more efficient.[32]

The seed for the subsequent widespread popularity of deposit money was thereby sown in this period. Whereas around 1900 only 20% of the money supply consisted of deposit money, by 1920 this figure exceeded 50%. The trend then stalled due to problems in the banking system in the early 1920s and growing concerns about the economic and political situation in the 1930s, with the share of deposit money falling to around 40% of the money supply at the start of the Second World War (see below).[33]

3.2.2 *Financing*

The Dutch banking system was still small and segmented after the First World War. Merchant banks provided short-term loans and current accounts for businesses and wealthy individuals. A few hundred savings banks (including Rijkspostspaarbank, established by the government in 1881) provided accounts for small savers in urban areas but did not lend to businesses; the assets side of their balance sheets mainly consisted of loans to public agencies (government bonds). In rural areas, savings and

[30]DNB (2002: 15)

[31]Peekel and Veluwenkamp (1984: 14); Van Zanden (1997b: 129)

[32]Lelieveldt (2017)

[33]Van Zanden (1997b)

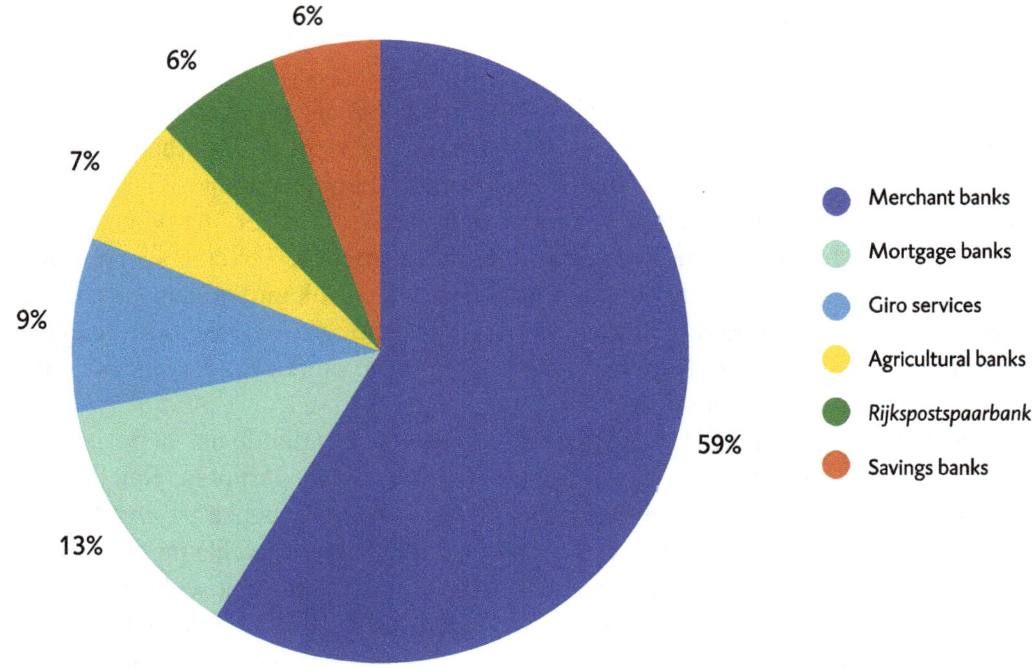

Fig. 3.3 Different types of banks by balance sheet total (1923)
Source: Van Zanden (1997b: 127)

credit facilities were provided by a network of around 1000 cooperative agricultural credit institutions, with the number of account holders more or less equal to the total number of agricultural businesses. Mortgage banks financed property on the basis of 'pandbrieven' (mortgage bonds). Non-cash payment services for individuals and small businesses became the preserve of the PCGD. Figure 3.3 shows the relationship between the different types of Dutch banks (in terms of balance sheet size) in 1923.

But banking was clearly on the rise. The closure of the stock exchange at the outbreak of the First World War forced businesses and lenders to rely more on banks. Economic growth also helped: partly due to neutrality during the war, the Dutch economy grew fairly quickly during the pre- and post-war periods. With 3.4% annual growth between 1913 and 1929, it outperformed the Western European average by more than a percentage point.[34] Industrialization continued, while profits from agriculture and commerce were increasingly deposited in banks. This encouraged (and was encouraged by) the further development of the banking system. Banks expanded to serve larger companies and became even more active in financing industrialization, at times playing key roles in establishing industrial companies. Between 1910 and 1923, banks doubled the number of seats they occupied on the supervisory boards of industrial companies, thereby gaining considerable influence. Banks became more interconnected with business, while many industrial companies,

[34]Van Ark and De Jong (1996: 201).

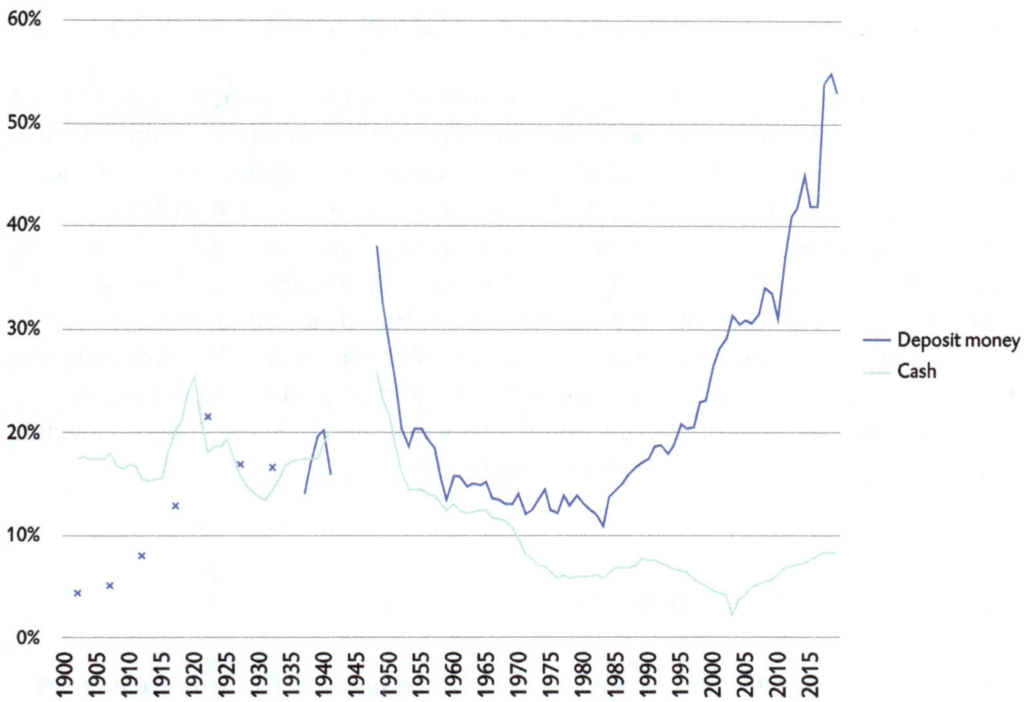

Fig. 3.4 Volume of deposit money and cash
M1, percentage of GDP, 1900-date
Sources for money supply: De Jong (1967); De Vries (1989); Statistics Netherlands Statline; DNB Statistics
Sources for GDP: Smits et al. (2000); Van der Bie (1997); Statistics Netherlands (2001); Statistics Netherlands Statline

SMEs and farms became dependent on (short-term) bank financing. The immediate post-war years witnessed very high demand for long-term finance for large-scale investments.[35]

After peaking in 1920 the Dutch economy stagnated, partly due to problems in Germany. After runs on a number of smaller banks in 1921, in 1922 authorities feared a systemic breakdown. DNB had to support a number of banks, including two medium-sized institutions (Bank-Associatie and Rotterdam-based Marx & Co) and numerous smaller banks. DNB incurred substantial losses, leaving it unable to support the large Rotterdamsche Bankvereeniging and compelling it to seek financial assistance from the government. A similar situation arose a year later in the reorganization of Centrale van Middenstandsbanken.[36]

Despite these problems, the 1921–1923 banking crisis had no major negative economic consequences. The economy even grew between 1922 and 1923. The lack of mass bank failures bolstered public confidence, although the growth of bank deposits as a proportion of the money supply stagnated. As Fig. 3.4 shows, banking

[35]Van Zanden (1997a: 128–131)

[36]Stoffer (1986); Van Zanden (1997b: 143–144)

problems affected the money supply, which rose sharply relative to GDP after 1910, before contracting in the 1920s.

What did change was the readiness of merchant banks to finance industry: close relationships with businesses were severed, the number of directorships held by banks fell sharply and banks' total assets declined as a proportion of national income. There was also a relative decline in the position of merchant banks, while more specialized institutions (agricultural and savings banks) expanded. The caution exercised by both banks and DNB allowed the Dutch banking system to weather the Great Depression of the 1930s. Unlike many other European countries, reserves held by banks and DNB were sufficient to avoid a crisis of confidence. The downside was that the Netherlands was able to remain on the gold standard, keeping the guilder expensive and prolonging its uncompetitive position. This had major negative consequences for the economy, as discussed below.[37]

3.2.3 *Policy and Regulation*

When the First World War broke out, the Netherlands – like other countries – suspended the exchangeability of money into gold. The statutory coverage ratio of DNB banknotes was reduced, from 40% of the value of issued banknotes in coins or metal to 20% in 1914. After the war, attempts were made to restore the pre-war monetary framework based on the gold standard. Many countries, including the Netherlands, decided to reintroduce the gold standard in 1925. But this subsequently caused a host of problems, eventually contributing to the Great Depression of the 1930s. This crisis started in the United States and spread rapidly around the world (see Box 3.4).[38]

Box 3.4 Crisis in the US: The Banking Act and the Chicago Plan

The US was hit by a severe financial and economic crisis in 1929. In the preceding years millions of Americans had invested their money in shares, often financed by bank borrowings. When the stock market crashed in October 1929 (Black Thursday), countless Americans saw their investments evaporate while many were unable to repay their loans. The banking sector was hit hard. Four waves of bank runs ensued, the fourth (in 1933) being the worst. A total of 7000 banks failed during this period. The Fed bore much of the blame as it was reluctant to support banks in distress. The criteria for providing emergency assistance were so strict that many banks ultimately went bust. This triggered a negative spiral of panic among banks and account holders, a

(continued)

[37]Van Zanden (1997a); Jonker (1999: 69)

[38]Eichengreen (1992)

Box 3.4 (continued)
worsening of economic conditions and corporate bankruptcies. The economic malaise was unprecedented: real national income fell by 30% and unemployment rose to more than 20% of the working population.[39]

The Roosevelt government introduced a wide range of reforms in response to the crisis. Interdependence between stock markets and the banking system was tackled by prohibiting merchant banks from engaging in securities trading.[40] The government also introduced a deposit insurance system, primarily in response to the many bank runs. The Fed was also given wider powers to support the banking system in case of emergency. A number of prominent economists associated with the Chicago School, including Frank Knight and Harry Simons, considered these measures insufficient. They called for even clearer lines of separation within the banking system: bank deposits should be separated from risky assets and backed entirely by cash, central bank reserves or government bonds. This would give the government greater control over the financial monetary system and with bank deposits fully covered, eliminate bank runs. Although these ideas were brought to the attention of the Roosevelt government, they did not carry the day.[41] Nevertheless, they still inspire many of the contemporary calls (including by Stichting Ons Geld) for fundamental reforms to the financial monetary system. We will consider these ideas in detail in Chap. 5.

European countries were deeply affected by the problems in the United States, beginning with crashes in Austria and Germany. American banks that had extended loans to banks in these countries collectively withdrew their money in response to the problems at home. Although Austrian and German central bank gold stocks were insufficient to provide credible support to their banking systems, no international aid was forthcoming. France in particular was sceptical about supporting these countries, for (geo)political reasons. The German and Austrian central banks then tried to convert their balances into gold at British banks, causing problems in the UK. As the Bank of England was powerless to stem the outflow of gold, the UK decided to leave the gold standard in 1931. Many other countries followed. While countries had cooperated to make the gold standard work prior to 1914, in the 1920s there was no willingness to do so. Sticking to the gold standard now contributed to instability.[42]

[39]Konzelmann et al. (2010); Coljé (1988); Romer and Romer (2003).

[40]The Glass-Steagall Act (officially the 1933 Banking Act) imposed four obligations. Banks affiliated with the Federal Reserve were no longer permitted to trade in securities for customers. They were also banned from trading and investing in securities on their own account, and from supporting securities issues. Finally, their staff were not permitted to be involved in financial institutions not subject to these restrictions (Sections 16, 20, 21 and 32).

[41]Benes and Kumhof (2013); Laina (2015)

[42]Temin (1993); Eichengreen and Temin (2000); Moessner and Allen (2010).

The Netherlands saw a strong inflow of gold, partly because DNB participated in the 'run' on the Bank of England. People also saw the Netherlands as a safe haven. DNB and the Ministry of Finance defended the guilder's link to gold in moral terms, portraying devaluation as tantamount to counterfeiting.[43] But as other countries allowed their currencies to depreciate by abandoning the gold standard, the 'remainers' paid a high price as their products became more expensive. Dutch farming in particular suffered badly, and as the economy deteriorated, unemployment climbed to almost 20% of the working population.[44] Calls from Dutch business for devaluation were therefore unsurprising. But it was only in September 1936, five years after the UK, that the Dutch government decided to abandon the gold standard – not because the authorities were persuaded of the benefits of leaving, but because the Dutch position had become untenable after Switzerland and France suspended exchangeability.[45]

The problems of many countries in the 1930s began with a financial crash. Authorities often responded by tightening financial regulation and oversight, splitting up banks, placing limits on international capital flows, imposing much stricter capital and liquidity requirements and introducing tight controls over bank lending. The Netherlands here was an exception. There was less urgency to reform the banking system, which had escaped many of the difficulties experienced in other countries. It was only after the Second World War that policy and oversight in financial regulation and supervision were tightened and formalized. We discuss these developments in the next section.

3.2.4 Summary: Money Creation in the Interwar Period

During the interwar period, most people in the Netherlands still relied on coins to make payments. Banknotes were mostly used by businesses and wealthy people, although the introduction of the ten guilder note and inflation during the First World War made banknotes more widely used. Although non-cash payments gained ground with the introduction of public giro services, it remained beyond the reach of many people. Non-cash payments were common for businesses, but bank services remained expensive and cumbersome. DNB in this period increasingly operated as a 'banker's bank', buying up loans granted by merchant banks. The creation of money was thus increasingly linked to the credit policies of merchant banks. Bank credit policies also saw changes in the interwar period, focusing on long-term industrial finance alongside short-term trade credits.

The reintroduction of the gold standard in 1925 meant that money creation, monetary policy and financial stability policy were once again tied to the supply

[43] Langeveld (2009)

[44] Statistics Netherlands (2009)

[45] Van Zanden (1997a: 148–151)

and demand for gold. The fixed link to gold played a key role in the global financial and economic malaise of the 1930s, preventing central banks from providing liquidity to banks in distress. National governments also had no appetite to support other countries in trouble: everyone wanted to retain gold or reclaim it from others. The result was a global run on gold that ultimately turned out badly for all. As in the nineteenth and early twentieth centuries, the Netherlands proved vulnerable to international trends. This time, however, it adopted a different strategy. While the country had previously chosen to review or abandon the guilder's link to metal when international developments prompted it, in the 1930s the gold standard was considered sacred. The Netherlands only abandoned gold when it was unable to do otherwise.

3.3 The Bretton Woods Period (1945–1973)

The Great Depression had already left the international financial monetary system highly fragmented. The Second World War caused even greater disruption, including in the Netherlands. In the years leading up to the war, people had turned to hoarding coins. In 1938 the Dutch Ministry of Finance ordered the printing of paper guilders and paper 'rijksdaalders', which became known as 'zilverbonnen' ('silver coupons') or 'muntbiljetten' ('coin notes'). The German occupiers continued this practice on a larger scale, dramatically increasing the money supply. The volume of deposit money likewise increased, leading to a structural increase in banks' leverage. Following liberation, the new Dutch government was forced to pursue a currency reform.[46]

After the war, countries sought to shape the international financial monetary system so that they would have more room to manoeuvre and international disruptions would less likely undermine the entire system. Although it was again decided to link money to precious metal – currencies were linked to the US dollar, which in turn was linked to gold – the Bretton Woods Agreement of 1944 amounted to a sea change, both in the formalization of international cooperation on monetary and financial matters and in its specifics, including restrictions on international capital flows. Control over financial markets was now part of broader government policy to ensure the financial sector would contribute to economic recovery and development. With growing prosperity, banks broadened their focus to serve the population as a whole, while changes in the banking sector included the fading of divisions between different types of banks.

[46]In the autumn of 1945 everyone in the Netherlands had to surrender their banknotes. In return they received a blocked account at banks and ten guilders per family member per week to meet living expenses; new banknotes became available afterwards. Known as the 'Lieftinck tenner' after the finance minister who introduced it, the reform sought to remove the excess banknotes that had entered into circulation during the German occupation and to wipe out the profits of those who had exploited the war-time black market.

3.3.1 *Money and Payments*

Deposit money became dominant in the decades following the Second World War. Until the late 1950s, the ratio of cash to deposit money remained more or less stable; thereafter, cash declined relative to GDP while the growth of deposit money broadly kept pace with economic growth. In 1975, the ratio was roughly 70%–30% in favour of deposit money.

By 1968 the public Postcheque- en Girodienst (PCGD) held over a million accounts.[47] Automation enabled wages to be paid electronically, favoured by employers and the government over the expensive, labour-intensive system of cash payments.[48] The PCGD and the municipal giro services introduced innovations that made electronic payments increasingly attractive. In 1961, Gemeentegiro Amsterdam became the first Dutch bank to issue debit cards that could be used to make payments in shops. In 1969 it became the first bank to install an automated teller machine.[49]

This period witnessed greater competition between different types of banks, which up until the 1960s had their own areas of operation and customer base. But with the growing prosperity of the Dutch population, commercial banks, which had previously focused on business, now tried to entice customers away from the PCGD. They did so by offering interest on payment accounts and by introducing guaranteed cheques that consumers could use in the Netherlands and abroad. The boundaries between different types of banks gradually faded, with many banks turning into universal banks. But despite this blurring of boundaries, there remained two separate payment systems: one operated by the public PCGD and the other by a partnership of commercial (private) banks.[50]

3.3.2 *Financing*

The Dutch economy was in bad shape after the Second World War. Material damage was extensive, factories lay idle and many businesses were shuttered. No more than 37% of imports were covered by exports, which would be untenable in the long run.[51] The government, which had to take drastic steps to stimulate reconstruction, saw regulating finance as essential to its strategy. As in other European countries, Dutch policymakers regulated the growth, allocation and price of credit. Banks had to obtain prior consent for loans exceeding 50,000 guilders while DNB had to ensure

[47]Peekel and Veluwenkamp (1984: 3)

[48]Lelieveldt (2017: 9)

[49]Van Engelen (2009: 37)

[50]DNB (2002)

[51]Van Zanden (1997a: 174)

that it only granted loans essential for reconstruction.[52] The government thus sought to ensure that credit was used productively (see also Sect. 3.3.3).

As in other European countries, the Dutch government set up financial institutions to promote recovery. A pre-war initiative (Maatschappij voor Industriefinanciering, founded in 1935) had collapsed due to undercapitalization. In contrast, the Nederlandse Herstelbank, established in 1945, successfully financed industrial companies with backing from the government. Another institution, the Export Financieringsmaatschappij established in 1951, helped stimulate Dutch exports.[53]

The financial sector reoriented itself as the economy recovered. Economic growth led to a sharp rise in business demand for loans. Many businesses also found that retained earnings were insufficient to finance investments and growth. With the Nederlandse Herstelbank and Export Financieringsmaatschappij unable to meet the growing demand for credit, merchant banks, after decades of restraint, took renewed interest in long-term lending to Dutch business. But this required a solid base of cash and central bank reserves, which proved problematic.[54]

The growing prosperity of the Dutch population and the more even spread of wealth meant that a fast-growing proportion of the money supply was entering the hands of wage earners. This money was still mostly paid out in cash. To the extent that people deposited this cash in giro and savings accounts, it was generally at PCGD and Rijkspostspaarbank. This meant that when banks granted loans to businesses, thereby creating new bank deposits, an increasingly large proportion of money ended up *outside* of the commercial banking system. The resulting outflow of cash and central bank reserves limited the ability of banks to grant new loans, thereby putting a brake on the creation of deposit money. To prevent the continued leakage of reserves, commercial banks began to focus on providing payment accounts to the general public. Business financing and household savings therefore became increasingly intertwined.[55]

Competition between banks encouraged mergers and consolidations. In 1964 Nederlandsche Handel-Maatschappij and Twentsche Bank merged to become Algemene Bank Nederland (ABN) while Amsterdamsche Bank and Rotterdamsche Bank formed Amsterdam-Rotterdam Bank (AMRO). In 1972 the umbrella bodies for agricultural cooperatives merged to form Coöperatieve Centrale Raiffeisen-Boerenleenbank (Rabobank). The smaller savings banks (there were still 266 in 1960), Rijkspostspaarbank and the giro institutions were hit hard by this competition. Despite the many mergers, savings banks lost their market share. The Amsterdam municipal giro became part of PCGD in 1976. PCGD and Rijkspostspaarbank also increased their collaboration, a prelude to their merger in the 1980s to form Postbank, which subsequently merged into ING in the 1990s.

---

[52]Barendregt and Visser (1997: 187)

[53]Posthuma (1955); Van Riel (2016)

[54]WRR (2016: 67–68)

[55]Peekel and Veluwenkamp (1984: 22–23)

3.3.3 *Policy and Regulation*

Many European countries in the post-war period used monetary policy to promote economic growth and employment. Political influence on monetary policy increased as finance ministries took over more control from central banks.[56] Although this trend was less pronounced in the Netherlands, ultimate responsibility for monetary policy lay with the Ministry of Finance, with the central bank operating in the 'shadow of hierarchy'.[57] Many central banks that had been private institutions were nationalized in the post-war period (DNB in 1948) in view of the public interest of monetary policy.[58]

To facilitate the pursuit of national policy goals, governments sought international cooperation. Here the Bretton Woods Agreement was a watershed. Under the Bretton Woods regime, governments linked their currencies to the US dollar, which in turn was linked to gold.[59] Compared to the old gold standard, governments placed much tighter restrictions on international financial transactions. Capital controls – which gave countries more freedom to gear their monetary policies to their domestic economies – were also standard in the newly formed European Economic Community.[60] According to the well-known 'monetary trilemma', countries can choose at most two of the following three policy goals: (1) fixed exchange rates; (2) autonomous monetary policy; and (3) full freedom of capital movements.[61] With the Bretton Woods Agreement, governments chose the former two.

The Bretton Woods regime departed from the preceding period in yet another way. To address temporary deficits in a country's current account, the International Monetary Fund was endowed with substantial capital resources to lend to countries in difficulty. In the event of structurally negative trade balances, countries could adjust exchange rates, thereby postponing real adjustments to wages and prices. The need for such regulated flexibility and international coordination was a crucial lesson from the interwar period.[62] The Netherlands used this option at the end of 1949 (following the example of the UK) and devalued its currency by 30% against the dollar.[63] But despite these changes, the Bretton Woods variant of the gold standard also ultimately proved untenable (see Box 3.5).

---

[56] Goodhart (2010)

[57] De Greef et al. (1997)

[58] Capie et al. (1994)

[59] Outside the US, households could no longer exchange their banknotes and coins for precious metal. This can be seen as the next step in the decoupling of national currencies and precious metal.

[60] Bakker (1996)

[61] Obstfeld and Taylor (1998)

[62] Feinstein et al. (1997: 204)

[63] Bakker and Van Lent (1989: 170)

Box 3.5 The Demise of the Gold-Dollar Exchange Standard

Although gold still played a role in the Bretton Woods system, the link with national currencies was more indirect, namely through the US dollar. Since the US Federal Reserve could increase international reserves (dollars rather than gold), this standard, unlike the gold standard, did not cause major problems for international economic stability. But as the designated provider of international reserves, the United States enjoyed major advantages over other countries.[64]

The United States' freedom to increase international reserves introduced a weakness into the Bretton Woods system; as identified by the Belgian-American economist Robert Triffin, but also already by Keynes during the Bretton Woods negotiations in 1944. As international reserves grew more 'abundant', the gold-dollar fixed exchange rate would gradually lose credibility. As foreign central banks had increasingly large claims on US gold stocks, a 'run' could ultimately arise, even with the US controlling two-thirds of global gold stocks.

This is precisely what happened in the late 1960s and early 1970s. The rapid rise of global trade and robust European growth led to a structural increase in the demand for international reserves, causing the gold coverage rate to fall from 55% in 1944 to 22% in 1970. Large US capital exports, associated with aid programmes and the Vietnam War, exacerbated the problem. After 1965, France in particular sought to undermine US dominance by converting dollars into gold and arguing for a return to the gold standard. In August 1971 US President Nixon decided to suspend the exchangeability of dollars into gold, severing both the link between money and gold and transatlantic monetary ties. The decoupling, which became permanent in 1973, saw previously linked currencies become floating currencies. The Netherlands soon moved to a *de facto* link to the Deutschmark.

The Banking Act of 1948 entrusted DNB with "regulating the value of the Dutch monetary unit in the manner most beneficial for the country's prosperity, while stabilizing its value as far as possible".[65] Monetary policy was thus linked to the public interest (the country's prosperity). Capital controls were originally meant to prevent an *outflow* of capital, to ensure that capital would be used in the Netherlands for reconstruction. But as the economy and trade balance recovered, capital controls were used to prevent excessive *inflows* of finance, which DNB feared would stoke inflation. The Netherlands was among the first countries in Europe to lift controls on capital outflows.[66] DNB also restricted short-term lending and overdrafts to curb

[64]Eichengreen (2011)

[65]Quoted in Renselaar and Stokman (2001: 8). Our translation.

[66]Bakker (1996)

excessive credit growth, which – with the associated growth of the money supply – could fuel inflation.[67]

While price stability was a key rationale for credit controls, they also contributed to financial stability.[68] The Act on the Supervision of the Credit System (1952) had given DNB formal responsibility for the stability of the Dutch banking system.[69] Credit controls, capital requirements and liquidity rules were part of the DNB arsenal. Capital rules addressed banks' equity positions, their ability to absorb losses without becoming insolvent, and stipulated that equity had to be at least 20% of risk-bearing assets.[70] Liquidity rules required banks to hold sufficient central bank reserves or readily saleable assets (such as government bonds). Meant primarily to control money creation,[71] they also sought to limit the mismatch between the term of bank loans and liabilities. Banks had to ensure that long-term loans (of more than 2 years) were fully matched by long-term liabilities (including savings deposits).

Another instrument was the so-called structural policy, which required divisions to be maintained *within* the banking system and *between* banks and other (financial and non-financial) sectors. Structural policy determined the types of activities banks were allowed to pursue and the types of regulation to which they were subject. The purpose was to maintain segmentation within the banking sector. Other goals were to prevent the emergence of excessively large banks or financial conglomerates and banks acquiring shares in non-financial businesses. This would limit banks' power and market dominance and guarantee transparent ownership to enable effective supervision. DNB thus gained influence over competition within the sector: merger and acquisition plans had to be submitted to DNB and could only proceed on the basis of a 'declaration of no objection'.[72]

In practice, however, DNB was highly flexible regarding mergers, as evidenced by the consolidation described above and the formation of universal banks in the 1960s. The idea was that Dutch banks would need to have a certain size to successfully compete in the emerging European market. Universal banks gradually grew dominant in the Netherlands; compared to specialised banks, they faced fewer restrictions on the types of activities they could pursue, thereby generating competitive advantages.

---

[67] Barendregt and Visser (1997: 189)

[68] De Greef et al. (1997)

[69] Coljé (1988: 11)

[70] Van Eekelen (1987); Coljé (1988)

[71] From 1954 there was a compulsory cash reserve: banks were required to maintain a certain level of central bank reserves relative to bank deposits. From the 1970s there was also a liquidity reserve requirement, based partly on banks' other liquid assets (Eijffinger 1983: 20–29).

[72] Van Eerden (2001)

3.3.4 Summary: Money Creation in the Bretton Woods Period

The use of deposit money finally became dominant in payments and savings during the post-war period. Automation, increased scale and professionalization made it much easier and cheaper for banks to provide deposit money accounts and process payment instructions. Increasing and more evenly spread prosperity implied that wage earners held a growing share of the money supply. But the continued preference of most people for the public giro system or cash, constrained commercial bank lending and hence money creation. The outflow of deposit money created by banks to the public banks (or its conversion into cash), restrained the commercial banks in the growth of their loan book. In response, commercial banks began to focus on offering payment accounts to consumers, thus gradually becoming all-purpose banks. This was accompanied by a process of increasing scale and a blurring of distinctions between different types of banks.

Government policy heavily affected bank lending. Policy instruments such as credit and interest rate limits and allocation rules sought to bolster the financial sector's economic contribution, curb inflation, limit upward pressure on interest rates, and prevent financial instability. Dutch policies were far from unique here as all Western governments used these types of instruments.[73]

At Bretton Woods, governments agreed to reshape the international financial monetary order, privileging international cooperation, capital controls and adjustable exchange rates. Still, the system maintained an (indirect) link to gold, thereby resembling the pre-war gold standard. But because countries used capital controls and the main international reserve currency (the dollar) was abundantly available, this time the link to gold did not lead to instability. Nevertheless, it was precisely the dollar's abundance that finally undermined the system: as international claims on US gold stocks grew, the dollar-gold link became less credible, encouraging countries to convert their dollars into gold. Ultimately, there was a run on US gold – just as there had been on British gold in the 1930s. And just as Britain was forced to abandon the gold standard in 1931, the US had to close the 'gold window' in 1971. This time, the link between gold and money was severed definitively, again illustrating how a fixed link between money and metal (or any other 'external anchor') ultimately fails to deliver the desired stability.

3.4 The Pre-crisis Period (1973–2008)

Trust in interventionist government policies evaporated in the 1970s when the economy stagnated and inflation rose to high levels. The 1980s thus witnessed the rising popularity of economic theories that embraced market forces and were more sceptical of government intervention. These theories presented the financial sector as

[73]Stellinga (2015)

a largely passive factor in the economy, as a kind of neutral 'intermediary'. Financial markets were not seen as fundamentally different from other markets: stimulating market forces was believed to improve efficiency.[74] Although policymakers did not embrace these pro-market ideas unconditionally, they were definitely inspired by them.

The Netherlands was quick to adopt these pro-market ideas. Restrictions on lending and international capital flows were almost entirely dismantled and the post-war structural policy abandoned. These reforms stimulated bank lending, in particular mortgages, as well as mergers and acquisitions, which ultimately led to the dominance of a small number of large financial institutions. The 'public' giro and savings segment was absorbed by the commercial banking sector through the creation of Postbank in 1986 and its subsequent privatization, while numerous local savings banks were merged into umbrella organizations (chief among them SNS, formed in 1987). As a result, Dutch households became almost entirely dependent on a small number of big, private institutions for all their savings, payments and borrowing needs.

3.4.1 *Money and Payments*

In the decades leading up to the 2008 financial crisis, the proportion of deposit money in the money supply (M1) rose from 70% in 1975 to 83% at the outbreak of the crisis (see Fig. 3.5).[75] Paying with bank deposits became the norm for a wide range of transactions. In addition to salary and rent or mortgage payments, the introduction of electronic bank payment cards and the PIN system meant that shopping and other retail payments also became electronic. Technological innovations played a key role, for example in the rollout of in-store payment facilities. Automation also cut the costs of giro payments.[76]

Almost everyone gained access to one or more bank accounts. In 1984 there were five million PCGD accounts and six million giro accounts at private banks.[77] By 2002 Dutch consumers collectively held over 20 million accounts (many more than the number of inhabitants), while businesses and government institutions collectively held two million accounts.[78] People of course still used cash for many transactions (from 2002 in euros instead of guilders), but cash payments were gradually dwarfed by giro payments.

The privatization of Postbank – itself the result of the merger of Rijkspostspaarbank and PCGD – after 1986 was a crucial development. Postbank merged with NMB to form NMB-Postbank, which in turn merged with Nationale

[74]Blyth (2002)

[75]The share of deposit money peaked around the time of the introduction of the euro. People held less cash so they would not have to change it into euros.

[76]Lelieveldt (2017)

[77]Peekel and Veluwenkamp (1984: 3)

[78]DNB (2002)

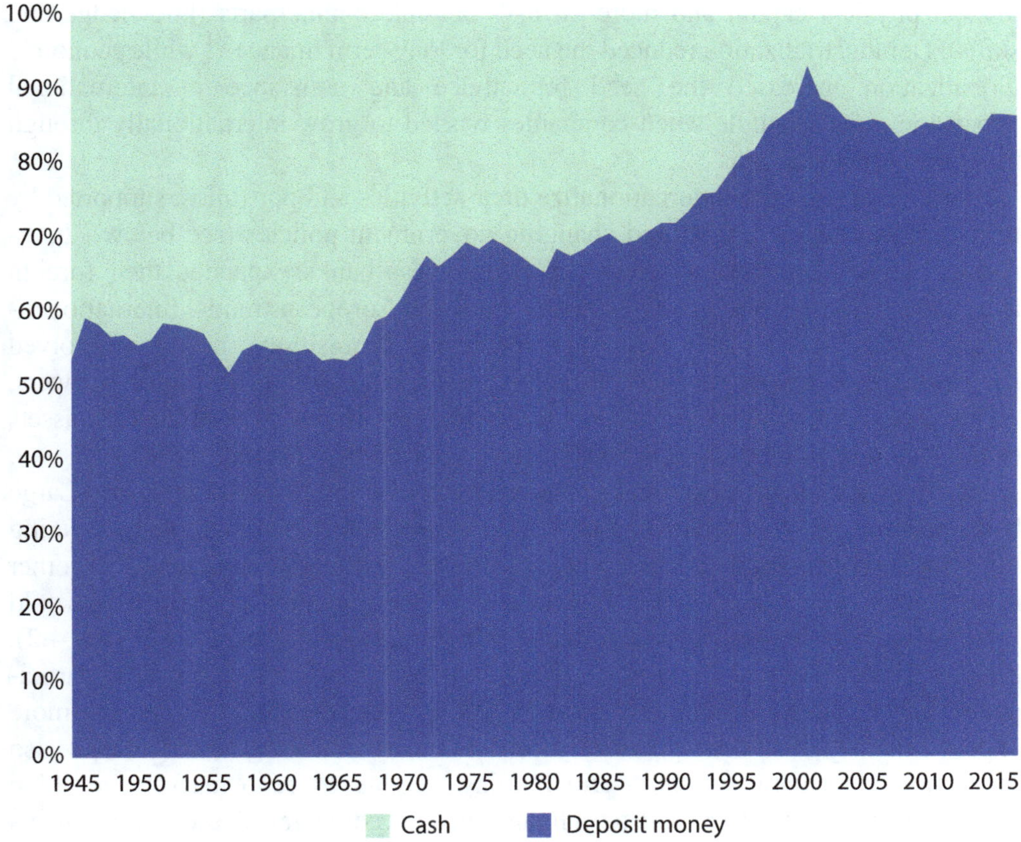

Fig. 3.5 The share of deposit money and cash over time
M1 in the Netherlands (1945–2015)
Source: Statistics Netherlands, Statline; DNB (direct data supply) (Data since 2002 are less reliable as the amount of cash in any euro area country can no longer be observed. In the euro area cash is allocated to different countries by means of a fixed allocation key)

Nederlanden to form the ING Group in 1991. This ended the 'public' part of the payment and giro system; cash was now the only form of 'public money'.[79] The privatization of Postbank took place amid broader consolidation in the Dutch banking sector. Since then, most customer deposits have been with four large universal banks (ING, ABN-AMRO, Rabobank and SNS), which in 2013 had a joint market share of around 89% of bank deposits.[80]

3.4.2 Financing

Since the 1980s, many countries have transitioned towards a knowledge-based economy, entailing further expansion of the service sector and greater internationalization and liberalization. Financing requirements changed as service sectors rely

[79]DNB (2002); Uittenbogaard (2017)

[80]DNB (2015: 19)

less on physical capital and more on its intangible counterparts (knowledge and skills). Deindustrialization reduced the need for long-term finance,[81] while economic globalization increased the need for advice and assistance in international expansion – for example when companies wished to grow internationally through mergers and acquisitions.

Banks also sought to internationalize their activities and portfolios, supported by technological developments and changing government policies (see below). International capital transactions grew exponentially as banks expanded their foreign activities. Here the Dutch banking sector followed European trends. Internationalization was achieved partly through mergers and acquisitions, but also involved the purchase of foreign financial products or direct lending to foreign borrowers. At the time of the credit crisis, foreign assets made up around 50% of the total assets of the Dutch banking system, with ING and ABN AMRO leading the way.[82]

Banking also became more closely interwoven with financial markets. Large banks increasingly focused on capital market transactions,[83] for example by offering investment products and assisting companies with stock market flotations.[84] Another important development was the emergence of 'securitization', where banks sold large volumes of loans to special purpose vehicles ('shadow banks' – see Box 4.2). Shadow banks financed these loans by selling securities to other financial participants such as pension funds and insurers. As a result, these parties became more exposed to risks that were previously confined to the banking sector. Banks also grew more dependent on short-term funding, relying on repo markets in which financial participants offer short-term finance against collateral. These developments made banks increasingly susceptible to the short-term dynamics of financial markets.[85]

At the same time, societal developments affected the operation of the financial sector. With growing prosperity and wealth, financial products and services such as facilities for savings, loans and insurance became mass products, no longer the preserve of the most prosperous households. Women's growing participation in the labour market and rising female incomes pushed up the price of housing, while welfare reforms privileged financial self-reliance and the individual contracting of services (savings and insurance) that had previously been organized collectively.[86]

These developments had a major impact on (and were themselves influenced by) the Dutch banking sector. Banks began to focus more on consumer lending, in particular mortgages. In banks' loan books, the proportion of 'loans to households' increased from 43% in 1990 to 57% today. This entailed an enormous rise in

---

[81] OECD (2000)

[82] WRR (2016: 109–110)

[83] The capital market relates to the supply and demand for longer-term financial resources. The money market relates to the supply and demand for short-term financial resources.

[84] WRR (2016: Chap. 4)

[85] WRR (2016: 96–100)

[86] Schelkle (2012)

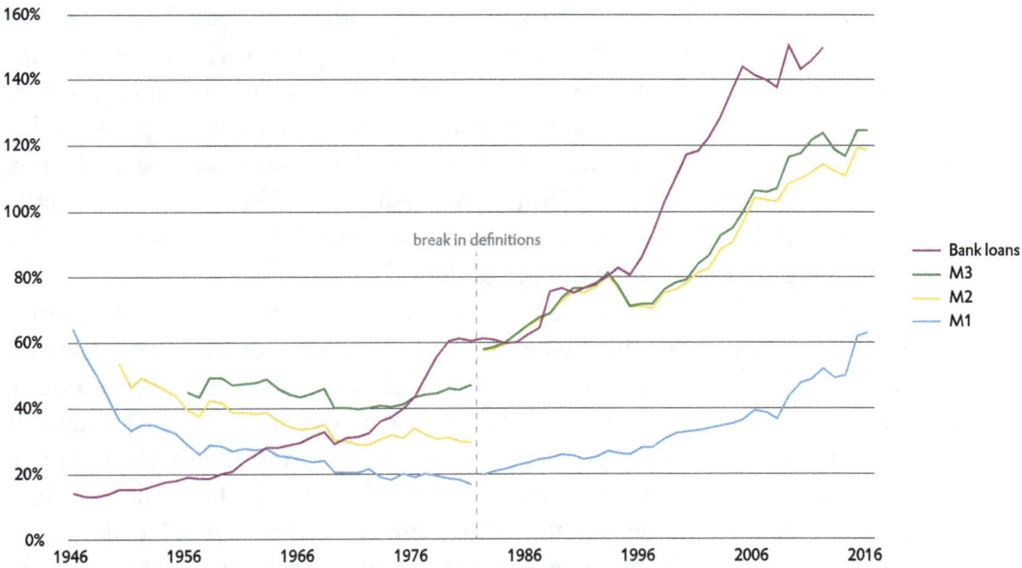

Fig. 3.6 Credit (bank loans) and money in circulation
The Netherlands, percentage of GDP
Source: DNB data (money supply) and Taylor and Schularick (bank loans)

household debt, from 27% of GDP in 1982 to 106% of GDP in 2011.[87] Increased lending and rising house prices reinforced one another, with increased borrowing pushing up property prices which in turn contributed to increased borrowing, and so on.

These developments were facilitated by changes in government policy, consolidation in the banking sector and the growing importance of deposit money. Lending by commercial banks was previously constrained by the leakage of reserves to the public part of the monetary system (cash and deposits at public banks). The increasing popularity of deposit money and the integration of the old PCGD and Rijkspostspaarbank into the commercial banking system effectively removed this constraint. The similarity between large banks further implied that they could be increasingly confident that the inflow and outflow of deposits would match (Fig. 3.6).

3.4.3 Policy and Regulation

Government policies facilitated these developments. Governments promoted freedom of movement for financial firms and capital flows, believing this would foster economic growth through more efficient services and financial innovation. As in other Western European countries, Dutch policymakers dismantled a wide range of

[87]WRR (2016: 122)

post-war rules governing the price, growth and allocation of credit.[88] By the late 1980s, practically all restrictions had been lifted, paving the way for the lending boom. Ballooning household debt was also facilitated by socioeconomic policies. Housing market policies in many countries encouraged home ownership; examples in the Netherlands included the National Mortgage Guarantee scheme and (to a lesser extent) the Encouragement of Home Ownership Act. The tax system's preferential treatment of debt finance – such as home mortgage interest deduction – also contributed to the growth of Dutch mortgage debt.[89]

Financial globalization was boosted by the elimination of restrictions on international capital flows. In Europe, the Netherlands, the UK and Germany were the first to lift all restrictions, with all other EU countries following suit in the 1990s. Policy initiatives at the European level also gave impetus to the internal market for financial services. The passporting system gave financial institutions the freedom, once established in one EU member state, to set up branches in all EU countries while being supervised in their home country. Governments harmonized legislation to create a level playing field for financial firms, for example with the 1999 Financial Services Action Plan. The introduction of Economic and Monetary Union further reinforced the Europeanization of financial markets.[90]

Western governments also dismantled their structural policies for the banking sector. The post-war principle that a segmented sector contributes to financial stability was discarded and replaced by a belief that institutions with diversified business models would not only operate more efficiently but would also be better able to spread their risks. Dutch structural policy ended around 1990 with the approval of a series of mergers. ABN and AMRO merged to form ABN-AMRO in 1991; the merger of VSB, AMEV and the Belgian insurer AG Group led to the creation of Fortis in 1990; while Postbank, NMB and Nationale Nederlanden merged to form the ING Group. Partitions and dividing lines between different parts of the financial system – including between insurance and banking – were practically a thing of the past.

While policymakers encouraged financial institutions' freedom of movement, they were aware of the risks. To ensure financial firms' stability, policymakers turned to capital requirements: rules that obliged banks to hold sufficient equity to absorb unforeseen losses. To facilitate integration, European countries harmonized their capital adequacy rules, basing them on the capital requirements advanced by the Basel Committee (established by central banks from ten OECD countries in 1974). The Basel I Accord (1988) was transposed into European rules, and subsequently implemented in European member states.

The Netherlands' formal framework for capital requirements dates back to 1957. As these requirements were eased between 1970 and 1985, Basel I resulted in no

[88]Barendregt and Visser (1997)

[89]Tijdelijke Commissie Huizenprijzen (2013)

[90]OECD (1997); Abdelal (2007); Lane (2013)

substantial changes.[91] Banks were now required to hold capital (equity) equivalent to at least 8% of their risk-weighted assets. Larger changes came with Basel II (2004), which gave banks more freedom to use their own advanced risk management systems to estimate the equity they needed. Supervisors sought to reconcile public and private interests, believing banks, in exchange for more freedoms, would better manage their risks.[92] Compared to post-war structural and credit policies, capital requirements were a much more indirect form of public control, with policymakers viewing them as a market-friendly way of regulating banks.[93]

Much also changed in the domain of (international) monetary policy. The demise of the Bretton Woods fixed exchange rate system in 1971 marked the abandoning of precious metal as the anchor of monetary policy. Whether countries should continue to pursue fixed exchange rates now became a key issue. Many economists called for their abandonment, or at least for regulated flexibility. But within the European Economic Community (subsequently the EU), flexibility was seen as undesirable; the common market, it was thought, would operate best when economic participants had certainty about exchange rates.

Following the demise of the Bretton Woods system, European countries sought to link their currencies as far as possible. From 1973 the Netherlands focused on Germany, not only because of the importance of trade with that country, but also due to its reputation for low and stable inflation.[94] From 1977 onwards there was a *de facto* Deutschmark zone comprising the Netherlands, Denmark, Luxembourg and Belgium – all taking their cues from decisions by the Bundesbank. Although European countries agreed to set margins within which their currencies could fluctuate, this proved difficult to maintain in practice, as seen in the many devaluations. As countries had deregulated cross-border capital flows, they were now susceptible to speculative attacks.

In 1990 France and Germany agreed that France would accept German reunification in exchange for monetary union. This was not the sequence the Netherlands had in mind, as it saw economic integration and convergence as a prerequisite for monetary union. The formal decision to establish a single European currency was taken in 1991 and was enshrined in the Maastricht Treaty in 1992. Economic and Monetary Union was completed in 2002 with the introduction of euro notes and coins.

In addition to fixed exchange rates, European central banks also increasingly focused on guaranteeing price stability – generally defined as inflation of around 2%. Many people saw the high and volatile inflation of the 1970s as proof of the need to overhaul monetary policy. Previously accepted (explicit or implicit) targets – for employment, economic growth and financial stability – were now relegated to the background of monetary policy. Inflation was measured mainly by growth in

---

[91] Van Eekelen (1987)

[92] Tarullo (2008)

[93] Hellwig (2010)

[94] De Greef et al. (1997)

consumer prices; movements in the price of financial assets such as houses and shares were generally ignored.

With the liberalization of financial markets, central banks saw little point in pursuing mechanisms of direct control and switched to indirect instruments: setting interest rates on short-term loans to banks, coupled with a 'communications strategy' to make their policies predictable for financial market participants. There was also a new consensus that both the development and implementation of monetary policy should be as far removed from politics as possible – reflected in the design of the European Central Bank. Politicians were deemed too fickle and opportunistic to conduct predictable monetary policy and to keep inflation in check.[95]

3.4.4 Summary: Money Creation in the Pre-crisis Period

The period before the credit crisis witnessed fundamental changes to the financial monetary system. In the Netherlands deposit money became the norm; virtually everyone had bank and savings accounts while cash payments declined. Banks became an indispensable part of the payment system, while the public institutions PCGD and Rijkspostspaarbank became part of the 'commercial banking system' through privatizations. Whereas before the 1970s two relatively separate worlds had coexisted – the commercial banks served businesses while PCGD, Rijkspostspaarbank and other savings banks served households – these activities became interwoven. There were now few partitions within banking, further witnessed in the emergence of conglomerates of banks and insurance companies.

In the area of financing, numerous constraints on lending were dismantled; policymakers eliminated practically all capital controls, credit ceilings, allocation rules and interest rate limits. The constraints that replaced them – broadly speaking, capital requirements – only functioned as indirect limits on credit creation (see Chap. 2). Bank lending – in the Netherlands particularly mortgage lending – took off. Banks also became more active internationally and began focusing on the capital market. As mergers and acquisitions led to ever larger institutions, a small group of very large banks came to dominate the financial monetary system.

Changes in international monetary policy had consequences for money creation and credit growth. As stated above, central banks abandoned direct control mechanisms and increasingly relied on the 'interest rate instrument' (their ability to vary interest rates charged on loans to banks). Since the main focus was on movements in the price of goods and services, central banks paid less attention to credit growth linked to the financing of financial assets and real estate. Given this paradigm, it is no surprise that the growth of intrafinancial and mortgage lending in the decade prior to the crisis remained largely outside the purview of central banks. How far they had underestimated the importance of these developments only became clear during the crisis.

---

[95]Forsyth and Notermans (1997); Hilbers (1998); Blyth (2002); Goodhart (2010); OECD (2011)

3.5 Conclusion

The financial monetary system has seen fundamental changes over the past two centuries. From a system dominated by coins (for households) and trade bills and DNB banknotes (for businesses) in the nineteenth century, we have moved to a system in which bank deposit money is by far the most important means of payment. The link between currency and precious metal (gold or silver) remained important for the operation of the system until well into the twentieth century, but no longer plays a role today. Instead, the crucial factors are credit supply and demand, the operation of the banking system and government policy.

Our current system did not develop from any explicit blueprint. The changes mostly came about gradually (in some cases rapidly) with no overall coordination. Numerous factors – international developments, social and economic changes, technological advances and policy developments – all had major impacts. Policymakers and central banks, for example, mostly saw the rise of deposit money as a positive development for efficiency and only gradually discovered that it enabled banks to significantly increase their lending. In short, the current design of our financial monetary system was not planned, let alone set in stone.

One common thread through monetary history is the perennial dilemma between the need to maintain currency stability and the need for monetary flexibility. Flexibility is essential to ensure economic growth and to allow authorities to intervene during crises. The tension between stability and flexibility was acutely felt during periods when money was tied to precious metal. On the one hand, people saw this link as essential to achieve certainty in an inherently uncertain world. On the other hand, the strict link created problems for financing economic activity and for combatting crises. Conversely, excessive flexibility in the monetary system can undermine stability. The flexibility of lending in the 1990s and 2000s ultimately led to the 2007–2009 financial crisis, thereby undermining both financial stability and economic growth. The subsequent debt hangover and economic malaise then threatened price stability – risking deflation rather than inflation.

As a small trading country, the Netherlands is vulnerable to the international environment. Although the country has some scope to chart its own course, the effects of its choices are largely determined by developments beyond the control of its policymakers. Over the decades the Netherlands has had to manage its scope for independent action as strategically as possible – and has not always done so successfully. In the 1930s the Dutch authorities retained the gold standard for too long when major countries were abandoning it, while evidence was mounting that the Netherlands was harming its economic interests. Conversely, the Netherlands has at times been too quick to uncritically follow international trends, for example when policymakers in the 1980s abandoned almost all limits on credit growth, concentration in the banking sector and capital flows. In sum, striking the right balance between a flexible response to international developments and charting a national course remains a constant challenge.

Bibliography

Abdelal, R. (2007). *Capital rules. The construction of global finance*. Cambridge, MA/London: Harvard University Press.

Bakker, A. F. P. (1996). *International financial institutions*. London: Longman.

Bakker, A. F. P., & van Lent, M. M. P. (1989). *Pieter Lieftinck, 1902–1989. Een leven in vogelvlucht*. Utrecht: Veen.

Barendregt, J., & Visser, H. (1997). Towards a new maturity. In M. 't Hart, J. Jonker, & J. L. van Zanden (Eds.), *A financial history of the Netherlands* (pp. 152–194). Cambridge: Cambridge University Press.

Benes, J., & Kumhof, M. (2013). The Chicago plan revisited. *IMF Working Paper, 12*, 202.

Blyth, M. (2002). *Great transformations. Economic ideas and institutional change in the twentieth century*. Cambridge: Cambridge University Press.

Boonstra, W. W. (2018). *Geld; Wat is het, wat doet het, waar komt het vandaag?* Amsterdam: VU University Press.

Capie, F., Goodhart, C., & Schnadt, N. (1994). The development of central banking. In S. Fischer, C. Goodhart, & N. Schnadt (Eds.), *The future of central banking: The tercentenary symposium of the Bank of England* (pp. 1–261). Cambridge: Cambridge University Press.

Coljé, H. (1988). *Het toezicht op de banken in Nederland*. Amsterdam: NIBE.

de Greef, I., Hilbers, P. L. C., & Hoogduin, L. H. (1997). *Moderate Monetarism: A brief survey of Dutch monetary policy in the post-war period* (DNB staff reports, no. 28). Available at: www.dnb.nl

de Jong, A. M. (1967). *Geschiedenis van de Nederlandsche Bank* (Vol. I-III). Haarlem: Joh. Enschedé.

de Vries, J. (1989). *Geschiedenis van de Nederlandsche Bank, V, De Nederlandsche Bank van 1914 tot 1948. Visserings tijdvak 1914–1931*. Amsterdam: NIBE.

DNB. (2001). *Kwartaalbericht December 2001*. Amsterdam: De Nederlandsche Bank.

DNB. (2002). *Tariefstructuren en infrastructuur in het Nederlandse massale betalingsverkeer*. Amsterdam: De Nederlandsche Bank.

DNB. (2015). *Visie op de structuur van de Nederlandse bankensector – Stabiliteit en efficiëntie door diversiteit en concurrentie*. Amsterdam: De Nederlandsche Bank.

Eichengreen, B. (1992). *Golden fetters. The gold standard and the great depression 1919–1939*. Oxford: Oxford University Press.

Eichengreen, B., & Temin, P. (2000). The gold standard and the great depression. *Contemporary European History, 9*(2), 183–207.

Eichengreen, B., El-Erian, M., Fraga, A., et al. (2011). *Rethinking central banking*. Ontario: Committee on International Economic Policy and Reform.

Eijffinger, S. C. W. (1983). *Het monetaire beleid van de Nederlandsche Bank* (Serie Researchmemoranda, no. 19). Amsterdam: Vrije Universiteit.

Feinstein, C., Temin, P., & Toniolo, G. (1997). *The European economy between the wars*. Oxford: Oxford University Press.

Forsyth, D. J., & Notermans, T. (1997). *Regime changes: Macroeconomic policy and financial regulation in Europe from the 1930s to the 1990s*. Oxford: Berghahn Books.

Goodhart, C. A. E. (2010). *The changing role of central banks* (BIS Working Paper 326). Basel: Bank for International Settlements.

Hellwig, M. (2010). Capital regulation after the crisis: Business as usual? *Preprints of the Max Planck Institute for Research on Collective Goods, 31*.

Hilbers, P. (1998). *Financial sector reform and monetary policy in the Netherlands* (IMF Working Papers No. 19).

Jonker, J. (1997). The alternative road to modernity. Banking and currency, 1814–1914. In M. 't Hart, J. Jonker, & J. L. van Zanden (Eds.), *A financial history of the Netherlands*. Cambridge: Cambridge University Press.

Jonker, J. P. B. (1999). De bakermat van het Nederlandse bankwezen, financiële markten in Nederland vanaf de Franse Tijd tot de opkomst van de handelsbanken, 1813–1870. In *Wereldwijd bankieren, ABN AMRO 1824–1999*. Amsterdam: ABN AMRO.

Knafo, S. (2006). The gold standard and the origins of the modern international monetary system. *Review of International Political Economy, 13*(1), 78–102.

Konzelmann, S., Wilkinson, F., Fovargue-Davies, M., & Sankey, D. (2010). Governance, regulation and financial market instability: The implications for policy and reform. *Cambridge Journal of Economics, 34*(5), 929–954.

Kymmell, J. (1992). *Geschiedenis van de algemene banken in Nederland 1860–1914, Part I*. Amsterdam: Nederlands Instituut voor het Bank- en Effectenbedrijf.

Kymmell, J. (1996). *Geschiedenis van de algemene banken 1860–1914, Part II-A+B*. Amsterdam.

Laina, P. (2015). Proposals for full-reserve banking: A historical survey from David Ricardo to Martin Wolf. *Economic Thought, 4*(2), 1–19.

Lane, P. R. (2013, April). *Capital flows in the Euro Area* (*European Economy Economic Paper* 497).

Langeveld, H. (2009). Grotendeels buitenspel. Het Nederlandse parlement en de crisis van de jaren dertig van de twintigste eeuw. In C. van Baalen et al. (Eds.), *Jaarboek Parlementaire Geschiedenis* (pp. 37–46).

Lelieveldt. (2017, September 7). Betalingsverkeer: hoe markt en regelgeving elkaar maken en breken. *ESB*.

Moessner, R., & Allen, W. A. (2010). *Central bank co-operation and international liquidity in the financial crisis of 2008–2009* (BIS Working Paper 310). Basel: Bank for International Settlements.

Murau, S. (2017). Shadow money and the public money supply: The impact of the 2007–9 financial crisis on the monetary system. *Review of International Political Economy*. https://doi.org/10.1080/09692290.2017.1325765.

National Bank of Belgium. (1957). Bijdrage tot de studie van het statuut der buitenlandse munten. *Tijdschrift voor documentatie en voorlichting 32, 2*(4), 257–375.

Obstfeld, M., & Taylor, A. M. (1998). *The great depression as a watershed: International capital mobility over the long run* (NBER working paper w5960).

OECD. (1997). *The OECD report on regulatory reform* (Sectoral Studies) (Vol. 1). Paris: Organisation for Economic Co-operation and Development.

OECD. (2000). *The service economy*. Paris: Organisation for Economic Co-operation and Development.

OECD. (2011). *OECD at 50 – Evolving paradigms in economic policy making*. Paris: Organisation for Economic Co-operation and Development.

Peekel, M., & Veluwenkamp, J. W. (1984). *Het girale betalingsverkeer in Nederland*. Amsterdam: Nederlands Instituut voor het Bank- en Effectenbedrijf.

Posthuma, J. E. (1955). Tien Jaar Herstelbank. In *Tien jaar economisch leven in Nederland* (pp. 1–45). The Hague.

Romer, C. D., & Romer, D. H. (2003). *Choosing the federal reserve chair: Lessons from history* (NBER working paper 10161).

Schelkle, W. (2012). In the spotlight of crisis how social policies create, correct, and compensate financial markets. *Politics & Society, 40*, 3–8.

Smits, J. P., Horlings, E., & Van Zanden, J. L. (2000). *Dutch GNP and its components, 1800–1913* (Monograph Series no. 5). Groningen: Groningen Growth and Development Centre.

Statistics Netherlands. (2001). *Tweehonderd jaar statistiek in tijdreeksen 1800–1999*. Den Haag: CBS.

Statistics Netherlands. (2009). *Werkloosheid jaren dertig hoogste ooit*. Available at: www.cbs.nl/nl-nl/nieuws/2009/12/werkloosheid-jaren-dertig-hoogste-ooit.

Stellinga, B. (2015). *Europese financiële regulering voor en na de crisis* (The Netherlands Scientific Council for Government Policy Working Paper 15). The Hague: Sdu Uitgevers.

Stoffer, J. (1986). *Het ontstaan van de NMB*. Deventer: Kluwer.
Tarullo, D. (2008). *Banking on Basel. The future of international financial regulation*. Washington, DC: Peterson Institute for International Economics.
Temin, P. (1993). Transmission of the great depression. *Journal of Economic Perspectives, 7*(2), 87–102.
Tijdelijke Commissie Huizenprijzen. (2013). *Kosten koper – Een reconstructie van 20 jaar stijgende huizenprijzen*. The Hague: Sdu Uitgevers.
Uittenbogaard, R. (2014). *Evolution of central banking. De Nederlandsche Bank 1814–1852*. Dissertation, Utrecht.
Uittenbogaard, R. (2017). Een korte geschiedenis van regulering van retailbetalingsverkeer. *Economisch en Statistische Berichten, 102*(4753S), 55–61.
van Ark, B., & de Jong, H. (1996). Accounting for economic growth in the Netherlands since 1913. *Economic and Social History in the Netherlands, 7*, 199–242.
van der Bie, R. (1997). *Een doorlopende groote roes. De economische ontwikkeling van Nederland, 1913–1921*. Dissertation, Vrije Universiteit Amsterdam.
van Eekelen, L. J. J. (1987). De ontwikkeling van het solvabiliteitstoezicht van De Nederlandsche Bank. *Maandschrift Economie, 51*, 134–149.
van Eerden, L. A. (2001). Structural regulation of the banking industry in the Netherlands: A shift of power, 1980–95. In M. Bovens, P. 't Hart, & B. G. Peters (Eds.), *Success and failure in public governance. A comparative analysis* (pp. 363–382). Cheltenham/Northampton: Edward Elgar.
van Engelen, W. (2009). *Blauw bloed: Opkomst en ondergang van de Postbank*. Amsterdam: Pearson Education NL.
van Goor, H. H. M. (2001). *Banken en industriefinanciering in de 19e eeuw. De relatie tussen Mees en Stork*. Van den Bergh gaat naar Engeland, Dissertation. Amsterdam.
van Renselaar, C., & Stokman, A. C. J. (2001). *Afscheid van de Nederlandse munt: gulden lessen* (WO&E research report no. 667). Amsterdam: De Nederlandsche Bank.
van Riel, A. (2016). *Het financieel stelsel in historisch perspectief*. The Hague: WRR.
van Riel, A. (2018). *Trials of convergence. Prices, markets and industrialization in the Netherlands, 1800–1913*. Dissertation.
van Zanden, J. L. (1997a). *Een klein land in de twintigste eeuw. Economische geschiedenis van Nederland 1914–1995*. Utrecht: Spectrum.
van Zanden, J. L. (1997b). Old rules, new conditions, 1914–1940. In M. 't Hart, J. Jonker, & J. L. van Zanden (Eds.), *A financial history of The Netherlands* (pp. 124–151). Cambridge: Cambridge University Press.
van Zanden, J. L., & van Riel, A. (2004). *The strictures of inheritance: The Dutch economy in the nineteenth century*. Princeton: Princeton University Press.
van Zwet, J. R. (2001). *De ontwikkeling van de Bankwet 1814–1998. Van 's Konings oudste dogter tot integrerend onderdeel van het ESCB* (WO&E research report 649).
Williams, D. G. T. (1968). The evolution of the sterling system. In C. Whittlesey (Ed.), *Essays in money and banking*. Oxford: Clarendon.
WRR. (2016). *Samenleving en financiële sector in evenwicht*, WRR report nr. 96. Den Haag: Sdu Uitgevers.

4

A Comprehensive Study of the Financial Monetary System

The previous chapter traced how our financial monetary system has evolved since the nineteenth century. The financial system is crucial for the functioning of society, enabling households, businesses and other institutions to make payments, save money, obtain finance (through debt or equity), and insure themselves against unforeseen events. Payments, savings, finance and insurance are the four classical functions of the financial sector.[1] A sector that performs these functions well contributes to economic development and prosperity; a malfunctioning sector can cause a great deal of damage.

Trust is essential for the functioning of the system. Sobel defines this complicated concept as a person's willingness to let others make decisions that affect one's well-being.[2] Two dimensions of trust are central for our purposes. First, trust is earned through reliability – through the fulfilment of justified expectations. A second aspect of building or maintaining trust is the ability to express dissatisfaction. This is tied to the system's (perceived) legitimacy. This chapter assesses our financial monetary system on the basis of four characteristics: its economic contribution (Sect. 4.1); its stability (Sect. 4.2); its fairness in the distribution of benefits, costs and risks (Sect. 4.3); and its legitimacy (Sect. 4.4).

Based on this analysis, we highlight key problems in the current system. As many of these problems are also emphasized by the advocates of monetary reform, this raises the question whether they can be traced back to how money is created in the current system. Unfortunately, this is no easy question to answer. In our current system, money and debt are inextricably linked. Money largely consists of bank deposits and is thus linked to the functioning of banks. This interconnectedness means that problems resulting from the organization of payments, savings, lending and money creation in our society – and specifically the role banks play in these activities – cannot be readily separated. Moreover, problems such as high levels of

[1]The insurance function falls outside of the scope of this report.

[2]Sobel (2002)

debt arise from many different factors. The problems discussed in this chapter therefore cannot be ascribed solely to how money is created. Chapters 5 and 6 will discuss to what extent these problems could be solved by transitioning to a different monetary system.

4.1 Economic Contribution

A well-functioning financial sector contributes to society, specifically to its economic development. In the wake of the financial crisis, many more people have been asking whether the financial sector is fulfilling this role. This section addresses this issue by first considering the functioning of the payment system. We then address concerns about high levels of debt and how far these can be reduced without causing economic damage.

4.1.1 The Payment System

The payment system is crucial for society's functioning.[3] We evaluate the Dutch payment system using five criteria: its cost, accessibility, convenience, security and reliability. Studies have found that the total cost of the Dutch payment system (relative to GDP) is lower than that of most other countries. At approximately 0.92% of GDP, the Netherlands is just behind Denmark, Sweden and Finland – the top three in Europe – where costs amount to approximately 0.80% of GDP.[4] The cost of payments in the Netherlands is also declining. Although cash payments have become more expensive (from €0.30 per transaction in 2002 to €0.39 in 2009), the cost of giro payments has fallen sharply, from €0.49 to €0.33.[5] Given the shift from cash to giro/electronic payments – most payments in the Netherlands are now made with debit cards – the total social costs have most likely decreased even more.[6]

How are these costs allocated? Dutch consumers incur relatively few *direct* costs: they must often pay a fee to maintain a bank account, but pay little or nothing in the way of transaction charges. The direct costs are borne by businesses and banks. Businesses incur costs for both cash and electronic payments. For cash payments, these include the cost of transport, deposit and security systems; for electronic payments, charges levied by the bank. While banks incur costs to process payments, they also derive benefits from their position in the payment system, including the possibility to link services (such as loans and payment accounts), the relatively low

[3]The payment infrastructure has characteristics of a public good. We return to this in Chap. 7.

[4]Schmiedel et al. (2012: 40)

[5]Jonker (2013)

[6]Jonker et al. (2018)

interest paid on payment account balances and the government's implicit or explicit support of banks (see Sect. 4.3). Nevertheless, a study by McKinsey & Company on behalf of the Dutch Banking Association (NVB) and De Nederlandsche Bank (DNB) shows these benefits did not offset the costs banks incur when handling cash and electronic payments.[7]

The second factor is accessibility. Here, low payment account charges encourage the use of the electronic infrastructure. The NVB signed in 2001 a pledge with the Salvation Army and the Ministry of Finance that all permanent residents aged 18 and above with a valid identity card (or a postal address at a recognized welfare or government agency) have the right to a basic payment account.[8] Under European rules, there is now a statutory obligation for banks to provide people with a payment account (Section 4:71f of the Financial Supervision Act). All consumers lawfully resident in the EU must have access to a bank account with basic functions and reasonable charges.

The dominance of electronic payments raises concerns about the accessibility of the cash payment system.[9] While it is relatively easy to obtain cash – 99.65% of all Dutch residents live within five kilometres of an automated teller machine – some stores and municipalities no longer accept cash payments. It is particularly problematic in case of public bodies, as there is often no alternative.[10] Although most places still accept cash, DNB has raised concerns about its declining use.[11]

A third aspect concerns payment convenience. The payment system is an area of constant innovation. As discussed in the previous chapter, in the Netherlands it was mainly the public bodies – particularly the Postcheque en Girodienst and Gemeentegiro Amsterdam – that led with innovations such as ATMs and POS terminals and promoting giro transfers. Dutch consumers today enjoy a high level of convenience due to innovations such as internet banking and contactless payments. One issue of concern is the ease with which consumers can switch banks: although there is a switching service that eliminates some of the inconvenience, switching banks poses difficulties as account numbers are not portable.

A fourth factor is security. According to the National Forum on the Payment System, safety has been improving with declining incidences of bank card skimming and fraud in internet banking.[12] Whereas the damage caused by this type of fraud amounted to around €81 million in 2012, by 2016 it had fallen to €10 million. But despite improvements, there remain grounds for concern. Protecting people from online threats (cyber-crime) remains a constant challenge. The more we use internet banking and online payments, the more criminals will operate online.[13]

[7]McKinsey and Company (2006)

[8]Louisse (2013)

[9]MOB (2017b)

[10]Nationale Ombudsman (2017)

[11]Voormeulen cited in Bremmer (2018); DNB (2018a)

[12]MOB (2017a)

[13]CPB (2016); MOB (2017b)

Finally there is the issue of reliability, or disruptions to the system. Although the payment system is generally reliable, the 2008–2009 financial crisis revealed its dependence on the banks: large-scale government intervention was necessary to ensure that the banking sector and hence the payment infrastructure remained operational. Apart from financial instability, cyber problems appear to pose the main danger, with banks in recent years facing major DDoS (distributed denial of service) attacks that disrupted access to internet banking. The digital payment infrastructure also depends on other critical infrastructure such as telecoms and electricity. DNB recently cited increased digitization and cyber-attacks as risks that continue to grow with the shift from cash to electronic payments.[14]

4.1.2 The Volume of Debt

Seen historically, global debt levels are exceptionally high.[15] According to BIS statistics, the total volume of private debt in the Netherlands (by consumers, businesses and other non-financial institutions) has risen from less than 40% of GDP in 1960 to over 250% today. This is high compared to other countries (see Fig. 4.1).

The sharp rise in private debt has many causes. Combined with financial liberalization and deregulation, the fact that banks can create money when granting loans implies that constraints on bank lending are limited. Financial innovations such as the securitization of loans have also contributed to high levels of private debt.[16] The deductibility of interest charges makes debt finance cheaper than equity finance. Another factor is compulsory saving through pension funds, meaning that first-time home buyers must borrow more.

Before the crisis, credit growth was largely seen as a positive development. Despite limited empirical evidence, economists broadly assumed that increased lending (as a percentage of GDP) was positively correlated with economic growth and even contributed to it.[17] Rising levels of individual indebtedness were also largely seen as positive, with economists framing it as the democratizing of financial services.[18]

There has been much more attention for the downsides of high private debt in the wake of the crisis. A new consensus holds that private debt can be excessive, with recent research showing an 'inverted U' relationship between lending and economic

---

[14]DNB (2018b)

[15]Buttiglione et al. (2014). This section focuses on private debt. We deal with public debt in Sect. 4.3.

[16]Securitization is the process whereby bank loans are 'packaged' and sold on to other financial players. This creates 'space' on banks' balance sheets, enabling them to grant new loans.

[17]Levine (1997); Bijlsma and Dubovik (2014: 2)

[18]Debelle (2004); Rajan and Zingales (2004)

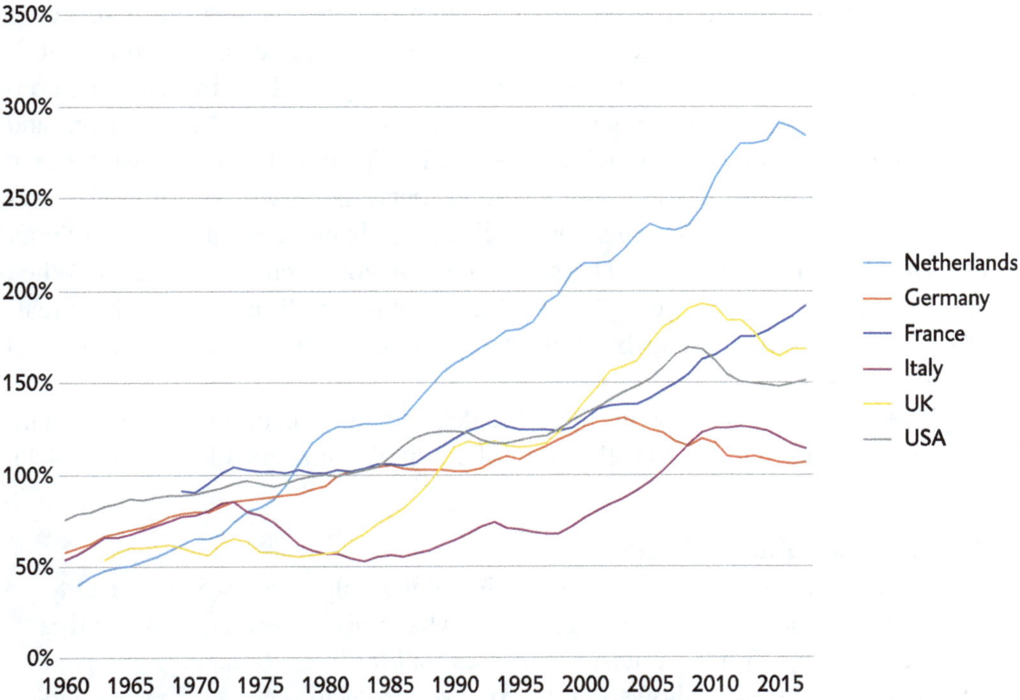

Fig. 4.1 Volume of outstanding private debt relative to GDP
Source: BIS statistics. Private debt defined as the debt of households and businesses, excluding financial firms. Figures differ depending on the source. For 2016, for example, debt relative to GDP ranges between 206% (World Bank), 231% (IMF), 262% (Eurostat), 264% (Statistics Netherlands) and 289% (BIS) of GDP. Business loans are not consolidated in the BIS data, so intragroup loans are included in the calculation. We use BIS figures in this report as they are the longest-running consistent and internationally comparative series. Despite the differences, all sources reveal the same upward trend.

growth.[19] This implies that although financially underdeveloped countries may benefit from increased lending, this does not apply to financially developed countries where lending above a certain limit may constrain economic growth.[20] Although the precise turning point remains elusive, the OECD concludes that most OECD countries – including the Netherlands – will not benefit from any further rise in private debt.[21]

Nevertheless, many economists still argue that high debt levels – given the low incidence of default – do not pose a problem for the Netherlands. Although it is true that Dutch banks' loan losses have been limited, high debt levels can still create macroeconomic problems. First of all, high levels of debt entail stability risks. A crisis is often preceded by strong credit growth,[22] while high debt levels can

[19]Arcand et al. (2015); OECD (2015); Cecchetti and Kharroubi (2012, 2015)

[20]Rousseau and Wachtel (2011); Arcand et al. (2015)

[21]OECD (2015); WRR (2016: 50–51)

[22]Borio (2012); Schularick and Taylor (2012); Drehmann et al. (2011)

constrain recovery after a financial crisis.[23] High debt levels also make spending more volatile. Dutch household consumption is highly volatile compared to that of other countries.[24] Due to high private debt and savings tied up in pensions, consumption patterns in the Netherlands are heavily influenced by house prices and interest rate fluctuations. In principle this works in both directions: with rising property prices homeowners feel wealthier and spend more; with downward movements the reverse occurs. This fuels pro-cyclical trends in the economy, the overall effects of which are negative.[25] The same phenomenon occurs in business. When debt levels are high relative to equity, business viability will more likely be threatened by a cyclical downturn. Debts must always be paid, whereas equity can be used to absorb losses.

High debt levels in society are therefore detrimental to economic development. Many authors point out that the allocation of credit also matters a lot (see Box 4.1).

Box 4.1 Allocation of Credit

While high private debt is a problem, it is not the only issue: we also need to consider who has access to credit and at what price.[26] We can distinguish between lending to households, businesses, public institutions and financial institutions. Figure 4.2 shows that the proportion of loans to businesses and public institutions in the total bank balance sheet has declined in recent decades while that of loans to households and financial institutions has increased sharply. This is tied to the growth of mortgage lending and changes in the financial system.

A number of economists argue that these trends in lending negatively impact economic development.[27] Clearly, the focus on mortgage finance and lending to other financial institutions has its downsides. Lending patterns and the price of assets such as houses and financial instruments become mutually reinforcing, exerting pro-cyclical effects on the banking sector and the economy at large.[28]

This, however, does not mean that banks are granting insufficient credit to businesses. If we look at loan volumes in terms of GDP, banks in recent decades have not reduced lending to businesses (on the basis of DNB Table 5.2.1). Moreover, bank credit is not the only source of (debt) finance for firms, with large companies having access to capital markets. There are nevertheless problems in business lending, primarily to smaller and medium

(continued)

[23]Mian and Sufi (2010); IMF (2012: 96–100); IMF (2016); Liu and Rosenberg (2013)

[24]Lukkezen and Elbourne (2015: 10)

[25]SER (2013); WRR (2016)

[26]Arcand et al. (2015); Beck et al. (2012); Cecchetti and Kharroubi (2012, 2015); Bezemer (2017)

[27]See e.g. Turner (2015) for the UK; Bezemer and Muysken (2015); Jordá et al. (2014)

[28]WRR (2016)

Box 4.1 (continued)
sized enterprises (SMEs). The past decades saw a shift from relationship to transactional banking, with bankers increasingly basing lending decisions on standardized criteria rather than on personal knowledge of the customer or sector.[29] While standardization has positive effects, it biases decisions towards measurable factors. This can negatively impact access to credit for small businesses and entrepreneurs, who already have less access to alternative financing. For example, SME loans, due to problems of scale, remain unattractive for pension funds.[30]

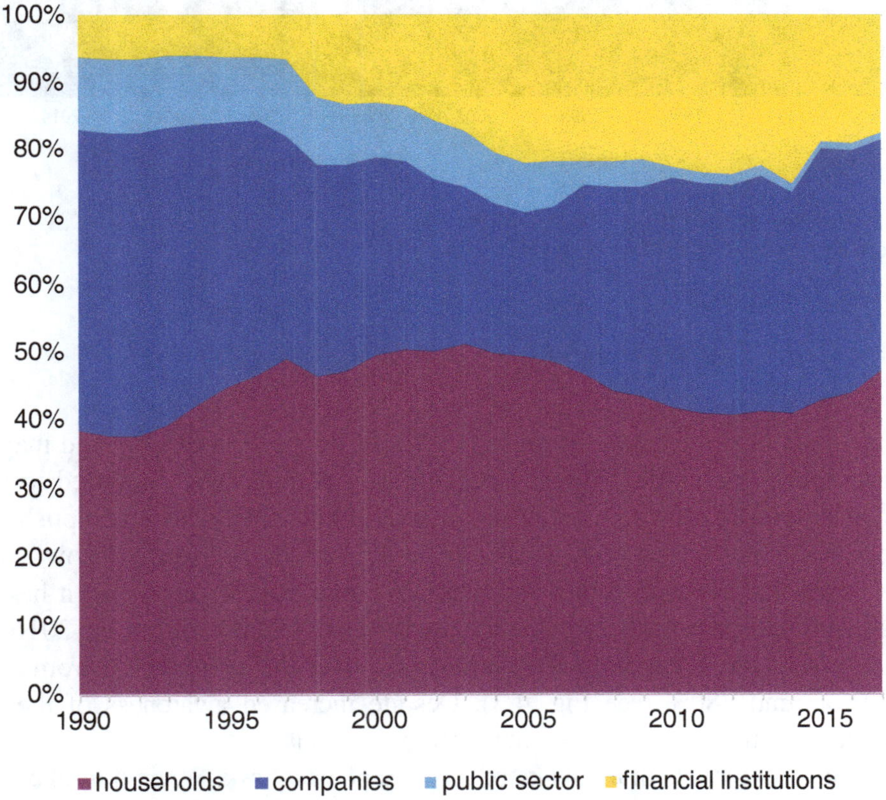

Fig. 4.2 Allocation of bank loans
Relative share of credit categories in total bank loans
Source: Compiled on basis of DNB Table 5.2.1

[29]Boot and Ratnovski (2016)

[30]SER (2013); European Commission (2013)

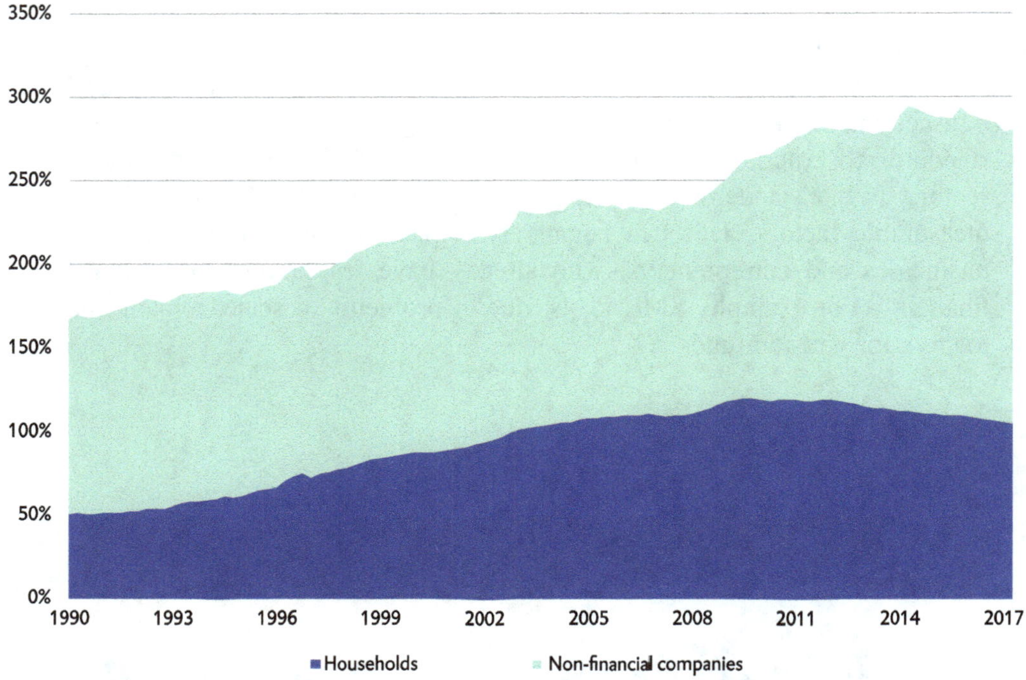

Fig. 4.3 Volume of debt in the Netherlands
Private sector debt as a percentage of GDP
Source: BIS

4.1.3 Reducing Debt Levels

Current levels of private debt increase the risk of financial instability and may well be constraining economic growth. Reducing outstanding debt – referred to in the jargon as deleveraging – may seem the obvious solution. How to accomplish this is far from self-evident, however. Total private debt in the Netherlands now exceeds pre-crisis levels in both absolute and relative terms. In absolute terms, it has risen from €1400 billion just before the credit crisis to €1600 billion in 2016 (BIS statistics). As a percentage of GDP, it has risen over the same period from around 230% to around 280% (see Fig. 4.3). Despite increased awareness of the risks, private debt is currently no lower than before the crisis.

Reducing debt levels in the wake of crises is no easy task. When households and businesses pay down their debts, their scope for spending shrinks, slowing economic growth, triggering unemployment and paradoxically increasing the volume of private debt as a percentage of GDP. There may also be deflationary (price-reducing) effects, further impeding economic growth. In short, although debt repayment can have economic advantages by increasing stability, it can cause short-term economic damage.[31] Still, there are ways to reduce debt levels without undermining

[31] Lo and Rogoff (2015); Mian and Sufi (2014); Pontuch (2014); Turner (2015). Economists refer to 'the paradox of thrift', popularized by the works of John Maynard Keynes and Irving Fisher.

consumption. For example, if debt is repaid through a transfer of wealth from parents to children, the negative effects on consumer spending are less severe.

While repayment is not the only way to reduce debt, alternative methods have shortcomings or may not be feasible in the current system. After a crisis one could restructure problematic household and business debt. Depending on the method, private debt levels could be reduced without directly leading to deflation and lower economic growth. While such debt reduction could stimulate consumption and investment, it would create losses for lenders (in particular banks) and could lead to financial instability.[32] One option would be for the government to play an active role in the restructuring. Either way, it would have distributive effects, with debtors receiving preferential treatment over non-debtors and lenders. It is also questionable whether this strategy would be feasible in our internationally interconnected financial system. Restructuring between debtors and creditors within a single legal system is already difficult[33]; spread across countries, the task becomes even more onerous.

We can also aim to reduce debt in relative rather than in absolute terms. If the economy grows but outstanding debt does not, debt levels decrease as a percentage of GDP. This can happen when growth is financed through equity and the broad money supply grows more slowly than the economy (because money creation always involves debt creation). The relative debt burden can also decrease due to inflation. In the long run, however, inflation implies a larger money supply. In our current system, where money creation takes place largely through lending, it is generally accompanied by increasing debt (regardless of whether monetary growth is caused by bank lending or quantitative easing).

There are ways to stimulate demand without rising private debt levels. It can be done through greater government spending (which would increase public debt) or through the monetary financing of government spending and 'helicopter money' (which would not). Monetary financing means that government spending is financed directly by the central bank, currently prohibited under Article 123 of the Treaty on the Functioning of the European Union. In the case of 'helicopter money', the central bank directly credits household accounts with new money. It is unclear whether this would also fall within the prohibition on monetary financing. Either way, these options raise issues that we only address later (in Sect. 7.1.3). What is clear is that reducing the debt burden following a crisis is a complex affair, made no easier by international interdependencies. In a system where money and debt creation are inextricably linked, it is even more difficult.

---

[32] Demertzis and Lehmann (2017)

[33] Reinhart et al. (2015: 2)

4.2 Stability

The second goal of any financial monetary system is stability. Financial instability has grave consequences for society. When a bank fails, account holders lose their money; if their deposits are insured, they temporarily lose access to their money. Although the latter may not sound dramatic, 90% to 95% of our money supply is made up of deposit money; a crisis in a large bank could make it impossible for millions of people and businesses to make payments, disrupting day-to-day business. Holders of the bank's bonds, shares and subordinated deposits[34] would lose their investments while bank lending would grind to a halt.

Instability of the entire financial system has much wider effects on society. In addition to direct costs such as bank bailouts, crises undermine economic growth, business investment, accumulated wealth and trust. Unemployment often skyrockets. Long-term unemployment entails the loss of knowledge and expertise, reinforcing negative economic outcomes and potentially leading to structurally higher unemployment.[35] Crises also undermine public finances (we return to this in Sect. 4.3). Even in the absence of a crisis, financial instability can have detrimental consequences for the real economy: when private assets (such as homes) plummet in value while liabilities (debts) remain unchanged, economic growth is constrained.[36]

We first examine the stability of individual banks and subsequently the stability of the system as a whole. The two are of course intimately linked: the instability of a systemic bank can cause the whole system to falter, while system instability threatens individual banks. Note that financial stability does not require the absolute stability of every individual institution; for systemic stability, it is important that institutions can be restructured or can be allowed to fail.

4.2.1 Stability of Individual Banks

The fragility of individual banks is primarily linked to the maturity transformation and risk transformation that take place within a bank. While both can positively affect the availability of finance and the return generated on savings deposits, they also make banks inherently unstable.

Maturity transformation means that the terms of a bank's assets differ from those of its liabilities. While mortgages may have a 30-year maturity, money market loans to the bank may mature after a day and deposit money can be withdrawn at any time. These term differences between the bank's assets and liabilities generate liquidity risks: the bank must be able to immediately repay account holders while other

[34] If a bank fails, the balances on these savings accounts are only repaid once all other creditors have been paid.

[35] WRR (2016: 160–1); Layard et al. (1991)

[36] Borio (2012); Turner (2014)

parties' debts to the bank have longer durations. When problems arise, the first to withdraw their deposits have the greatest chance of seeing their money again. If a bank's creditors (account holders and providers of short-term loans) withdraw their funds *en masse*, the bank will have insufficient central bank reserves or other liquid assets to meet these requests. This is the risk of a bank run.

The bank will then have to sell some of its assets or borrow (against collateral) from the central bank.[37] Whether the bank succeeds depends on the extent of the withdrawals, whether it is able to borrow from other parties and whether it has sufficient assets to sell. Selling assets will be less problematic in normal times than during a crisis. In a crisis many markets dry up, meaning that either there are no buyers or a bank can only sell its assets at prices far below their book value.

There are various ways to discourage runs on a bank. Central banks can provide emergency liquidity, while deposit insurance schemes guarantee account holders' deposits (in Europe currently up to €100,000).[38] But deposit guarantee schemes often only guarantee certain types of deposits and only up to a certain amount; they thus cover only part of a bank's liabilities.[39] The large sums managed by professional parties are generally not covered by deposit insurance and are often the first to be withdrawn. The risk of a bank run therefore remains.

The maturity mismatch between banks' assets and liabilities widened in the years preceding the crisis as banks increasingly financed their activities through short-term borrowing in money and capital markets. Confident that they could always obtain new funds, individual banks felt protected against liquidity risks. But the crisis revealed that these funding markets can dry up.[40] While this risk has received more attention since the crisis, Dutch banks still depend fairly heavily on market finance and are therefore vulnerable to turbulence in financial markets.[41]

Risk transformation means that one side of a bank's balance sheet contains risky assets that can fluctuate in value while the other side has debts of fixed amounts. While a bank can make losses on its loan book and financial assets, it has promised its creditors to repay debts in full. A bank with an account on its books with a balance of €1000 must always be able to pay out €1000, plus any interest.

Losses can be absorbed by the bank's equity; when equity is wiped out, the bank is bankrupt. The bank's solvency determines whether it has sufficient equity to absorb shocks in the value of its assets. The risks of insolvency and illiquidity are

---

[37]Bank of England (2013)

[38]Deposit guarantee schemes were institutionalized in Europe fairly late: in Germany in 1977, in France and the Netherlands in 1979, in the UK in 1982, and in Belgium in 1985. The United States is the pioneer, having introduced a guarantee system in 1933 during the Great Depression (Baltensperger and Dermine 1986: 14).

[39]Cannas et al. (2014)

[40]Brunnermeier et al. (2009)

[41]DNB (2017: 17)

intimately linked. In times of crisis, liquidity problems can rapidly turn into solvency problems and vice versa.[42]

Banks' equity levels declined sharply in the decades before the crisis as growing bank balance sheets were financed mainly through additional debt. In other words, the share of equity relative to the total balance sheet (the leverage ratio) declined. Low leverage ratios make banks more susceptible to shocks and fuel pro-cyclical behaviour. When ratios are low, relatively small losses (or gains) translate into major reductions (or increases) on the balance sheet.[43] Since the crisis, we have seen efforts to increase banks' equity, with Dutch banks' leverage ratios rising from around 3% in 2007 to around 6% today.[44] Elsewhere in Europe it is not much better.[45] Improvements notwithstanding, bank equity levels remain low, especially when compared to non-financial companies: around 33% for SMEs and around 48% for large firms.[46]

4.2.2 Systemic Instability

As we saw during the 2007–2009 crisis, systemic stability is not simply the aggregate of the stability of individual banks. The financial system must also contend with systemic risks, "a risk of disruption to financial services that is caused by an impairment of all or parts of the financial system and that has the potential to have serious negative consequences for the real economy".[47] The literature usually distinguishes between vulnerabilities resulting from: (1) the build-up of large imbalances, such as high debts and the development of bubbles; and (2) the structure of the sector, including interdependencies and financial institutions being too big to fail.[48]

Economic and financial cycles are accompanied by periods of collective optimism and pessimism. As Rien Nagel, former director of Rabobank, puts it: "As a bank we're part of the herd. You can linger on the edge of the herd, but if you move too far away you won't survive. So if favourable economic developments suddenly lead everyone to grant mortgage loans of five times annual salary, instead of the maximum of three times, you're bound to go with the herd".[49] Market players' expectations crucially affect the functioning of financial systems, both in the run-up

[42]Goodhart (2007)

[43]Schoenmaker and Wierts (2015)

[44]DNB Table 10.1. Based on data gathered for the IMF *Coordinated Compilation Exercise on Financial Soundness Indicators.*

[45]WRR (2016)

[46]Verhoeven et al. (2010)

[47]FSB, IMF and BIS (2009: 2)

[48]DNB (2016); IMF-FSB-BIS (2016); Stellinga (2020)

[49]Cited in Keuning (2017). Our translation.

to crises and during their aftermath.[50] Banks grant loans with expectations about future income streams and the value of collateral, while the price of other financial instruments also depends on future expectations. Shares drop in value when profit outlooks are adjusted downwards; bonds fall in value when the future looks less rosy.[51] These forecasts are not only based on calculations of known risks. The financial world is beset by uncertainty; decisions are often based on intuition, narratives and social norms. Changing expectations or declining trust can lead to very different judgements, affecting people's willingness to purchase financial assets.[52]

Changing expectations about the future fuel the pro-cyclicality of the financial system. In times of confidence, estimates of future incomes are positive, loans are readily granted and financial assets are highly valued. Rosy expectations also mean that households and businesses are willing to incur greater debt. This can inflate the value of assets such as houses and shares, reinforcing the optimism and increasing the value of collateral. Rising house prices and credit growth are thus mutually reinforcing. All this contributes to higher profits and growth, further reinforcing the overall trend. A financial boom is born, fuelled by strong credit growth.

Relatively minor, unexpected changes such as disappointing profits can undermine general confidence. This can cut into the value of banks' financial assets, leading to a disruption of financial markets, thereby reinforcing banks' problems. Doubting their investments, financial actors will try to sell them off. Panic can ensue. Previously positive, self-reinforcing effects now operate in reverse, only more strongly as asset values collapse and market liquidity dries up.[53] Financial institutions lose access to funding, with accompanying doubts about their solvency. As the boom turns into a crisis, banks become less willing to grant loans. Households and businesses become reluctant to take on more debt or attempt to pay down what they have already borrowed. Homeowners see a collapse in housing prices while their mortgages are fixed. They feel compelled to consume less, often with further negative effects on the economy. The financial crisis turns into economic turmoil.[54]

Alternating waves of collective optimism and pessimism recur in history. Although designing a crisis-proof financial system may be unrealistic, the system should be able to absorb moderate shocks. But this has become less and less the case over the past decades as imbalances have accumulated, the probability of shocks has grown and shock-absorbing capacities have declined. After decades of relative calm,

---

[50]Stellinga and Mügge (2017); Stellinga (2018, 2019)

[51]Bonds issued by governments deemed reliable are exceptions. Safe havens in times of crisis, they can rise in value.

[52]King (2016: 150)

[53]Adrian and Shin (2008). This means there are no further buyers; there is no longer a 'market' where these products can be traded.

[54]Borio (2012); King (2016). This dynamic was already recognized in the works of economists such as Kindleberger (1978) and Minsky (1986).

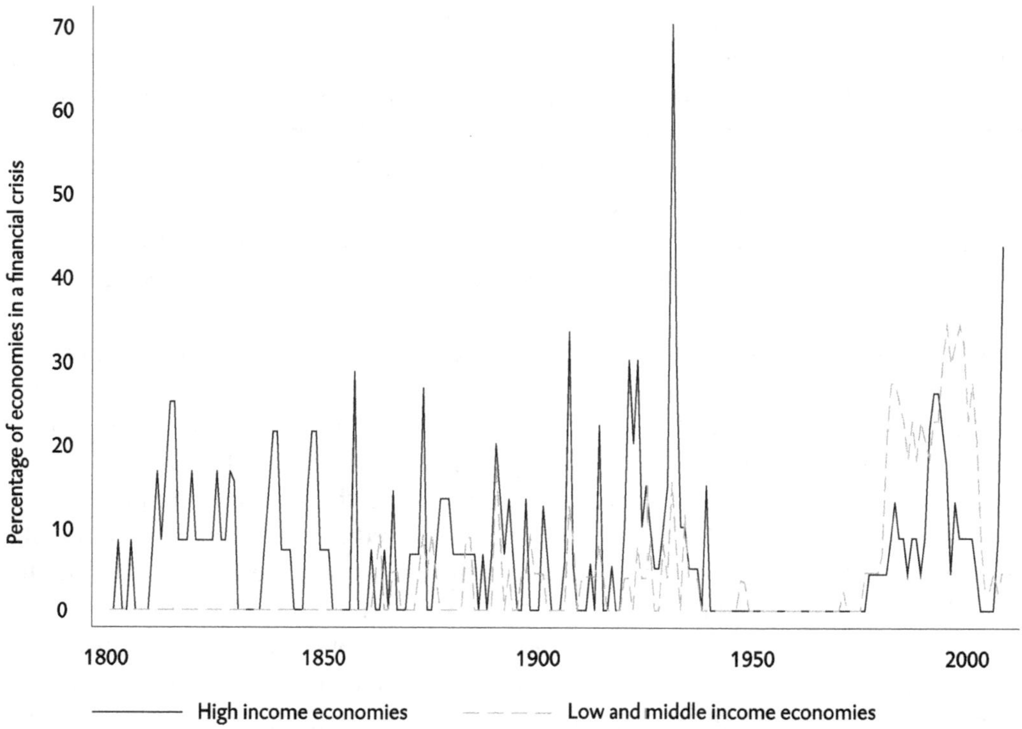

Fig. 4.4 The frequency of banking crises since 1800

financial instability has returned since the 1970s as a structural problem (see Fig. 4.4).[55]

Imbalances in our current system are evident in the financial and non-financial private sectors' ballooning levels of debt. Private debt is at historic highs. Limited equity relative to this debt means that all actors have less scope to absorb shocks. We observed that despite post-crisis improvements, banks still have little equity, while corporate and household debt-to-equity levels have also risen in recent decades.[56] Small economic fluctuations can thus rapidly create problems for financial institutions, businesses and households. A society in which all economic actors are highly indebted is more sensitive to systemic shocks.[57]

Systemic fragility has also been fuelled by structural changes in financial markets. Financial globalization, the blurring of boundaries between financial institutions, and the growing uniformity of major banks have changed financial sectors markedly. Previously national financial systems have been internationalized with the liberalization of capital flows and the dismantling of other barriers. Although financial globalization has some major benefits, it allows local problems to spread rapidly to the global level and vice versa. Financial activities have also become interwoven. Whereas financial systems in the post-war period remained segmented, the lines

[55]Taylor (2012); WRR (2016: 70–71);

[56]Schularick and Taylor (2012); WRR (2016)

[57]Bezemer and Muysken (2015); WRR (2016)

between different types of financial institutions have been blurred. Banks today combine a wide range of financial activities; although this may bolster the ability of individual banks to absorb shocks, the system as a whole is more susceptible to instability.[58] Day-to-day movements in banks' share prices are more interrelated than those of businesses in other sectors, indicating that investors are aware of these systemic risks.[59] Banks have become intertwined not only with other banks but with other financial institutions (see Box 4.2). Finally, we see the emergence of institutions that are so big or important for the system – institutions that are too-big-to-fail – that their problems can threaten the entire system.

Box 4.2 The Shadow Banking System

The 2007–2009 crisis revealed that the source of systemic instability can lie outside of the formal banking system. Many argue that the crisis was largely a 'shadow banking crisis' where problems arose in institutions that were not strictly speaking banks (they had no banking licences) and only later spread to banks. Although this framing suggests that the shadow banking system is a separate segment of the financial sector, it is closely intertwined with banking, either because banks had granted these institutions loans and guarantees or because banks were financed by them. Many shadow banks that experienced difficulties had been set up by banks to circumvent laws and regulations.

There are competing definitions of the shadow banking system. Broadly defined, it comprises all financial institutions that are not banks, pension funds or insurance companies.[60] The weakness of this definition is that it lumps together disparate institutions that differ greatly in their activities and stability risks. The FSB therefore uses a narrower definition, including only institutions that pursue activities and incur risks that closely resemble those of banks (such as lending based on short-term debt).[61] Examples of shadow banks in this narrower definition include institutions involved in securitization, 'open-ended' investment funds and broker dealers.

How one defines shadow banking affects estimates of its size. Broadly defined, the Dutch shadow banking system had a total balance sheet of €5552

(continued)

[58]Haldane (2009). Holding similar types of financial assets as well as pursuing similar strategies can increase systemic instability. In the stock market crash of 1987, all large institutional investors in the United States were using the same risk management system and received automatically generated advice to sell.

[59]De Vries (2005); Muns and Bijlsma (2015). Hartmann et al. (2004) show that stock prices in the EU and US react more to movements in an index of bank shares than movements in the broader market index. Muns and Bijlsma (2015) compare linkages between bank share prices and linkages in other sectors and find banking to have the highest systemic risk. De Vries (2005) traces this to the high probability of large outliers, coupled with banks pursuing the same activities.

[60]See for example ESRB (2018)

[61]FSB (2015)

Box 4.2 (continued)
billion (826% of GDP) in 2014; according to the narrow definition it was €207 billion (31% of GDP) (see Van der Veer et al. 2015). The difference is mostly due to the many 'special financial institutions' registered in the Netherlands – institutions set up by multinationals to take advantage of the flexible tax regime – which do not fall within the narrow definition of shadow banking and are not directly linked to banks.

For financial stability, three questions follow: (1) what are the vulnerabilities within the shadow banking system? (2) how do they impact society (possibly through regular banking)? and (3) what policies are required to eliminate these vulnerabilities? Although policymakers have devoted much attention to these matters following the crisis, issues remain. Many institutions still fall outside the scope of policy and supervision. We still know little about how different types of shadow banks may contribute to future financial instability. While growth in non-bank financial intermediation can contribute to financial stability and economic growth, the potential risks cannot be underestimated.

Financial instability may also be caused by very different factors, such as cyber-attacks on crucial parts of the system. These are occurring with increasing frequency and are becoming more dangerous. Cyber security is now a top priority for banks. Cyber risks can threaten the overall system and, like financial risks, are exacerbated by high levels of interconnectedness in the financial system.[62]

4.3 Fairness

An important requirement of the financial monetary system is that it is fair in the allocation of costs, benefits and risks. Financial crises are a key problem in this respect, as they entail high public costs. These include *direct* costs (for example the costs of bailing out financial institutions) and *indirect* costs (such as unemployment and the deterioration of public finances). Another question concerns the financial benefits that banks enjoy as a result of implicit or explicit government guarantees, the position they occupy in the payments system and through competitive distortions. Finally, there are questions about the allocation of costs, benefits and risks from higher private debt levels.

[62] BIS (2014: 1); Bank of England (2015)

4.3.1 The Public Costs of a Crisis

Profits before the crisis went to the bank whereas the costs were borne by the government and the general public – this is what many said in the wake of the crisis.[63] How valid is this statement? We first consider the costs of a financial crisis before discussing the allocation of benefits in the pre-crisis period.

Financial crises have major economic and social consequences. These include the evaporation of wealth, business bankruptcies, increasing unemployment and house evictions. To stop further deterioration and prevent systemic collapse, public authorities (governments and central banks) normally intervene in various ways – through liquidity or capital injections, taking over problematic loans, issuing guarantees or even nationalizing financial institutions.

While the idea that public authorities must intervene during a crisis is far from new, the size of implicit or explicit public guarantees has mushroomed in recent decades. This is largely due to the greater size of banks relative to GDP,[64] while the growth of the shadow banking system and its interconnectedness with banks means that central banks must also worry about the stability of financial institutions that are not strictly speaking banks. The collapse of Lehman Brothers in September 2008 triggered a global crisis. Since then, no government has seriously considered allowing a major financial institution to fail.[65]

The enormity of public guarantees became evident during the crisis as public authorities had practically no choice but to provide financial support. Support to banks from the Dutch state – in the form of capital injections, acquisitions of problematic financial assets and guarantees – amounted to 27.3% of GDP or approximately €174 billion.[66] Providing support does not immediately imply *losses* for the government: if a government purchases bank shares or takes over problematic loans, it obtains financial assets that may ultimately generate value. The Dutch government, for example, benefitted from its guarantee for ING.[67] Moreover, guarantees do not always have to be called on.

Still, the *net costs* of support are often substantial.[68] This was certainly true for the 2007–2008 crisis. Between 2008 and 2014, the *direct* losses borne by euro area governments for supporting financial institutions amounted to 4.7% of GDP or roughly €470 billion. There were substantial differences between countries, with the outliers being Ireland (30% of GDP), Greece (22% of GDP) and Cyprus (19% of

---

[63]See e.g. https://www.nemokennislink.nl/publicaties/winst-is-voor-de-bank-verlies-voor-de-burger/

[64]ESRB ASC (2014: 7)

[65]DNB (2015: 35) argues that if guarantees are given to other financial players, they should also be more tightly regulated.

[66]DNB (2011)

[67]Netherlands Court of Audit (2016)

[68]IMF (2015)

GDP). The Netherlands, with losses of 4.8% of GDP, was close to the average.[69] Direct government support led to the deterioration of government finances, rapidly rising public debt and often to austerity.

Alongside the *direct* costs, a crisis also entails *indirect* costs for the government. Recessions, bankruptcies and unemployment cause government finances to deteriorate due to both lost tax revenues and higher social security expenditures. During recessions households and companies decrease spending and investment, often encouraging governments to stimulate the economy through greater spending, thereby impairing public finances (in any case in the short term).

Although the direct costs of a bailout are highly visible, the indirect costs are generally much higher.[70] Unemployment in the Netherlands doubled from 3.7% before the crisis to 7.4% in 2014 (Statistics Netherlands). Dutch government debt rose from €260 billion in 2006 to €450 billion in 2014 (Statistics Netherlands). For all euro area countries together, government debt as a percentage of GDP rose by 27 percentage points, with only 4.7 percentage points resulting from the *direct* costs.[71] The total growth of government debt in the Netherlands (25 percentage points) was around the average, with Ireland (86 percentage points), Greece (73 percentage points), Spain (62 percentage points) and Cyprus (53 percentage points) being the negative outliers.[72] Figure 4.5 shows the growing post-crisis government debt for selected EU countries.

Social discontent with the enormity of the crisis' costs was – and remains – high. Discontent was also fuelled by the broadly shared sentiment that the boom's benefits accrued disproportionately to a select group of employees, managers and shareholders in the financial sector. But bankers were not the only ones to benefit from the preceding boom: governments, businesses and households did so as well.[73] Who benefits from a boom is difficult to calculate with any precision. For governments, it is clear that the negative effects of a financial crisis exceed the preceding *positive* effects of a boom on government finances. Overall, the cycle of boom and bust leaves countries worse off.[74]

Before the crisis, employees in the financial sector earned substantially more than those in other sectors (even when controlling for education). This certainly applied to executive remuneration.[75] Bank shareholders also enjoyed golden times, rapidly

[69]ECB (2015)

[70]Turner (2015: 82); WRR (2016: 160); ECB (2015)

[71]This represents the difference between the initial (debt of *x*% of GDP) and post-crisis situations (debt of *x* + 27% of GDP). As debts are expressed as a percentage of GDP, the crisis-induced shrinking of GDP raises this percentage.

[72]ECB (2015)

[73]This does not mean that good times for the financial sector are automatically good times for the country as a whole. Although the financial sector is crucial for economic growth, its further growth given current debt levels may well have a dampening effect on GDP – even without considering the effects of the financial crisis (Cournède and Denk 2015).

[74]IMF (2015: 13–15)

[75]Philippon and Reshef (2012); Denk (2015)

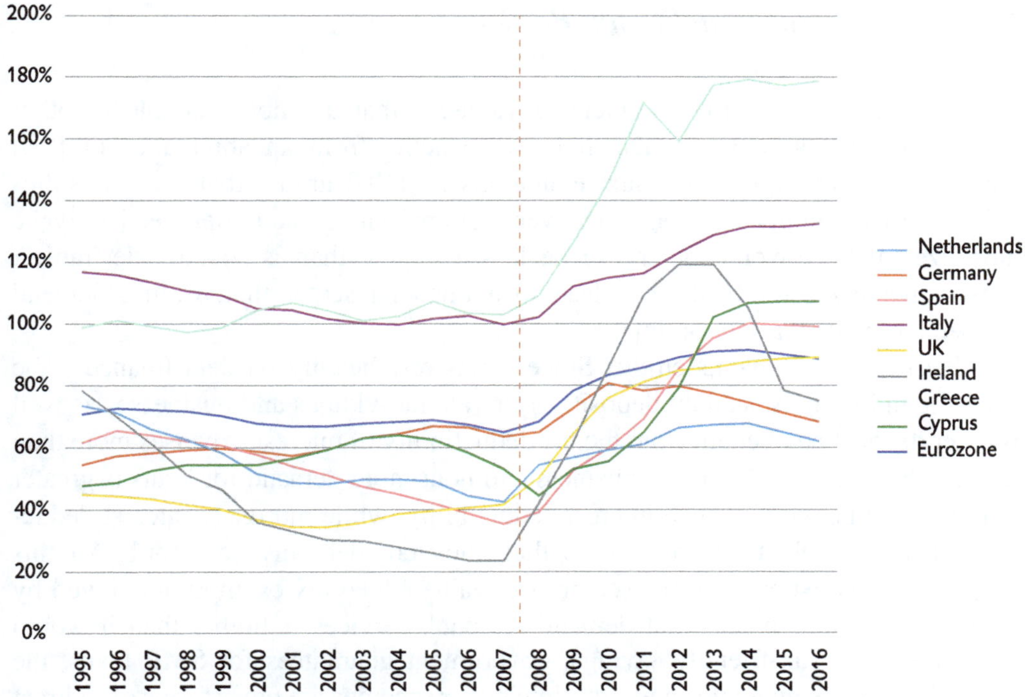

Fig. 4.5 Government debt of EU countries
Percentage of GDP
Source: Eurostat data (2018)

earning large sums from profit distributions and share repurchases.[76] Nevertheless, the claim that profits are private and losses are public is overly simplistic: the benefits of the pre-crisis boom spread beyond the banking sector, while those directly involved in finance also suffered losses. Still, there is truth to the notion that the benefits disproportionately accrued to the financial sector while the costs were borne more widely.[77]

Measures taken following the crisis sought to address this problem, including the European *Bank Recovery and Resolution Directive* (BRRD) which aimed to reduce the *direct* public costs of crises by making shareholders, bondholders and large savers responsible for the cost of future bank bailouts; public support should only be a last resort. While an important step, the BRRD has yet to prove itself in practice (see Chap. 7).

[76]Haldane et al. (2010)
[77]WRR (2016)

4.3.2 Financial Benefits for Banks

The financial sector enjoys financial advantages that are not available to other sectors. According to DNB, Dutch banks benefit "from an abundance of [...] subsidies, arising largely from tax regulations".[78] DNB argues that such subsidies "stimulate oversupply and lead to lower welfare" since "activities need only be subsidized if they would otherwise be less available than is socially desirable". These advantages for banks can lead to a financial sector that, from a societal perspective, is larger than optimal.

What benefits do banks enjoy? Since banks rely heavily on debt finance – the payment and savings account deposits of private individuals and businesses as well as other debts – they benefit from the tax deductibility of interest expenses more than ordinary businesses. Moreover, business and household demand for loans is greater than it would be without such interest deductibility, while mortgage interest deductions enable people to borrow more than they could otherwise afford. All this provides indirect support to the sector. The value added tax exemption enjoyed by the financial sector means that demand for bank services is higher than it would otherwise be.[79] Tax-friendly savings, government guarantees for SME loans, the national mortgage guarantee and first-time buyer schemes are other forms of indirect support for the banking sector.[80]

Banks also receive government support because of their social and economic importance. With crucial functions in the field of payments, finance and insurance, some banks are simply too big to fail and will always be supported in case of problems. Account holders' deposits are also guaranteed up to a certain level.[81] These implicit and explicit public guarantees mean that individuals and companies are prepared to accept lower interest rates on their bank accounts than if they incurred greater risks.[82] This latter point bears on the broader issue of financial benefits for commercial banks given their role as money-creating institutions (see Box 4.3).

---

[78]DNB (2015: 31)

[79]Bettendorf and Cnossen (2014). Other sectors enjoying this exemption are education and healthcare. Exemptions for financial services are described in the Turnover Tax Act 1968, Article 11(1)(i-k), pursuant to Article 135(1) of the European VAT Directive. Difficulties calculating VAT on bank services stem from whether they are end- or intermediate use.

[80]DNB (2015: 31–33)

[81]While the deposit insurance scheme is officially a guarantee between banks, the state is expected to act as the ultimate guarantor.

[82]OECD (2012)

Box 4.3 Seigniorage for Banks?

The House of Representatives motion requesting the WRR to study money creation called for an examination of "the extent of seigniorage".[83] Seigniorage is traditionally seen as the difference between the production cost of money and its purchasing power. If the government produces a €10 note and the production cost is 10 cents, the seigniorage when it is spent amounts to €9.90. Of course, this is far from the full story. The cost of generating the social trust required to allow a piece of paper to serve as money is much greater than just the production cost. Money depends on numerous institutions including an effective legal system and a central bank.[84]

More importantly, this traditional perspective provides scant insight into the financial advantages and disadvantages of money creation in our current system. After all, it concerns a form of money creation – the government prints money and spends it itself – that is prohibited in the EU and most other countries. In our current system, money is created by commercial and central banks when they grant loans or purchase financial assets, the lion's share by commercial banks. Banks do not spend this money themselves but make it available to the borrower in the form of bank deposits.

The academic literature focuses mainly on revenue from seigniorage for public institutions (central banks), not on gains accruing to private institutions (commercial banks). According to economists at the New Economics Foundation and Copenhagen Business School, private seigniorage consists of the funding advantages banks enjoy as a result of being able to create deposit money.[85] They calculate this advantage by comparing the interest banks pay on deposits and the interest they would have to pay if they had to finance themselves by other means (the 'alternative cost method').

While this is a rather straightforward methodology to calculate private banks' seigniorage, it has three shortcomings. First, it is far from obvious how to determine the interest rate that banks 'would otherwise have to pay'. Should we use the rates that banks pay on other debts? Those paid by other (financial or even non-financial) institutions? What about terms of maturity? Second, the method takes scant account of the real costs, for example that banks must maintain a payment infrastructure to finance themselves through bank deposits. The provision of bank accounts is also so intertwined with other

(continued)

[83]Kamerstukken II, 2015–2016, 34346, no. 19

[84]Giannini (2011: 14–15)

[85]Bjerg et al. (2017); Macfarlane et al. (2017)

Box 4.3 (continued)
bank activities that it is difficult to allocate costs.[86] Finally, the financing benefit says nothing about who enjoys it: is it the bank's borrowers (with lower interest on bank loans), employees (with higher pay) or shareholders (with higher dividends)?

This does not mean that banks do not derive financial benefits from their status as money creating institutions. But for society, the crucial question is not which part of bank income can be seen as 'seigniorage', but the extent to which banks' indispensable role in the payment system and the sector's concentration is giving banks an excessive piece of the pie. As various studies have concluded, competition in Dutch banking leaves much to be desired.[87] DNB points to "high market concentration, entry barriers, and products that are difficult to compare with each other" while banks benefit from various implicit and explicit government guarantees.[88] All point to excessive bank profits.[89] Focussing on these excess profits seems more promising than figuring out the level of private seigniorage.

The 'alternative cost method' is generally not used to determine gains from public money creation (the issuing of bank notes and central bank reserves). The euro area uses the concept of 'monetary income': the interest income that national central banks earn by implementing monetary policy. To calculate it, expenditure on debts is deducted from income on assets. The assets include loans to commercial banks and securities such as bonds purchased as part of quantitative easing; the debts are central bank reserves and cash. The monetary income of all national central banks is pooled and then allocated to the central banks, using an allocation key. For DNB the monetary income over the period 2002–2017 averaged €770 million per year (an average of approximately 0.12% of GDP).[90] This monetary income, together with income on other assets, makes up DNB's total income. After the deduction of various costs and provisions, the profit is paid to the Dutch government.

Banks and bank services receive implicit or explicit support through a number of channels. This, however, does not determine who benefits. Benefits may be passed on to bank customers through the interest rates they pay and receive. But given the concentration of the financial sector, it is doubtful that banks pass on these advantages to customers in full. The OECD states that high implicit support contributes to

[86]How do accounting methods recognize joint production costs? While a number of methods are available, these remain arbitrary as the costs incurred do not specifically concern individual products in the joint production process.

[87]DNB (2015); ACM (2014)

[88]DNB (2015: 41); see also ESRB ASC (2014); OECD (2015)

[89]WRR (2016: 39)

[90]DNB reports this amount in its annual reports.

the "financial sector wage premia", with employees of financial institutions earning substantially more than employees of non-financial institutions with comparable profiles in age, education, etc.[91]

Benefits are also unevenly distributed *within* the financial sector, with funding advantages mainly accruing to systemically important banks. Since the government has no choice but to bail out banks that are vital to the system, these banks are not allowed to fail. This is the too-big-to-fail problem. CPB, the Netherlands Bureau for Economic Policy Analysis, estimates that this advantage for the systemic banks amounts to 0.4% of GDP, or approximately €2.5 billion annually. The OECD puts this number higher at around 0.5% of GDP.[92] The advantage for systemic institutions derives from credit rating agencies taking into account implicit government support. This leads to lower interest costs and hence a funding advantage.[93] Given that large banks know that they will receive public support, also means that they incur more risks by providing riskier loans and operating with lower equity buffers. This can have self-reinforcing effects, making these crucial institutions ever larger.[94]

Policymakers have sought to address the too-big-to-fail problem since the crisis, opting for a strategy of dissuasion by imposing levies or taxes on systemic relevance. European bank regulation allows regulators to impose higher capital requirements on systemically relevant institutions. The idea is that banks see this as a 'tax' on systemic relevance while higher requirements reduce risks of failure. Policymakers have thus far avoided more direct approaches such as splitting banks into different units, while a European plan to 'ring-fence' their crucial parts to make it easier to save them has been shelved. Instead, regulators are drawing up bank resolution plans to facilitate their winding up in crises or to keep their vital parts in operation. The too-big-to-fail problem has been addressed but has not disappeared. Then G30 Executive Director Mackintosh describes the situation as follows: "If a major international bank once again teeters on the brink of collapse, no one in finance believes they would be allowed to fail."[95] The ECB's recently expressed preference to create even larger banks is of no help in this respect.[96]

4.3.3 Benefits and Costs of Increased Indebtedness

How are the benefits, costs and risks of increased private indebtedness allocated? Theoretically, rising debt levels could be pointing to a 'democratization of financial services' as less prosperous people can now obtain funding and shape their lives as

[91]OECD (2015)

[92]Bijlsma and Mocking (2013); OECD (2012)

[93]DNB (2018c: 47)

[94]Adfonso et al. (2014); Carney (2014: 9); Liikanen Report (2012: 23)

[95]Mackintosh (2014: 410)

[96]Nouy (2018)

they wish.[97] While few would argue against broader access to secure and affordable financial products, this 'financialization' of society has its associated risks. Various studies have suggested that the financialization of society can contribute to increasing economic inequality and that economic inequality and people's reliance on financial services are mutually reinforcing.[98] People with higher incomes and more assets benefit more from the ability to make lucrative investments and obtain cheap finance.[99] People with lower incomes and fewer assets often have higher interest expenses (in relation to their income), have to go take on relatively higher debts and are often the first to lose their jobs in a downturn. If people have problems to pay interest and must borrow more to make ends meet, the problem gets worse.[100] Indebtedness causes stress, affecting people's ability to perform well, exacerbating the debt problem. While access to credit can help households shape their lives, problematic debt makes it more difficult.[101]

These problems appear to be especially severe in countries such as the United Kingdom and the United States where many people borrow for private consumption and where social security benefits are modest.[102] But in the Netherlands as well, a growing number of households – currently more than one million – have problematic debt, although these more often concern payday loans, debt collector's fees and taxes than bank debt. People regularly fall below the subsistence minimum due to problematic debt, while applications for debt assistance continue to rise (see Fig. 4.6).[103] This brings to the fore the issue of rights and obligations of creditors and debtors. Debtors have a relatively weak position vis-à-vis creditors in case of difficulties in redeeming loans.

Mortgage debt likewise raises questions about the distribution of risk between creditors and debtors. This is an important issue in the Netherlands. Fitch Ratings describes the Netherlands (alongside the UK) as the European country with the "*the most lender-friendly legal system*".[104] This means that mortgage borrowers must do their utmost to meet their obligations. Should they fail to do so, the bank can sell their home while any residual debt is still owed and the bank has a claim on the debtor's income for years to come. The debtor can only escape payment obligations by filing for personal bankruptcy.[105]

It goes without saying that debtors must fulfil their obligations and should only be able to escape them in exceptional circumstances. But this statement requires qualification. Financial products such as mortgages are long-term products with

[97]Beck (2011)

[98]Turner (2015: 119–124); OECD (2015)

[99]OECD (2015: 24)

[100]Turner (2015: 123)

[101]Tiemeijer (2016); WRR (2017)

[102]Mian and Sufi (2014)

[103]Tiemeijer (2016)

[104]Fitch Ratings (2012); cited in De Ruijter (2012)

[105]NVB (2014)

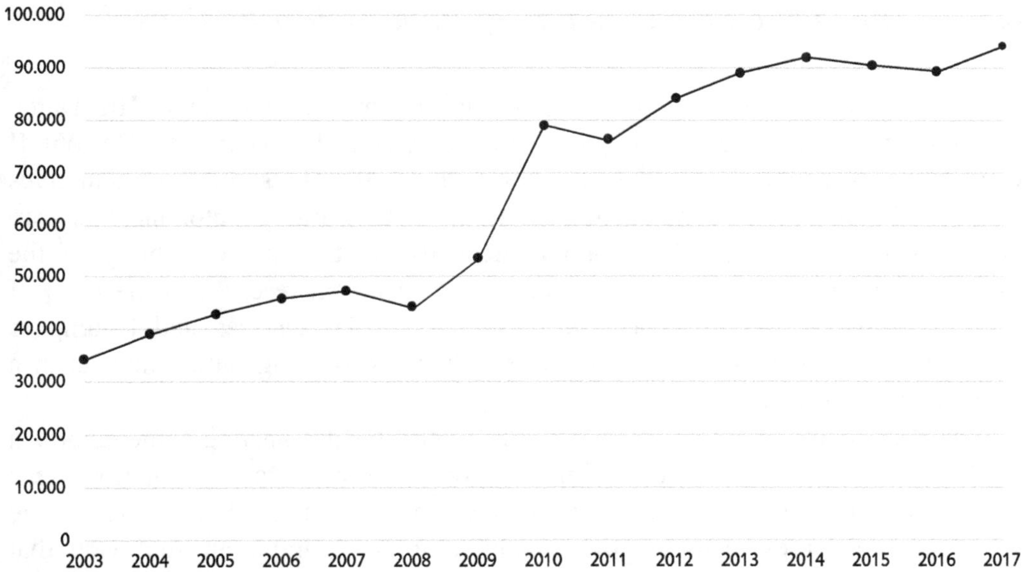

Fig. 4.6 Applications for debt assistance in the Netherlands (The NVVK is the sector organization for debt assistance and social banking)
Source: NVVK

which the customer has only occasional experience. The borrower thus has a major disadvantage in information and experience, while the risks can have far-reaching consequences.[106] For mortgage debt there is an additional factor: the uncertainty surrounding house prices over time. The dynamics of the housing market reflect the combined actions of a large number of players: consumers, estate agents, mortgage lenders and policymakers. When a homeowner is left with residual debt after being forced to sell her home, it is doubtful whether this is entirely her own fault. Measures since the crisis have reduced these risks by limiting the value of loans relative to that of the home and through financing rules that consider the ratio of income to mortgage expenses.

4.4 Legitimacy and Influence

Public trust in the financial monetary system requires justified expectations to be met and opportunities to express dissatisfaction and exert influence. Problems here are rife. The public-private character of banks muddies what can be expected of them while options for democratic control have been curtailed in recent decades. The ability of households to exert direct influence on banks is limited.

[106]European Parliament (2014)

4.4.1 *The Public-Private Nature of Financial Institutions*

Society needs an efficiently functioning financial monetary system. The Dutch Parliamentary Committee of Enquiry into the Financial System (the De Wit II Committee) that investigated the financial crisis for the House of Representatives formulated it as follows: "The financial sector is not an ordinary sector and banks are not ordinary companies. The economy depends greatly on the stability of the financial system. Payments, the development of personal reserves in the form of savings, pensions and insurance, the system of social services and lending to business rely on the financial sector. Hence there is a strong public interest in a stable financial sector".[107]

The discipline of economics has various criteria for designating something as a public interest. The existence of a public good or service is one criterion. This requires that two conditions are met: no one can be excluded and its use by one person does not prevent its use by someone else. An example are the dykes that protect everyone in the Netherlands from floods. The payment infrastructure likewise has the characteristics of a public good. No one can be excluded from the use of cash, and while exclusion would be possible from the electronic infrastructure, legislation requires that all people in principle have access to a bank account (Section 4:71f of the Financial Supervision Act). The use of the electronic or cash payment infrastructure by one party does not hinder its use by another, but rather promotes it. With the declining use of cash, the electronic infrastructure for payments has become crucial for the functioning of society.

A well-functioning system for credit provision is also in the public interest. Lending has far-reaching positive and negative external effects. It can contribute to economic development, but both excessive lending and the limited availability of credit can damage the economy. Precisely because of these external effects, an efficient lending system is vital.

The network effects between individual institutions distinguishes banking from other sectors. The functioning of bank A directly affects the functioning of bank B. This means that the actions of individual banks affect the banking system as a whole and hence its fulfilment of public interests: the bankruptcy of a systemic bank can threaten people's savings, the payment system and lending. In other sectors, the (impending) insolvency of a private company is generally less problematic for the system as a whole. The proper functioning of a bank thus concerns not only the bank and its direct stakeholders but has wider social implications.

Banks thus have two faces. On the one hand, a bank is an organization with public functions essential for society. There are sound reasons to regulate the sector and for the government to bail it out during crises. The bank resembles a public organization and is expected to operate in the public interest and not lavish upper management with exorbitant salaries and bonuses. On the other hand, a bank is a private organization driven by market forces and competition, and customers should make

[107] De Wit II Committee (2012: 540). Our translation.

informed decisions when buying financial products. The legal standards applying to public and private organizations also differ.[108] As these views are formulated in different contexts, it is understandable that expectations regarding bank actions at times clash.

4.4.2 *Options for Democratic Control*

Public involvement in the financial monetary system is unavoidable given its importance. The government even has a constitutional duty to regulate the monetary system (Article 106).[109] That public interests are at stake does not mean that services should be in public hands. In the Netherlands, education and healthcare are also provided by private institutions, while there are major public interests at stake. It does mean, however, that the conditions and policy goals should ultimately be determined democratically. In particular we can expect the public institutions responsible for the development and implementation of financial monetary policy to act within a democratic mandate and to be democratically accountable. Several developments, however, have limited the scope for democratic oversight.

First, financial institutions increasingly operate internationally, aided by the deregulation of international capital flows. Much of the policy is developed on the European or global levels, with the Basel Committee playing a central role in banking regulation. While international policies are necessary to prevent a legislative race to the bottom, it also means that it is increasingly difficult for national governments to deviate from the international standard without facing a loss (or threatened loss) of financial activities.[110] This is partly due to a second trend: the sweeping liberalization of the financial sector since the 1980s. This included the abandoning of post-war policy instruments such as the separation of different banking activities, credit ceilings and restrictions on capital movements.

Third, technocratic decision making also limits democratic influence. Monetary and financial policy are complex issues, and policy development and implementation are increasingly outsourced to technocratic forums such as the Basel Committee. In such forums, trade-offs between political goals often disappear under a layer of expertise. Major financial players also have resources to influence policy developments at the supranational level, which is not the case for other stakeholders (smaller players, consumer organizations or NGOs).[111]

Finally, many rules are enshrined in the European treaties ("constitutionalization"). Agreements in monetary and financial policy are set out in the Treaty on the Functioning of the European Union, including the goal of monetary policy (Article

[108]Jak (2014)

[109]This article states: "The monetary system is governed by law." Our translation.

[110]Pettifor (2017)

[111]Pagliari (2012)

127(1) TFEU) and the prohibition of monetary financing (Article 123 TFEU). Changes can only take place with the consent of all EU member states. Governments have boxed themselves in to such an extent that they have limited scope to take different paths based on new insights or changing circumstances.[112]

Internationalization, liberalization, technocratic decision making and constitutionalization introduce specific problems for democratic accountability and control. Key institutions in the field of monetary and financial policy are remote from politics, while policy-making within central banks is hermetically isolated from parliamentary influence. This applies in particular to the European Central Bank, but also to national central banks. Although politics still influences central banks through appointments to governing boards and various accountability mechanisms, participation in economic and monetary union requires the central bank to be formally independent of day-to-day politics. A lot of financial sector policy is also developed within the same policy forums that are largely independent of national and European politics. The scope for political control and influence appears to be limited.[113]

A somewhat different problem is that changing laws and regulations can more rapidly create problems in contexts of high debt, limited equity and limited social capacity to absorb change. Policy adjustments must be made with great caution. For example, abolishing the tax advantages of debt may lead to long-term gains but also to greater short-term uncertainty and instability for highly leveraged households and institutions. For banks as well, improvements will be more difficult starting from low equity levels. High debt therefore also limits policy discretion.

4.4.3 Position of Citizens

Finally, we need to consider people's ability to exert influence on the system. Consumers can reward or penalize specific banks by taking their business elsewhere. But the exit option in the financial sector is impeded by various factors. Switching from one bank to another poses administrative hurdles; especially the lack of account number portability makes it unattractive for many consumers to change banks. It is also almost impossible for uninitiated consumers to assess whether banks are behaving appropriately when it is already difficult for regulators and direct stakeholders to understand what banks are doing. Finally, the highly concentrated Dutch banking landscape offers consumers little in the way of alternatives.

People can also exert influence on the workings of the financial system by means of voice, for example when they organize into NGOs. But their resources and capabilities are dwarfed by the resources of large financial players to organize and exert influence on politics and policy. The fragmentation of policy across many

---

[112]Van der Sluis (2017)

[113]Stellinga (2015)

different forums is also advantageous for large players; they can be active in numerous areas, while counterforces with less capacity can only focus on a few.[114]

The limited scope for influence takes another dimension when we consider the gulf between the perceptions of citizens and banks. Haldane, Chief Economist at the Bank of England, calls it a "*Great Divide*".[115] Many bank and financial institution mangers perceive the post-crisis period as one in which they have been overwhelmed by new legislation and regulations, but are again on track to regain the trust of consumers. Many people, however, associate the period with the absence of fundamental change and the financial sector with greed and corruption. There is a gulf between how post-crisis developments have been perceived.[116]

4.5 Conclusion

The financial monetary system showcases deficiencies in all four areas: economic contribution, stability, fairness and legitimacy. Our analysis highlighted two underlying problems: (1) the unbalanced and uncontrolled growth of money and debt; and (2) a distorted balance between public and private interests.

The excessive growth of money and debt can undermine the economic contribution of our financial monetary system. Although efficient lending fuels economic development, there is a point at which more lending no longer contributes to economic growth. High debt levels also pose risks to stability. Crises are often preceded by debt accumulation while post-crisis recovery takes longer when debts are high. Excessive debt also raises issues of fairness, for example regarding the unequal distribution of the costs and benefits of booms and busts. The excessive growth of money and debt is also related to the system's legitimacy, as it limits politicians' ability to make policy adjustments when even small changes can have major economic consequences.

The second underlying problem is the balance between public and private interests. The financial sector fulfils crucial public functions, namely the facilitation of payments, savings, finance and insurance. Many of the problems we described in this chapter can be traced to the changing balance between private and public interests. With the growing use of deposit money and the disappearance of a public option for electronic payments, banks have become semi-public institutions – a transformation that has largely gone unnoticed. The current imbalance between private and public interests also undermines the system's contributions to the economy. In the run up to the credit crisis banks behaved as if they were purely private firms without a public role. This contributed to the instability and led to an unfair distribution of costs and benefits. Their actions also fuelled problems of

---

[114] Anheier (2013)

[115] Haldane (2016)

[116] Haldane (2016)

legitimacy, as it became less clear for politicians and citizens about precisely what they could expect from banks.

This does not mean that all of our problems can be traced to commercial banks creating our money. Nor is this what advocates of an alternative system are suggesting. What they do argue, however, is that a financial monetary system in which payments and financing are strictly separated – in which commercial banks no longer create money – will resolve or reduce many of the problems described in this chapter. We analyse this alternative system in the next two chapters. Chap. 5 outlines the potential design of an alternative system. Chap. 6 discusses its advantages and disadvantages.

Bibliography

ACM. (2014). *Barrières voor toetreding tot de Nederlandse bancaire retailsector*. Den Haag: ACM.

Adfonso, G., Santos, J. A. C., & Traina, J. (2014). Do "Too-big-to-fail" banks take on more risk? *Federal Reserve Bank of New York Economic Policy Review, 20*(2), 41–58.

Adrian, F. T., & Shin, H. S. (2008). Liquidity and financial contagion. *Financial Stability Review, Special Issue on Liquidity, 11*, 1–7.

Anheier, H. K. (2013). Institutional voids and the role of civil society: The case of global finance. *Global Policy, 5*(1), 23–35.

Arcand, J. L., Berkes, E., & Panizza, U. (2015). Too much finance? *Journal of Economic Growth, 20*(2), 105–148.

Baltensperger, E., & Dermine, J. (1986). *The role of public policy in insuring financial stability: A cross-country, comparative perspective*. Fontainebleau: INSEAD.

Bank of England. (2013). *Quarterly Bulletin 2013 Q3*. Available at: bankofengland.co.uk.

Bank of England. (2015). Cyber risk. *Financial Stability Report, 37*, 31–33.

Beck, T. (2011). The role of finance in economic development: Benefits, risks, and politics. *CentER Discussion Paper, 141*.

Beck, T., Büyükkarabacak, B., Rioja, F. K., & Valev, N. T. (2012). Who gets the credit? and Does it matter? Household vs. firm lending across countries. *The B.E. Journal of Macroeconomics, 12* (1) Art. 2.

Bettendorf, B., & Cnossen, S. (2014). *Bouwstenen voor een moderne btw, CPB Policy Brief 02*. The Hague: CPB Netherlands Bureau for Economic Policy Analysis.

Bezemer, D. (2017, March 14). *Oratie Dirk Bezemer: Waarom schuldverschuiving Nederlandse hoogconjunctuur kwetsbaar maakt*.

Bezemer, D., & Muysken, J. (2015). *Dutch financial fragilities, WRR Working Paper 13*. The Hague: WRR, The Netherlands Scientific Council for Government Policy.

Bijlsma, M. J., & Dubovik, A. (2014). *Banks, financial markets and growth in developed countries – A survey of the empirical literature* (CPB Discussion Paper 266). The Hague: CPB Netherlands Bureau for Economic Policy Analysis.

Bijlsma, M., & Mocking, R. J. M. (2013). *The private value of too-big-to-fail guarantees* (CPB Discussion Paper 240). The Hague: CPB Netherlands Bureau for Economic Policy Analysis.

BIS. (2014). *Cyber resilience in financial market infrastructures*. Basel: Bank for International Settlements.

Bjerg, O., McCann, D., Macfarlane, L., Nielsen, R. H., & Ryan-Collins, J. (2017). *Seigniorage in the 21st century: A study of the profits from money creation in the United Kingdom and Denmark*. Available at: https://doi.org/10.2139/ssrn.2921225

Boot, A., & Ratnovski, L. (2016). Banking and trading. *Review of Finance, 20*, 2219–2246.

Borio, C. (2012). *The financial cycle and macroeconomics: What have we learnt?* (BIS Working Paper 395). Basel: Bank for International Settlements.

Bremmer, D. (2018, October 29). *Minder dan 4 op de 10 betalingen nog contant, DNB is bezorgd*, in AD. https://www.ad.nl/economie/minder-dan-4-op-de-10-betalingen-nog-contant-dnb-is-bezorgd~a7a3fb34/

Brunnermeier, M. K., Crocket, A., Goodhart, C., Persaud, A. D., & Shin, H. S. (2009). *The fundamental principles of financial regulation*. Geneva: International Center for Monetary and Banking Studies (ICMB) and Centre for Economic Policy Research (CEPR).

Buttiglione, L., Lane, P. R., Reichlin, L., & Reinhart, V. et al. (2014). *Deleveraging? What deleveraging?*

Cannas, G., Cariboni, J., Kazemi Veisari, L., & Pagano, A. (2014). *Updated estimates of EU eligible and covered deposits*. European Commission, Joint Research Centre, Institute for the Protection and Security of the Citizen.

Carney, M. (2014, September 9). *Speech given at the 146th Annual Trades Union Congress, Liverpool*. Bank of England.

Cecchetti, S. G., & Kharroubi, E. (2012). *Reassessing the impact of finance on growth* (BIS Working Paper 381). Basel: Bank for International Settlements.

Cecchetti, S. G., & Kharroubi, E. (2015). *Why does financial sector growth crowd out real economic growth?* (BIS Working Paper 490). Basel: Bank for International Settlements.

Cournède, B., & Denk, O. (2015). *Finance and economic growth in OECD and G20 countries* (OECD Working Paper 1223).

CPB. (2016). *Risicorapportage Cyberveiligheid Economie*. The Hague: CPB Netherlands Bureau for Economic Policy Analysis.

De Ruijter. (2012). *Scenario's Woningmarkt – Risico's voor de woningmarkt en inventarisatie van beleidsopgaven*. Amstelveen: De Ruijter Strategie BV.

de Vries, C. G. (2005). The simple economics of bank fragility. *Journal of Banking & Finance, 29*, 803–825.

De Wit Committee II. (2012). *Parlementaire enquête financieel stelsel. Eindrapport*, Kamerstukken II, 2011–2012, 31980, no. 61.

Debelle, G. (2004). *Household debt and the macroeconomy* (BIS Quarterly Review). Basel: Bank for International Settlements.

Demertzis, M. and A. Lehmann (2017) 'Tackling Europe's crisis legacy: a comprehensive strategy for bad loans and debt restructuring', Policy Contribution 11: 1–15, Brussels: Bruegel.

Denk, O. (2015). *Financial sector pay and labour income inequality: Evidence from Europe* (OECD Economics Department Working Papers No. 1225). Paris: OECD Publishing.

DNB. (2011). *Overheidssteun aan financiële instellingen*. Available at: https://www.dnb.nl/nieuws/nieuwsoverzicht-en-archief/dnbulletin-2011/index.jsp

DNB. (2015). *Visie op de structuur van de Nederlandse bankensector – Stabiliteit en efficiëntie door diversiteit en concurrentie*. Amsterdam: De Nederlandsche Bank.

DNB. (2016). *De financiële stabiliteitstaak van DNB*. Amsterdam: De Nederlandsche Bank.

DNB. (2017). *Overzicht Financiële Stabiliteit – Voorjaar 2017*. Amsterdam: De Nederlandsche Bank.

DNB. (2018a, November 7). *DNBulletin: 'Contant of pin? Wie betaalt, bepaalt.*

DNB. (2018b). *Jaarverslag 2017*. Amsterdam: DNB.

DNB. (2018c). *Overzicht Financiële Stabiliteit – Najaar 2018*. Amsterdam: De Nederlandsche Bank.

Drehmann, M., Borio, C., & Tsatsaronis, K. (2011). *Anchoring countercyclical capital buffers: The role of credit aggregates* (BIS Working Paper 355). Basel: Bank for International Settlements.

ECB. (2015). *The fiscal impact of financial sector support during the crisis* (ECB Economic Bulletin 6). Frankfurt am Main: ECB.

ESRB. (2018, September). *EU shadow banking monitor* (No. 3). Frankfurt am Main: ECB.

ESRB ASC. (2014). *Is Europe overbanked?* (Reports of the Advisory Scientific Committee No. 4). European Systemic Risk Board.

European Commission. (2013). *Green paper on long-term financing of the European economy.*

European Parliament. (2014). *Consumer protection aspects of financial services.* Available at: www.europarl.europa.eu

FSB. (2015). *Global shadow banking monitoring report 2015.* Basel: FSB.

FSB, IMF, & BIS. (2009). *Guidance to assess the systemic importance of financial institutions, markets and instruments: Initial considerations.* Report to the G-20 Finance Ministers and Central Bank Governors. Available at: https://www.imf.org/external/np/g20/pdf/100109.pdf

Giannini, C. (2011). *The age of central banks.* Cheltenham/Northampton: Edward Elgar.

Goodhart, C. A. E. (2007). *Liquidity Risk Management* (Special Paper 175, LSE Financial Markets Group Paper Series).

Haldane, A. G. (2009, April 28). *Rethinking the financial network.* Speech by Mr Andrew G. Haldane, Executive Director, Financial Stability, Bank of England, at the Financial Student Association, Amsterdam.

Haldane, A. G. (2016, May 18). *The great divide.* Speech given by Andrew G. Haldane, Chief Economist, Bank of England, New City Agenda Annual dinner.

Haldane, A. G., Brennan, S., & Madouros, V. (2010). What is the contribution of the financial sector: Miracle or mirage? In *The Future of Finance: The LSE Report.* London School of Economics and Political Science.

Hartmann, P., Straetmans, S., & de Vries, C. G. (2004). Bank system stability: A cross-atlantic perspective. In M. Carey & R. M. Stultz (Eds.), *The risks of financial institutions. NBER* (pp. 133–192). Chicago/London: The University of Chicago Press.

IMF. (2012). Chapter 3: Growth resuming, dangers remain. In *Dealing with household debt.* Washington, DC: International Monetary Fund.

IMF. (2015). *From banking to sovereign stress: Implications for public debt* (IMF Policy Papers). Washington, DC: International Monetary Fund.

IMF. (2016). *Debt, use it wisely, Fiscal monitor October 2015.* International Monetary Fund.

IMF-FSB-BIS. (2016). *Elements of effective macroprudential policies.* Available at: www.imf.org/external/np/g20/pdf/2016/083116.pdf

Jak, N. (2014). *Semipublieke instellingen; De juridische positie van instellingen op het snijvlak van overheid en samenleving.* Dissertation.

Jonker, N. (2013). *Social costs of POS payments in the Netherlands 2002–2012: Efficiency gains from increased debit card usage* (DNB Occasional Studies, Vol. 11, No. 2). Amsterdam: DNB.

Jonker, N., Hernandez, L., de Vree, R., & Zwaan, P. (2018). *From cash to cards. How debit card payments overtook cash in the Netherlands* (DNB Occasional Studies, Vol. 16, No. 1). Amsterdam: DNB.

Jordá, O., Schularick, M., & Taylor, A. M. (2014). *The great mortgaging: Housing finance, crises, and business cycles* (Federal Reserve Bank of San Francisco Working Paper Series No. 23).

Keuning, W. (2017, October 6). Rabo-directeur: "Ik heb ook meegewerkt aan overkreditering". *Het Financieele Dagblad.*

Kindleberger, C. P. M. (1978). *Manias, panics, and crashes: A history of financial crises.* London: Palgrave Macmillan.

King, M. (2016). *The end of alchemy: Money, banking and the future of the global economy.* New York: W.W. Norton & Company.

Layard, R., Nickell, S., & Jackman, R. (1991). *Unemployment – Macroeconomic performance and the labour market.* Oxford: Oxford University Press.

Levine, R. (1997). Financial development and economic growth: Views and agenda. *Journal of Economic Literature, XXXV,* 688–726.

Liikanen Report. (2012). *High-level expert group on reforming the structure of the EU banking sector.* Brussels: European Commission.

Liu, Y., & Rosenberg, C. B. (2013). *Dealing with private debt distress in the wake of the European financial crisis. A review of the economics and legal toolbox* (IMF Working Paper Series, WP/13/44). Washington, DC: IMF.

Lo, S., & Rogoff, K. (2015). *Secular stagnation, debt overhang and other rationales for sluggish growth, six years on* (BIS Working Paper 482). Basel: Bank for International Settlements.

Louisse, M. L. (2013). Het wettelijk recht op een betaalrekening is een feit, maar wel een zeer beperkt feit. *Vennootschap & Onderneming*, (1), 11–15.

Lukkezen, J., & Elbourne, A. (2015). *De Nederlandse consumptie – Goede tijden, slechte tijden* (CPB Policy Brief 2015/03). The Hague: CPB Netherlands Bureau for Economic Policy Analysis.

Maatschappelijk Overleg Betalingsverkeer. (2017a). *Rapportage 2016*. Amsterdam: MOB.

Maatschappelijk Overleg Betalingsverkeer. (2017b). *Pin-only beleid publieksbalies gemeenten – verzoek aan IPO*. Amsterdam: DNB.

Macfarlane, L., Ryan-Collins, J., Bjerg, O., Nielsen, R., & McCann, D. (2017). *Making money from making money. Seigniorage in the Modern Economy*. London: New Economics Foundation.

Mackintosh, S. P. M. (2014). Crises and paradigm shift. *The Political Quarterly, 85*(4), 406–412.

McKinsey & Company. (2006). *Payment services in the Netherlands: An analysis of revenues and costs for banks. Final report*. Amsterdam: McKinsey & Company.

Mian, A., & Sufi, A. (2010). Household leverage and the recession of 2007–09. *IMF Economic Review, 58*(1), 74–117.

Mian, A., & Sufi, A. (2014). *House of Debt – How they (and you) caused the great recession, and how we can prevent it from happening again*. Chicago: The University of Chicago Books Press.

Minsky, H. P. (1986). *Stabilizing an unstable economy*. New Haven: Yale University Press.

Muns, S., & Bijlsma, M. (2015). Tail dependence: A cross-study comparison. *Journal of Portfolio Management 41, 3*, 109–116.

Nationale Ombudsman. (2017). *Een onderzoek naar pinbetaling als enige mogelijkheid bij betalingen aan de balie van de gemeente*. The Hague.

Netherlands Court of Audit. (2016). *Brief aan de Tweede Kamer over Ontwikkelingen interventies kredietcrisis*. The Hague: Netherlands Court of Audit.

Nouy, D. (2018, September 18). The European banking sector – Towards a single jurisdiction, Speech by Danièle Nouy, Chair of the Supervisory Board of the ECB, ACPR Conference, "Financial supervision and the role of national authorities in Europe", Paris.

NVB. (2014). The Dutch Mortgage Market, Memorandum of the Dutch Banking Association.

OECD. (2012). *Implicit guarantees for bank debt: Where Do we stand?* Paris: Organisation for Economic Co-operation and Development.

OECD. (2015). *Finance and inclusive growth*. Paris: Organisation for Economic Co-operation and Development.

Pagliari, E. (Ed.). (2012). *Making good financial regulation – Towards a policy response to regulatory capture, international centre for financial regulation*. Guildford: Grosvenor House Publishing.

Pettifor, A. (2017). *The production of money: How to break the power of the banks*. London: Verso.

Philippon, T., & Reshef, A. (2012, November 1). Wages and human capital in the U.S. financial industry: 1909–2006. *The Quarterly Journal of Economics, 127*(4), 1551–1609.

Pontuch, P. (2014). Private sector deleveraging: where do we stand? *Quarterly Report on the Euro Area 13, 3*, 7–19. European Union Publications Office.

Rajan, R. G., & Zingales, L. (2004). Making capitalism work for everyone. *Journal of Applied Corporate Finance, 16*, 101–108.

Reinhart, C. M., Reinhart, V., & Rogoff, K. (2015). Dealing with debt. *Journal of International Economics, 96*(Supplement 1), S43–S55.

Rousseau, P. L., & Wachtel, P. (2011). What is happening to the impact of financial deepening on economic growth? *Economic Inquiry, 49*(1), 276–288.

Schmiedel, H., Kostova, G., & Ruttenberg, W. (2012). *The social and private costs of retail payment instruments. A European perspective* (ECB-Occasional Paper Series, no. 137). Frankfurt am Main: DNB.

Schoenmaker, D., & Wierts, P. (2015). *Regulating the financial cycle: An integrated approach with a leverage ratio* (Duisenberg school of finance – Tinbergen Institute Discussion Paper). Amsterdam.

Schularick, M., & Taylor, A. M. (2012). Credit booms gone bust: Monetary policy, leverage cycles, and financial crises, 1870–2008. *American Economic Review, 102*(2), 1029–1061.

SER. (2013). *Nederlandse economie in stabieler vaarwater*. The Hague: Social and Economic Council.

Sobel, J. (2002). Can we trust social capital? *Journal of Economic Literature, 40*(1), 139–154.

Stellinga, B. (2015). *Europese financiële regulering voor en na de crisis* (The Netherlands Scientific Council for Government Policy Working Paper 15). The Hague: Sdu Uitgevers.

Stellinga, B. (2018). *The financial valuation crisis. The inherent limits to taming unstable markets (PhD-manuscript)*. Amsterdam: University of Amsterdam.

Stellinga, B. (2019). Why performativity limits credit rating reform. *Finance and Society, 5*(1), 20–41.

Stellinga, B. (2020). The open-endedness of macroprudential policy. Endogenous risks as an obstacle to countercyclical macroprudential policy. *Business and Politics, 22*(1), 224–251.

Stellinga, B., & Mügge, D. (2017). The regulator's conundrum. How market reflexivity limits fundamental financial reform. *Review of International Political Economy, 24*(3), 393–423.

Taylor, A. M. (2012). *The great leveraging* (NBER Working Paper Series 18290). Cambridge, MA: National Bureau of Economic Research.

Tiemeijer, W. (2016). *Eigen schuld? Een gedragswetenschappelijk perspectief op problematische schulden* (WRR Investigation). Amsterdam: Amsterdam University Press.

Turner, A. (2014). *Escaping the debt addiction: Monetary and macro-prudential policy in the post crisis world*. Frankfurt: Centre for Financial Studies.

Turner, A. (2015). *Between debt and the devil – Money, credit, and fixing global finance*. Princeton: Princeton University Press.

van der Sluis, M. (2017). *In law we trust: The role of EU constitutional law in European monetary integration*. Florence: European University Institute.

van der Veer, K., Klaaijsen, E., & Roerink, R. (2015). *Scherper licht op financiële stabiliteitsrisico's van het schaduwbankwezen* (DNB Occasional Studies, 13: 7). Amsterdam: DNB.

Verhoeven, W. H. J., van Essen, C., Folkeringa, M., Ruis, A., & Smit, C. K. (2010). *Het buffervermogen van het mkb. Omvang, achtergronden en een internationale vergelijking*. Zoetermeer: Panteia.

WRR. (2016). *Samenleving en financiële sector in evenwicht*, WRR report nr. 96. Den Haag: Sdu Uitgevers.

WRR. (2017). *Weten is nog geen doen. Een realistisch perspectief op redzaamheid*, WRR report nr. 97. Amsterdam: Amsterdam University Press.

5

Exploring the Workings of the Sovereign Money System

The previous chapter assessed our financial monetary system according to four criteria: (1) its economic contribution, (2) its stability, (3) its fairness in the distribution of benefits, costs and risks, and (4) its legitimacy. According to citizens' initiatives around the world (including *Ons Geld* in the Netherlands), fundamental reforms are necessary to fix the flaws in the financial monetary system. Although their proposals for reform differ, many support a *sovereign money system*[1] in which all money is directly or indirectly in public hands.[2] This means that money can only be created by the central bank; commercial banks lose their ability to create money.[3] It also means that the institutions that lend money (we call them financing institutions) are strictly separated from those that make up the payment system.

The sovereign money system has a long lineage. Its forerunners include the architects of the *Chicago Plan* in the 1930s (see Box 5.1), Nobel laureate Milton Friedman in the early post-war period and economist James Tobin in the 1980s.[4] Since the latest financial crisis, variants of a sovereign money system have been proposed by economists John Kay, Laurence Kotlikoff, Jaromir Benes and Michael Kumhof.[5] *Financial Times* columnist Martin Wolf has proposed similar ideas.[6] These ideas have also been debated in national parliaments. A proposal for a sovereign money system was subject of a Swiss referendum in June 2018, in which it was rejected.

---

[1] Also known as full reserve banking, 100% money, limited purpose banking, or *Vollgeld*.

[2] Dyson et al. (2016); Huber (2017)

[3] The proposals refer to an independent public institution. Ons Geld calls it the monetary authority, others call it the central bank (for the sake of clarity, we use the more common latter term). In our view, the question of whether such an institution should have a balance sheet or the ability to grant loans is a separate matter.

[4] Friedman (1948); James Tobin (1985)

[5] Kay (2009); Kotlikoff (2010); Benes and Kumhof (2013)

[6] Wolf (2014)

Box 5.1 The Chicago Plan

Calls for a sovereign money system often build on ideas advanced in the 1930s by economists associated with the University of Chicago, particularly Frank Knight and Henry Simons. Against the backdrop of the Great Depression and the Roosevelt government's reforms, they called for an even more radical overhaul of the banking system and monetary policy. Their ideas later came to be known as the Chicago Plan.

The Chicago Plan emerged against the backdrop of unprecedented economic contraction, deflation, unemployment and many bank failures. To prevent a further escalation of the banking crisis, all banks in the United States were closed in March 1933. After inspection of banks' balance sheets, some remained shuttered and some were recapitalized, while others were expected to continue operations on their own. To avert further panic, the government provided a temporary, unlimited guarantee for deposits. The Banking Act of June 1933 introduced a deposit guarantee system that set the insured sum at $2500, which covered around 97% of account holders and 23.7% of the total value of bank deposits. The Banking Act also specified that commercial banks could no longer engage in securities trading (the Glass-Steagall Act), thereby limiting the interdependence of the banking system and securities markets.

Around the same time as the 1933 Banking Act, Knight, Simons and six other economists sent the first version of the Chicago Plan privately to several members of the US government. They advocated a new type of bank that would be required to back all deposits with central bank reserves. Credit would be provided by separate institutions which would no longer be allowed to operate on the basis of self-created bank deposits. In short, the aim was to split the banking system into payment and financing sections. The idea inspired Irving Fisher in his 1935 book *100% Money*, which argued that "there should be a further separation of functions and that the banks which have slow assets [...] should not have demand deposits against them".[7]

But the Chicago Plan came too late, with the most important reforms already having been pushed through in 1933. Subsequent discussion mainly concerned how monetary policy could be adapted to better support economic growth and employment. The Banking Act of 1935 therefore primarily concerned the organization and policy of the Federal Reserve System. The Chicago Plan nevertheless continued to play a background role in one element of the Act, namely in the rules concerning the reserves that commercial banks were required to hold with the Fed. The idea was that by varying these requirements the Fed could curb or stimulate lending. One of the drafters of the 1935 Banking Act, Lauchlin Currie, supported the Chicago Plan and had

(continued)

[7]Cited in: Phillips (2015 [1995]: 50)

Box 5.1 (continued)
formulated the rules in such a way that the Fed could demand that bank deposits be backed 100% by reserves. In other words, the rules would open the way to full reserve banking. But in the passage of the Act, Congress capped the figure at 30%.[8]

This chapter addresses the broad outlines of a sovereign money system as advocated in recent proposals.[9] We do not delve into the details of each proposal but focus on their overarching characteristics. We first outline what these proposals imply for the payment system (Sect. 5.1) as well as for investing and lending (Sect. 5.2). We then turn to the government's role and responsibilities in the new system, including how money is created and enters society (Sect. 5.3), and discuss transition paths to the new system (Sect. 5.4). The advantages and disadvantages of a sovereign money system will be discussed in the following chapter.

5.1 The Payment System

In the sovereign money system, all money is – directly or indirectly – sovereign money, held either at the central bank or at payment institutions where deposits are 100% backed by central bank reserves. In our current system, the only sovereign money is cash, issued by the central bank; bank deposits – which make up more than 90% of the current money supply – are debts owed by a private party (the bank) to the account holder.

That money largely consists of bank deposits entails risk. As we saw in Chap. 2, banks can fail, suffering such losses on their assets (mortgage loans, corporate loans, bonds, shares, derivatives) that their equity evaporates, rendering them technically bankrupt. Banks can also run out of liquidity when account holders try to withdraw their balances in cash or transfer them to other banks *en masse*. Since the bank only covers a fraction of these deposits with central bank reserves and other liquid assets, it may be unable to meet these requests (see Fig. 5.1).[10] While the failure of a small bank will rarely threaten the integrity of the payment system, a systemic crisis involving a large bank or many banks simultaneously may well do so.

In our current set-up, the payment system is tied up with banks' other, riskier activities. The advocates of an alternative system want to end this. In the proposals,

---

[8]Phillips (2015 [1995]: 115–135)

[9]Benes and Kumhof (2013); Dyson et al. (2016); Kotlikoff (2010); Huber (2017); Sigurjónsson (2015); Ons Geld (2015); Ons Geld (2016); Kay (2009)

[10]Liquidity problems can also arise from the short-term loans banks obtain in financial markets. While these loans are normally rolled over or replaced by loans from other lenders, major funding problems can ensue when lenders doubt the soundness of the institution.

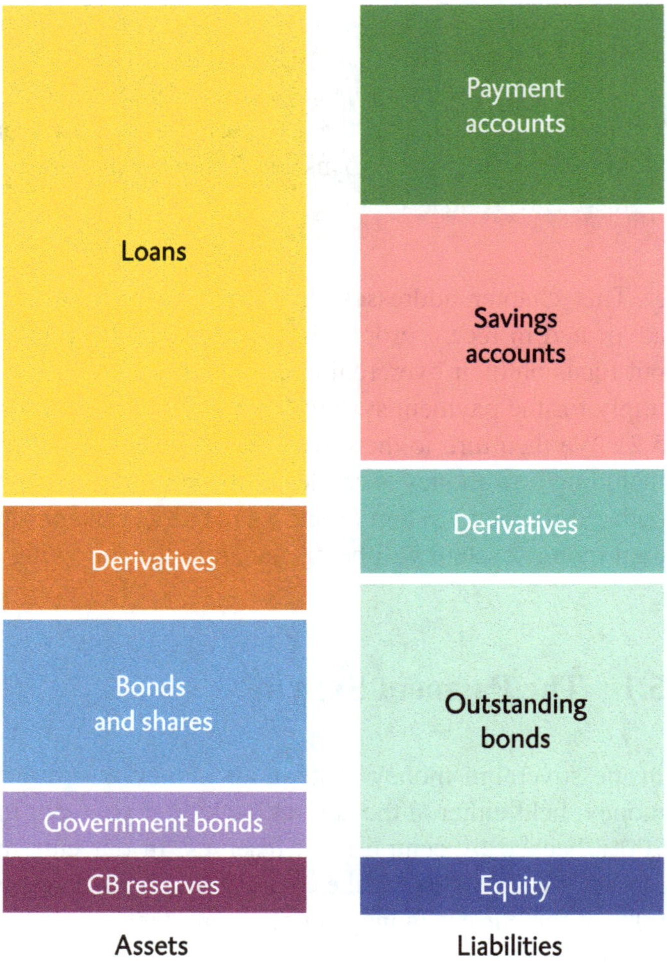

Fig. 5.1 Simplified bank balance sheet

deposits in payment accounts would from now on be entirely sovereign money or covered fully by sovereign money. To that end the payment part must be separated from the rest of the financial system.[11] Although the precise design differs between the proposals, we can identify two broad variants: (1) payment accounts at banks are fully covered by central bank reserves or government bonds (Sect. 5.1.1), and (2) payment accounts are held directly by the central bank (Sect. 5.2.2) (see Fig. 5.2).

5.1.1 Payment Accounts at Payment Institutions

This option entails separate (or at least separated) banks for payment services. As is currently the case, money would enter the bank's balance sheet as a debt to the account holder. The difference is that the corresponding assets are restricted as

[11]Benes and Kumhof (2013); Kay (2009); Kotlikoff (2010); Dyson et al. (2016); Huber (2017); Ons Geld (2016)

Fig. 5.2 Options for payment

deposits must be fully covered by central bank reserves or, in some proposals, government bonds.[12] This would obviate the need for deposit insurance schemes.

Payment accounts would be held either at specially established subsidiaries of financial institutions or at independent institutions. In the former scenario, payment accounts would be separated *within* the bank, with the bank's riskier activities confined to its other subsidiaries. Such ring-fencing would mean that in principle, the bank's other activities cannot affect the payment system. In the latter scenario, independent institutions would administer payment accounts, 100% backed by central bank reserves. The banks' business model would then consist of account holders paying for services (a flat fee or per transaction). This would then be the price account holders pay for the security of their electronic means of payment. Earnings could also be generated by marketing customer data, although financial data quite

[12]Benes and Kumhof (2013); Kotlikoff (2010); Kay (2009)

rightly enjoy special protection. Another possibility is that earnings would be generated by the interest the central bank pays on central bank reserves.[13]

Most proposals for a sovereign money system involve full coverage by central bank reserves and cash.[14] A slightly less radical variant is Kay's narrow banking proposal in which payment accounts are fully covered by secure, liquid assets, mainly government bonds.[15] Although Kay's plan allows narrow banks to hold other (relatively) secure assets on their balance sheets, he believes it both feasible and desirable to restrict eligible assets to government bonds.[16] Whether this plan meets the requirements of sovereign money depends on whether eligibility is limited to government bonds of the bank's home country and whether governments can 'print money' if necessary – the latter no longer being an option for euro area countries that have transferred their powers to the European Central Bank. As Kay's plan is not explicit on this point, it is unclear whether it should be seen as a variant of a sovereign money system.

5.1.2 Payment Accounts at the Central Bank

The second option is to transfer all payment accounts to the central bank.[17] The money in these accounts could then be seen as an electronic form of cash (which is also issued by central banks). *Positive Money* argues that account holders in this scenario would have to be the legal owners of the money.[18]

Transactions could then be processed in several ways. Responsibility for payments could fall to the central bank or be left in the hands of private payment institutions. These private institutions would not enter the money on their balance sheets but act as administrative intermediaries. The point of deferring tasks to private institutions is that central banks might be unwilling to provide services to millions of individual customers – services that could be offered by private institutions responsible for operations that are currently the preserve of banks: opening accounts, verifying customer identity, enforcing anti-money laundering regulations, issuing bank cards and maintaining the payment infrastructure, including the ATM network. Customers would have to pay for these services per account, per transaction or through a flat fee, while competition would keep these costs as low as possible.[19]

[13]Based on the 'normal' situation where the interest paid by the ECB on central bank reserves is not negative.

[14]Benes and Kumhof (2013)

[15]Kay (2009)

[16]Kay (2009: 31)

[17]Dyson et al. (2016); Huber (2017); Ons Geld (2016)

[18]Dyson et al. (2016)

[19]Dyson et al. (2016: 20)

Payment institutions would not be permitted to do anything with the money without the express instruction of the account holder. Were the payment institution to fail, the money would remain at the central bank. If the payment institution is a subsidiary of a financial institution, it would be legally and financially shielded from risks arising from the parent company's other activities.[20]

Ons Geld argues that the money should not be on the central bank's balance sheet but in a basic register (similar to the land registry) held by a monetary authority.[21] Money would then no longer represent a debt and would be shielded from financial risks. Given the particular nature of a central bank, the practical difference as compared to entering money on a central bank's balance sheet is limited, however (see Box 5.2).

Box 5.2 The Balance Sheet of a Central Bank

The central bank's peculiar nature is reflected in its balance sheet. In the new system, the right side of the balance sheet comprises electronic sovereign money (similar to cash in the current system). Although cash money is conventionally recorded as a debt in accounting terms, it is not a debt in economic terms; it does not have to be repaid and nothing else can be demanded in its place. The other specific feature on the liability side is that a central bank may have negative equity without having to close down.[22]

The left side of the central bank's balance sheet contains its assets. Although in the current system the convention is that new central bank reserves will only be created on the basis of corresponding transfers from commercial banks, the central bank can also create reserves or money when there are no matching assets of actual value. In a sovereign money system, a central bank will be able to create new money by recording corresponding assets without actual value (such as a 'money creation certificate') in its accounts.[23]

This peculiarity means that money is equally secure whether it is recorded on a central bank's balance sheet or in a different type of accounting system. Most debts (cash or electronic money) will not be repayable on demand while the central bank cannot go bankrupt (unless it is saddled with foreign debts). This peculiarity also means that accounting practices are irrelevant to the question of whether central bank money can be considered 'debt-free'. Although money held on a central bank's

[20]Dyson et al. (2016: 19)

[21]Ons Geld (2016)

[22]Problems may arise if a central bank has liabilities in foreign currencies. Although the central bank can have negative equity, central bankers would be wary of the effect on legitimacy (see Cohen-Setton 2015).

[23]Dyson et al. (2016: 30) propose the newly created money to be 'covered' by perpetual zero-coupon bonds issued by the government and bought by the central bank.

balance sheet is recorded as debt for accounting purposes, it is not a debt in economic terms.

5.1.3 Conclusion

All proposals for a sovereign money system assume a separate payment system where all money is 100% sovereign money. While the proposals differ on how this is to be implemented, the differences have no practical consequences. The logical result is that the central bank will assume full responsibility for the creation of *new* money. The proposals assume that payment accounts will be secure and stable (although problems due to cybercrime or failing ICT-systems are not discussed). As money is not exposed to financial risks, no deposit guarantee scheme is needed.[24] The underlying principle is that no interest is paid on payment accounts and services will have to be paid for. Guaranteed interest-bearing savings accounts will no longer exist.

5.2 The Financial System

The financial monetary system must not only ensure an efficient and reliable structure for payments but also facilitate the financing of economic activity. This section examines how proposals for a sovereign money system envisage the operation of financial institutions. A key issue is how these institutions finance *themselves*. In our current system, banks are largely financed by bank deposits, created when they grant loans. In the new system, financing institutions would not be allowed to do this; they would have to raise money before lending it. Here the proposals point to two broad possibilities: financing based on debt (discussed in Sect. 5.2.1) and financing based on equity (discussed in Sect. 5.2.2) (see also Box 5.3). The proposals also differ in the envisioned extent of public lending, which we discuss in Sect. 5.2.3.

Box 5.3 Financing: Equity and Debt

A company can be financed in two ways: through equity or debt. In the former, the financier buys a share in a public or private company.[25] This share gives

(continued)

[24]Van Dixhoorn (2013: 15); Dyson et al. (2016: 19)

[25]For cooperatives it is more complex. In principle, members are liable for operations, thereby guaranteeing solvency. But in practice, this liability is almost always excluded in the articles of association or limited to a specific amount. Equity can then be accrued in different ways. Some

Box 5.3 (continued)
the investor a degree of influence over the company's decisions and a share of profit in the form of dividend. The financier has no guarantee of recovering the invested sum. To do so he must sell his share, if possible, to another party or back to the company. The value of the share may fluctuate. If the company goes bankrupt, the shareholder is at the back of the queue when it comes to distributing the company's residual value. The creditors must be repaid first.

When a loan (debt finance) is granted, lender and borrower enter an agreement with provisions on the repayment terms and interest payments. In principle the invested money is thus fully repaid to the financier. If the company goes bankrupt, its debts may have to be repaid through the sale of its assets. Some debts are negotiable; these are generally referred to as bonds. Bank deposits are a special form of debt as they are in principle repayable on demand and are easy to transfer, including in specific amounts.

5.2.1 Financing Institutions Operating on the Basis of Debt

In this variant, private financing institutions operate largely on the basis of debt and partly on the basis of equity (to absorb any losses). These institutions must first borrow money from households and companies before lending it to other households and companies. When companies and individuals take out loans, the financing institution transfers them money in exchange for a debt contract. Conversely, those who lend money to the financing institution receive debt securities in return. Financing institutions then have debts to those who have deposited money. These can be registered debts (investment accounts) or negotiable debts (bonds). In contrast to our current system, these debts are not repayable on demand.

Figure 5.3 illustrates this process with the aid of balance sheets. While this example uses investment accounts, the same process applies in principle to negotiable debts (bonds). For convenience, we assume that the central bank administers the payment system and that financing institutions have accounts at the central bank. We can see how the process operates when Elisabeth makes €1000 available to the financing institution, which then lends it to Company X. This is a simplified example, with the illustration showing the *changes* that ensue from lending.

We note that financing institutions borrow and then lend *existing* money; they thus operate as true intermediaries. The money supply does not grow or contract as a result of these activities, but remains unchanged at €2000. At the same time, something happens in the financial system, where *new* claims are created. Elisabeth now has a claim of €1000 (plus interest) against the financing institution and this

---

cooperatives have members' accounts where members deposit money. Cooperatives can also build up equity through retained profits, with equity certificates purchased by members or in exceptional cases by external parties (Van der Sangen 2012).

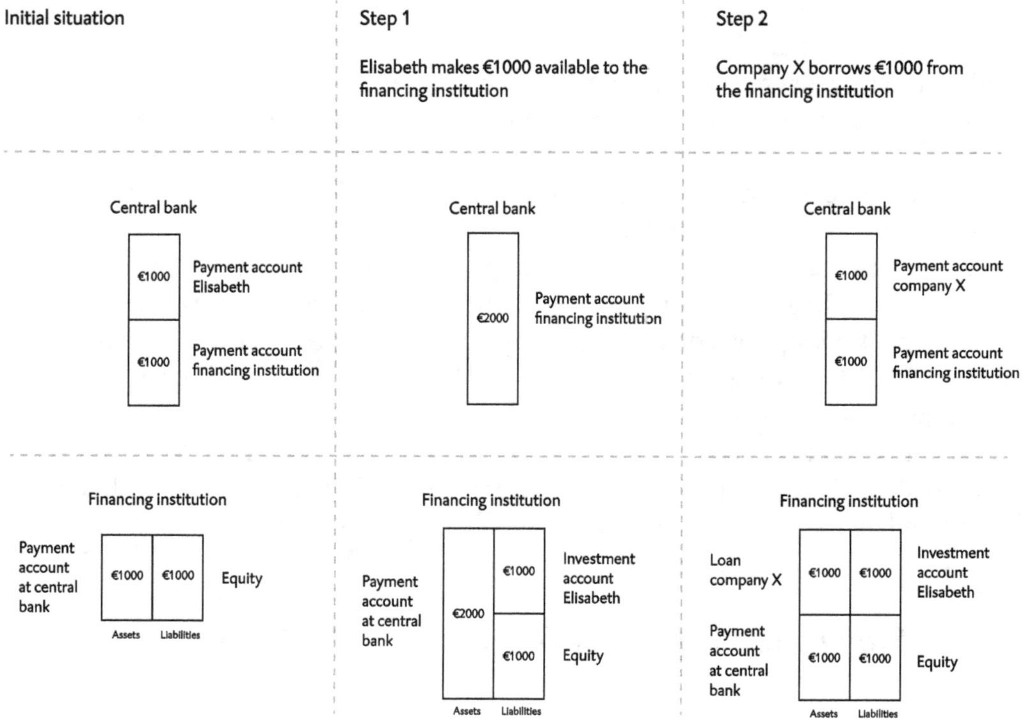

Fig. 5.3 Lending in the sovereign money system

institution has a claim of €1000 (plus interest) against company X. These claims disappear if the company repays its debt and the financing institution then repays Elisabeth. Finally, note that although the lending has no effect on the *money supply*, it does affect the size of the claims. If the company borrowing the money purchases something from another company, it is possible that this other company makes the money available to a financing institution. New loans can then be granted. Hence the credit supply is not fixed (see also Sect. 6.1).

If financing institutions operate on the basis of debts (bonds or investment accounts), a crucial question concerns their maturity period. Some proposals do not require debts and loans to have the same maturity period; as in our current system, we will then have maturity transformation. But although a financing institution may have outstanding loans with an average maturity of 10 years against debts with an average maturity of one year, the debts are not repayable on demand. Investment accounts will also have either a predetermined maturity or a particular notice period before they can be turned into central bank deposits.[26]

If financing institutions operate on the basis of debts with shorter maturity than their assets, bank runs and failures remain possible. If large numbers of people simultaneously seek to convert their investment accounts into central bank deposits, at maturity or after the notice period, the financing institution may have difficulties honouring their requests. The financing institution will likewise encounter problems

[26]Dyson et al. (2016); Huber (2017)

if it cannot issue new bonds, as it will then have to sell its long-term loans. If this happens in a recession at below cost price, the institution may collapse. This would amount to a slow-motion bank run. The sovereign money proposals consider this risk as part of the game; hence they do not support public guarantees for investment accounts or bonds issued by financing institutions.[27] Positive Money argues that the financial part of the system should operate on the basis of shared losses, with investment account holders also suffering losses if that is necessary to prevent bankruptcy.[28]

5.2.2 Financing Institutions Operating on the Basis of Equity Only

In another variant – for example in Kotlikoff's *Limited Purpose Banking* plan – financing institutions are financed only with equity. They thus only issue negotiable *shares*; in other words, they offer investment funds. Many different types of investment funds can be created, each with a different risk profile and maturity: mortgage funds, corporate loan funds, etc.[29]

The main difference with the former variant is that profits and losses are now shared evenly among all financiers. In the Kotlikoff plan, everyone is a shareholder. If the value of the portfolio falls, the value of the share also falls. No risk transformation takes place within the investment fund as all shareholders reap the profits as well as the losses; nor is there any maturity transformation. Funds can be differentiated by the *type* of maturity. A fund with a 30-year maturity is liquidated after 30 years, at which time shareholders receive the proceeds.[30] But shareholders can try to sell their shares at any time.

The allocation of risks in a financial system where financing institutions operate on the basis of debt differs substantially from a system where institutions operate entirely on the basis of equity. The latter suffers neither bank runs nor refinancing risks. On the other hand, investors are directly exposed to losses on their investments.

[27] See e.g. Dyson et al. (2016: 24)

[28] Dyson et al. (2016: 25)

[29] Cf. Chamley et al. (2012). Kotlikoff's proposal also includes money market funds, which are in fact payment institutions. These funds are only permitted to hold government bonds or central bank reserves, so their value is stable. A share of this money market fund can be used to buy a share in an investment fund. Conversely, borrowers can receive money from a financing institution in the form of new shares in the money market fund.

[30] Kotlikoff and Goodman (2009: 8); Van Dixhoorn (2013: 28)

5.2.3 *Private and Public Lending*

The proposals for sovereign money differ amongst themselves regarding the government's role in lending. Benes and Kumhof allow for the possibility that private financing institutions are partly financed by the central bank.[31] The central bank would lend money to the financing institution at a particular interest rate; this would mean that, in principle, the central bank can influence the interest rates charged by private financing institutions. If the central bank finds that sufficient credit is unavailable or only available at an excessive price, it can make more money available at a lower rate. Conversely, excessive lending can be curbed by reducing central bank loans or raising their price.

Other proposals acknowledge the advantages of this set-up but remain more cautious.[32] In normal circumstances, lending should be a purely private matter; lending sovereign money to private financing institutions should only happen in exceptional circumstances. The caution is understandable given the aim of stopping financing institutions from creating money by granting loans. We can imagine a situation in which financing institutions, being 'short of money', cannot meet the demand for credit. If the central bank then creates new money to lend to financing institutions, this resembles the current situation in which money is created in response to demand for credit.

5.3 Monetary Policy and Financial Regulation

A fundamental reorganization of the financial monetary system would have major consequences for monetary policy and financial regulation. We first address the creation, allocation and destruction of money before turning to financial regulation and the independence and legitimacy of the central bank.

5.3.1 *The Creation, Allocation and Destruction of Money*

A common feature of the proposals discussed in this chapter is that new money can *only* be created by public institutions. The liabilities of private financing institutions no longer serve as money; at any rate, this is the aim. In most proposals for an alternative system, the task to create money is assigned to an independent public institution or commission.[33] Various proposals refer to this body as a fourth,

[31]Benes and Kumhof (2013)

[32]Huber (2017)

[33]Huber (2017: 147); Ons Geld (2016)

money-creating power alongside those of the legislature, executive and judiciary.[34] For the sake of convenience, we assume the responsibility of money creation rests with the central bank.

To be clear, our current system allows central banks to create or destroy money, both cash and (indirectly via commercial banks) deposit money. The crucial difference is that in the current system the central bank does so only in exchange for the financial assets of other institutions. In the proposals for an alternative system, the central bank can create money 'out of nothing'. This raises numerous questions, which we briefly address below. What objectives should central banks pursue? How do central banks know how much money should be created or destroyed? Who determines the *allocation* of the newly created money? Will central banks still pursue an interest rate policy?

What goals central banks pursue is ultimately a political decision. We saw earlier that monetary policy does not have fixed goals. In response to runaway inflation in the 1970s, many European countries decided that central banks should aim primarily for price stability, generally defined as inflation stabilized at around 2%. In the United States, the Fed has additional formal objectives, namely contributing to maximum employment and low long-term interest rates. Central banks also often have a range of other goals such as financial stability, an efficient and reliable payment system and protecting depositors. In any case, the money-creating authority could pursue a range of goals or limit itself to the common objective of price stability.[35]

How does the central bank determine how much new money to create? One possibility is adhering to a particular rule, for example allowing the money supply to rise as fast as nominal economic growth (i.e. real growth plus price rises). Another possibility, one closer to the current situation, is to give the central bank decision-making discretion. Although it could apply a rule of thumb ('let the money supply rise in line with economic growth'), it would be possible to deviate from it. Because the interplay between consumer prices, asset prices, interest rates, exchange rates and debt volume are complex and variable, and because economic cycles are influenced by more than just money supply, Huber argues that it is impossible to adhere to a fixed rule.[36] Both Huber and *Ons Geld* therefore give the money-creating authority discretionary powers.[37]

All this relates to the transmission mechanism of money creation: the effect of the central bank's actions on the ultimate policy goals. The *allocation* of the new money plays an important role in this regard. New money can be used to:

- increase government spending (or maintain it at current levels while cutting taxes);

[34]Dyson et al. (2016); Ons Geld (2016)

[35]Dyson et al. (2016)

[36]Huber (2017: 157)

[37]Huber (2017); Ons Geld (2016)

- pay down outstanding government debt;
- transfer money directly to households (helicopter money);
- lend money to financing institutions.[38]

How new money enters the economy will affect the macroeconomic impact. For example, transferring money directly to households will have a different effect on price stability than lending it first to financing institutions. *Positive Money* argues that the central bank cannot predict with precision the effects of new money entering the economy.[39] If people use it to purchase consumer goods, it can cause immediate price pressure. But households may also decide to save the money. The creation of money affects purchasing power, but how this translates into wider objectives such as employment, economic growth and inflation depends ultimately on the decisions of a large number of actors.

Who decides how the new money is allocated? Most proposals assume a clear separation of responsibilities. *Positive Money*, for example, argues that politicians should decide how the new money is spent.[40] The central bank would then decide on the appropriate *size* of the money supply in light of monetary policy objectives. We thus see a convergence of money creation policy and fiscal policy, requiring the central bank to be well informed of political decisions. Consultation between central banks and politicians is nothing new; monetary policy affects fiscal policy in the current system through interest rate policy, inflation (which reduces the value of government debt) and the buying up of government bonds. Nevertheless, the relationship between the central bank and politicians would change in a sovereign money system. We address this in greater detail in the next chapter.

Although the proposals for an alternative system devote a great deal of attention to how new money enters the economy, there is scant attention to what should happen if, in the central bank's view, too much money is in circulation. On this subject *Ons Geld* states: "The government would be given the power to adjust the demand for and distribution of these funds. Redistribution traditionally takes place through taxation. Instruments can also be put in place which restrain or boost demand for government money."[41] Huber, *Positive Money*, and Benes and Kumhof do not address this issue.[42] Whether the threat of inflation should be tackled only by *reducing* money creation or also by 'taking money out of circulation' (for example by increasing taxes) remains unclear.

[38]See for example Huber (2017: 162); Dyson et al. (2016: 28); Wortmann (2017)

[39]Dyson et al. (2016: 51)

[40]Dyson et al. (2016: 30)

[41]Ons Geld (2016). Our translation.

[42]Huber (2017); Dyson et al. (2016); Benes and Kumhof (2013)

5.3.2 Regulating the Financial System

Most advocates of sovereign money emphasize that the government would not need to regulate financing as intensively as in the current system. Since the payment system would be protected from financial risks, the government can afford to be less involved. The plans thus mainly emphasize what will *no longer* be required: deposit guarantees, thousands of pages of financial legislation and costly bailouts.[43] Most proposals nevertheless acknowledge that a degree of government involvement would be desirable. What responsibilities would the government have in the new system?

Kotlikoff argues that the government should be in the business of assessing credit risks. He calls for a new supervisory body, the Financial Authority, to examine and rate all financial instruments.[44] People looking to invest their money would thus know that a public authority has examined all available products and assessed their risks. Financing institutions could also make use of private rating agencies, as could the Financial Authority to help with risk analyses, provided that these rating agencies have no financial interests in the companies being assessed. The government's primary responsibility would thus be certification and verification to ensure that financing operates smoothly.

The proposals differ on whether financing institutions should be subject to regulation. In Kotlikoff's system, all financing institutions take the form of investment funds and operate entirely on the basis of equity, rendering current policies on capital and liquidity superfluous. A body similar to the Netherlands Authority for Financial Markets (AFM) or the UK's Financial Conduct Authority could ensure that investors are not misled (for example with false promises about returns or incorrect information on investment portfolios) and that no fraud is committed. Competition law could also play a role.

If financing institutions finance themselves through a combination of equity and debt, there is greater need for regulation. *Positive Money* refers explicitly to the need for capital regulations. Here policymakers could choose between *risk-weighted* capital requirements, unweighted capital requirements (a minimum leverage ratio) or a combination thereof.[45] This would ensure a buffer against losses, thereby protecting the holders of the financing institution's debt.

If maturity transformation is permitted – i.e. a financing institution's assets have a longer maturity than its liabilities – liquidity may also need to be regulated. It is crucial to ensure that financing institutions do not issue deposits that are repayable on demand, as this would look suspiciously similar to current bank deposits. The consequence would be the emergence of a parallel private payment system – shadow money – which is precisely what proposals for an alternative system are seeking to avoid. To prevent them from being used as shadow money, regulators need to ensure

[43]Dyson et al. (2016: 12–13); Kotlikoff (2010: 132)

[44]Kotlikoff (2010)

[45]Dyson et al. (2016: 25–6)

that the deposits issued by financing institutions have a minimum maturity or notice period.

A key question is how the government should address instability and crises. The proposals all agree that governments should no longer provide guarantees and not be obliged to rescue private institutions from collapse (since the payment system will remain intact). There would be no need for the government to act as a lender of last resort; institutions would simply be allowed to fail. The general principle is that since the payment system is secure, the government can leave financing to its own devices. Chapter 6 will discuss whether this is a tenable position.

5.3.3 Independence and Accountability

In the alternative system, the creation of money is the preserve of public institutions. The proposals therefore emphasize that these bodies must be sufficiently independent from politics and politicians. Although parliament and government can set the objectives of monetary policy and determine how new money is allocated, they would not be permitted to control the money *supply*. The central bank must be independent, much like the judiciary. Huber proposes that the governor and board members of the central bank be appointed for fixed terms with the possibility of reappointment. During this period, their positions would not be at risk. Their independence, however, must include a degree of accountability to elected politicians.[46]

5.4 Transition to the New System

The proposals discussed in this chapter call for a monetary financial system in which all money is either fully covered by sovereign money (central bank reserves) or *is* itself sovereign money. How can this be achieved? The transition has two elements, which we discuss below: (1) the payment system must be kept separate from the financial system, and (2) changes must be made to the current system of financing.

5.4.1 Towards a New Payment System

How do we achieve the new payment system? The first question is which bank deposits are eligible for conversion into sovereign money. Here the proposals differ. *Positive Money* argues that only sight deposits should be eligible, while customer

[46]Huber (2017)

Table 5.1 Payment and savings account deposits on Dutch bank balance sheets (in billions of euros; August 2018)

	Payment accounts	Savings accounts	Savings accounts with fixed maturity	Total	Total as % of bank balance sheet
Dutch account holders	273	406	88	768	32%
Account holders in rest of euro area	58	8	10	76	3%
Account holders outside euro area	118	27	60	205	8%
Total	449	441	159	1048	43%
Total as % of bank balance sheet	18%	18%	7%	43%	

Source: DNB Table 5.2.5

savings and time deposit accounts are not.[47] *Ons Geld* uses a broader definition comprising "all savings and payment accounts (bank money deposits) that account holders currently consider to be their money, i.e. regardless of the maturity".[48] The scope of the deposits to be converted is no insignificant matter. Table 5.1 shows that in the Netherlands the difference amounts to €600 billion (the difference between €449 and 1.048 billion).

A choice must also be made about the design of the new payment system. As discussed above, there are two options. The first is that all payment accounts are placed with independent payment institutions, which are required to cover them 100% with central bank reserves. The central bank would thus have to create and lend to the banks reserves equal to the fully covered bank deposits. The payment part of the institution will then be separated from the rest – either as an independent company or as a subsidiary of the wider financial institution. This transition is illustrated in Fig. 5.4.

The second option is placing all payment accounts at the central bank. This would entail transferring the eligible bank deposits at the commercial banks to the central bank, simultaneously accompanied by new loans from the central bank to these banks to replace the transferred deposits.

The transition could take place gradually or, following a preparatory period, overnight. In the gradual variant, the central bank would offer households the possibility of opening an account. If households transfer their money from a commercial bank to the central bank, the central bank can lend this amount back to the commercial bank in the form of a loan to stabilize the commercial bank's balance sheet. Bank deposits would gradually be replaced by central bank accounts, giving rise to a parallel *public* payment system. The result would be a hybrid

[47]Dyson et al. (2016: 40)

[48]Ons Geld (2016: 15). Our translation.

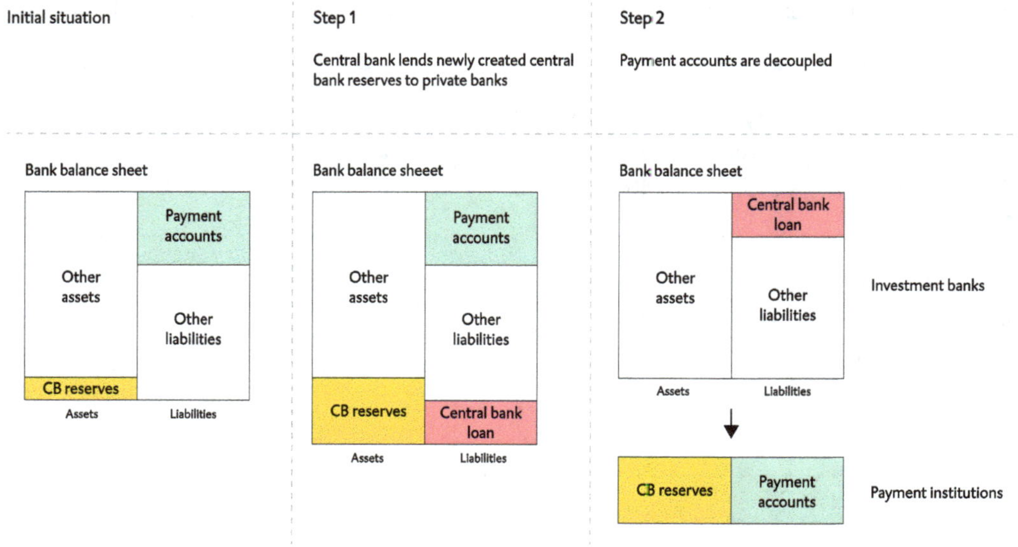

Fig. 5.4 Towards separate payment and financing institutions
Note: The ratios in the bank balance sheet are merely indicative. They would depend on how 'payment accounts' are defined and whether the deposits of non-Dutch account holders are also transferred.

system – with payment accounts that are not yet fully covered by central bank reserves and banks that are still able to create new money through lending.

To move from the hybrid system to a fully sovereign money system, there must be an end date by which all payment accounts have been transferred to the central bank. After this date, bank deposits (except central bank loans) would be converted into investment accounts, bonds or shares, while banks would no longer offer payment accounts.

5.4.2 *Towards a New Financial System*

Once the above transition has been completed, adjustments would need to be made in the financial system. After the transition, as shown in Fig. 5.4, financing institutions would have substantial debts to the central bank. How could this debt be reduced? Financing institutions could use the government bonds they hold to repay part of it. The remainder could be repaid over the long run on the basis of interest payments and repayments of outstanding loans from households and businesses. This could take a long time, for example in the case of mortgages. Benes and Kumhof suggest the government could create sovereign money to pay everyone a citizen's dividend to instantly reduce private debt.[49]

[49]Benes and Kumhof (2013)

There is also the question of what would happen to the financing institutions' other liabilities (savings deposits and bonds). In the limited purpose banking model, all outstanding liabilities would have to be converted into shares.[50] The lenders to the bank would thus become shareholders. If financing institutions were still permitted to operate on the basis of debt, savings accounts would be converted into investment accounts or bonds.[51]

Positive Money devotes specific attention to whether the financial part of the system would continue to operate during and immediately after the transition period. As financing institutions will need to raise money before they lend it, they may initially have no or little money to lend. *Positive Money* leaves the option open for a temporary period in which financing institutions can borrow new money from the central bank in order to meet the demand for credit. At the same time, they can increase their stock of money through interest income on outstanding loans and raising money from the payment system. In their view, financing must ultimately be able to operate on an entirely private basis.[52]

5.5 Conclusion

This chapter examined plans to restructure our current financial monetary system into a sovereign money system. All proponents agree that the system for payments must be strictly separated from the system for financing. In the new payment system, all money is directly or indirectly sovereign money. New money can no longer be created by private institutions; only the central bank can do this. Lending by financing institutions must take place on the basis of *existing* money. Financing institutions must raise money from households and businesses before they can lend it.

Alongside these commonalities, the plans harbour some significant differences. Some want payment accounts to be held directly at the central bank; others, at payment institutions that fully back this money with central bank reserves. The plans also envision different ways in which new money enters the economy. In some plans, financing institutions are only permitted to operate on the basis of equity; in others, they are also permitted to issue debt certificates. The proposals also differ in the type of policy and supervision to which financing institutions are subject; nor are the objectives of monetary policy and relationships between the central bank and politicians set in stone. Finally, there are multiple – gradual or rapid – transition options. Table 5.2 provides an overview of the differences and similarities.

While this chapter has discussed variations in the design of the sovereign money system, we have yet to consider its possible advantages and disadvantages.

[50]Kotlikoff (2010: 152)

[51]Dyson et al. (2016)

[52]Dyson et al. (2016)

Table 5.2 The core and variations of the sovereign money system

	The core of the sovereign money system	Variations in the sovereign money system
Money	All money is directly or indirectly public.	Money is placed in an account at the central bank or in a payment institution that covers it 100% with central bank reserves.
Money creation	Money cannot be created by commercial banks, only by the central bank.	Newly created money can be used for: (1) government spending, (2) paying down government debt, (3) direct transfers to households, and (4) lending directly or indirectly through financing institutions.
Lending	The institutions that grant credit (financing institutions) are clearly separate from the payment institutions (or the central bank) at which the money is held. Financing institutions cannot create new money to grant loans; they must raise the money first.	Proposals disagree on the extent to which the maturity of loans and the maturity of the institution's financing can differ, and on how institutions finance themselves: Are deposits fixed in value (a debt contract between institution and financier) or do they rise and fall with the performance of the institution (such as shares in an investment fund)?

Proponents contend that it scores much better on economic contribution, stability, fairness and legitimacy than our current system. The following chapter considers their arguments and the objections from critics.

Bibliography

Benes, J., & Kumhof, M. (2013). The Chicago plan revisited. *IMF Working Paper, 12*, 202.

Chamley, C., Kotlikoff, L. J., & Polemarchakis, H. (2012). Limited-purpose banking – Moving from "Trust me" to "Show me" banking. *American Economic Review, 102*(3), 113–119.

Cohen-Setton, J. (2015). *Blogs review: QE and central bank* (continued). http://bruegel.org/2015/01/blogs-review-qe-and-central-bank-solvency-continued/

Dyson, B., Hodgson, G., & van Lerven, F. (2016). *Sovereign money. An introduction*. Available at: http://www.positivemoney.org.

Friedman, M. (1948). A monetary and fiscal framework for economic stability. *The American Economic Review, 38*(3), 245–264.

Huber, J. (2017). *Sovereign money. Beyond reserve banking*. Cham: Palgrave Macmillan.

Kay, J. (2009). *Narrow banking: The reform of banking regulation*. London: Centre for the Study of Financial Innovation.

Kotlikoff, L. J. (2010). *Jimmy Stewart is dead. Ending the world's ongoing financial plague with limited purpose banking*. Hoboken: Wiley.

Kotlikoff, L. J., & Goodman, J. C. (2009). *Solving our nation's financial crisis with limited purpose banking* (Working Paper). Boston: Boston University.

Ons Geld. (2015). *Initiatieftekst Burgerinitiatief Ons Geld*. Available at: http://onsgeld.nu/burgerinitiatief.pdf

Ons Geld. (2016). *Memorandum over het geldstelsel.* Available at: http://onsgeld.nu/kamerdebat-memo-geldstelsel.pdf

Phillips, R. J. (2015 [1995]). *The Chicago plan and new deal banking reform.* New York: Routledge.

Sigurjónsson, F. (2015). *Monetary reform. A better monetary system for Iceland.* Reykjavik.

Tobin, J. (1985). Neoclassical theory in America: J. B. Clark and Fisher. *The American Economic Review, 75*(6), 28–38.

van der Sangen, G. J. H. (2012). De evolutie van de coöperatie en haar financiering. In *R.C.E. Galle Handboek Cooperatie*. Dordrecht: Convoy.

van Dixhoorn, C. (2013). *Full Reserve Banking: An analysis of four monetary reform plans.* Utrecht: Sustainable Finance Lab.

Wolf, M. (2014, April 24). Strip private banks of their power to create money. *Financial Times.*

Wortmann, E. (2017). *Deleverage without a crunch* (Working Paper, Stichting Ons Geld).

6

Sovereign Money System: Benefits and Demerits

This chapter considers the advantages and disadvantages of the sovereign money system. It is structured following the four goals of any well-functioning financial monetary system that we identified in Chap. 4: its contribution to the economy (Sect. 6.1); stability (Sect. 6.2); fairness in the distribution of costs, benefits and risks (Sect. 6.3); and legitimacy (Sect. 6.4). Section 6.5 addresses the international dimension, the transition, and system dynamics and innovation. Section 6.6 provides a summary of the chapter.

Caution is required when discussing the advantages and disadvantages of the sovereign money system, as it has never fully operated in practice. This means that there is no direct empirical evidence of its advantages and disadvantages. Macroeconomic models analysing its expected effects should likewise be treated with a grain of salt.[1] We also need to remember that uncertainty surrounds many economic relationships in our existing system; definitive statements about the operation of a yet-to-be-implemented system are thus even more problematic. Finally, there are different variants of the sovereign money system, in particular concerning how lending is organized. The various proposals thus harbour different potential advantages and disadvantages.

6.1 Economic Contribution

The first question is whether a sovereign money system would better contribute to society. In Chap. 4 we outlined the financial monetary system's two key functions: organizing payments and finance. Although there are concerns about the security of payments during crises, our current system handles payments efficiently. But the

[1] For example: Benes and Kumhof (2013); Flaschel et al. (2010); Chiarella et al. (2011); Yamaguchi (2011); Van Egmond and De Vries (2016).

volatility of lending and high levels of indebtedness are problematic in our current system. How might this change in the sovereign money system? This section addresses: (1) the operation of the payment system; (2) the financial system's procyclicality; (3) the availability and price of credit; and (4) the possibility of a one-off debt reduction.

6.1.1 The Operation of the Payment System

A sovereign money system would not likely lead to any immediate improvement or deterioration in the payment system's functioning. Although some authors worry that centralizing payments at the central bank could stifle innovation,[2] this would not apply if independent payment banks are competing for customers. Moreover, there is no reason to believe that public institutions would be less innovative than private ones. In the Netherlands, the main innovations in payments up to the 1970s, including ATMs and electronic payments, were introduced by public institutions. In most cases, private banks followed their lead (see Sect. 6.3).

There is no immediate reason to expect the total cost of payments to rise or fall in a sovereign money system; what is unclear is *who* will pay the costs. Banks currently use income from their assets and the benefits they derive from cheap financing to fund the payment system, which would no longer be possible in the sovereign money system.[3] As the only assets payment banks would have on their balance sheets are central bank reserves, they will have little or no interest income. If the interest on central bank reserves does not cover banks' costs, this will likely lead to higher costs for consumers.[4] If the government decides to subsidize the payment system, the allocation of costs would also differ from our current system. In sum, no major changes in the payment system are expected under normal circumstances.

An important difference would be that in the sovereign money system, payment accounts would theoretically no longer be exposed to financial risks: a financial crisis would not directly affect the payment system. The emergence of shadow money in the financial part of the sovereign money system could undo this benefit; we will return to this in Sect. 6.2. In addition, cyber risks could, just as in our current system, threaten the payment system's integrity.

---

[2]See e.g. Van Dixhoorn (2013: 33); Swiss National Bank [SNB] (2018).

[3]This cross-subsidy may mean that while payment accounts become more expensive, other products will become cheaper.

[4]KPMG (2016: 14).

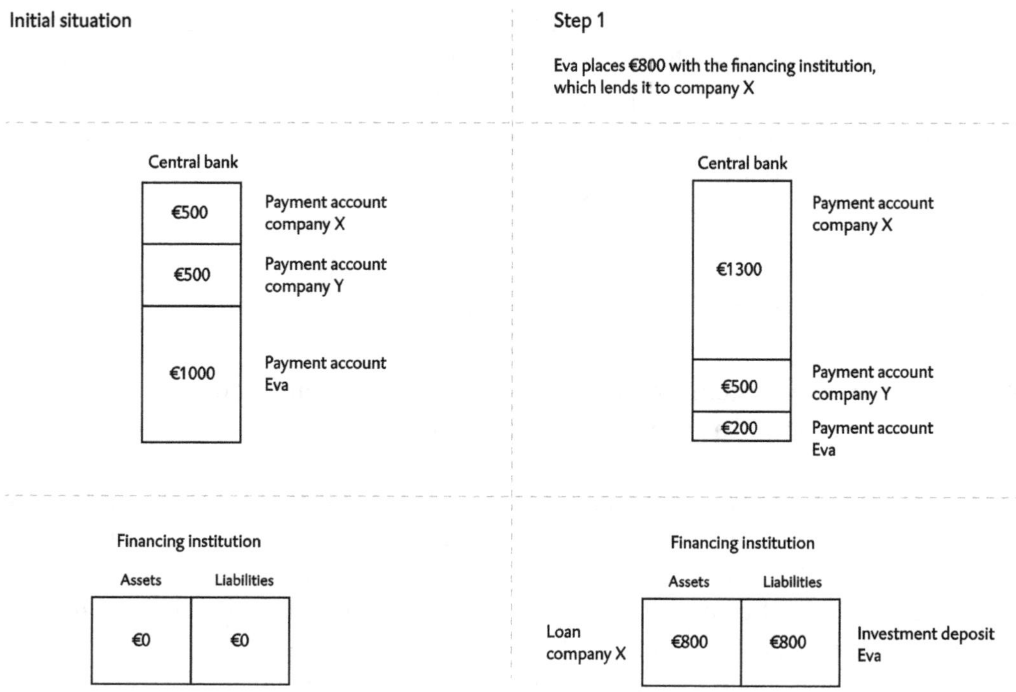

Fig. 6.1 Structure of debts in a sovereign money system part I

6.1.2 *The Financial System's Procyclicality*

Proponents of the sovereign money system argue that periods of collective optimism and pessimism will no longer be reinforced due to stronger curbs on lending.[5] This requires some explanation. In our current system, rising demand for credit can be met relatively easily. Banks create new money when they grant loans, and although there are some constraints, there are no hard limits. Lending therefore mushrooms in good times. In times of crisis, banks will see a decline in the value of their assets and will scale back lending to maintain a sound balance sheet.

In a sovereign money system, financing institutions must raise money before they can lend. They cannot increase the money supply; only the central bank can do so. This means lending is unlikely to rise and fall as rapidly as in our current system. Nevertheless, limits on lending are less rigid than may appear at first sight; credit can grow without the money supply growing as well. Consider an example: Eva places €800 with a financing institution operating on the basis of investment deposits, which then lends this amount to company X (see Fig. 6.1).

Company X purchases goods from company Y. Company Y then makes the money (€800) available to the financing institution, which in turn lends it to company X (see Fig. 6.2). Hence a fixed amount of money can result in an increased amount of credit. In our example credits have risen by €1600.

[5]Benes and Kumhof (2013); Dyson et al. (2016); Ons Geld (2016).

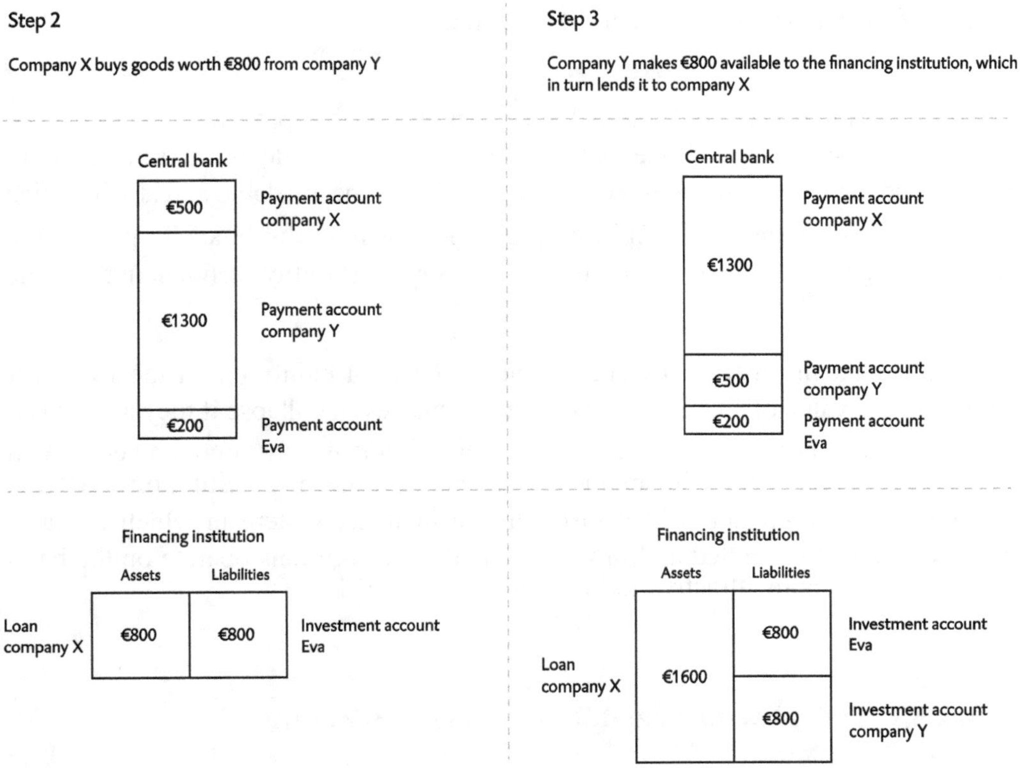

Fig. 6.2 Structure of debt in a sovereign money system part II

Although limiting the money supply does not mean the volume of credit is fixed, we can realistically expect that lending is more constrained in a sovereign money system. The speed of net credit growth (new lending minus repaid debts) will be limited by people's readiness to turn their money into investment deposits. Financing institutions will try to entice people who have their money in secure payment accounts to make it available for financing, meaning people will incur risks. Financing institutions will only be able to do this by offering higher returns, which will ultimately affect the interest charged on loans. More expensive credit may then dampen demand. Proponents claim this is an effective way to prevent credit bubbles.[6]

Still, the link between lending and money creation is by no means the only factor that contributes to procyclicality. For example, the demand for credit largely follows market sentiment (collective optimism or pessimism), while the price of financial assets depends on supply and demand, again informed by future expectations and the behaviour of other market players. These procyclical effects will also be present in the sovereign money system.[7]

---

[6]For example Benes and Kumhof (2013). See Van Dixhoorn (2013); Sustainable Finance Lab (2015); Dommerholt and Van Tilburg (2016).

[7]Dow et al. (2015).

6.1.3 Price and Availability of Credit

The availability of credit is crucial for economic development. In Chap. 4 we encountered the inverted U phenomenon where both too little and too much credit can have adverse consequences. How much credit will be available and at what price in the sovereign money system largely depends on how the financial part of the system is organized. There is a trade-off between the stability of financing and the availability of credit.

When financing institutions operate on the basis of equity (as in the Kotlikoff proposal), the value of shares will fluctuate and may even collapse if they are sold *en masse*, but there is no risk of bank runs. The question is whether enough people will be prepared to invest sufficient money to enable financing institutions to lend. Although there is greater risk of instability, a financial system in which maturity transformation is permitted and in which financing institutions operate on the basis of debt may be more attractive to investors (see Box 6.1).

Box 6.1 The Advantages and Disadvantages of Maturity Transformation

Variants of the sovereign money system differ in whether they allow maturity transformation – differences between the maturity of deposits and the maturity of granted loans. For example, deposits may have a maturity of 1 month while loans have a maturity of 10 years.

Maturity transformation has an important economic function. The availability of long-term financing provides businesses and households the certainty that enables them to take economic risks, thereby contributing to economic development. But for individual financiers, providing long-term finance is risky: they lose access to their money for long periods without knowing whether they will need it in the intervening period. If every financier must make an individual assessment, the availability of long-term finance will suffer.

If maturity transformation is permitted, financial institutions can offer a solution: they can provide long-term loans based on short-term funding. This relies on the 'law of large numbers' where, under normal circumstances, the inflow and outflow of financing is almost the same. Maturity transformation therefore has major economic advantages, but at the same time it poses stability risks: when people want to withdraw their money *en masse*, the financial institution might fail.

(continued)

Box 6.1 (continued)

If maturity transformation is not permitted, the availability of long-term finance will suffer. According to Boonstra, "the possibility that consumers or businesses will want to tie up their savings for a number of years, let alone decades, is (...) zero".[8] If financing institutions are financed with negotiable bonds or shares, part of the problem is eliminated as these can be sold at any time. There will nevertheless be greater uncertainty about the proceeds, which may reduce readiness to provide money for financing.

The proposals differ on how to organize financing to such an extent that it is impossible to say whether sufficient affordable credit will be available in the sovereign money system. It is nevertheless likely that less credit will be available than in the current system. In the sovereign money system, the risks of lending shift from banks towards individuals who place their money with the financing institution. This may mean that they will be less inclined to make money available for financing, or are prepared to do so only in exchange for higher remuneration.

Whereas proponents see this as a positive development, others do not. Critics argue that it will lead to a permanent rise in the price of credit and a permanent reduction in its availability, thereby harming economic development.[9] New promising initiatives may receive no financing.[10] Tighter access to credit could also have major social consequences. As stated earlier, the relationship between lending and economic development has an inverted U shape, with both insufficient and excessive lending having negative effects. It is difficult to predict with any precision where the scale of lending in the sovereign money system would figure in the inverted U. Alongside its longer-term effects, the declining availability and higher price of credit may pose more immediate problems, which we will address in the context of the transition (Sect. 6.5.2).

Proponents of the sovereign money system argue that the fear of insufficient, overly expensive credit is exaggerated.[11] First, it is unlikely that a readjustment of financial risks would lead to an exponential rise in interest rates given the current global glut in capital. Positive Money points out: "the economic context at the moment is one of large pools of capital and a 'search for yield', implying that rather than there being a shortage of credit, there is a shortage of useful projects to invest

[8]Boonstra (2015: 30). Our translation.

[9]Pettifor (2017); Fontana and Sawyer (2016); Goodhart and Jensen (2015); SNB (2018).

[10]Pettifor (2017).

[11]Laina (2015); Dyson et al. (2016). Proponents of the sovereign money system claim it is misleading to state that lending will become too expensive because the price of credit better reflects actual financing costs. Credit is currently artificially cheap because the government covers part of the risk. Ons Geld (2016: 28) claims it will be different in the new system: "Interest rates will be market-driven and will hence be a pure reflection of the risk, demand and supply of the lending concerned." Our translation.

in".[12] Second, the central bank could always intervene if interest rates were considered too high: "the central bank would always be able to create money and inject it into key markets to bring interest rates down".[13] As detailed in Chap. 5, the new organization of financing could include a facility for financing institutions to borrow money from the central bank. If the central bank believes credit is too scarce and expensive, it could intervene, although this would require accurately assessing the need for credit. While Pettifor believes this is expecting too much foresight, Positive Money argues it is not very different from the central bank's current role in forecasting inflation (we return to this in Sect. 6.3).[14]

Thus far, we have examined the availability of credit based on the decisions people make to store or invest their money. Advocates of the sovereign money system have another reason to believe there will be less debt in the alternative system.[15] In the current system, the creation of money implies the creation of debt. In the sovereign money system, so its proponents argue, the government can create new money without creating debt.[16] This means the money supply can expand without the concomitant rise in debt. This reasoning seems to assume that the expanding money supply drives debt rather than vice-versa. But Fig. 3.6 shows that credit has risen more rapidly than the money supply. It is therefore difficult to argue on this basis that the decoupling of money and debt necessarily leads to less debt.

How would a sovereign money system affect other financial products such as options and derivatives? Although banks are not the only providers of loans and financial products, they play key roles here. We therefore expect that a shift towards the sovereign money system consequences will affect these markets as well, although it is difficult to assess in what ways and what effects it will have on the economy. Most proposals for a sovereign money system do not answer this question.

6.1.4 One-Off Debt Reduction

According to its proponents, transitioning to a sovereign money system will allow a large, one-off reduction in public and private debt.[17] The previous chapter (Sect. 5.4) detailed how the transition would entail large loans from the central bank to the commercial banking system. These loans on the balance sheets of newly formed financing institutions would replace the payment accounts that have moved

[12]Dyson et al. (2016: 47).

[13]Dyson et al. (2016: 47).

[14]Pettifor (2017); Dyson et al. (2016).

[15]See e.g. Dyson et al. (2016: 14).

[16]See Box 1.3 for a discussion of whether public money is debt.

[17]Benes and Kumhof (2013); Dyson et al. (2016); Sustainable Finance Lab (2015); Wortmann (2017).

elsewhere. Proponents see this as a chance to reduce both private and public debt, with positive consequences for financial stability and economic development.

To the extent that government debt is held by commercial banks, the central bank can offset its loans against government bonds on banks' balance sheets.[18] Government debt, however, is normally spread among numerous national and international institutions.[19] This limits the scope of offsetting public debt against loans issued by the central bank. All this also assumes that public debt *should* be reduced as much as possible. However, Visser points to the importance of government bonds for the allocation of risk in investment portfolios.[20]

Benes and Kumhof go a step further and propose that during the transition citizens should be given a dividend with which to repay their private debts.[21] Commercial banks could then use this money to repay their loans from the central bank. If this citizens' dividend were paid only to people with debts, it would have major redistributive consequences. If everyone received the same amount, citizens with no or lower debts would be free to spend it. If the dividend is small, the decline in private debt would be limited; if large, the risk of inflation would grow.

6.1.5 Summary

This section considered the possible advantages and disadvantages of the sovereign money system as it bears on its contributions to the economy. We examined both payments and financing. There is no reason to believe that the payment system will improve or deteriorate in the new system. The allocation of costs, however, would change. In the current system, banks fund the payment system partly with income from their assets; in the new system, this would either be impossible or difficult (depending on the interest rate on central bank reserves). Account holders could thus face higher direct costs. If payment accounts are held at the central bank, an option is that costs are met by the public purse.

Much would likely change in the area of lending. Volatility in lending will likely decrease as rising demand for credit will more quickly feed into interest rates, thereby dampening demand. Curbs on lending in the sovereign money system will be less severe than they may seem as decoupling the money supply from the credit

---

[18]The reality is more complex. The central bank grants loans to commercial banks, which can then repay these loans by transferring government bonds to the central bank. This could be made a requirement for granting the loan. The central bank can then write off the government debt. While the central bank's balance sheet will grow in the transition, its debt is for accounting purposes and not a debt in economic terms, thus differing from current government debt.

[19]Even under the current system, the central bank can always try to use newly created money to buy up outstanding government debt. Incidentally, it is difficult to state precisely who holds Dutch government debt (Tokmetzis 2013).

[20]Visser (2015).

[21]Benes and Kumhof (2013).

supply will not imply an absolute ceiling on credit. The economic cycle will not be a thing of the past. Factors that fuel volatility in our current system, such as the fact that financial assets cannot be objectively priced, will remain. Market sentiment will continue to affect the financial system.

It is difficult to predict how much credit will be available and at what price; this will largely depend on how the financial part of the system is regulated and organized. There will be a trade-off between financing institution stability and credit availability: the more risks the financiers of these institutions bear, the more stable the institutions will be. But people will be less inclined to make their money available for financing or expect higher returns. If the government demands that financing institutions operate entirely on the basis of equity, or if they are required to align the maturities of their debts and assets, individual institutions will be more stable but citizens and businesses may be more reluctant to enter into credit transactions. The negotiability of debts or shares will only alleviate part of this problem.

Less lending is not necessarily harmful in the long term: after all, it is possible to have too much credit. Both excessive and insufficient lending will have negative consequences for economic development and it is difficult to predict with any precision where the sovereign money system will fall on this axis. A sharp decline in the availability of credit may have severe short-term consequences, quite apart from any long-term effects.

The transition to the new system could lead to a one-off reduction in debt through the offsetting of the central bank's loans to financial institutions against debts on these institutions' balance sheets. While this is conceivable for public debt, for private debt there would be thorny political issues concerning implementation, winners and losers in redistribution, and heightened risks of inflation. Although it is easy to offset these debts in a model, it will be much more complex in practice.

6.2 Stability

The problem of financial instability concerns both individual institutions and the financial system as a whole – and the interplay between them. To what extent would a sovereign money system reduce instability? We first discuss the stability of individual institutions before considering systemic stability.

6.2.1 The Stability of Individual Institutions

Will a sovereign money system lead to more stable institutions? This question needs to be answered separately for payment and financing institutions. Payment institutions will be stable as they operate on the basis of full reserves; it is no longer possible for them to fail as a result of a bank run.[22] However, if shadow money were to arise in the financial part of the system – with the debts of financing institutions used as a means of payment – this would still mean that not all money is secure. We will return to this in Sect. 6.5.

A more complex question is whether financing institutions will be more stable. This will largely depend on the laws and regulations specifying what they are and are not permitted to do. If these institutions operate entirely on the basis of equity (as in the Kotlikoff plan), there is no risk of a bank run and much lower risks of bankruptcy, although investors may still suffer major losses (as in our existing stock markets). Stability risks are greater if financing institutions can operate on the basis of debt and if there remain differences between the maturity of their assets and liabilities. In the event of declining asset values, refinancing may become problematic and there may yet be runs on the financing institution. This in turn may lead to instability among other institutions. Capital regulations – requirements concerning equity levels – could provide a partial solution to this problem.

According to its proponents, a sovereign money system will lead to more stable financing institutions as their financiers exert a strong disciplining effect. Proponents expect that this market discipline results from the absence of government guarantees that distort the current system. This requires some explanation. In a sovereign money system, payments are insulated from credit risks. As financing institutions will no longer have to be rescued to protect the payment system, a key market-distorting factor – implicit and explicit government support for private institutions and account holders encouraging riskier behaviour – would disappear. According to its proponents, the absence of government guarantees is a key requirement for the sovereign money system. Ons Geld states that "it must be established beyond doubt that the authorities will provide no guarantee or compensation for losses on self-selected risk positions".[23]

With investors now actually bearing risk, proponents argue, they will exercise better control over financing institutions and demand that they are adequately capitalized. This will have a disciplining effect on institutions: "Transparency and good risk assessment is then rewarded. Banks can excel in the way in which they make risks transparent and handle the resources entrusted to them. Banks that are insufficiently competent or competitive in that regard will disappear from the scene due to market forces".[24] In short, financing institutions will become more stable by being exposed to genuine market discipline.

The first question is whether it is realistic to expect that government guarantees will truly disappear; we will address this in Sect. 6.3. Another question is what can realistically be expected from market discipline. Will it be strengthened and will this contribute to financial stability? Will investors be able to exert effective discipline on financing institutions? Experience in the years before the financial crisis gives no

---

[22]Certain risks such as cyber risk will continue to exist.

[23]Ons Geld (2016: 30). Our translation.

[24]Ons Geld (2016: 27). Our translation.

cause for optimism. Professional investors purchased financial products such as securitized mortgage packages but barely understood their risks. The credit rating agencies responsible for assessing financial products often issued much more positive ratings than were justified.[25] If it is difficult for professionals to assess risks accurately, can the average citizen be expected to do so?

In his proposal for Limited Purpose Banking, Kotlikoff therefore advocates a single national rating agency – a Federal Financial Authority – that would publish all ratings.[26] Some of the perverse incentives in the current design of the credit rating sector would then disappear, with financial institutions no longer shopping around among various credit rating agencies.[27] But it remains inherently difficult to give objective financial ratings, partly because the ratings themselves affect the value of financial assets.[28]

Finally, we need to bear in mind that – as in the current system – the stability of individual institutions does not automatically lead to the stability of the wider system. Comparisons of individual institutions cannot prevent financial assets from being wrongly priced throughout the market. It is difficult for individual market participants not to share in the general sentiment, encapsulated in the famous statement by Citibank's CEO Charles Prince: "*As long as the music is playing, you've got to get up and dance.*" Strengthening the stability of individual institutions by strengthening market mechanisms will not necessarily deliver system stability at the macro level.[29]

6.2.2 Systemic Risks

According to its proponents, the sovereign money system will lead not only to more stable institutions but to a more stable system. Stronger curbs on lending will constrain credit bubbles, a major source of instability. And *even if* instability occurs, it will remain limited to the financial part of the system, as the payment system is secure. There will be no bank runs in the payment system: all money is held directly at the central bank or fully backed by central bank reserves. If a large number of people simultaneously wish to withdraw their money in cash or transfer it to another payment bank, no problems will ensue. The essence of the sovereign money system is that money is secure and incurs no risk.[30]

The existence of secure payment institutions and risky financing institutions without public guarantees may prompt worried citizens to seek refuge in the former –

[25] FSA (2009).

[26] Kotlikoff and Goodman (2009).

[27] This could also occur in the current system.

[28] Stellinga and Mügge (2017); Stellinga (2018, 2019).

[29] White (2008); Turner (2015); King (2016); Warwick Commission (2009); Goodhart (2016).

[30] Benes and Kumhof (2013); Kotlikoff (2010).

a development which critics believe could contribute to instability. The extent to which this scenario is possible largely depends on how the financial part of the system is organized. If it operates on the basis of equity or bonds, these instruments will sharply decline in value, making it difficult for financing institutions to raise new money and grant new loans. If financing institutions are financed on the basis of term deposits with a notice period, a slow-motion systemic bank run is still possible.[31]

The stability of financing may also be threatened by new or existing financial products – for example CDS (credit default swaps) products that insure bondholders against the risk of bond defaults – that are not used to invest in the real economy. During the credit crisis, the insurer AIG sold off so many of these products that it had to be bailed out just 3 days after the fall of Lehman Brothers. These types of instability may also continue to exist in the sovereign money system.

6.2.3 Summary

Will a sovereign money system contribute to financial stability? Its major advantage is that payment institutions will be stable. But how about financing institutions? This will largely depend on the statutory requirements governing how they are financed. They will be more stable if they have to operate entirely (or largely) on the basis of equity, or if they have to observe strict maturity matching between the loans they grant and the debts they owe. But this may reduce the availability of credit and thus the new system's contribution to economic growth.

According to its proponents, stronger market discipline in the sovereign money system will render financing institutions more stable than the current commercial banks; since governments will no longer bail them out, investors will require them to be more cautious. But this is by no means a given. First, it is questionable whether governments will actually cease to provide support. Second, the ability of investors to monitor and discipline should not be overstated. Furthermore, market discipline will only partially be able to counter the build-up of systemic risks. The financial crisis of 2007–2009 showed that investors and banks can collectively misprice assets. Banks did their utmost to rival or outperform their peers, ratcheting up systemic risks as all joined in the hype. Investors may negatively judge underperforming financial institutions, but this will not necessarily prevent the build-up of systemic risks and may even increase it.

On the other hand, systemic risks will arguably develop less easily in a sovereign money system. Stronger curbs on lending would dampen procyclical pressures, while instability would be less problematic as the payment system is secured. Nevertheless, critics argue that it is precisely the strict separation between payments and financing that contributes to systemic risk: in good times people are enticed to

[31]Goodhart and Jensen (2015).

invest their money, but if prospects deteriorate, they will seek refuge in secure payment institutions. This in turn may disrupt the financial part of the system.

6.3 Fairness

Chapter 4 addressed problems related to the fair distribution of costs, benefits and risks in our current financial monetary system. How would things differ in a sovereign money system? We address in turn: (1) the abolition of implicit and explicit government support; (2) the benefits of money creation; and (3) the benefits and costs of debt.

6.3.1 Abolition of Implicit and Explicit Public Support

Explicit and implicit government guarantees to the financial sector create two sets of problems: (1) profits are private while the costs of crisis are largely public; and (2) banks – especially large banks – enjoy major advantages over smaller banks and ordinary companies. Proponents argue that in a sovereign money system, the separation of payments and financing will end the need for public guarantees.

Even if national arrangements differ, deposit guarantee schemes are ultimately backed by the government. In the event of a systemic crisis or the collapse of one of the major banks, people turn to the government for a bail-out. In the new system, payments would be secure and the government would no longer have to provide this guarantee, according to proponents. As failures in the financial part of the system no longer threaten the payment system, the problem of 'private profits, public losses' would no longer exist; from now on it would be 'private profits, private losses'. The financing advantages enjoyed by systemically important institutions – which benefit from cheaper finance as investors know the government will rescue them – would end. In the new system, the government would simply no longer bail out individual financing institutions.[32]

Although the downside of public support for banks is widely recognized, the question is whether the absence of government guarantees can be set in stone in any new system. For a number of reasons, this cannot be assumed.

First of all, politicians take the fate of their voters seriously; if a large number of people are affected by collapsing financing institutions, the government will come under extreme pressure to help them. Although we cannot apply the experiences of the current system directly to the new system, the bail-in problem illustrates how difficult it is for politicians to refuse support when problems arise. The debate surrounding the rescue of the Italian banks *Popolare di Vicenza* and *Veneto Banca*

[32]Benes and Kumhof (2013); Kotlikoff (2010); Dyson et al. (2016); Ons Geld (2016).

in 2017 shows how difficult it is to force a bank's creditors to meet the full costs of a rescue. Out of fear of undermining broader trust, the Italian government decided to shoulder a large part of the rescue costs itself.

A second reason is that a well-functioning financial system is in the public interest, that can be undermined by bankruptcies. Even if the payment system is secured, a financial crisis can cause massive economic and social harm. An isolated bankruptcy will not necessarily threaten lending, but a systemic crisis certainly may, making state intervention desirable.[33] If a large number of citizens see their investments evaporate and companies lose access to revolving credit, the damage may be severe. The loss of prosperity and increasing uncertainty will cause households to rein in spending. This could trigger a negative spiral of corporate insolvency, failures of financing institutions and personal bankruptcies as assets evaporate.

A third reason is the possibility that 'shadow money' emerges in the financial sector. It is possible that over time the investment deposits and financial instruments issued by financing institutions will be used to make payments and will hence serve as money.[34] As we saw in Chap. 3, deposit money grew in importance after the nationalization of banknotes in the United Kingdom, Switzerland and the United States. If this shadow money plays a major role in the economy, the government will likely provide guarantees in the event of a crisis.[35]

Apart from its realism, one may reasonably ask whether it desirable to assume that no implicit or explicit public guarantees will exist in the financial sector. Guarantees can eliminate uncertainty, prompting people to take risks and bolstering stability. Guarantees can be private, such as collateral requirements and insurances from third parties. But public guarantees may prove necessary to create the trust needed for people to invest their money and to avert that minor doubts about institutions trigger major panics.

6.3.2 *Seigniorage*

According to its advocates, a key advantage of the sovereign money system is that the financial benefits of money creation accrue to the government, while in the current system it is the commercial banks that reap the benefits. But banks themselves do not spend the money created when they grant loans; they therefore receive no conventional seigniorage – the difference between the production cost of money and its value to society. They nevertheless have a financing advantage as they can create a part of their funding themselves on which they generally pay relatively low

[33] Bachetta (2017).

[34] Goodhart and Jensen (2015); Laina (2015); Dow et al. (2015).

[35] See also Murau (2017)

interest. On the other hand, they bear the costs of maintaining the payment system (see also Box 4.3).[36]

Advocates argue that seigniorage should in principle accrue not to private companies but to the government.[37] Since the central bank can create and spend money almost free of charge, the new system would allow conventional seigniorage and it would be public.[38] According to Dommerholt and Van Tilburg, the additional sum created in the Netherlands would amount to around €20 billion annually.[39] Used for government spending, it would contribute around 7% of the Netherlands' current budget. This entails monetary financing; the government would not have to incur additional debt or raise taxes, it can simply spend the money created by the central bank. What the government spends the money on is then a political choice.

Critics see a system that enables the government to create money 'out of thin air' and then to spend it as fraught with danger.[40] Additional new money cannot be created without consequences; it increases the claim against current and future production. To the extent that money creation leads to inflation, it can be seen as an indirect tax.

Critics argue that the government's ability to create money can lead to abuse. Political pressure could lead the central bank to create so much money that it fuels excessive inflation. The creation of new money and rising prices could reinforce each other in such a way that it gets out of control and triggers hyperinflation. Critics often point to the dangers of public money creation by referring to hyperinflation in the Weimar Republic in the early 1920s, Hungary after the Second World War, and Zimbabwe from the mid-2000s. In these situations, the 'gains' for government were mirrored by 'losses' for society in the form of a high inflation tax.[41]

But advocates of sovereign money believe this is cherry-picking from history. Hyperinflation occurs primarily in exceptional situations, i.e. immediately following a war or under a dysfunctional dictatorship. Many properly functioning states (including the Netherlands) have used monetary financing in the past without triggering hyperinflation. Dyson points out that monetary financing is technically possible in our current system but the government has deliberately restricted its own

---

[36]Huber (2017).

[37]Ons Geld (2016); Dyson et al. (2016); Huber (2017).

[38]As discussed in Box 4.3, the costs of generating the social trust required for any monetary system to function extend far beyond the production costs of money. The functioning of money requires numerous institutions. This holds for both the current system and the sovereign money system.

[39]Dommerholt and Van Tilburg (2016). They state: "This €20 billion is an estimate of the annual seigniorage with 2% inflation, 2% growth and a money supply of €500 billion. This estimate assumes that the circulation speed of money remains unchanged, even with possibly higher interest rates in the future" (Dommerholt and Van Tilburg 2016: 680 [our translation]). The estimate suggests a direct relationship between money supply and economic growth and inflation and does not include the cost of money creation.

[40]See e.g. Boonstra (2018).

[41]Boonstra (2015); Ryan-Collins (2015).

freedom to use it. In Europe this would require an amendment to the Treaty on the Functioning of the European Union.

For proponents, it is a question of ensuring that public money creation proceeds in a responsible manner. To a certain extent, the government must 'lash itself to the mast', for example by having an independent central bank determine how much new money can be created. The right checks and balances must be in place.[42]

6.3.3 The Benefits and Costs of Debt

Advocates of the sovereign money system believe it will lead to less debt and less inequality. Less debt implies lower net interest expenses; according to Positive Money, "less income is transferred upwards to the top 10% of the population".[43] Note, however, that lower debt levels do not automatically lead to lower interest payments. If the interest rate rises because less credit is available, interest payments may still increase.

Pettifor believes that the sovereign money system will disadvantage people with lower incomes or fewer assets, as they will find it more difficult to obtain loans, reducing their financial independence. What matters is not the *average* interest rate that debtors pay: people with low incomes and few assets already pay higher rates than others and this effect would be reinforced in the new system when less credit is available.[44] It is difficult to make meaningful statements about the sovereign money system's impact on inequality. Too many different factors are involved.

6.3.4 Summary

Will costs, benefits and risks be better distributed in the sovereign money system? We have addressed three issues: (1) the extent to which public guarantees can be dismantled; (2) seigniorage; and (3) the benefits and costs of debt.

Proponents expect the new system to lead to greater fairness because private losses will at last be genuinely 'private' and financing institutions will no longer have to be rescued with taxpayers' money. The question is whether this will be so under all circumstances. Public interests remain at stake in the financial sector, which may be jeopardized if private financing institutions perform poorly or go bankrupt. If a systemic crisis hits the sector, there will be major consequences even if the payment system is not compromised. In that case the government may still be expected to intervene. This is not only because politicians want to protect their

[42]Dyson et al. (2016).

[43]Dyson et al. (2016: 16).

[44]Pettifor (2017).

constituencies, but because government guarantees and interventions also have positive effects. After all, efficient financing is essential for the functioning of society. Although it is unlikely that private institutions would be bailed out as readily, it is questionable that losses in the new system would always remain 'private'.

In the sovereign money system seigniorage accrues to the government. Where excessive additional money creation may lead to inflation, this can be viewed as an indirect form of taxation (however, to the extent that money creation leads to inflation, this applies to our current system as well). Monetary financing harbours the danger that the government will abuse its ability to create money, in the worst case leading to hyperinflation. Adequate checks and balances are therefore essential.

It is difficult to make definitive statements about the benefits and costs of debt. Advocates expect lower debt to lead to less inequality while opponents expect more expensive credit to lead to more inequality.

6.4 Legitimacy

How does the sovereign money system fare in terms of legitimacy? Here we address three issues: (1) the separation of public and private activities; (2) public control and democratic oversight; (3) the position of citizens.

6.4.1 The Separation of Public and Private Activities

Advocates claim that the transition to a sovereign money system will result in a clearer division of the financial monetary system into a public part (the payment part) and a private part (the financing part). This would clarify the status of financial institutions as private institutions that can go bankrupt and will receive no support whatsoever from the government. Proponents believe the advantages extend beyond the aspect of costs and benefits; it would also lead to an improvement in public control and legitimacy. Since the proper functioning of banks and payments is crucial for the economy, politicians and policymakers are inclined to equate the interests of banks with those of the public. But if the public interest of the payment system is secured, the government may no longer feel responsible for the viability of financing institutions. The influence of private institutions on public decision-making would then be reduced.

The main objection to this line of reasoning is that the financial part of the system will continue to harbour public interests. Although the bankruptcy of a small institution is not necessarily a problem, that of a systemically important one – or many institutions at the same time – may well jeopardize the public interest in a well-functioning credit system. It seems unrealistic to expect that financing can ever be entirely 'private' as it will always remain vital to society.

6.4.2 Public Control and Democratic Oversight

Proponents expect the government to be better able to achieve inflation targets and other macroeconomic outcomes in a sovereign money system. Benes and Kumhof, who advocate a strict target for inflation, argue that the government could keep inflation at zero.[45] Ons Geld is likewise optimistic about the government's ability to influence the value of the currency: "Such a monetary target [constant purchasing power of the currency] is also conceivable in a sovereign money system. After all, the state monetary authority could steer the public money supply in any required direction. Both inflation and deflation could be effectively targeted and combated."[46]

Other proponents are more cautious about the government's ability to control macroeconomic outcomes. The transmission mechanism from money creation to price stability is complex and to a certain extent unpredictable. Inflation, like every other macroeconomic objective, is influenced by countless factors. Huber writes: "the higher degree of exposure to foreign influences, including exposure to foreign monetary influences, [...] the lower the degree of national 'autonomy'" – which certainly holds for countries like the Netherlands.[47] For Huber and Positive Money, the issue is not so much about perfect control over policy outcomes as having greater influence than in the current system.

The assumption that inflation can simply be controlled by adjusting the money supply is incorrect. First, it overestimates the power of predictive models used by the central bank; the economy contains fundamental uncertainties and real-time data is unavailable.[48] Second, it assumes that there is a clear, direct link between the money supply and inflation, while in fact many more factors play a role.[49] Monetary transmission is a complex issue in *every* system, frustrating any attempt to achieve precise targets. It is possible, however, that the option of monetary financing will make it easier to tackle deflation in the alternative system than in the current system.

National macroeconomic outcomes are also informed by international developments. Particularly in open economies such as the Netherlands, international trends heavily influence national outcomes. Central banks in a sovereign money system will still have to take account of international developments – as the Dutch central bank always had to do.

For the proponents of sovereign money, greater public control over money creation also represents a gain in *democratic* legitimacy. Ons Geld argues that money creation must take place within a framework of democratic oversight;[50] Positive Money believes that decisions on how to allocate new money should be

[45]Benes and Kumhof (2013: 56).

[46]Ons Geld (2016: 23). Our translation.

[47]Huber (2017: 190–192).

[48]Dow et al. (2015: 10).

[49]See e.g. Borio (2017).

[50]Ons Geld (2016: 10).

entrusted to the government.[51] Hence they believe that a crucial political decision – where new money should be spent – will also become a matter of democratic oversight.

In the proposals, decisions about the money supply rest with an independent public institution. To prevent political abuse, this independence must be safeguarded.[52] Pettifor, however, warns of the possible antidemocratic consequences of such safeguarding: “it would place great financial and economic power in the hands of a few technocrats”.[53] Many other critics point to the likelihood of political pressure being exerted on the central bank.[54]

6.4.3 The Position of Citizens

Advocates argue that the position of citizens vis-à-vis financing institutions will improve in the new system, with the abolition of implicit government guarantees making it more important for financing institutions to secure consumer loyalty. Alongside switching to a different financing institution, citizens have another option, namely the use of payment accounts. If a financing institution underperforms or incurs excessive risk, citizens will not invest in it and leave their money in payment accounts. This would have a disciplining effect on financing institutions.[55]

A sovereign money system would indeed give citizens another option. But this does not mean that all factors that in our current system weaken citizens’ positions vis-à-vis banks will be immediately resolved. Financing institutions will retain considerable informational advantages. The question is whether consumers can bridge the information gap when even professionals struggle to do so. Moreover, a quick exit option is not guaranteed. How far citizens can punish financing institutions in the short term for poor performance will largely depend on the permitted maturity transformation and the negotiability of financial instruments in the new system.

6.4.4 Summary

Proponents of the sovereign money system expect the transition to the new system will provide greater clarity about public and private interests. Although the entanglement of ‘the public’ and ‘the private’ in our current system clearly has

[51]Dyson et al. (2016).

[52]Ons Geld (2016: 18).

[53]Pettifor (2017: 107).

[54]Dow et al. (2015); Visser (2015); SNB (2018); Dommerholt and Van Tilburg (2016).

[55]Ons Geld (2016).

problematic aspects, the strict separation of the two is not as easy as it sounds. Public interests are at stake in financing. If private financing institutions perform poorly or go bankrupt, public interests may yet be threatened. The financial part of the system will continue to have a public dimension, even if in formal terms the institutions are entirely private.

Advocates expect the sovereign money system to result in greater public control over inflation and different macroeconomic outcomes. Some even argue that it will open the way to constant zero-percent inflation. Economies, however, are too complex for central banks to have such control, in part because they must always contend with developments in other countries. How far a sovereign money system would lead to *greater* control over inflation remains unclear. The central bank would change its primary policy instrument from adjusting interest rates to adjusting the money supply. If the exclusive focus is on the money supply, interest rates will most likely become more volatile. Nor has it been proven that managing the money supply is more effective than influencing market interest rates, as in both cases the transmission mechanism is uncertain. What monetary financing does offer in the sovereign money system is a more direct means of combating deflation.

If the government gains the power to create new money, checks and balances will be required to manage it effectively. The immediate question is whether the system will then lead to an improvement in terms of democratic influence.

Similar reservations apply to assessments of the position of citizens in the new system. The position of investors vis-à-vis financing institutions may improve as households have another option, namely storing their money in payment accounts. Asymmetries will still exist, however, as citizens will continue to be at an informational disadvantage. The position of citizens will also depend on the extent to which maturity transformation is permitted and the financing institution's debts are negotiable, as this affects to what extent investors can 'vote with their feet'.

6.5 Other Issues

This section addresses issues that, strictly speaking, fall outside of the criteria of economic contribution, stability, fairness and legitimacy but which are nonetheless crucial for assessing the feasibility and thus desirability of the sovereign money system. These are: (1) how the new system could be integrated in the international context; (2) prospects for a smooth transition; and (3) the extent to which system dynamics and innovation may undermine the new system over time.

6.5.1 The International Dimension

An initial question is how any *national* introduction of a sovereign money system would relate to the *international* context. The proposals mostly argue on the basis of a 'closed system' and pay scant attention to this international dimension.

The international dimension, however, is crucial. As we saw in Chap. 3, countries are far from autonomous in their financial monetary policies; developments in other countries heavily influence national macroeconomic objectives and countries must respond accordingly. Between the end of the Bretton Woods system and the introduction of the euro, the Dutch central bank in fact took its cues from its German counterpart. Another important question, particularly for open economies, is what the introduction of a sovereign money system would do to the exchange rate. Will the currency rise or fall in value? Will it be possible to achieve exchange rate stability? These matters are difficult to predict and have major economic consequences. Moreover, financial services are currently so international that there are countless interdependencies with foreign countries that would influence how plans from the drawing board turn out in practice.

Practically speaking, would the Netherlands be able to introduce a sovereign money system in the current international context? The Netherlands is part of the euro area, so it could not be introduced without the Netherlands withdrawing from the euro or persuading other euro area member states that a joint transition would be desirable. Quite apart from the likelihood of all euro area countries opting to do so, this would make any transition and its implementation much more complex. Many other questions arise. Who would be authorized to issue the newly created money? Who would make this decision? Would it happen at the European level or at the level of individual states? And based on what allocation? Plans for a sovereign money system, however, envision the system being introduced in individual countries. They therefore provide no answers to these questions.[56]

6.5.2 The Transition

A second question concerns the transition to a sovereign money system. Although the various proposals discuss the transition in terms of the effects on commercial and central bank balance sheets, they pay less attention to uncertainties in the dynamics

[56] Wortmanns' (2017) argument for a 'virtual euro' is an exception and briefly discusses how a 'citizens' dividend' should be distributed among EU states: "Member States are entitled to dividends on equal footing, irrespective of their debt with the banking system. For that, an appropriate allocation key must be applied. For Citizens, an equal share per capita seems most suitable, irrespective of individual debt with the banking system" (ibid.: 4). To allocate the new money, Wortmann simply writes that it should be made available to "the European Union and the Eurozone Member States combined" (ibid.: 8). The argument pays scant attention to the complications that could arise.

that a transition would create. Positive Money presents the option of a *gradual* transition which would allow people to grow accustomed to the new situation (see Sect. 5.4).[57] A more rapid transition may require public guarantees for the financial sector to forestall panic, even if this contradicts the idea that the government will no longer support private financing institutions. Proponents, however, focus primarily on the more technical aspects of the transition, discussing the transition mostly in terms of balance sheet changes.

Kroll believes this largely underestimates the complexity of the transition and the risk of systemic failure.[58] The monetary financial system is also a social system built on trust where people do not always act predictably or rationally. In the financial sector, market participants' expectations about the behaviour of other participants crucially inform their own choices. Precisely for this reason, self-reinforcing effects can easily emerge. These are important considerations for a transition to a sovereign money system since they imply that it is not a technical exercise in which everyone acts exactly in the way that is envisaged. If people believe a transition entails major risks – or if they believe other people believe so – this can become the reality. The government is unable to control such expectations.

One of the risks is a crisis in the banking system. As noted earlier, bank deposits (payment accounts only or both payment and savings accounts) would be converted into payment accounts that are declared 100% secure. The downside is that all bank debts that fall *outside* of this definition will thereafter incur risk. Lenders may fear that banks will encounter difficulties due to the transition and decide to move their assets to a bank in another country, leading to capital flight. If the government opts to switch to the new system overnight after a preparatory period, there is a real likelihood of panic, with people wanting to move *en masse* out of the financial part of the system.[59] In such an eventuality, the financial sector could cease to operate or require rescuing by the government. Of course it is impossible to say with any certainty whether this will happen. The point is that the trust required for the sovereign money system to function cannot be taken for granted.

6.5.3 Dynamics and Innovation

A third question is whether system dynamics and innovation will ultimately cause the sovereign money system to evolve into a system that resembles the set-up we currently have. The most important question here is whether the government can prevent the emergence of shadow money: private liabilities that serve as money but

[57]Dyson et al. (2016).

[58]Kroll (2015).

[59]This relates to whether savings accounts are also transferred to the new payment banks alongside current bank deposits. The proposals are often unclear on this point. If yes, the transition would be much larger. If not, savings accounts could change overnight from 'secure' to risk-bearing deposits.

are not *public* money.[60] It is possible that investment deposits or other financial instruments will come to be used as money, as has often happened in history (see Chap. 3). Bank deposits that are now widely used as money also started out as 'shadow money'. Shadow money most likely arises if financing institutions allow it to be used for payments between them. If this parallel payment system grows important enough, it will be even more problematic if the government decides to allow the financial part of the system to collapse in a crisis. As such, it increases the likelihood of government guarantees for financing institutions.

The advocates argue that this will not happen. The government can enforce rules and supervision to prevent the creation of shadow money. This can be done, for example, by banning the immediate repayability of debts or requiring financing institutions to disclose information on the associated risks.[61] Furthermore, the development of a *full-fledged* parallel monetary system is no simple feat. According to Positive Money, it took many decades for bank deposits to become a full-fledged alternative to cash, and did so only because the government issued all kinds of guarantees to intervene in the event of problems. As such, the development of a parallel system would be 'easier said than done'.[62] Ons Geld argues that the creation of shadow money would not be an entirely negative phenomenon: its popularity could be seen as an "indicator of the quality and operation of the sovereign money system".[63] Nor would shadow money necessarily pose a threat to the operation of the monetary system: "It would be sufficient for the government to focus on its own public money supply and dismantle all its support for private funds".[64] As long as this remains the case, it does not matter so much whether private operators introduce new means of payment; these will bear risks and the government will not have to rescue the system if it fails.[65] The question is whether such a policy is feasible and desirable in the case of a generally accepted means of payment.

Here both proponents and opponents offer important insights. The proponents rightly argue that something can only serve as 'money' if it enjoys broad trust. Such trust is not automatic: it has to be built up over time and must be supported by numerous formal and informal institutions.[66] On the other hand, this is precisely what has happened repeatedly in the past. Banknotes, bank deposits and, more recently, shares in money market funds in the United States all gradually began to serve as money, illustrating the dynamics and innovation in the financial monetary system. The fact that we now pay with bank deposits is not the result of a deliberate plan, but of numerous interacting developments over time (see Chap. 3). The idea that the organization of the financial monetary system remains stable over time is

[60]Goodhart and Jensen (2015); Laina (2015); Dow et al. (2015).

[61]Dyson et al. (2016: 24); Musgrave (2014).

[62]Dyson et al. (2016: 48).

[63]Ons Geld (2016: 29). Our translation.

[64]Ons Geld (2016: 29). Our translation.

[65]Ons Geld (2016).

[66]Mitchell-Innes (1913).

flawed. System dynamics, innovation and arbitrage are inherent to the system and make it unlikely that a strict separation between public payment institutions and private financing institutions can be maintained over the longer term.[67]

6.6 Conclusion

Trust is essential in every financial system. Trust is ultimately something that must be earned, and it is impossible to determine in advance whether it will arise in the sovereign money system. We previously pointed to key characteristics of the financial system that can generate trust: its economic contribution, stability, fairness and legitimacy. This chapter discussed the advantages and disadvantages of the sovereign money system on the basis of these four goals.

We started with the alternative system's contribution to the economy. There is no *prima facie* reason to expect that a sovereign money system will result in a more or less efficient payment system. A key advantage is that the payment system is in principle no longer susceptible to financial instability and the instability of financing institutions. Citizens would probably have to pay more for services as payment banks would have no other income. Lending would be more tightly regulated and possibly be less procyclical, with positive economic consequences. However, if lending fell sharply and credit became too expensive, this could negatively impact economic development. The transition would entail large loans from the central bank to commercial banks. The possibility of offsetting outstanding public debt against these loans could lead to a one-off reduction in public debt.[68]

Contribution to the economy	• The payment system is secure during a financial crisis. • The volume of lending will probably be lower, but possibly more stable. The effect on economic development is unspecified. • Possible one-off partial reduction in public debt.

For stability, we distinguished between that of individual institutions and that of the system as a whole. A sovereign money system will mean stable payment banks against which bank runs will either be impossible or will not lead to bankruptcy, even if there is residual operational risk. But financing institutions will still face the risks of instability. Although proponents argue that they will become more stable as they are genuinely exposed to market discipline, the question is whether shareholders, bondholders and holders of investment accounts will actually be able to discipline financial institutions more effectively. Furthermore, stronger market discipline for individual institutions does not preclude the build-up of systemic risks. Advocates believe, however, that systemic risks will arise less quickly due to better

[67]Visser (2015).

[68]The central bank's balance sheet will increase during the transition. Government debt (with interest payments and a repayment obligation) differs from the accounting debt of the central bank.

constraints on lending. Crises will also not directly jeopardize the payment system. Nevertheless, some authors believe the strict separation between financing and payment will *increase* the risk of a systemic crisis, because in case of doubt people will seek refuge *en masse* in secure payment institutions.

Stability	*Stability of individual institutions* • A bank run on a payment bank is not problematic. • Risk of instability in financing institutions will not disappear, but will diminish. The size of this risk depends on the organization of the system. How are financing institutions permitted to finance themselves? There may be a trade-off against the volume of lending: measures necessary for more stable institutions could constrain lending. *Stability of the system* • To the extent that the new system leads to less volatility in lending, it contributes to financial stability. • For the stability of the system as a whole, the means by which financing institutions are financed is crucial. For financing that can be withdrawn in the short term, systemic risks can arise because in a crisis people will seek refuge e*n masse* in public payment institutions. But financing institutions could take account of this risk and implement measures that would contribute to systemic stability.

Third, we considered fairness in the distribution of benefits, costs and risks. Advocates expect the current problems associated with implicit and explicit government guarantees will not arise in the new system, and see the withdrawal of government guarantees as a crucial precondition for its proper functioning. The question is whether this will always be tenable as the public interest in lending may require the government to step in during a systemic crisis to prevent further deterioration. In a sovereign money system the government collects seigniorage; whether this will benefit society as a whole depends on whether money creation remains under control. Finally, how the new system will affect the allocation of debt income and expenses remains unclear.

Fairness	*Allocation of profits and losses* • For the public cost of financial instability, much depends on how financing is organized. Private financing institutions will no longer have to be rescued to keep the payment system secure, but they may need to be rescued to sustain lending. • The benefits of money creation accrue to the government. Whether this benefits society as a whole will largely depend on how much money is created and how it is spent.

As for its legitimacy, the sovereign money system will more clearly demarcate private from public interests. Splitting payments from financing may mean that the private interests of financing institutions will be less readily equated with public interests. But lending is so crucial for the functioning of society that public interests will continue to be harboured in the financial part of the sovereign money system. It is impossible to predict whether the sovereign money system will be seen as more legitimate. While both the current and envisioned systems shield the central bank from political influence, this may become more challenging in the sovereign money system as efforts will be made to exert political influence, particularly when much is at stake. Citizens may have greater direct influence on financing institutions, particularly as they now have a clear alternative in the payment institutions. At the same time, information asymmetries in the new system should not be underestimated.

Legitimacy	• Public interests will be less dependent on the viability of private institutions. The payment system will no longer be interwoven with private activities. But efficient financing is also in the public interest; private financing institutions will thus also have a public dimension. • It is difficult to predict whether the sovereign money system will be seen as more legitimate. A central bank that takes decisions on the money supply may invite attempts to exert political influence. Distance from politics will be crucial.

All of this suggests that no conclusive answer can be given as to whether the sovereign money system is preferable to our current system. We can nevertheless make explicit all the assumptions we have to make to conclude that the sovereign money system as a whole is preferable:

- the central bank is able to properly manage the growth of the money supply, while the government will at all times remain committed to balanced money creation;
- the liabilities of financing institutions will not serve as money so that they become money-creating institutions and begin to resemble today's banks;
- financing institutions no longer need to be bailed out by the government because they can fail without disrupting the economy, thereby eliminating the problem of perverse incentives and 'private profits, public costs';
- sufficient and appropriate financing will be available in the new system through lending by the financing institutions or through market financing;
- institutions (central banks, payment banks, financing institutions) will be able to generate trust among citizens, businesses and investors necessary for the system to function properly;
- the system can operate in an international context with strong financial interdependencies without all countries switching to the sovereign money system.

In addition, there is the question of feasibility, in particular concerning the transition and international interdependencies. The complications that would accompany a transition should not be underestimated. If all players are uncertain about the new situation, there is a significant risk of a crisis during the transition. When policies and systems change, there are often unexpected, unintended and usually also undesirable side-effects. The choice to transition to a sovereign money system amounts to a large-scale experiment with the backbone of the economy. International interdependencies cannot be overlooked in the assessment of feasibility. The Netherlands is part of the euro area; for this reason alone, the system change has to take place at the European level unless the Netherlands leaves the euro area. Aside from the euro, many other international interdependencies constrain the Netherlands to pursue an unconventional monetary and financial policy and would turn such a transition into an unprecedented experiment. These international interdependencies feature scarcely, if at all, in the plans for a sovereign money system.

Bibliography

Bachetta, P. (2017). The sovereign money initiative in Switzerland: An assessment. *Swiss Finance Institute Research Paper*, 17–25. https://doi.org/10.2139/ssrn.2994926.

Benes, J., & Kumhof, M. (2013). The Chicago plan revisited. *IMF Working Paper, 12*, 202.

Boonstra, W. W. (2015). *Hoe werkt geldschepping?* Utrecht: Rabobank.

Boonstra, W. W. (2018). *Geld; Wat is het, wat doet het, waar komt het vandaag?* Amsterdam: VU University Press.

Borio, C. (2017, September 22). *Through the looking glass*. OMFIF City Lecture.

Chiarella, C., Flaschel, P., Hartmann, F., & Proaño, C. (2011). *Stock market booms, endogenous credit creation and the implications of broad and narrow banking for macroeconomic stability* (New School for Social Research, Working Paper 7).

Dommerholt, B., & van Tilburg, R. (2016). De voor- en nadelen van publiek geldschepping, *ESB* January 2017.

Dow, S., Johnson, G., & Montagnoli, A. (2015). *A critique of full reserve banking* (Sheffield Economic Research Paper Series). The University of Sheffield.

Dyson, B., Hodgson, G., & van Lerven, F. (2016). *Sovereign money. An introduction*. Available at: http://www.positivemoney.org.

Flaschel, P., Hartmann, F., Malikane, C., & Semmler, W. (2010). Broad banking, financial markets and the return of the narrow banking idea. *Journal of Economic Asymmetries, 7*(2), 105–137.

Fontana, G., & Sawyer, M. (2016). Towards post-Keynesian ecological macroeconomics. *Ecological Economics, 121*(C), 186–195.

FSA. (2009). *The turner review: A regulatory response to the global banking crisis*. London: The Financial Services Authority.

Goodhart, C. A. E. (2016). *Determining the quantity of bank deposits* (The Basel Issue, Banking Perspectives).

Goodhart, C. A. E., & Jensen, M. (2015). Currency School versus Banking School: An ongoing confrontation. *Economic Thought, 4*(2), 20–31.

Huber, J. (2017). *Sovereign money. Beyond reserve banking*. Cham: Palgrave Macmillan.

King, M. (2016). *The end of alchemy: Money, banking and the future of the global economy*. New York: W.W. Norton & Company.

Kotlikoff, L. J. (2010). *Jimmy Stewart is dead. Ending the world's ongoing financial plague with limited purpose banking*. Hoboken: Wiley.

Kotlikoff, L. J., & Goodman, J. C. (2009). *Solving our nation's financial crisis with limited purpose banking* (Working Paper). Boston: Boston University.

KPMG. (2016). *Money issuance: Alternative money systems*. Report commissioned by the Icelandic Prime Minister's Office. Available at: www.kpmg.com

Kroll, M. (2015). *The monetary system in crisis: Monetary reform proposals, and a simple suggestion for a more effective monetary policy* (World Future Council, Future Finance – Discussion Paper No. 1).

Laina, P. (2015). Proposals for full-reserve banking: A historical survey from David Ricardo to Martin Wolf. *Economic Thought, 4*(2), 1–19.

Mitchell-Innes, A. (1913, May). What is Money? *The Banking Law Journal*, 377–408.

Murau, S. (2017). Shadow money and the public money supply: The impact of the 2007–9 financial crisis on the monetary system. *Review of International Political Economy*. https://doi.org/10.1080/09692290.2017.1325765.

Musgrave, R. S. (2014). *The solution is full reserve/100% reserve banking* (MPRA Paper No. 57955).

Ons Geld. (2016). *Memorandum over het geldstelsel*. Available at: http://onsgeld.nu/kamerdebat-memo-geldstelsel.pdf

Pettifor, A. (2017). *The production of money: How to break the power of the banks*. London: Verso.

Ryan-Collins, J. (2015). *Is monetary financing inflationary? A case study of the Canadian economy, 1935–75* (Levy Institute Working Paper, No. 84).

Stellinga, B. (2018). *The financial valuation crisis. The inherent limits to taming unstable markets (PhD-manuscript)*. Amsterdam: University of Amsterdam.

Stellinga, B. (2019). Why performativity limits credit rating reform. *Finance and Society, 5*(1), 20–41.

Stellinga, B., & Mügge, D. (2017). The regulator's conundrum. How market reflexivity limits fundamental financial reform. *Review of International Political Economy, 24*(3), 393–423.

Sustainable Finance Lab. (2015). *De Geldkwestie*. Utrecht: Sustainable Finance Lab.

Swiss National Bank. (2018). *Arguments of the SNB against the Swiss sovereign money initiative (Vollgeldinitiative)*.

Tokmetzis, D. (2013, October 2). Niemand weet wie onze staatsschuld bezit. *de Correspondent*.

Turner, A. (2015). *Between debt and the devil – Money, credit, and fixing global finance*. Princeton: Princeton University Press.

van Dixhoorn, C. (2013). *Full Reserve Banking: An analysis of four monetary reform plans*. Utrecht: Sustainable Finance Lab.

van Egmond, N. D., & de Vries, B. J. M. (2016). *Monetaire hervorming; de mogelijkheid van een gezond financieel-economisch bestel*. Available at: www.sustainablefinancelab.nl

Visser. (2015, May 21). *Praktische kant burgerinitiatief ons geld weinig aantrekkelijk*. Me Judice.

Warwick Commission. (2009). *The Warwick Commission on international financial reform: In praise of unlevel playing fields*. Warwick: University of Warwick.

White, W. R. (2008, March 3). Past financial crises, the current financial turmoil, and the need for a new macrofinancial stability framework Speech by Mr William R White, Economic Adviser and Head of Monetary and Economic Department of the Bank for International Settlements, at the LSE Financial Markets Group and Deutsche Bank Conference "The structure of regulation: Lessons from the crisis of 2007", London.

Wortmann, E. (2017). *Deleverage without a crunch* (Working Paper, Stichting Ons Geld).

Yamaguchi, K. (2011). Workings of a public money system of open macroeconomies. In *Modeling the American monetary act completed. Paper at the 29th international conference of the system dynamics society*. Washington, DC.

7

Balancing the Current System

The previous chapter examined the advantages and disadvantages of the sovereign money system. Although we do not argue to move towards such a system, the problems raised by the advocates of sovereign money are real and urgent. Their plans moreover provide a solid basis for measures that could be usefully introduced into the current system.

In Chap. 4 we identified two challenges: we need a more balanced and controlled growth of money and debt as well as a better balance between public and private interests. This chapter focuses on the steps that can be taken to bring this about. We discuss both measures taken since the crisis and measures that have been proposed but were not implemented.

7.1 Taming the Money and Debt Cycle

The first challenge is taming the money and debt cycle. The balanced growth of money and debt matters not only for the stability of the financial system but for maximizing its contributions to the economy. As we saw in Chap. 3, finding the right balance between flexibility and rigour is a perennial challenge. If the monetary system is too strictly regulated – for example when currency was strictly tied to gold – this ultimately creates problems for economic growth and exacerbates crises. Flexibility in money creation and lending is necessary to anticipate cyclical fluctuations. On the other hand, a too-flexible monetary system leads to speculative bubbles and/or high inflation. Self-fulfilling effects can arise, where credit and money creation and rising financial asset prices all reinforce each other.

The decades leading up to the last financial crisis witnessed a trend towards greater flexibility. Numerous constraints on lending were removed while the money creating role of banks grew due to the increasing dominance of deposit money.

Public policies also encouraged private debt growth.[1] This flexibility led to historically high levels of debt as well as greater volatility in lending and hence in the economy at large. We discussed the downsides of this in Chap. 4: excessive credit growth heightens the probability of financial crises, while high levels of debt can undermine economic development and lead to the unfair allocation of costs and benefits in society.

This section discusses the main policy initiatives and suggestions to achieve a more balanced growth of money and debt. These are: (1) better curbs on and elimination of incentives for the growth of debt; (2) policy coherence and the structure of the financial sector; and (3) measures to cushion financial crises.

7.1.1 Curbing the Growth of Debt

In the wake of the crisis, macroprudential policy emerged as the main method to counter the excessive growth of debt. Initial steps have also been taken to eliminate tax incentives for debt finance.

7.1.1.1 Macroprudential Policy

Macroprudential policy focuses specifically on countering systemic risks, defined as "the risk of developments that threaten the system as a whole and ultimately cause severe damage to the economy".[2] To gauge such risks, analysts assess the emergence of imbalances (such as high debts and the growth of bubbles) and the structure of the financial sector (high concentration and interdependencies).[3]

Macroprudential policy makes use of the same instruments as banking supervision (also referred to as microprudential policy) such as capital and liquidity requirements. The main difference is the *purpose* for which the instrument is deployed: reducing risks to individual institutions (microprudential) or to the financial system as a whole (macroprudential). The macroprudential framework offers various possibilities for national supervisors to impose additional requirements to counter systemic risks (see Box 7.1).

---

[1]WRR (2016)

[2]DNB (2016a: 8)

[3]DNB (2016a); IMF-FSB-BIS (2016)

Box 7.1 Macroprudential Policy

The main macroprudential instruments are included in the European Capital Requirements Directive and Regulation, known as the CRD IV package.[4] Based largely on international agreements in the Basel III framework, the main instruments are additional capital buffers *on top of* microprudential requirements. An example is the countercyclical capital buffer. In good times, when lending grows too rapidly, the national supervisor (DNB in the case of the Netherlands) can impose on banks an additional capital requirement of 2.5%, which can be drawn upon in bad times. National supervisors can also (temporarily) increase the minimum risk weighting for mortgage loans if they believe the housing market is overheating. Systemically important institutions face additional capital requirements. National supervisors can also tighten other parts of the capital framework if they can demonstrate the remaining instruments are insufficient. This is referred to as the flexibility package (see Table 7.1). The CRD V package (2019) modified several aspects of these rules (mainly activation requirements and buffer limits) but did not change their essence, nor did it introduce additional instruments.

Alongside this European macroprudential framework, many countries have requirements on mortgage loans. In the Netherlands, for example, there is a maximum loan-to-value ratio of 100%, which means the loan cannot exceed the appraised value of the home.

Responsibility for macroprudential policy is shared by a range of organizations. A distinction can be drawn between: (1) the detection and reporting of systemic risks, and (2) the activation of instruments. The first is carried out at the European level by the European Systemic Risk Board (ESRB), which is part of the European Central Bank. In the Netherlands this responsibility rests with DNB and the *Financial Stability Committee*, comprising representatives of DNB, the Ministry of Finance and the Authority for Financial Markets.[5] Primarily a national matter, the activation of instruments is the responsibility of DNB, while mortgage loan limits are the responsibility of the Ministry of Finance. To activate certain instruments, DNB must obtain approval from European organizations such as the ESRB and the European Banking Authority. The advent of the European banking union has also given the ECB specific macroprudential responsibilities: it can activate the CRD IV instruments implemented by national member states or increase their stringency if it deems this necessary to counter systemic risks.

[4]European Commission (2014); Stellinga (2021)

[5]Cavelaars et al. (2013)

Table 7.1 Overview of macroprudential instruments in the CRD IV package

	Brief Description	Legal Basis
Countercyclical capital buffer	A capital surcharge (ranging from 0% to 2.5%, possibly higher) to counter risks of the financial cycle. If a country introduces this surcharge, it also applies to credit granted by other European banks in the country.	Articles 130 and 135-140 of CRD IV
Systemic buffer	A capital surcharge for one or more systemically important banks.	Articles 133-134 of CRD IV
G-SII/O-SII buffer	A capital surcharge for 'global systemically important institutions' or 'other systemically important institutions'.	Article 131 of CRD IV
Sectoral risk weights	The risk weighting for mortgage loans can be increased to counter systemic risks.	Article 124 and Article 164 of the Capital Requirements Regulation (CRR)
Flexibility package	Various measures (including an increase in liquidity requirements or risk weightings) if other macroprudential instruments are insufficient.	Article 458 of the CRR

One of the main issues is how to measure systemic risks.[6] Deviation in the growth trend of credit is a key indicator when deciding to apply the countercyclical capital buffer (CCB). The question is whether the Netherlands should rely on this indicator as the 'baseline' is very high; since lending rose so rapidly in the run-up to the crisis, it would take extreme credit growth to turn this warning light red. While DNB has thus far concluded that there is no reason to activate the CCB in the Netherlands, other indicators suggest serious grounds for concern.[7] Precisely because one indicator alone does not reliably point to the build-up of systemic risks, the ESRB recommends activating the buffer on the basis of multiple indicators.[8] Sweden notably applied the buffer in March 2017 although according to the standard indicator (growth trend of credit) it was not required to do so.[9]

A crucial follow-up question is how far these instruments can actually curb the risks. While macroprudential instruments have thus far been a part of capital regulation, capital requirements are primarily meant to make banks more shock-resistant to potential problems, not to curb the growth of debt. BIS economist Claudio Borio, one of the developers of the CCB, argues that it is not suited to curbing credit growth and that the relationship between *risk-weighted* capital

[6]Cf. Stellinga (2020)

[7]ESRB (2016)

[8]ESRB (2014)

[9]Finansinspektionen (2018: 4).

requirements and lending is too indirect to serve as an effective brake.[10] One of the reasons for this is that, particularly in good times, the risks to banks' assets (such as outstanding loans) are underestimated.[11]

This raises the question of whether macroprudential policy needs to be broadened. The countercyclical raising of liquidity requirements is highly complex in the existing framework and can only be implemented through the flexibility package, which is not easy to deploy (see Table 7.1).[12] Furthermore, the non-bank financial sector mostly falls outside the purview of macroprudential policy. The current framework's exclusion of shadow banks – financial institutions that strongly resemble banks as they issue short-term debt to fund long-term loans – is a particular ground for concern. The crisis was largely caused by ballooning credit growth among financial institutions that subsequently proved untenable. Nevertheless, these institutions largely remain outside of the scope of macroprudential policy.[13]

Macroprudential instruments not only target financial institutions but also specific loans. A key macroprudential instrument is the maximum loan-to-value (LTV) ratio: the maximum loan that can be granted relative to the value of collateral. In the Netherlands the maximum permitted LTV ratio for mortgage loans has been reduced in stages since 2012; since 1 January 2018, the maximum is 100%. Various institutions are calling for a further reduction of the LTV ratio to 90% or even 80%.[14] On the other hand, the Netherlands Bureau for Economic Policy Analysis (CPB) warns against the high social costs associated with further reducing the LTV ratio, particularly for first-time buyers in the housing market.[15]

Although capping the LTV ratio curbs lending, it is not an absolute ceiling. So long as the value of homes continues to rise and market prices are used to determine value in the LTV ratio, more credit can be granted. This in turn can further inflate house prices. A loan-to-income (LTI) ratio that ties the amount of the loan to the applicant's income is in theory a stronger curb on lending. While the Netherlands has no direct LTI limits, there are limits on financing costs. One's income and the interest rate determine the maximum that can be spent on a mortgage (about which NIBUD, the National Institute for Family Finance Information, issues an annual recommendation). This constitutes a loan ceiling although the lender may apply a different limit if it can be justified.

---

[10]Borio (2010)

[11]Carmassi and Micossi (2012); Danielsson et al. (2012)

[12]See also ECB Task Force on Systemic Liquidity (2018)

[13]ESRB (2016)

[14]Financial Stability Committee (2015); IMF (2017); DNB (2017); Wijffels Committee (2013)

[15]Veldhuizen et al. (2015); Van Dijk and Voogt (2017)

7.1.1.2 Tax Incentives

A second strategy to limit private debt growth is the reduction of tax incentives to incur debt. The tax treatment of debt makes it more advantageous for households, businesses and banks to use debt rather than equity finance. Households and businesses can deduct interest payments from their taxable income. Cautious steps have been taken since the crisis. The maximum mortgage interest deduction was reduced from 52% in 2014 to 49.5% in 2018; it will fall further to 37% by 2023. Steps have also been taken to limit interest deductions for private equity operators. The Dutch government also intends to set an upper limit for deductible interest expenses (interest ceilings) for banks and insurance companies. Tax benefits of so-called cocos – special debt instruments issued by banks – have been abolished in 2019.[16]

Some countries have tried to tackle the unequal tax treatment of debt and equity by introducing deductibility for equity. Belgium, for example, introduced a *notional interest deduction* in 2006 (see Box 7.2). Other countries such as Cyprus, Italy, Croatia, Latvia, Liechtenstein, Austria and Turkey have also introduced equity deductibility in recent years. The relevant base (all equity or only new equity) and the notional interest rate differ from country to country.

Box 7.2 Equity Deductibility in Belgium

In 2006 Belgium introduced the deductibility of equity costs for business. This 'deduction for risk capital' means a notional interest rate can be deducted from adjusted equity; in the 2015 assessment year this notional rate stood at 2.63%.[17] Since the deduction did not apply to the equity of subsidiaries, the European Commission and the European Court of Justice ruled that it violated the free movement of capital within the EU.[18] Belgium accordingly amended the law. Now the deduction is only permitted on the increase in equity over the average of the previous five years. While this measure primarily focuses on 'ordinary' businesses, Schepens shows that this measure has also contributed to an increase in the equity of Belgian banks.[19] A major criticism of the measure is that it facilitates international tax arbitrage by multinationals.[20]

In general, it is desirable for different types of funding to be treated equally in order to combat avoidance behaviour; this is provided for in the deductibility of equity. Limits on the tax deductibility of interest expenses implies that unequal treatment between debt and equity is not eliminated, which may have undesirable

[16]Ministry of Finance (2018)

[17]Federal Public Service Finance (2018)

[18]The European Commission (2012); the European Court of Justice (2013)

[19]Schepens (2016)

[20]Hebous and Ruf (2017)

consequences. Nevertheless, it does meet the desired objective of discouraging excessive reliance on debt finance.[21]

Although attention since the crisis has focused on the preferential tax treatment of debt, there have been few concrete steps to address the problem. Whereas the gradual reduction of mortgage interest deductibility has been successful, the tax advantage for businesses has only been partially addressed. Given the free movement of capital within the European Union, the equal tax treatment of equity and debt requires coordination at the European level to prevent tax arbitrage. For banks the situation is more complex since debt finance (and its associated interest expenses) is at the core of the business model (lending by means of money creation). The question is whether this core includes *all* forms of bank's debt finance (such as short-term market funding) and whether more differentiated interest deduction would be appropriate.

7.1.2 Policy Coherence and the Structure of the Financial Sector

Policy reforms since the crisis have focused on the constraints and incentives for the growth of debt. Less attention has been devoted to policy coherence and the structure of the financial sector.

7.1.2.1 Policy Coherence

The macroprudential policy framework is now largely an independent policy area with its own instruments and responsible organizations.[22] The question is whether this demarcation acknowledges the many factors that play a role in the boom-bust dynamics of lending. Here it is particularly important to examine the relationships between macroprudential policy, banking supervision (microprudential policy), monetary policy and socioeconomic policy.

Macroprudential policy largely uses the same type of instruments as banking supervision, particularly capital requirements. At the same time, macroprudential policy has been set up as a separate policy area with its own objectives and framework. One of the founders of the macroprudential framework, Claudio Borio of the Bank for International Settlements, nevertheless believes it is mistaken to speak of two separate policy areas. It is more a case of different perspectives: one focused on the stability of individual banks (micro perspective) and one focused on

[21]Annex II compares the effects of introducing an interest rate ceiling and introducing equity deductibility.

[22]IMF-FSB-BIS (2016)

system stability (macro perspective).[23] This implies that the distinction between banking supervision and macroprudential policy is fluid and complex. Particularly in the field of risk weightings, microprudential logic may clash with macroprudential logic (see Box 7.3).[24]

Box 7.3 Procyclical Effects of Risk Weightings

Bank capital requirements look at the size of the bank's *risk-weighted* assets to determine the required equity level. Although risk weightings may appear rational from the perspective of an individual bank (having few risky loans such as mortgages means less need for equity), they may be imprudent from the macro and long-term perspective.

The first international capital framework, the Basel I Accord of 1988, used a system of broad categories to determine risk weightings. Over time, both banks and supervisors became dissatisfied with what they considered imprecise measures of risk. Basel II of 2004 gave banks with approved risk management systems more latitude to assess the riskiness of their assets. Risk assessments issued by credit rating agencies were also given more prominence. Policymakers hoped that this would better align capital requirements with the actual risks that banks faced. In addition, they expected that banks would put their risk management in order and engage in less rule-avoiding behaviour.

One of the disadvantages of the Basel II approach is that it can reinforce procyclical effects. Banks' risk models often have short-term horizons. In good times with few bankruptcies, the models report low risk, encouraging banks to grant more loans. During a crisis, all signals suddenly turn red, prompting banks to hit the brake. A similar dynamic is found in credit ratings. At the aggregate level, this can strengthen the cycle of boom and bust.

Limited changes have been made in this area since the crisis. Policymakers require banks to apply longer time horizons in their risk models and to factor in worst-case scenarios. There are also lower limits for risk weighting and banks must no longer place blind trust in credit assessments. The Basel III Accord (2010) and the recent Basel IV Accord (2017) nevertheless continue to rely on both risk models and credit ratings.[25]

As an adjacent policy area, monetary policy merits greater attention in light of the debt problem. In its current form, monetary policy is primarily aimed at stabilizing the value of money, which in many countries is construed as limited inflation for

[23]Borio (2010: 2–4)

[24]The current practice of giving a zero weighting to government bonds on bank balance sheets poses other risks. It means countries with higher risk can finance themselves more cheaply than would be the case on a market basis.

[25]Stellinga (2018, 2019)

goods and services. The price of houses and financial assets falls outside its direct purview. Critics believe this narrow focus contributed to the financial crisis, with central banks in Europe and the United States keeping their interest rates low, thereby contributing to the growth of credit bubbles.[26] In the wake of the crisis, critics charged that the policy of low interest rates and quantitative easing was again contributing to excessive debt. This raises the question of whether monetary policy should also explicitly address financial stability.

There are two reasons to keep monetary policy separate from other policy areas. First is the question of whether the principal instrument of monetary policy, the interest rate, is an appropriate means of countering credit bubbles. It is doubtful that raising interest rates is on its own sufficient to counter excessive credit growth, while doing so can cause serious damage to the rest of the economy.[27] Second, monetary policy's exclusive focus on price stability gives the central bank a clear objective, making it easier to argue that it should be independent from politics. In addition, pursuing a single goal also improves oversight by and accountability to politicians. Financial stability is a vaguer concept and more difficult to measure and account for.

On the other hand, there are good arguments for monetary policy to focus more on financial stability. Although the interest rate may be too blunt an instrument to tackle credit bubbles, this does not mean that central banks should ignore sharp rises in lending when deciding on interest rates. The interest rate instrument is so powerful that other instruments alone will probably be insufficient to curb excessive credit growth.[28] Since the crisis, the ECB has started to interpret its mandate more broadly while Banking Union has given the ECB a key role in supervision. The time thus seems opportune to reflect more broadly on the relationship between monetary and financial stability policy and its associated instruments.

Finally, socioeconomic policy fields such as housing, pensions and tax policy affect the volume of debt in society. High mortgage debts in the Netherlands cannot be viewed apart from broader housing market policy, where a stagnant rental market and the deductibility of mortgage interest render home ownership attractive. Likewise, the pension system mandating employees to save significant portions of their salaries contributes to long balance sheets where high debts are combined with high, but mostly inaccessible savings. Countering our dependence on debt requires a broader strategy than just macroprudential policy. Brakes such as the loan-to-value ratio will be more effective if they are tied to the elimination of incentives to borrow rooted in socioeconomic policy.[29]

---

[26] Eichengreen et al. (2011)

[27] See e.g. Haldane (2010); Constancio (2015); Fahr and Fell (2017)

[28] Caruana (2016)

[29] See WRR (2016)

7.1.2.2 Structural Measures

Post-crisis deliberations on how to constrain credit growth have devoted less attention to the structure of the banking sector. The current Dutch banking landscape with its three large universal banks is liable to encourage money creation and credit growth. As the big three are relatively certain that newly created bank deposits will remain available to them as a source of funding, they face less constraints in credit creation. A more diverse banking sector in which newly created money does not automatically remain within the big three banks may indirectly constrain money creation; as was the case, for example, in the 1960s and 1970s (see Chap. 3). Greater diversity in the banking landscape, as advocated by proponents of the sovereign money system, would help. Some of their ideas can be pursued without switching fully to the alternative system. Two recent proposals are particularly noteworthy: (1) the introduction of a central bank digital currency; and (2) the formation of a bank focused primarily on payments and savings.

There have been ongoing discussions about whether the central bank should allow citizens and businesses to hold payment accounts at the central bank.[30] In the debate this is referred to as the introduction of central bank digital currency (CBDC). In the current system, only commercial banks and a number of other financial institutions have access to digital accounts at the central bank. Since these deposits do not count as part of the money supply, these are called central bank reserves rather than central bank money. While citizens and businesses can access central bank money in the form of cash (coins and banknotes), for digital money they can only rely on commercial banks. The question is whether a digital, public means of payment should be developed, allowing households, businesses and other financial institutions to save directly with and make payments through the central bank. As a public alternative to payment accounts at commercial banks, it could be organized as a relatively independent payments system that can provide a back-up in the event of disruptions to the private payments system.[31]

The debate on CBDC mostly focuses on financial stability issues. In the current system, citizens can either convert their bank deposits into cash or transfer them to another bank. The introduction of a central bank digital currency would enable this money to be transferred to the central bank. Critics fear that this possibility would *increase* instability as warning clouds on the horizon may prompt citizens to transfer their balances *en masse* to the central bank, thereby triggering a bank run across the *entire* commercial banking sector.[32] This would then require the central bank to rescue the commercial banks, with a substantial expansion of its role as lender of last resort.[33]

---

[30]Bardearr and Kumhof (2016); BIS (2018); Bordo and Levin (2017); Broadbent (2016); Fung and Halaburda (2016); Mersch (2017); Ordoñez (2018); Skingsley (2016)

[31]Sveriges Riksbank (2017)

[32]Danmarks Nationalbank (2017)

[33]BIS (2018)

Proponents argue that there are ways to mitigate such problems, for example by limiting the convertibility of bank deposits into central bank digital currency and capping the amount allowed to be held on the central bank account.[34] Additionally, the deposit guarantee system would continue to discourage bank runs. It is also possible that digital public money will result in more diversity in the financial system, helping to curb systemic risks. If a full-fledged alternative to bank deposits is available, this would put a stronger brake on money creation than our current homogenous system. In Chap. 4 we pointed out that the forerunners of the Postbank (PCGD and Rijkspostspaarbank) fulfilled such a function for decades.[35] In short, the diversity introduced by central bank digital currency may have a disciplining effect on banks. Finally, the fact that a safe haven could destabilize the current system points to flaws in our current system rather than shortcomings of CBDC. After all, the forerunners of the Postbank did not cause instability.

Another possibility would be granting licences to banks whose only assets are central bank reserves, thereby giving citizens indirect access to 'secure' money. But financial stability would remain a concern as this variant also provides a safe haven for bank deposits, potentially exacerbating the risk of a systemic bank run. But as with central bank digital currency, greater diversity in the sector may have positive effects on stability. In the Netherlands, such a deposit bank has been proposed by the Full Reserve Foundation (see Box 7.4).

Box 7.4 A Deposit Bank

The Full Reserve Foundation's plans for a deposit bank focus less on volatile lending than on ensuring that "taking risk becomes a choice". The foundation seeks to "reduce and ultimately abolish" the deposit guarantee system so that "banks can once again fail without the payment system coming to a standstill".[36] To date, no such deposit bank has materialized.

The Full Reserve Foundation applied for a licence for a deposit bank, i.e. a bank whose sole assets comprise central bank reserves. The idea was that citizens would have a secure option for payments and savings with a bank that incurs no financial risks. The finance minister, however, ruled that no such banking licence could be issued. The discussion largely focused on participation in the deposit guarantee scheme.

The Full Reserve Foundation wanted the deposit bank to have access to TARGET2, the interbank payment system. But the minister ruled that access to TARGET2 would require participation in the deposit guarantee scheme.[37] The Full Reserve Foundation did not believe the deposit bank should shoulder the

(continued)

[34]Kumhof and Noone (2018)

[35]Peekel and Veluwenkamp (1984)

[36]Full Reserve Foundation 2018. Our translation.

[37]Letter from the Minister of Finance TK 32013 No. 142

Box 7.4 (continued)
costs of other banks' riskier activities; the deposit guarantee scheme is, after all, a mutual insurance which would put the deposit bank in difficulty should other banks collapse. Other solutions to cover this risk, such as insuring the deposits through a private insurer, were deemed unacceptable.

DNB proposed organizing the deposit bank as a money market fund so it would not have to participate in the deposit guarantee scheme.[38] This was unacceptable for the Full Reserve Foundation as it would mean exclusion from the payment system (a money market fund does not have access to TARGET2). These obstacles ultimately led to the entire plan being abandoned.

The idea that greater diversity in the commercial banking sector can limit excessive debt growth has received scant attention since the crisis. Of course, there have been debates about the importance of greater diversity.[39] But concentration in the sector has only increased since the crisis. The share of the three major banks grew from 71% in 2006 to 75% in 2016 (measured by balance sheet size), while that of the five largest banks grew from 84% to 89%.[40] New supervision requirements were a factor in Rabobank's decision to centralize its operations, with its local branches giving up their own banking licences. In short, in many ways, diversity seems to have decreased.

7.1.3 *Preparedness for the Next Financial Crisis*

In addition to limiting excessive debt growth, it is also important to prevent financial collapse once problems materialize. The first step is to prevent a shock from immediately becoming a crisis. Tightening banking requirements have been key in this respect. If a crisis nevertheless arises, we need to ensure that money and credit do not enter a downward spiral. Here we discuss how to deal with banks that are in distress and the tools available for monetary policy to combat the next crisis.[41]

---

[38]Letter from the Minister of Finance TK 32013 No. 131

[39]See e.g. DNB (2015b); Ministry of Finance (2016)

[40]Committee on the Global Financial System (2018)

[41]As previously noted, this is a translation of a report that was published in January 2019. The response to the 2020 COVID-19 crisis and its possible effects on financial stability are outside the scope of this translation.

7.1.3.1 Tightening of Banking Supervision

Bank regulation and supervision have been tightened since the crisis, with the Basel III Accord (2010) and its implementation in European laws and regulations introducing tighter capital requirements as well as rules for liquidity.

Capital requirements have been strengthened in different ways. The requirements for the risk-weighted capital ratio have been increased. As the crisis revealed deficiencies in this area, policymakers have made further adjustments, gradually reducing banks' room for manoeuvre in weighting risks. Capital requirements have also been strengthened by introducing an unweighted capital requirement (the leverage ratio). This is intended as a backstop for the risk-weighted capital ratio, not as a replacement. Banks' equity must be at least 3% of the total size of the balance sheet (EU rules: CRR II). In the Netherlands, the current requirement is 4% for systemic banks. This requirement will be aligned with European requirements once these enter into force (June 2021).[42]

Liquidity rules help ensure that banks have sufficient liquid assets and stable sources of funding. Up until the 2007-2009 crisis, policy in this area was developed at the national level but was of marginal importance compared to capital regulation. The crisis showed this to be a blind spot. Basel III therefore introduced liquidity rules. The liquidity coverage ratio (LCR) states that banks must have sufficient liquid assets to deal with short-term stress. The net stable funding ratio (NSFR) states that banks must have appropriate financing sources for long-term liabilities.

Although these steps go in the right direction, we should not overstate the nature of the changes. Risk weighting still plays a central role in capital requirements, but during booms risk models indicate that risk is low.[43] The danger remains that banks will not have access to equity if they need it to absorb shocks. While the introduction of the leverage ratio is an improvement, many believe the 3% minimum is too low to absorb significant setbacks.[44] Liquidity requirements also remain rather insignificant in practice. Since its introduction in 2010, the LCR was eased first by the Basel Committee itself and then implemented in the EU in a more flexible form due to fears that banks would otherwise be hit too hard.[45] The same applies to the NSFR: its implementation has been postponed in the EU with policymakers fearing it would impede economic recovery. It will now become operational in June 2021, more than 11 years after the Basel Committee first proposed this measure.[46]

[42]DNB (2019)

[43]Carmassi and Micossi (2012); Danielsson et al. (2012)

[44]See e.g. Admati et al. (2010); Admati and Hellwig (2013); Wolf (2017); Benink (2018)

[45]Stellinga and Mügge (2017)

[46]DNB 2019

7.1.3.2 Problem Banks

The 2007-9 crisis revealed policy frameworks for dealing with failing banks to be insufficient; there were few if any emergency plans in place and it was unclear which bodies were responsible (particularly in the case of cross-border banks) and what powers they had.[47] There were few options besides nationalizing banks, granting them large loans or buying up their shares, which meant taxpayers ended up meeting a large part of the costs.

Much has changed since then. First of all, banks are obliged to have recovery plans in place to tackle any eventualities. These include, for example, possibilities for recapitalization, access to emergency funding, and the sale of assets or specific parts of the business. The recovery plan is part of a broader policy framework for dealing with problem banks. The European Single Resolution Mechanism (SRM) has been in force since 2015 as part of the Banking Union. This framework sets out the various options available to supervisors if a bank encounters solvency problems. It comprises the national resolution authorities (in the Netherlands: DNB) and a European body, the Single Resolution Board (SRB), which plays a leading role for banks supervised by the ECB.

These authorities draw up a resolution plan for each bank. Resolution means "a controlled and careful means of winding up a bank threatened by collapse".[48] They have various options. They can: (1) pass on the losses to the shareholders and creditors (bail-in); (2) sell parts of the bank, without the shareholders' approval; (3) transfer the essential parts of a bank to a public 'bridge bank', in which the bad parts are allowed to fail; and (4) transfer the bad parts to a separate vehicle (a bad bank) that will then be gradually liquidated. The authority can also choose to allow the bank as a whole to fail.[49]

Although the single resolution mechanism is an important step forward, it has barely been tested in practice. We should not have undue expectations of the bail-in in the event of a major crisis. Although it may work for an individual bank or a number of small banks, whether it will also work in a systemic crisis is highly questionable.

Alongside the immediate challenges of absorbing the 2007-9 crash, the EU has had particular problems with the prolonged negative effects of the weakened banking sectors. After the crisis, some EU countries were very slow to recognize problem loans. Many banks actually needed capital injections and a writing off of bad loans to strengthen their financial positions, but many governments were reluctant to enforce this. There are good reasons for being reticent about writing off loans: it is quite possible that the economy will revive and reduce the volume of problem loans.[50] The

[47] See De Wit Committee II (2012); De Larosière (2009)

[48] DNB (2018a)

[49] DNB (2018a)

[50] The write-down of a problem loan on the bank's books may impair the bank's position if the debtor goes bankrupt.

writing off of problem loans leads to losses for the bank and a deterioration in its equity position; if there is no simultaneous plan for recapitalization, early loan write-downs may exacerbate the crisis.

Yet delaying writing off problem loans may also result in 'muddling through', with the wait-and-see attitude impeding recovery. If problem loans remain on bank balance sheets, banks remain financially unhealthy, potentially reinforcing the downward spiral. Recapitalization plans are required to avoid this. Recapitalization based on retained earnings always takes longer than recapitalization with new shares (which existing shareholders will oppose). Policymakers in the United States have tackled this issue by demanding that banks recapitalize during the 2007-9 crisis, with the government acting as a backstop if they fail to raise enough capital. American banks thus improved their financial positions faster and resumed lending sooner. In Europe policymakers were much more reticent; the result was that the recovery took much longer.[51] Bail-in rules mean that banks must be recapitalized in the event of problems, but these rules are aimed at individual banks. European rules do not currently provide a means to force a group of banks – including banks that are not in acute difficulties – to recapitalize during a crisis.

7.1.3.3 Monetary Policy in the Next Crisis

During the 2007-9 financial crisis, central banks sought to support vital markets and lower interest rates. The US and the UK resorted fairly quickly to quantitative easing, which had long been used in Japan. Quantitative easing involves the central bank buying up government and corporate bonds. The European Central Bank chose this path in 2015 as the threat of deflation loomed in the wake of the euro crisis. Combined with low (even negative) interest rates, the ECB sought to encourage borrowing in the hope that this would boost the economy and bring inflation to the desired level. Monetary policy thus moved into unfamiliar terrain.

Another crucial question is what instruments governments have at their disposal to revive the economy in a forthcoming crisis. Many governments have very high levels of debt. Even higher public debt in a subsequent crisis could fuel investor mistrust, which in turn could lead to a new debt crisis. What additional room for manoeuvre would governments have then?[52]

Public money creation through monetary financing is one option.[53] In monetary financing, the central bank creates new money without any corresponding debt. There are various ways in which this money can be brought into the economy, including through government spending or the central bank transferring money directly to citizens ('helicopter money'). Monetary financing is the standard way

[51]Cf. The Economist (2017)

[52]Reid et al. (2017); BIS (2015: 22)

[53]See e.g. Turner (2015)

to create new money in the sovereign money system. Could it be an option in the current system in case of an emergency?

The main objection is that monetary financing can spiral out of control, even leading to hyperinflation (see Chap. 6). Having this option may also make governments less inclined to control public spending. It is also doubtful whether many countries would actually need to resort to monetary financing in a future crisis: some governments, including those of the Netherlands and Germany, would be able to implement generous countercyclical fiscal policies in the event of a crisis.

Although the monetary financing of government spending is now rare, it used to be quite common, including in Western countries. The historical experience is thus not as clear-cut as opponents would have us believe. Although monetary financing has the potential to spiral out of control, it has often proved to be effective.[54] Some observers believe the policy of quantitative easing already has characteristics of monetary financing, particularly when the ECB buys up newly issued government bonds and it remains unclear whether it will ultimately sell them.

Monetary financing is currently prohibited in Europe under the Treaty on the Functioning of the European Union (Article 123 TFEU). It is therefore generally assumed that monetary financing would require an amendment to this treaty. Saravelos et al. argue that although monetary financing through *government expenditure* is prohibited in the EU, it is unclear whether this would apply if the ECB opted to transfer newly created money directly to citizens.[55]

7.1.3.4 Interim Conclusion

Macroprudential policy has been the main post-crisis initiative to manage the growth of debt. Additionally, small steps have been taken to eliminate fiscal incentives to accumulate debt. Despite these measures, in the Netherlands the level of private debt as a percentage of GDP is no lower than before the crisis (see Fig. 4.3). It is thus uncertain whether the range of instruments to limit debt growth are a match for all the forces that still encourage it. These include tax and other incentives, the structure of the financial sector, and lenient monetary policies.

7.2 Balance Between Public and Private Interests

The second major challenge is restoring the balance between public and private interests. As we discussed in Chap. 4, crucial public interests are at stake in the financial sector. The payment infrastructure has the characteristics of a public good while lending has significant positive and negative external effects. That public

---

[54]See Saravelos et al. (2016); Ryan-Collins (2015)

[55]Saravelos et al. (2016)

interests are at stake implies that the government needs to take responsibility for these issues. This of course does not mean that the government will completely take over the provision of these services itself. In many public-interest services such as energy, food supplies and healthcare, private parties play an important role in promoting public interests.[56] Likewise, in the financial sector both public and private actors have a responsibility to contribute to the public interest.

The public-private relationship has changed over the past decades. Fifty years ago, payments and savings in the Netherlands were primarily ‘public’: people used cash for most payments and mostly relied on the publicly owned predecessors of the Postbank for non-cash payments. Financing, on the other hand, was more often the domain of private institutions although the government had an important role through public investment banks. Since then, commercial banks have expanded to serve households while the public banks have been privatized. With the shift to deposit money, society now largely depends on private banks for payments and savings.

The financial crisis reminded us how dependent society has become on financial institutions, particularly the major commercial banks. Since their operation has a direct impact on important public functions, public and private interests are interwoven. Commercial banks cannot be seen as purely private institutions. Indeed, their public dimension came to the fore in the dispute over a pay raise for ING’s chief executive in 2018. According to Dutch Prime Minister Rutte, banks do not have the same freedom as other companies to set their chief executive’s pay as they are “semi-public institutions”.[57]

Since the crisis, various steps have been taken to strike a better balance between public and private interests in the financial sector. Attempts have been made to: (1) draw a clearer boundary between public and private interests and institutions, and (2) to embed public interests more firmly in the banking sector.

7.2.1 A Clearer Boundary Between Public and Private Interests

Since the crisis, efforts have been made to better balance public and private interests in the financial sector. The first step was to draw a clearer boundary between the two. Attention has been paid to whether banks’ more public activities can be separated from their more private activities. Efforts have also been made to limit the public guarantee for the financial sector.

---

[56]WRR (2000); WRR (2012); WRR (2013)

[57]NRC 9 March 2018

7.2.1.1 The Ring-Fencing of Public Activities

Following the crisis, a great deal of attention was devoted to the need to separate banks' public activities from their riskier private endeavours. Critics claimed that by pursuing risky activities such as trading in complex financial instruments, large banks had jeopardized their 'public functions'. Institutions had become so large and complex that governments felt obliged to rescue the *entire* bank to safeguard its public functions. A clear separation of activities would ensure that public activities were protected and that governments would not have to bail out the entire bank in the event of a crisis.

A range of proposals – some of them implemented – were advanced to introduce such a separation.[58] How this separation would work differed between the proposals. Broadly speaking, there were two options which could be combined if necessary: (1) prohibiting banks that perform utility functions from pursuing certain risky activities; and (2) obliging banks to 'ring-fence' certain activities within the bank. In the case of ring-fencing, the bank would not be prohibited from pursuing riskier activities, but would have to ensure that specific business units are independent in their operations and their funding basis.

The United States chose the first option: the Volcker Rule (adopted and gradually introduced in 2012) states that banks offering payment and savings accounts are not allowed to pursue certain activities such as trading on own account (so not on behalf of customers). In the United Kingdom banks have been required to ring-fence their domestic retail activities since 2019 so that these can operate independently; other activities must be kept outside of the ring-fenced entity (Vickers Rule). In the EU, the European Commission presented a plan to keep certain trading activities separate, on the advice of the Liikanen Committee,[59] combined with a variation of the American Volcker Rule. But the Commission withdrew this plan in 2017.

No separation measures have been implemented in the Netherlands although the subject has arisen in social and political debates. The De Wit Committee called for 'utility bank activities' (payments, savings and loans) to be ring-fenced from more speculative activities.[60] But the government found such a separation difficult to achieve in practice and feared negative consequences for the Dutch economy.[61] As the debate persisted, the government appointed a separate committee to investigate whether structural measures were required. The committee (chaired by Herman Wijffels) counselled adopting the Liikanen proposal on the ring-fencing of trading activities and, if necessary, prohibiting banks from own-account trading.[62] The

[58]See for example De Wit Committee (2010, 2012); Vickers Report (2011); Liikanen Report (2012); Wijffels Committee (2013)

[59]Liikanen Committee (2012),

[60]The De Wit Committee (2010: 18–19)

[61]Ministry of Finance (2010): Section 2.12

[62]Committee on the Structure of Dutch Banks (2013: 24–25)

government, however, decided to await European regulations, which to date have not materialized.[63]

7.2.1.2 Reducing the Public Guarantee

Realization of the scale of the government's guarantees to the major banks led to a public outcry. Following the crisis, European policymakers set up a recovery and resolution framework and a European authority to respond to bank failures. Policymakers also sought to reduce the public guarantee by making professional investors in banks bear more of the financial risk and having banks contribute to the deposit guarantee scheme in advance.

The main way in which professional investors can contribute financially in a crisis is through the 'bail-in'. If a bank gets into difficulty, its shareholders, bondholders and other creditors (if they are not covered by the deposit guarantee system) must meet the costs. It is hoped that this will reduce the public costs of bailing out failing banks and lead to less risky bank behaviour. Laudable though this measure is, we should not have overly high expectations. Particularly in the event of a systemic crisis, a bail-in can reinforce panic and hence exacerbate the crisis.[64] In such cases, the government must stand ready to intervene and offer guarantees.

Changes have also been made to the deposit guarantee scheme. Although it is primarily a safety net between banks, it is publicly enforced and the government is required to intervene in emergencies. During the crisis, European countries increased the guaranteed amount to €100,000. Whereas banks previously had to contribute when another bank collapsed, in the Netherlands a fund was created in 2015 requiring pre-financing by banks. By 2024 this fund will amount to 0.8% of all guaranteed deposits, with the bank's mandatory contribution largely depending on its risk profile.[65] This fund, however, is insufficient to repay the guaranteed deposits should one of the large Dutch banks collapse; in this case the government would have to step in. The relevance of the deposit guarantee system is thus questionable, in any event for the large banks. If a systemic bank is on the brink of collapse, the deposit guarantee system would not be called upon; rather, a solution would be sought for the entire bank instead.

7.2.1.3 Better Representation of Public Interests in the Banking Sector

The clearer separation is one way to achieve a healthier balance between public and private interests. Another is to ensure the better representation of public interests in the banking sector.

[63] Ministry of Finance (2014)

[64] Turner (2015: 173)

[65] DNB (2015a)

7.2.1.4 Greater Awareness of Public Duty

Measures have been implemented since the crisis to better represent public interests within banks. Employees in the financial sector must now swear an oath. This was first inserted into the Dutch Banking Code, which banks implement on a 'comply-or-explain principle'.[66] The code was later incorporated into the Financial Supervision Act and thus extended to the entire financial sector (although reference is still made to the 'banker's oath'). The oath must now be sworn by all executive and supervisory board members, customer-facing staff and employees able to influence the institution's operations. In the oath, the person promises to act honestly, to consider the interests of all stakeholders when taking decisions, and to keep the interests of the customer central. Breaches lead to disciplinary consequences.

Further rules of conduct have been added to the banker's oath. The banking sector now pledges to work in the interests of society and to consider the interests of all stakeholders. Individual banks have also sought ways to ensure that the interests of different stakeholders are protected (see Box 7.5).

Box 7.5 Balance Between Different Stakeholders
De Volksbank (formerly SNS Bank, nationalized in 2013) has an internal agreement stating that decisions must consider the interests not only of shareholders but those of customers, employees and society at large. Solutions must be sought that balance these interests. For example, De Volksbank now waits longer before engaging bailiffs and debt collection agencies in cases of default. The customer is first approached by the bank itself. A bailiff is only used if the debtor is able but unwilling to pay.[67]

Rules for remuneration have been introduced to counter excessive pay and perverse incentives. That the bonuses paid to bankers in good times could not be clawed back when governments had to incur the bail out costs were perceived by many people to be grossly unfair. Critics also claimed bonuses reward misconduct, namely pursuing short-term profit at the expense of long-term stability.[68] Recent European rules limit bonuses for bank executives to 100% of their annual salary, while unjustified bonuses can be reclaimed. The Netherlands now has stricter rules for *all* financial employees, capping their bonuses at 20% of their annual salary.

While clear steps have been taken, cultural changes do not happen overnight; these measures must prove themselves over the longer term. A crucial question is whether these initiatives are enough to counter the forces within banks that lead to

[66] NVB (2009)

[67] De Volksbank (2017)

[68] E.g. De Wit Committee I (2010)

their purely commercial focus.[69] One may legitimately ask whether organizational changes within banks are required.

7.2.1.5 Position of the Citizen

Other efforts to change bank behaviour have focused on providing greater counterweight to powerful commercial interests in the financial sector. The crisis showed that banks had previously encountered little resistance to their activities, in large part due to the massive informational advantages they enjoyed over their customers, shareholders and financiers.

Consumers were in particularly weak positions.[70] Although pre-crisis policies required financial institutions to offer sufficient and factually accurate information, this often led to information *overload* where customers could no longer see the forest for the trees.[71] Information alone is insufficient; behavioural research shows that consumers, contrary to the assumptions of rational choice theory, sometimes take excessive risks.[72]

Since the crisis, policies have sought to strengthen the position of consumers. Since 2014, banks have a statutory duty of care towards customers.[73] The Netherlands Authority for Financial Markets has the power to ensure that customer interests are sufficiently heeded when financial institutions develop new, potentially risky products. The position of consumers has also been strengthened by the creation of a complaints office, while the government has strengthened its commitment to mandatory financial information. The Money Wise Platform (*Wijzer in Geldzaken*), established in 2013, seeks to encourage responsible financial behaviour through better information. A similar initiative, the National Financing Guide (*Nationale Financieringswijzer*), addresses businesses.[74]

Other factors have weakened the position of consumers. Standard products have not been developed to give consumers greater certainty about the suitability of financial products. The process of switching banks also remains complex, rendering the exit option less practical for account holders (see Box 7.6).

---

[69] See e.g. Luyendijk (2015) on the situation in the UK

[70] Advisory Committee on the Future of Banks (2009)

[71] ‘t Hart and Du Perron (2006)

[72] Tiemeijer et al. (2009); WRR (2014)

[73] This duty of care had already existed for a long time in case law (De Vré 2014).

[74] WRR (2016: 199–200)

Box 7.6 Exit Option for Account Holders

Europe uses an account number system, the *International Bank Account Number* (IBAN), to simplify international transfers. The disadvantage of this system is that account numbers are linked directly to banks, rendering number portability impossible. If account holders wish to change banks, they are issued a new account number. This is an obstacle even if a switching scheme is in place.

Discussions have been under way for many years, including in the Dutch Lower House, on ways to introduce number portability into the IBAN system. DNB has concluded it will be difficult, requiring technical adjustments at both the national and European levels. "It appears technically possible to allow switching in the current infrastructure while retaining the NL IBAN. However, in view of the expected complexity of the introduction in terms of technology, operations and processes, and the consequences for banks and processors, including outside the Netherlands, it is not recommended".[75] But this has not silenced the discussion. A motion was adopted in parliament on 4 April 2018 to embed number portability in the Banking Act. Minister Hoekstra has promised to study other options (Handelingen II, 2017/18, 69, item 10, p. 37).

One possibility is to use aliases in the payment system. The National Forum on the Payment System recently stated: "To give a real boost to bank account switching, a new type of alias is required: a standardized, self-checking number that preferably belongs to consumers and businesses and can be used throughout the euro area [. . .]. Given the need for a solution at the European level, the MOB will share these findings with the European Commission as input for the cost benefit analysis for European number portability that the Commission will institute in 2019".[76]

A better exit option may strengthen the position of consumers vis-à-vis banks, but a genuine dialogue between consumers and financial institutions would require consumers to be involved in other ways. Here there is an interesting parallel with the position of citizens in the healthcare system (see Box 7.7).

Box 7.7 Position of Citizens in the Healthcare System

Like the financial system, healthcare in the Netherlands is a mixed public-private system. The position of the citizen is guaranteed in a number of ways, vis-à-vis both care institutions and insurance companies. Some care institutions are required to establish client advisory boards. Health insurers are

(continued)

[75]DNB (2016b: 29)

[76]DNB (2018b)

Box 7.7 (continued)
required to guarantee in their articles of association that they give policyholders reasonable influence over company policies (Article 28 (1) (b) of the Healthcare Insurance Act).

This influence was deemed insufficient. Two motions were adopted in the Lower House in 2014 requiring policyholders to be given more influence over health insurers.[77] The Council for Public Health and Healthcare (2014) recommended giving citizens greater say to improve the legitimacy of the system. The 2017 coalition agreement stated: "legal provisions will be adopted giving policyholders, patients and clients a greater say on the policy of their health insurer and care provider."

There are currently two bills pending. The new Care Institutions Client Participation Act (2018) mandates the establishment of a client advisory board in all care institutions with more than 10 care providers (this obligation previously applied only to publicly financed care institutions). Whereas the previous law contained the right of consultation in decisions affecting clients, the new act contains the right to consent to these decisions.[78]

A further bill has been tabled to strengthen the position of policyholders vis-à-vis health insurance companies (Act on Influence of Policyholders under the Healthcare Insurance Act). The government believes the opinions and wishes of policyholders must carry more weight in the health insurer's decision-making.[79] Minimum requirements must be drawn up, giving individual policyholders a say and guaranteeing their permanent advisory representation. This can take the form of a members' council, but the insurer can also use alternative means.

People must deal with the financial sector not only as consumers but also as citizens. Here, the voice of citizens is interpreted in the first place by parliament. Financial regulation has received much more attention since the crisis, with elected representatives being much more engaged with financial laws and regulations. A meaningful representation of the public voice in the financial sector also requires public organizations to be more informed about societal wishes, a requirement the United Kingdom is seeking to meet in an innovative way (see Box 7.8). Finally, there is greater recognition of the importance of 'watchdogs'. An example is Finance Watch, an NGO operating as a counter-lobbying organization, established following the crisis.

[77]Kamerstukken II, 2013–2014, 33,362, no. 35; Kamerstukken I, 2013/14, 33,362, no. N

[78]Kamerstukken II, 2017–2018, 34,858, no. 3

[79]Kamerstukken II, 2017–2018, 34,971, no. 3

Box 7.8 Involving Citizens in Financial Regulation
According to Andrew Haldane, Chief Economist at the Bank of England (BoE), central banks have a twin deficit problem: citizens have insufficient understanding of economics and there is a lack of public trust. To address both of these deficits, the BoE announced in March 2018 that it was setting up regional citizen panels. According to Haldane, the aim is to initiate a structured and systematic dialogue between the BoE and citizens on the economy, the financial system and monetary policy. The aim is not only to ensure that citizens are better informed, but to learn from them.[80] Actively informing and consulting citizens is part of a broader approach to involve them more in the Bank of England's policy. This includes a layered communications strategy that involves communicating in a language free of financial jargon, a national education programme and regional tours.

7.2.2 *Interim Conclusion*

The Dutch government ultimately decided not to separate the activities of commercial universal banks. Nor has such a measure been implemented at the European level, although individual countries (including the UK) have advanced a number of initiatives. Governments have taken steps to prepare themselves for the next banking crisis. Key among these are bail-in measures to pass on the costs of a bail-out to the bank's financiers. It nevertheless remains unclear how these measures will operate during a major crisis.

That universal banks have numerous public utility functions implies that they are semi-public institutions. Banks have been more aware of this since the crisis, evidenced by initiatives such as the Banking Code and the banker's oath. Whether such initiatives within the sector's sphere of influence will lead to actual change remains uncertain, raising the question of whether greater attention should be devoted both to the organization of banking and how to increase the influence of certain stakeholders. When considering the balance between public and private interests, we cannot forget the need for greater diversity and competition in banking.

7.3 Conclusion

Two important challenges must be addressed to arrive at a more stable, fairer and legitimate financial monetary system: the more balanced growth of money and debt and a better balance between public and private interests. This chapter has

[80]Haldane 2018: 3

considered the extent to which such steps have been taken in the current system and what further possibilities exist, partly inspired by plans for a sovereign money system.

Although measures have been taken to achieve a more balanced growth of money and debt, they have not been robust enough to reduce the current mountain of debt. This means further attention is required for incentives to borrow and lend, policy coherence and the structure of the financial sector.

Regarding the balance between public and private interests, we first considered the possibilities of separating the financial system's public and private functions. Attempts to achieve a clear boundary have foundered for various reasons. Since the major universal banks have public utility functions, they have become *de facto* semi-public institutions. It is thus particularly important to assess how public interests are safeguarded in these institutions. The organizational structure of banks can also be assessed in this light.

Bibliography

Admati, A. R., & Hellwig, M. (2013). *The bankers' new clothes: What's wrong with banking and what to do about it*. Princeton: Princeton University Press.

Admati, A., Allen, F., Brealey, R., et al. (2010, November 9). Healthy banking system is the goal, not profitable banks. *Financial Times*.

Adviescommissie Toekomst Banken. (2009). *Naar herstel van vertrouwen*. Amsterdam: Dutch Banking Association.

Bardearr, J., & Kumhof, M. (2016). The macroeconomics of central bank issued digital currencies. Available at: bankofengland.co.uk.

Benink, H. (2018, October). Banken hebben nog steeds onvoldoende buffers. *ESB, 103*(4766S), 11.

BIS. (2015). *85th annual report*. Basel: Bank for International Settlements.

BIS. (2018). *Central bank digital currencies*. Basel: BIS.

Bordo, M. D., & Levin, A. T. (2017). *Central bank digital currency and the future of monetary policy* (NBER Working Papers).

Borio, C. (2010). *Implementing a macroprudential framework: Blending boldness and realism*. Basel: Bank for International Settlements.

Broadbent, B. (2016, March 2) *Central banks and digital currencies*. Speech at London School of Economics.

Carmassi, J., & Micossi, S. (2012). *Time to set banking regulation right*. Brussels: Centre for Economic Policy Research.

Caruana, J. (2016, November 26). *Monetary policy for financial stability, Keynote speech by Jaime Caruana, General Manager, Bank for International Settlements*. In 52nd SEACEN governors' conference, Naypyidaw, Myanmar.

Cavelaars, P., de Haan, J., Hilbers, P., & Stellinga, B. (2013). Uitdagingen voor financieel toezicht na de crisis. In P. Welp et al. (Eds.), *De staat van toezicht. Sector- en themastudies* (WRR investigations no. 27). Amsterdam: AUP.

Committee on the Global Financial System. (2018). *Structural changes in banking after the crisis* (CGFS Paper 60).

Constancio, V. (2015, February 13). *Financial stability risks, monetary policy and the need for macro-prudential policy*. Speech by Vítor Constâncio, Vice-President of the ECB, Warwick Economics Summit.

Danielsson, J., Shin, H. S., & Zigrand, J. -P. (2012). *Endogenous and systemic risk* (NBER chapters, no. 12054).
Danmarks Nationalbank. (2017). *Central bank digital currency in Denmark?* (Analysis no 28).
de Larosière, J. (2009). *The high-level group on financial supervision in the EU, Report*. Brussels: European Commission.
De Volksbank. (2017). *Jaarverslag Volksbank NV*. Utrecht: de Volksbank.
de Vré, H. (2014). De bijzondere zorgplicht van financiële dienstverleners onder toezicht. In *Wetenschappelijke Bijdragen, Bundel ter gelegenheid van het 35-jarig bestaan van het wetenschappelijk bureau van de Hoge Raad der Nederlanden*. The Hague: Boom Juridische uitgevers.
De Wit Committee. (2010). *Parlementair onderzoek financieel stelsel. Rapport*, Kamerstukken II, 2009–2010, 31980, no. 4.
De Wit Committee II. (2012). *Parlementaire enquête financieel stelsel. Eindrapport*, Kamerstukken II, 2011–2012, 31980, no. 61.
DNB. (2015a). *Nederlands depositogarantiestelsel wordt meer risicogebaseerd*. Available at: https://www.dnb.nl/nieuws/nieuwsoverzicht-en-archief/persberichten-2015/dnb334375.jsp.
DNB. (2015b). *Visie op de structuur van de Nederlandse bankensector – Stabiliteit en efficiëntie door diversiteit en concurrentie*. Amsterdam: De Nederlandsche Bank.
DNB. (2016a). *De financiële stabiliteitstaak van DNB*. Amsterdam: De Nederlandsche Bank.
DNB. (2016b). *Technische mogelijkheden IBAN-portabiliteit in Nederland*. Amsterdam: De Nederlandsche Bank.
DNB. (2017). *Overzicht Financiële Stabiliteit – Voorjaar 2017*. Amsterdam: De Nederlandsche Bank.
DNB. (2018a). *DNB en resolutie*. Available at: www.dnb.nl
DNB. (2018b). *Resultaten van de MOB-vergadering 16 mei*. Available at: www.dnb.nl
DNB. (2019). *Banking package main changes of CRD/CRR/BRRD/SRMR review*. Amsterdam: DNB.
ECB Task Force on Systemic Liquidity. (2018, October). *Systemic liquidity concept, measurement and macroprudential instruments* (Occasional Paper Series, No. 214).
Eichengreen, B., El-Erian, M., Fraga, A., et al. (2011). *Rethinking central banking*. Ontario: Committee on International Economic Policy and Reform.
ESRB. (2014). *Recommendation of the European systemic risk board of 18 June 2014 on guidance for setting countercyclical buffer rates*. Available at: www.esrb.europa.eu
ESRB. (2016). *Confidential transmission of ESRB Warning on medium-term vulnerabilities in the residential real estate sector of the Netherlands*. Available at: www.esrb.europa.eu
European Commission. (2012). *Taxation: The European Commission requests Belgium to amend its rules on the notional interest deduction*. Brussels: European Commission.
European Commission. (2014). *Economic review of the financial regulation agenda*. Brussels: European Commission.
European Court of Justice. (2013, July 4). C-350/11 (*Argenta Spaarbank NV vs Belgische Staat*).
Fahr, S., & Fell, J. (2017). Macroprudential policy – Closing the financial stability gap. *Journal of Financial Regulation and Compliance, 25*(4), 334–359.
Federal Public Service Finance. (2018). *Notionele interestaftrek: uniek en innoverend belastingvoordeel in België*. Available at: https://financien.belgium.be/nl/ondernemingen/internationaal/buitenlandse_investeerders/Notionele_interestaftrek/#q1
Financial Stability Committee. (2015). *Aanbeveling van het Financieel Stabiliteitscomité over de LTV-limiet na 2018*. Amsterdam: Financial Stability Committee.
Finansinspektionen. (2018). *Countercyclical buffer rate*. Available at: www.fi.se
Fung, B. S. C., & Halaburda, H. (2016). *Central bank digital currencies: A framework for assessing why and how* (Bank of Canada staff discussion paper 2016–22). Available at: bankofcanada.ca
Haldane, A. G. (2018). *Climbing the public engagement ladder*. Speech 6 March, Royal Society for the encouragement of Arts, Manufactures and Commerce (RSA).

Haldane, A. G., Brennan, S., & Madouros, V. (2010). What is the contribution of the financial sector: Miracle or mirage? In *The Future of Finance: The LSE Report*. London School of Economics and Political Science.

Hart, 't, & du Perron, C. E. (2006). *De geïnformeerde consument*. Deventer: Kluwer.

Hebous, S., & Ruf, M. (2017). Evaluating the effects of ACE systems on multinational debt financing and investment. *Journal of Public Economics, Elsevier, 156*(C), 131–149.

IMF. (2017). *Netherlands financial system stability assessment* (Country Report No. 17/79). Washington, DC: International Monetary Fund.

IMF-FSB-BIS. (2016). *Elements of effective macroprudential policies*. Available at: www.imf.org/external/np/g20/pdf/2016/083116.pdf

Kamerstukken (Parliamentary Papers) I, 2013/14, 33362, no. N.

Kamerstukken (Parliamentary Papers) II, 2013–2014, 33362, no. 35.

Kamerstukken (Parliamentary Papers) II, 2017–2018, 34858, no. 3.

Kamerstukken (Parliamentary Papers) II, 2017–2018, 34971, no. 3.

Kumhof, M., & Noone, C. (2018). *Central bank digital currencies — design principles and balance sheet implications* (Bank of England Staff Working Paper 725).

Liikanen Report. (2012). *High-level expert group on reforming the structure of the EU banking sector*. Brussels: European Commission.

Luyendijk, J. (2015). *Dit kan niet waar zijn: Onder bankiers*.

Mersch, Y. (2017). *Digital Base Money: An assessment from the ECB's perspective*. Available at: https://www.ecb.europa.eu/press/key/date/2017/html/sp170116.en.html

Ministry of Finance. (2010). *Kabinetsreactie eindrapport Tijdelijke commissie onderzoek financieel stelsel (Commissie-De Wit)*, Kamerstukken II, 2010–2011, 31980, no. 16.

Ministry of Finance. (2014). *Update on recommendations of De Wit Committee, Annex II to Answers to written questions on Government view of the Dutch banking sector*, Kamerstukken II, 2013–2014, 32013, no. 50.

Ministry of Finance. (2016). *Kamerbrief over Hervormingen en resultaten in de Nederlandse financiële sector*, Kamerstukken II *2015–2016*, 32013, no. 132.

Ministry of Finance. (2018). *Aankondiging afschaffing fiscale aftrek op vergoeding aanvullend tier 1-kapitaalinstrumenten*, Kamerstukken II, 2017–2018, 32013, no. 195.

NVB. (2009). Code Banken, Amsterdam: NVB.

Ordoñez, M. F. (2018, February 6). The future of banking. Secure money and deregulation of the financial system, Speech at the Areces Foundation.

Peekel, M., & Veluwenkamp, J. W. (1984). *Het girale betalingsverkeer in Nederland*. Amsterdam: Nederlands Instituut voor het Bank- en Effectenbedrijf.

Reid, J., Nicol, G., Burns, N., & Chanda, S. (2017). *Long-term asset return study. The next financial crisis*. London: Deutsche Bank.

Ryan-Collins, J. (2015). *Is monetary financing inflationary? A case study of the Canadian economy, 1935–75* (Levy Institute Working Paper, No. 84).

Saravelos, G., Brehon, D., & Winkler, R. (2016, April 15). *Helicopters 101: Your guide to monetary financing* (Deutsche Bank Special Report).

Schepens, G. (2016). Taxes and bank capital structure. *Journal of Financial Economics, 120*(3), 585–600.

Skingsley, C. (2016, November). Should the Riksbank issue e-krona?, Speech.

Stellinga, B. (2018). *The financial valuation crisis. The inherent limits to taming unstable markets (PhD-manuscript)*. Amsterdam: University of Amsterdam.

Stellinga, B. (2019). Why performativity limits credit rating reform. *Finance and Society, 5*(1), 20–41.

Stellinga, B. (2020). The open-endedness of macroprudential policy. Endogenous risks as an obstacle to countercyclical macroprudential policy. *Business and Politics, 22*(1), 224–251.

Stellinga, B. (2021). The rise and stall of EU macro-prudential policy. An empirical analysis of policy conflicts over financial stability, market integration, and national discretion. *JCMS: Journal of Common Market Studies*. https://doi.org/10.1111/jcms.13195

Stellinga, B., & Mügge, D. (2017). The regulator's conundrum. How market reflexivity limits fundamental financial reform. *Review of International Political Economy, 24*(3), 393–423.

Sveriges Riksbank. (2017, September). *The Riksbank's e-krona project, report 1.*

The Economist. (2017). *American banks have recovered well; many European ones much less so.* London: The Economist.

Tiemeijer, W. L., Thomas, C. A., & Prast, H. M. (Eds.). (2009). *De menselijke beslisser: over de psychologie van keuze en gedrag* (WRR Investigation). Amsterdam: Amsterdam University Press.

Turner, A. (2015). *Between debt and the devil – Money, credit, and fixing global finance.* Princeton: Princeton University Press.

van Dijk, M., & Voogt, B. (2017, June 6). *Actualisatie economische effecten van een verdere verlaging van de LTV-limiet* (CPB Background Document to the Financial Markets Risk Report 2017).

Veldhuizen, S., Groot, S., & Van Dijk, M. (2015). *De economische effecten van een verdere verlaging van de LTV-limiet.* The Hague: CPB Netherlands Bureau for Economic Policy Analysis.

Vickers report. (2011, September). *Independent commission on banking: Final Report Recommendations.*

Wijffels Committee. (2013). *Commissie-Structuur Nederlandse Banken: Naar een dienstbaar en stabiel bankwezen.*

Wolf, M. (2017, September 21). Banking remains far too undercapitalised for comfort. *Financial Times.* Available at: www.ft.com/content/9dd43a1a-9d49-11e7-8cd4-932067fbf946

WRR. (2000). *Het borgen van publiek belang*, WRR report nr. 56. Den Haag: Sdu Uitgevers.

WRR. (2012). *Publieke zaken in de marktsamenleving*, WRR report nr. 87. Amsterdam: Amsterdam University Press.

WRR. (2013). *Toezien op publieke belangen. Naar een verruimd perspectief op rijkstoezicht*, WRR report nr. 89. Amsterdam: Amsterdam University Press.

WRR. (2014). *Met kennis van gedrag beleid maken*, WRR report nr. 92. Amsterdam: Amsterdam University Press.

WRR. (2016). *Samenleving en financiële sector in evenwicht*, WRR report nr. 96. Den Haag: Sdu Uitgevers.

8

Summary and Reflections

This book has discussed the necessity and desirability of reform of the Dutch financial monetary system. It is the result of a widely supported parliamentary motion calling on the government to request the Netherlands Scientific Council for Government Policy (WRR) to investigate the monetary system and the advantages and disadvantages of alternative monetary systems. The parliamentary debate was the result of a play by the theatre group *De Verleiders* (The Seducers) and a subsequent citizens' initiative *Ons Geld* calling for money creation to be placed exclusively in public hands.

The Netherlands is far from the only country to have witnessed public debate over sovereign money in the wake of the last financial crisis. Commentators such as Martin Wolf (2014), the well-known Financial Times columnist, have called for similar reforms. Economists from the IMF and the Bank of England are investigating alternatives and the Icelandic parliament has drawn up a specific proposal. In Switzerland a referendum was held on a similar proposal in June 2018 in which 24% of the votes cast were in favour of the introduction of a 'Vollgeld' system. The recent calls for an alternative system are hardly new; they are variations of the Chicago Plan developed in the 1930s by leading economists in the United States and subsequently endorsed by luminaries such as Milton Friedman and James Tobin. The recent calls for a sovereign money system can also be seen as a variant of the ban on commercial banks issuing their own banknotes, as happened in the US, the UK and Switzerland in the nineteenth century. This time, the ban would concern deposit money creation by commercial banks.

The citizens' initiative *Ons Geld* (Our Money) has triggered a fundamental debate in the Netherlands on the role of money and debt. While its focus on 'money creation' may suggest that *Ons Geld* is primarily concerned about monetary policy and the payment system, this is far from the case. Money in our current system is inextricably linked to debt as the creation of deposit money goes hand in hand with the issuing of loans. Money in our current system is also inextricably linked to commercial banks as the bulk of our money supply consists of deposit money, which is a debt owed by the bank to the account holder. This means that in our current system, money cannot be viewed in isolation from debt and the role of banks. Therefore, changing how money is created would amount to a fundamental reorganization of the entire system. Advocates of sovereign money see it not only as a way to ensure safe deposit money, but also to address other problems. These include financial crises, excessive private and public debt, housing bubbles, inflation, the loss of sovereignty and democratic deficits.[1]

The functioning of the financial monetary system has far-reaching effects on economy and society. Understanding how it works is essential and *Ons Geld* has made an important contribution to the discussion. In its 2016 study *Finance and Society: Restoring the Balance*, the WRR drew up recommendations for a more harmonious and productive relationship between the financial sector and society.[2] In this present study, we have delved further into detail and evaluated our current system in light of the goals of public utility, stability, fairness and legitimacy. Both of our studies highlight the same core problems: the unbalanced growth of debt and the imbalance between public and private interests. The recommendations in this report draw on and complement those in *Finance and Society: Restoring the Balance*.

In this final chapter we discuss the book's key findings. We first recap the operations of our current system and the problems it presents. We then discuss how the alternative of sovereign money would work and whether switching systems would be desirable. Finally, we consider what steps can be taken to address the major problems posed by the current system.

8.1 How Does Money Creation Work?

Money is the generally accepted means of making payments and repaying debt, although the form it takes differs between countries and over time. Nowadays there are two generally recognized forms of money: (1) banknotes and coins (cash) issued by public bodies, and (2) bank deposits, which are debts owed by the bank to account holders. Bank deposits make up around 93% of the current money supply.[3]

New deposit money is created by commercial banks when they grant loans. When Peter borrows €1000 from the bank, €1000 is credited to his bank account.[4] This is the point at which new money is created. It becomes a debt owed by the bank to the

[1]Ons Geld website: https://onsgeld.nu/geldsysteem/problemen

[2]This study is available in Dutch only; an English summary is available on the website www.wrr.nl/en

[3]This is based on M2 (cash, bank deposits and savings deposits with a maturity of up to two years or a notice period of up to three months).

[4]This new money then enters circulation. If it is used to make payments, it is transferred to other bank accounts.

borrower, who simultaneously has a debt of €1000 to the bank. Conversely, money is destroyed when the loan is repaid.

Banks are therefore not merely 'intermediaries' between savings and loans, but crucial participants in the process of money and debt creation. This, however, does not mean that banks can create money without limit. The main driver of money creation is lending, so there must be demand for loans. In addition, the granting of loans can pose risks for the bank's balance sheet. This constraint on money creation can be reinforced by regulations, for example capital requirements. Finally, monetary policy – particularly interest rates set by the central bank – can constrain money creation. But although these factors influence the creation of money, they do not impose any *absolute* limits.

Money creation cannot be understood apart from the dominant role of deposit money, which has given commercial banks a very prominent position in our current financial monetary system. We must also bear in mind that our current system was not designed according to a particular blueprint, but evolved over time as a response to social, technological, political and economic developments. While this means that our current system is not set in stone, it also implies that no new system designed on a drawing board can be implemented exactly according to the plan.

8.2 The Goals of the Financial Monetary System

A financial monetary system must be stable, contribute to our economy, it must be fair, and enjoy public legitimacy. Proponents of an alternative system of money creation rightly draw attention to a number of major deficiencies in these areas. While we do not claim that these problems are entirely due to the current system of money creation, they are related to the design of payments, finance and savings and the role banks play in these areas.

Economic Contribution

A well-functioning financial sector with efficient systems for payments and finance is crucial for economic development. Given the role of banks in maintaining the infrastructure, the main concern is that a crisis will disrupt the payment system, as threatened to happen in the crisis of 2008. Although growth is enabled by the availability of finance, excessive lending can harm economic development. Public and private debt in many European countries is at an all-time high. The pro-cyclical volatility of lending, with growth in good periods followed by contraction in downturns, is detrimental to balanced economic development. As well as the *volume* of credit, there are problems with its *allocation*. Especially mortgages and interbank loans have grown sharply, casting doubt on whether the current nature and volume of lending is optimally contributing to the real economy. A reduction of the debt mountain is desirable but not easy to achieve. To avoid major macroeconomic shocks, it can only take place in small steps.

Stability

Crises in the financial sector have far-reaching consequences for society. Although individual institutions in distress can have cascading effects, what really matters is the stability of the system as a whole. Following several decades of stability in the wake of the Second World War, deregulation and growing levels of debt have fuelled periodic crises since the 1980s. Since the latest crisis, a great deal of academic attention has focused on the relationship between financial crises and the growth of credit. Not only are crises preceded by large build-ups of especially private debt; when debt is high, it also takes longer for the economy to recover. Alongside excessive credit, the uniformity, scale and (international) interdependence of financial institutions fuel systemic instability.

Fairness

Fairness in the distribution of benefits, costs and risks is necessary for the public to support the financial system. The widespread dissatisfaction that followed the last crisis can be traced to the idea that banks reaped the rewards and the public bore the costs. Although the reality is not so black and white, banks received a disproportionate share of the benefits during the preceding boom, whereas the public costs of the crisis were astronomical. Even outside crisis periods, banks benefit from government support, for example the implicit public guarantee for systemic banks. A large financial sector with a mountain of debt has major distributional consequences, both during the build-up to a crisis and in its aftermath.

Legitimacy

The legitimacy of any financial system depends on its ability to meet society's justified expectations. There are a number of problems in this area. Banks are private institutions motivated by profit, but they also have public functions. Their mixed public-private character makes it unclear what we can expect from them. The limited scope for meaningful democratic influence, the lack of appropriate accountability mechanisms, and the banking sector's influence on policy all dent the legitimacy of our current system. Citizens have little direct influence on a bank's operations as both 'voice' and 'exit' possibilities are limited.[5]

8.3 Is the Sovereign Money System a Solution?

All of these deficiencies have prompted calls for a fundamentally different system – most prominently for a sovereign money system where money would, either directly or indirectly, be entirely 'public'. New money creation would be the preserve of the central bank, implying a strict separation of the payment and financing parts of the system. Although the proposals for a sovereign money system share these

[5]For example, voice could be more influential in the operation of cooperative banks.

Table 8.1 The core and variations of the sovereign money system

	Core of the sovereign money system	Variations of the sovereign money system
Money	All money is directly or indirectly public.	Money is placed directly in an account at the central bank or stored in a payment bank that backs it 100% with central bank reserves.
Money creation	Money cannot be created by commercial banks, only by the central bank.	Newly created money can be used for: (1) government spending, (2) paying down government debt, (3) direct transfers to citizens (helicopter money), (4) lending, directly or indirectly through financing institutions.
Lending	Institutions that grant credit (financing institutions) are clearly separated from payment banks (or the central bank) at which the money is held. Financing institutions cannot create new money with which to grant loans; they must raise the money first.	The proposals differ in: (1) how far the maturity of an institution's loans and debts can diverge, (2) how the institution finances itself: through fixed-value deposits or shares whose value rise and fall with the institution's performance (equity – comparable to shares in an investment fund).

underlying principles, they differ in their details and plans for implementation (see the overview in Table 8.1).

In a sovereign money system, money creation and lending are no longer inextricably linked. Money is 100% public and payment accounts can be opened directly at the central bank or indirectly at a payment bank that holds only central bank money (or keeps it entirely separate from its other activities, shielding it from risks). The risky financial part of the system is thus separated from the infrastructure for payments. The financing institutions have to raise money before they can extend credit. When money is made available to a financing institution, investors take risks in exchange for the possibility of higher returns. Proposals for an alternative system differ on how financing is organized and whether there is a government role in lending and its regulation.

Would a sovereign money system effectively address the concerns about the current system's performance on economic contribution, stability, fairness and legitimacy? Caution is required when answering this question. Although we can draw parallels from history – for example the rise and fall of the Amsterdamse Wisselbank – a sovereign money system has never operated in practice. We must therefore rely on extrapolations of assumed economic relationships and lessons from the past. Assessments about the advantages and disadvantages of an alternative system are therefore based on many assumptions.

It is impossible to state at the outset whether the alternative system would be better than what we have now. We can nevertheless identify a number of assumptions that we need to make if the alternative system as a whole is to function better. These include:

- the central bank is able to properly manage the growth of the money supply, while the government will at all times remain committed to balanced money creation;
- deposits held with financing institutions will not (over time) serve as money so that they become money-creating institutions and start to resemble today's banks;
- financing institutions no longer need to be bailed out by the government because they can fail without disrupting the economy, thereby eliminating the problem of perverse incentives and 'private profits, public costs';
- sufficient and appropriate financing will be available in the new system through lending by the financing institutions or through market-based instruments such as bonds and equity;
- institutions (central banks, payment banks, financing institutions) will be able to generate trust among citizens, businesses and investors necessary for the system to function properly;
- the system can operate in an international context with strong financial interdependencies without all countries switching to the sovereign money system.

There is also the issue of feasibility. Given the importance of the financial system to the functioning of society, we cannot underestimate the risks of an overhaul of the system. There is a real possibility that such a change has unintended negative consequences; a crisis during the transition cannot be ruled out. It is also unclear how international interdependencies would affect the transition. The Netherlands is part of EMU; for this reason alone, the change has to take place at the European level unless the Netherlands leaves the euro. Uncertain effects combined with the risks of transition mean the switch to a sovereign money system would amount to an unprecedented experiment with the backbone of the economy. For these reasons, we do not recommend a switch to a sovereign money system.

We nevertheless argue that proposals for such an alternative system should be taken seriously. First, because they allow us to better appreciate the advantages and limitations of our current system. The advocates of sovereign money rightly point to fundamental problems in our current set-up. Second, we believe that their plans can inspire reforms within the current system.

8.4 Two Major Challenges for the Current System

Although various reforms have been introduced since the crisis, actual changes to our financial monetary system have been modest. More than 10 years after the crisis, the commitment to reform among politicians and policymakers has given way to reform fatigue. But the facts don't justify the complacency. To realize a stable financial system that can fulfil its public utility functions, fairly distribute benefits, costs and risks, and enjoy public legitimacy, we need to address two major challenges: achieving more balanced growth of money and credit, and improving the balance between private and public interests.

We need to do this in an uncertain environment; in many ways we are in uncharted territory. Central banks have been pursuing 'experimental' policies for almost a decade without fully understanding the consequences. Private debt remains at historic highs while financial innovation and technological developments have far-reaching effects for the operation of money, debt and financial institutions. While new technologies offer opportunities for innovation and improvement in financial services, they come with both familiar and new risks (such as systemic risks resulting from cyber attacks) that threaten the public interest and the stability of the financial system. Precisely at this time of uncertainty, fast-moving developments and lack of clear-cut solutions, we can take inspiration from the advocates of sovereign money.

8.4.1 Balanced Growth of Money and Debt

The balanced and controlled growth of money and debt is necessary for stability and economic development. Both too little and too much flexibility in credit and debt have far-reaching negative consequences. As we saw in Chap. 3, striking the right balance between flexibility and rigidity in a world of financial innovation and uncertainty is a perennial challenge for policy-makers.

Over the past decades the balance has swung towards flexibility. There are now few constraints on lending and private (deposit) money creation, while many other factors including tax incentives and housing market policy encourage lending. The growing importance of deposit money, mainly held on the balance sheets of a few major Dutch banks, means these banks are much less constrained in their lending. Indebtedness is at historic highs despite measures taken since the crisis.

Why is this a problem? Research published since the crisis suggests that excessive credit growth leads to instability. Not only are financial crises often preceded by high build-ups of debt; post-crisis recovery takes longer when debt levels are high. Credit growth and economic development go hand in hand up to a certain point; beyond this level, the further growth of credit negatively affects the economy. High debt levels and volatile lending can also lead to the unfair distribution of costs and benefits in society. In an upturn, the financial sector enjoys many of the benefits; in a downturn, it is society that bears the costs, for example in the form of high unemployment.

Although there have been stricter curbs on lending since the crisis, such as the tightening of loan-to-value ratios for mortgages, these curbs are usually indirect and have limited effect. Action to tackle the incentives for credit growth has been limited while the structure of the banking industry has remained fundamentally unaltered. Many of the catalysts of debt growth remain while the level of private debt in the Netherlands is no lower than before the crisis.

The challenge in a crisis is to keep the economy going. During the last crisis, central banks took far-reaching measures including low and even negative interest rates and the large-scale purchase of government and corporate bonds. As these measures remain in force today, it raises the question of what means remain available to cushion the next crisis.[6]

8.4.2 *Balance Between Public and Private Interests*

The financial monetary system fulfils essential functions. It enables us to make payments, finance economic activities, save for retirement and insure ourselves against risks. Financial services are an essential prerequisite for all other economic activities. The payment system in particular plays a key infrastructure role.

Historically, both public and private players had important roles in payments and finance. Fifty years ago, savings and payments for a large share of the Dutch population were facilitated by public financial institutions. There was little lending to consumers and business financing was largely in private hands. Since then, deposit money has eclipsed cash, ordinary people have become consumers of financial services, public institutions and their services have been privatized (Postbank), and large universal banks have emerged. The public functions of the banking system now depend on private operators. The paradox is that an ever-larger part of the banking industry has been operating on a purely commercial basis for the past 50 years, while banking has taken on an ever-greater public role. This creeping transition in the role of commercial banks is reflected neither in legislation nor in economic analysis. Advocates of a sovereign money system rightly draw attention to this transformed landscape.

The fulfilment of public interests largely depends on private operators, particularly systemically important commercial banks. As their operations directly affect society as a whole, they cannot be seen as purely private actors. This means the banking sector must be much more firmly anchored in society.

8.5 Recommendations

We face two major challenges: (1) achieving the balanced growth of money and debt, and (2) restore the balance between public and private interests. Measures taken since the last crisis have not reduced the level of debt while the financial sector remains insufficiently anchored in society. Our recommendations are four-fold:

- Promote diversity in the financial sector
- Curb excessive debt growth
- Be better prepared for the next crisis
- Anchor the banks' public dimension

[6]As this book is a translation of a report published before the COVID-19 crisis, we do not address how central banks have responded to the economic and financial challenges raised by this new crisis.

8.5.1 Promote Diversity in the Financial Sector

A uniform banking landscape leads to herd behaviour and an expansion of the credit cycle. Dependence on systemic banks also makes it more difficult to strike a balance between public and private interests. This is a burning issue in the Netherlands, where concentration in banking has only grown since the crisis. The market share of the three largest banks measured by balance sheet size increased from 71% in 2006 to 75% in 2016 (see Chap. 7). The sector needs greater diversity. There must be genuine alternatives for payments and savings, and challenger banks must be supported.

Alternatives for Payments and Savings

There are currently few options outside of the big commercial banks. While cash is an alternative to deposit money, large cash holdings and payments are unrealistic today. In the past there were more alternatives, with the predecessors of the Postbank (Postcheque- en Girodienst and Rijkspostspaarbank) providing a public variant of deposit money.

Giving people the option to store money at a bank that only holds central bank reserves or is only permitted to carry out relatively secure activities would constitute a significant brake on excessive debt and money creation. It would also be a way to anchor the 'public dimension' of banking.

We recommend to provide a publicly anchored alternative for payments and savings alongside existing facilities. This can be done, for example, by facilitating a payment bank that only holds central bank reserves. Such a bank could be created by the government. The development of central bank digital currency also merits serious consideration.

The alternative could take different forms. It could be a bank engaged only in payments and savings, holding only central bank reserves as assets. The current negative interest rates on central bank reserves would hamper the viability of such a bank, but we are (hopefully) in an exceptional situation. Existing banks can provide payment accounts at low cost due to their other activities; a payment account at a payment bank would probably cost more for the consumer. Another possibility is for the government to establish such a bank.

A more radical change would be to allow citizens to open payment accounts at the central bank. Currently, only banks can have accounts at the central bank, while cash is the only central bank money citizens can hold. Central banks in various countries are studying the possibility of introducing central bank digital currency – a digital counterpart to cash.

The most common objection to providing a safer alternative – whether the private or public payment bank or citizen accounts at the central bank – is that it would make the system as a whole more unstable. The fear is that in a crisis, people will withdraw money *en masse* from commercial banks and place it with the safer bank. These concerns are legitimate. Still, it is unclear whether the risks would significantly increase. Also in our current system major institutional operators, businesses and citizens with substantial assets will quickly withdraw their deposits if they have doubts about the (national) banking system. For small account holders – both in the current system and in the case of a central bank digital currency – a deposit guarantee scheme discourages runs on the bank.

That our current financial system could be destabilized with the creation of a safe haven says more about the flaws of the current system than about the destabilizing effects of a safe haven. After all, Postbank and its predecessors existed for decades without causing such stability problems. Although a bank run can occur more quickly in our electronic age, this is more a difference of degree than in kind. One could just as easily reverse the reasoning: the creation of a secure alternative bank contributes to a more stable system through the disciplining effect on incumbent banks. It will force commercial banks to finance themselves more responsibly, with more equity and long-term bonds, thereby placing a more effective limit on the creation of money and debt.

Reduce the Dominance of Systemic Banks

The current system favours the large established banks and hampers newcomers and smaller banks. Both implicit and explicit government guarantees give systemically important banks funding advantages over smaller institutions. Extensive and complex regulations benefit the large incumbent banks because the costs impede the entry and profitability of (smaller) newcomers. The market power of the major banks also enables them to cross-subsidize their activities, again making it more difficult for newcomers to gain market share.

The Dutch banking sector has not always been so concentrated. Up until the 1980s, it included savings banks, giro services, mortgage banks, agricultural (cooperative) banks and general banks – all serving their own areas, subject to different rules, and differing in their organizational models. Since the 1980s, institutions have grown in size and have become more similar. Greater diversity in the financial sector would contribute to more balanced lending and make society less dependent on indispensable systemic banks. We need a more robust approach to tackle the market power of the major commercial banks and to support potential challengers.

We recommend to increase the diversity of the banking landscape by supporting challengers and making it less attractive for banks to be systemically important. This could be done, for example, by means of differentiated supervision or the imposition of heavier taxes on large banks that create systemic risks.

To diversify the banking landscape, policy needs to support potential challengers (both in and outside of banking proper) to the big incumbent banks. Current laws and regulations are geared towards the systemic banks and are less appropriate for the activities and risks of challengers. We need a differentiated policy framework, for example lighter banking licences for players with limited banking activities.[7] Another possibility is a more lenient supervisory regime for banks that have high (non-risk-weighted) equity buffers and stable funding. Compulsory participation in the deposit guarantee scheme as well as differentiation within this system should address actual risks; steps should be taken to prevent low-risk institutions from absorbing the costs of greater risks incurred elsewhere. The amended Dutch deposit guarantee scheme does not meet this requirement.

The main commercial banks derive considerable market power from their positions. To discourage market dominance, the government could impose significantly higher capital requirements or a higher (direct) tax on systemic risk, which would create incentives for banks to organize themselves differently or to dispose of business units. If this does not produce the desired result, the government could take more drastic measures. Like American competition law, European competition law should allow for the breaking up of banks considered 'too big to fail'.

The European Central Bank is encouraging cross-border mergers as part of the European Banking Union.[8] But seen from the perspective of 'too big to fail', systemic risk, market power and manageable complexity, larger banks than we have now are undesirable. If the aim is to create a European market for bank services, there could be a role for more specialized players. Cross-border mergers between banks would require selling off existing units; financial supervisors and competition authorities would need to be strengthened.

8.5.2 Curb Excessive Debt Growth

Ballooning debt can undermine both the financial sector's economic contribution and its stability. Although the problematic aspects of high indebtedness have received greater attention since the crisis, in the Netherlands total private debt as a percentage of GDP is now higher than before the crisis. We need to tackle the preferential tax treatment of debt and to make macroprudential factors a more explicit and integral part of policy.

Eliminate Incentives for Borrowing

The current tax regime renders borrowing attractive to households, businesses and banks. For Dutch households, the incentive to borrow in the form of mortgage

[7]In addition to the broad banking licence, there are 'A' and 'B'-type opt-in licences. In the A variant, the institution cannot solicit sight deposits from the public (but can do so from business customers). The institution lends on its own account and can access central bank reserves (TARGET2). The B variant is a licence for investment institutions which must raise money from the public. They do not provide credit but invest, and have no access to central bank reserves (TARGET2).

[8]Nouy (2018)

interest deductibility is being gradually reduced. But there has been less progress for companies and banks. Reducing banks' incentive to borrow is especially complex as much of their debt (payment and savings accounts) is linked to their money-creating function and their role in payments. We nevertheless need to combat excessive debt financing among banks and companies.

The preferential tax treatment of debt finance for banks, companies and households should be further reduced. Policy-makers should aim for neutrality between equity and debt finance.

To counter excessive money creation, tax incentives to borrow must be further reduced. This applies to both mortgage interest deductibility for citizens and interest deductibility for corporations. While national policies can address the incentives to borrow, major steps will require European coordination. Equity financing can be made more attractive to achieve the equal tax treatment of debt and equity. This can be done on a tax-neutral basis – there are a number of international examples of this – by allowing equity deductions accompanied by a slight overall rise in the tax rate. Although the interest rate ceiling proposed in the Dutch government coalition agreement discourages equity financing, it does not eliminate the advantages of financing through debt (see Chap. 7).

Stronger Curbs on Debt Growth

The risk of ballooning debt will remain even when the incentives for borrowing are reined in. In the decades following the Second World War, the government kept debt levels in check. But since the 1980s, credit and money growth have no longer been the focal points of financial regulation and monetary policy. Although there has been greater attention to controlling debt under the banner of macroprudential policy since the crisis, the available instruments are inadequate and insufficiently coordinated with other policy areas.

Macroprudential considerations should be given a more prominent place in the policy toolkit. This means both strengthening existing macroprudential policy and better coordination with banking supervision, monetary policy and socioeconomic policy.

While there has been more attention to the danger of credit bubbles since the crisis, the macroprudential policy framework has been interpreted narrowly and implemented mainly within the bank capital adequacy framework. National supervisors can raise capital requirements counter-cyclically and impose stricter requirements on systemically important banks. But these capital requirements are designed to absorb setbacks after the fact, not to counter the excessive growth of debt. A countercyclical risk-weighted capital requirement of 2.5% is insufficient to counter the build-up of credit bubbles (due to both the risk weighting and its size). The loan-to-value ratio also aims to counter excessive credit growth but is of limited effect given the context of rising house prices.

The macroprudential framework needs a stronger set of instruments to counter excessive credit growth. One possible instrument is an unweighted counter-cyclical capital requirement. The liquidity requirement for the bank's financing (the net stable funding ratio) can also be placed within the macroprudential framework, enabling the supervisor to counter excessive credit growth based on short-term debt. Other examples include instruments commonly used in the post-war period such as credit ceilings. The macroprudential policy framework needs to be extended in scope to cover institutions such as shadow banks.

Macroprudential policy is often seen as an island separate from banking supervision, monetary policy and socioeconomic policy. Historically, these policy areas were much more interconnected and different goals – financial and monetary stability – were assessed together. Excessive debt growth cannot be countered without involving banking supervision and monetary policy.

Capital and liquidity requirements – the core of banking supervision – rely on risk weightings mainly geared towards risks to individual institutions. Mortgages are seen as relatively secure loans for banks and have lower risk weightings than corporate loans. But from a macroprudential perspective, mortgages present higher risks. As we saw in the last crisis, property bubbles entail stability risks even when banks do not directly suffer large losses on their portfolios. Macroprudential considerations deserve greater attention when determining the risk weighting of portfolios.

Non-risk-weighted requirements need to play a greater role. The unweighted leverage ratio is a potentially powerful instrument for countering excessive lending. This requirement is primarily viewed from a micro-prudential perspective, the central question being whether it enables individual institutions to absorb losses. While the current requirement of 3% is also low from a micro-prudential perspective, its level is even more problematic seen from a macroprudential perspective. In good times, the low requirement enables banks to rapidly increase their balance sheets by providing more credit; in bad times, it obliges banks to keep their purse strings tight. It is desirable to tighten the minimum requirements for the leverage ratio and to vary them counter-cyclically.

Monetary policy needs to pay attention to excessive lending. Interest rates have been especially low since the crisis. This, coupled with the policy of quantitative easing, contributes to the growth of private debt. How far financial stability risks are factored into decision-making remains unclear. Monetary policymakers need to heed the deliberations of their macroprudential colleagues and broaden their focus on consumer price inflation to include the stability risks of inflation in financial assets (such as houses and shares).

Policies to reduce debt must coordinate with other policy areas including socioeconomic policy.[9] The high level of Dutch mortgage debt cannot be divorced from

[9]WRR (2016)

pension policy (which amounts to a mandatory transfer of a large proportion of savings) and housing market policy (for example a stagnant rental sector). The credit question cannot be narrowed to a single policy area; it requires coordinated action.

8.5.3 Be Better Prepared for the Next Crisis

Money and debt can reinforce one another both upwards and downwards. Even if a crisis can initially be cushioned by emergency public support and guarantees, the aftermath can be painfully drawn out. This particularly applies if banks, businesses and households enter the crisis with high levels of debt. The question now is how further shocks can be absorbed as interest rates are already at historic lows, the ECB is flush with debt securities, and public debts in many countries are sky high. A political discussion is needed on how best to absorb shocks in a subsequent crisis. Preparations should focus on recognizing losses quickly to create room for recovery. In addition we need to assess what other measures could be deployed in the next crisis.

Recognize Losses Quickly

Financial crises can have major consequences for citizens, businesses and banks. If problematic positions are not addressed in time, the aftermath can be disproportionate and society can be destabilized over the long term. Countries differ in how the risks of problematic debt are distributed. In the Netherlands, almost all of the loan risk is borne by the debtor. In light of both fairness and rapid post-crisis recovery, we need a more balanced allocation of debt-related risks. The compulsory recapitalization of the main banks after a crisis would allow them to more rapidly restructure problem loans, creating room for recovery.

After a crisis it is key to recognize losses in a timely manner to create space for recovery through: (1) better risk allocation when settling unsustainable debts, and (2) requiring a general recapitalization of banks.

To achieve a fairer distribution of the costs, benefits and risks of a fluctuating housing market, banks should be required to sell repossessed homes for at least 95% of the market price (as has been the case under the National Mortgage Guarantee since 2013). The problem of risk allocation extends beyond households to small and medium enterprises. The aim needs to be a more balanced allocation of risks, which would contribute to faster post-crisis recovery and benefit society as a whole.

Banks' financial positions often deteriorate in a crisis and it may take a long time to restore banks' equity positions through retained earnings. If banks are reluctant to resume lending, the crisis can be prolonged. A faster way to resume lending is for banks to recapitalize by issuing new shares.[10] Since existing shareholders rarely support this move, the United States during the last crisis opted for the compulsory recapitalization of all major banks. This instrument, which contributed to faster recovery, merits serious national and European consideration.

Explore Options to Combat the Next Crisis
A range of measures were taken during the last crisis to sustain the financial sector. They included the central bank acting as the lender of last resort, government bail-outs of banks and more unorthodox measures such as negative interest rates and the central bank buying up government and corporate bonds (quantitative easing). The question is how effective these instruments will be in the next crisis as interest rates are now close to or below zero and central banks are already awash with government bonds. The fact that, by and large, money can only be created if a debt is created at the same time limits the current system's ability to absorb shocks.

Extensive and controversial measures will again be proposed during the next crisis, without sufficient time to reflect on the probable consequences. It is important to study in advance, for example through scenario analyses, the advantages and disadvantages of different, possibly unconventional, policy options.

We recommend to investigate the measures which may be necessary in the next crisis.

Before 2007, many believed that financial crises in the Western world were a thing of the past. There will always be another crisis, and we need to be prepared. During a crisis there is very little time to take decisions. During the last crisis, it was decided to raise the deposit guarantee overnight from €38,000 to €100,000.[11] We need to explore and discuss policy options and frameworks in advance. Since central banks have already deployed many of their instruments, it is possible that in the next crisis more controversial measures will be proposed without preparation, such as buying up the government bonds of a specific country (the as yet unused OMT programme), monetary financing or helicopter money.

8.5.4 Anchor the Banks' Public Dimension

As a result of the gradual transition to deposit money, increased lending and the huge increase in the size of banks, the public functions in the field of payments, savings

[10]This is not an option for cooperative banks, which have different ways to build up equity. In addition to retained earnings, these include attracting more members or issuing securities for sale to members and non-members.

[11]Ireland decided to do so and other countries had to follow suit.

and finance have become increasingly dependent on banks. Although they are formally private, they also have a public dimension. This mixture of private activities and public functions gives rise to permanent tensions. These tensions can be mitigated to a certain extent by better separating public and private interests, for example through a publicly anchored alternative for payments and savings. But given the public interest in lending, some intertwining of public and private interests is unavoidable. Addressing the resulting tensions requires structurally anchoring the public dimension in banking. We call for strengthening the public dimension in the organization of banks and greater counter-balance by citizens, NGOs and politics.

Changes in the Organization of Banks

The safeguarding of public interests in the financial sector now depends on private banks. Much has changed in this private sphere over the past decades, with banks focusing more strongly on short-term profits and shareholder value.[12] The acknowledgement that banks are semi-public institutions requires changes to the organization of banks.

We recommend to strengthen the public dimension in the organization of banks. This requires changes in both the organizational structure and the corporate governance of banks.

The semi-public nature of banks requires balancing the interests of consumers, employees, lenders, shareholders and society as a whole. It is often claimed that listed banks have no choice but to privilege shareholder interests. We therefore need to examine other available organizational models whereby banks can address the interests of different stakeholders. Cooperative banks deserve special reconsideration.

The public dimension of banks can also be buttressed through corporate governance, for example by establishing a social advisory council to deliberate on bank policy and strategy. Alternatives include assigning voting rights to a foundation that guarantees the bank's public mission, a cooperative model in which a members' council is responsible for maintaining the bank's position in society, or appointing a public official to the supervisory board. Ultimately, banks need to see themselves as semi-public institutions. This requires adjustments to their organizational status and legal requirements to guarantee the fulfilment of their public tasks.

Facilitating Countervailing Powers

In the years leading up to the 2007–2009 financial crisis, banks and supervisors mostly dealt with each other and became increasingly detached from reality. Far less effort was made to build links with other stakeholders such as citizens, NGOs and politicians. The financial sector was seen as any other sector in which bank decision-making was the preserve of bankers, with policy and supervision being considered

[12]WRR (2016)

'technical issues'. The crisis has changed this understanding. The strengthening of the public dimension in banking requires the voice of citizens to be heard much more clearly, including in politics.

The strengthening of the public dimension in banking requires the voice of citizens to be heard more clearly.

The position of citizens would be strengthened if there were more 'exit' possibilities. A publicly anchored alternative for payments and savings would give citizens an exit option they currently lack. The position of citizens would also be strengthened if it was easier to switch banks. As it is unrealistic to change the European system of account numbers (IBAN) in the short term, consideration could be given to the use of aliases for bank accounts. Such an alias would enable citizens to change banks while retaining their account numbers. If such an alias does not refer to the country of the bank, it would even ease switching to foreign banks.

Since exit options in the current system are limited, it is all the more important for 'voice' options to be strengthened. The social advisory council suggested above is one example. Parliament of course is best placed to interpret the voice of citizens; in a previous report, we recommended parliament be more involved in financial policy.[13] Financial supervisors need to involve citizens in policy formation by actively consulting them. The Bank of England, which has set up regional councils to involve citizens in regular dialogue on the economy and the financial sector, provides a promising example. Finally, the voice of citizens can be strengthened by facilitating social bodies such as NGOs. The financial sector needs watchdogs that can warn against dangerous developments and keep banks and supervisors focused on their tasks.

8.6 Conclusion

Although how we organize money creation, payments and lending is vital to our economies and societies, many people find the intricacies difficult to understand. The design of the financial monetary system affects us all and concerned citizens are calling for fundamental reforms. The recurring social upheaval caused by the banking sector shows the breadth of dissatisfaction with our current system.

We therefore recommend restoring the balanced growth of credit and debt, and striking a better balance between public and private interests. This entails fostering greater diversity in the financial sector, curbing the excessive growth of debt, being prepared for the next crisis, and anchoring the public dimension of the banking system.

[13]WRR (2016)

Bibliography

Nouy, D. (2018, September 18). The European banking sector – Towards a single jurisdiction, Speech by Danièle Nouy, Chair of the Supervisory Board of the ECB, ACPR Conference, "Financial supervision and the role of national authorities in Europe", Paris.

Wolf, M. (2014, April 24). Strip private banks of their power to create money. *Financial Times*.

WRR. (2016). *Samenleving en financiële sector in evenwicht*, WRR report nr. 96. Den Haag: Sdu Uitgevers.

Annexes

Annex I: List of Experts Consulted

Position at time of interview.

Steef Akerboom	Senior Expert Market Intelligence, De Nederlandsche Bank
Barend van Amerongen	General Manager, De Nederlandsche Bank
Barbara Baarsma	Director of Knowledge Development, Rabobank
Joost Baeten	Coordinating Policy Advisor, Ministry of Finance
Jan Bartman	Statistical Analyst, De Nederlandsche Bank
Jan Marc Berk	Divisional Director for Economic Policy and Research, De Nederlandsche Bank
Dirk Bezemer	Professor of Economics of International Financial Development, University of Groningen
Michiel Bijlsma	Head of Competition and Regulation Sector, CPB Netherlands Bureau for Economic Policy Analysis
Paul den Boer	Statistical Researcher, CBS Statistics Netherlands
Wim Boonstra	Special Advisor and Endowed Professor of Economic and Monetary Policy, Rabobank and Vrije Universiteit Amsterdam
Ed Broekhuizen	Business Controller, De Nederlandsche Bank
Teunis Brosens	Senior Economist, ING
Mark Buitenhek	Global Head of Transaction Services, ING
Rutger Claassen	University Associate Professor of Ethics & Political Philosophy, Utrecht University
Hannie de Cloe-Vos	Strategy and Policy Advisor, Dutch Authority for the Financial Markets
Elbert Dijkgraaf	Finance Spokesman for SGP, Lower House of Dutch Parliament
Jeroen Dijsselbloem	Former Minister of Finance and President of the Eurogroup
Charlotte Dixhoorn	Engagement Manager, McKinsey & Company

(continued)

Bas Dommerholt	Supervisor, Dutch Authority for the Financial Markets
Klaas van Egmond	Professor of Geosciences, Utrecht University, Sustainable Finance Lab
Wouter Elsenburg	Senior Economist, General Financial and Economic Policy Directorate, Ministry of Finance
Oscar Gelderblom	Professor of Financial History, Utrecht University
David Gerber	Head of the Financial Market Policy Department and Deputy Head of the Markets Department, Staatssekretariat für Internationale Finanzfragen
Rik Grashoff	Finance Spokesman for GroenLinks, Lower House of Dutch Parliament
Mark Harbers	Finance Spokesman for VVD, Lower House of Dutch Parliament
Bonne van Hattum	Policy Officer, Dutch Authority for the Financial Markets
Ruben van der Helm	Policy Advisor, De Nederlandsche Bank
Nils Herger	Researcher, Study Center Gerzensee, Swiss National Bank
Joost Jonker	Researcher/University Lecturer, Utrecht University
Rein Kieviet	Senior Policy Advisor, De Nederlandsche Bank
Henk Klein Teeselink	Economist/Policy Advisor, De Nederlandsche Bank
Clemens Kool	Professor of Monetary and Financial Economics, Utrecht University
Wouter Koolmees	Finance Spokesman for D66, Lower House of Dutch Parliament
Jeroen Kremers	Chairman of the supervisory boards of bunq and Robeco
Arnold Merkies	Finance Spokesman for SP, Lower House of Dutch Parliament
Paul Metzemakers	Economist, De Nederlandsche Bank
Cyril Monnet	Swiss Doctoral Programme Manager and Professor of Economics, Study Center Gerzensee and Swiss National Bank
Reinier Musters	Founding partner, Orange Growth Capital
Dirk Niepelt	Director, Study Center Gerzensee, Swiss National Bank
Henk Nijboer	Finance Spokesman for PvdA, Lower House of Dutch Parliament
Bart Nooteboom	Emeritus Professor, Tilburg University
Pieter Omtzigt	Finance Spokesman for CDA, Lower House of Dutch Parliament
Christiaan Pattipeilohy	Head of Monetary Policy Department, De Nederlandsche Bank
Reinier Pollman	Programme Manager Innovation & Fintech, Dutch Authority for the Financial Markets
Sebastiaan Pool	Researcher, De Nederlandsche Bank
Maarten Postma	Policy Economist, Foreign Financial Relations Department, Ministry of Finance
Dion Reijnders	Policy Advisor, De Nederlandsche Bank
Vincent Rietvink	Policy Advisor, Ministry of Finance
Sergio Rossi	Professor of Economics, Université de Fribourg
Mark Sanders	University Associate Professor of International Macroeconomics, Utrecht University, Sustainable Finance ab
Carola Schouten	Finance Spokesman for ChristenUnie, Lower House of Dutch Parliament
Ivo Specker	International Economist, Ministry of Finance
Job Swank	Director of Monetary Affairs and Financial Stability, De Nederlandsche Bank

(continued)

Rens van Tilburg	Director, Sustainable Finance Lab
Jasper Timmermans	Senior Policy Officer, Ministry of Finance
Roland Uittenbogaard	Policy Officer and University Lecturer, Ministry of Finance and Erasmus University Rotterdam
Hans Visser	Emeritus Professor of Economics, Vrije Universiteit Amsterdam
Peter Wierts	Senior Economist, De Nederlandsche Bank
Wilte Zijlstra	Supervisor of Consumer Behaviour Expertise Centre, Dutch Authority for the Financial Markets

Consulted Citizens' Initiatives

Ons Geld

Jacqueline Haarsma
George van Houts
Martijn Jeroen van der Linden
Gerrit van Malkenhorst
Luuk de Waal Malefijt
Edgar Wortmann
Ferdinand Zanda
Frans Doorman (supplementary Ons Geld plan)

Stichting Full Reserve/Depositobank

Richard van der Linde

Vollgeld/Monnaie pleine

Martin Alder
Christian Gomez
Jean-Marc Heim

Virtueel goud

Kees van Hee
Jacob van Wijngaard

Plan B

Ada van Dijk
Rene Visser

Mathematically Perfected Economy

Mike Montagne
Jacob Schot

Mises Instituut

Ger van Gils
Jan Vis

Plan Volksbank

Ad Broere
Hans van Steenbergen

Annex II: Tax Regime, Debt and Banks' Risk Attitude

Banks are financed by debt, to a large extent through bank deposits; equity makes up only a small part of a bank's balance sheet. Debt finance is an important component in businesses, but less so than in banks. Consumers also borrow frequently, for example to buy a house. High levels of debt increase the likelihood of financial crises and make society more vulnerable. This is because debt implies an obligation to repay a fixed amount, which is difficult to do in adverse economic times, whereas a reduction in equity will not necessarily cause immediate problems. One of the key drivers of debt finance is the deductibility of interest for tax purposes, which places equity at a comparative disadvantage. In this annex we examine how this tax motive operates for banks. We discuss a number of alternative tax regimes that would discourage the use of debt finance and analyse how they could influence banks' risk behaviour.

1. **The tax shield**

For the purposes of corporate income tax (abbreviated to CIT), the interest payable on loans and bonds can be deducted from earnings before tax is levied. This provides the *tax shield* which increases the company's value. Shareholders thus have a motive to prefer debt finance.

While the tax shield encourages both companies and banks to use debt finance, the position for banks is more nuanced. If no corporate tax is levied, the value of the assets on the left side of the balance sheet determines the company's value, while the type of finance on the liabilities side is immaterial (this is the well-known Modigliani-Miller theorem). The situation differs for banks, as their value partially depends on the quality of the bank deposits on the liabilities side of the balance sheet. This quality depends on the payment services provided by the bank, the interest the bank pays on them, and the possibility that they will be withdrawn (which determines the level of liquid assets held by the bank). These differences between bank and company balance sheets notwithstanding, the principle of the tax shield applies to both companies and banks. The major difference between bank and company balance sheets lies in the share of debt finance, which for banks is much higher. This means banks have a larger tax shield when corporate tax is levied.

The tax shield is a factor on the demand side for non-financial companies and on the supply side for banks. Debt finance for companies is provided by banks and the bond and money markets. If it is provided through a bank loan, the bank increases the company's deposit when it grants the loan (see Chap. 2). The bank's debt thus increases, including in relation to equity. A loan from the bank to the company increases the debt of both parties. Both the company and the bank can then deduct interest expenses, increasing the tax shield for both (Fig. 1).

How do the CIT and the interest deduction work, and why does it create a tax shield? The figure above illustrates the effects of different types of profit tax by means of a stylized bank balance sheet. Let R be the interest rate received on loan L issued by the bank. On the deposits and other loans the bank requires for its

Fig. 1 Simple bank balance sheet

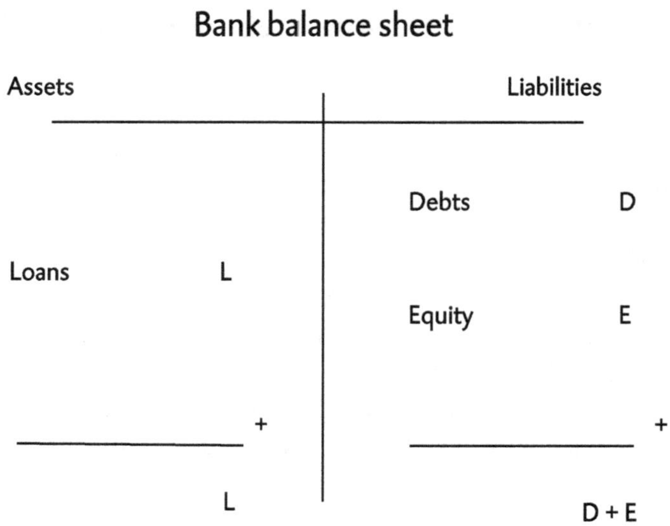

financing D (debt), it pays an interest rate of I. If a bank is viable, generally $R > I$. The difference $R - I$ is known as the interest margin. The bank's total earnings or income amounts to LR (L times R). The total costs are the interest payments on the debt DI (D times I). Since the fixed costs for personnel and overhead are marginal compared to LR or DI, for the sake of simplicity our analysis disregards them (it is straightforward to allow for a fixed cost item). The profit is the difference between the revenues and costs $LR - DI$. Excluding tax, this is what remains available to shareholders.

If we disregard the liquidity advantages that deposit finance enjoys over equity finance, it makes no difference to the value of the bank which part of the loan is financed with equity and which with bank deposits and bonds. The value of the bank is the value of the package of loans L (and how well they are repaid). If R is received on loans each year and we discount the future income stream to the present value at this interest rate, we obtain:

$$\left[1 - 1 + \frac{1}{1+R} + \frac{1}{(1+R)^2} + \frac{1}{(1+R)^3} + \dots\right] RL = \left[\frac{1}{1 - \frac{1}{1+R}} - 1\right] RL = L$$

The value of the bank is L, the market value of the package of loans that it has outstanding. The infinite series of the discount rates is a geometric progression, which can be written as:

$$1 + \frac{1}{1+R} + \frac{1}{(1+R)^2} + \frac{1}{(1+R)^3} + \dots = \frac{1}{1 - \frac{1}{1+R}} = \frac{1+R}{R}$$

The fact that the bank is worth L is somewhat dissociated from the type of finance on the liabilities side of the balance sheet, but not entirely. For simplicity, we disregard this effect. The general principle then applies that without corporate tax the value of a company or bank is determined entirely by its assets and what it expects to receive on them in the future (discounted to the present value). The financing mix E (equity/shares) and D (debt) plays no role in the valuation of the company, although the return on shares (but not the share price) depends on the amount of leverage. The precise relationship is as follows. Let Y be the expected return per share, then:

$$Y = R + (R - I)(D/E).$$

As soon as a corporate tax is levied, the value of the company is affected by the type of finance. Under the current CIT regime, interest paid on loans can be deducted from revenues. The company's value thus varies with the amount of leverage: the higher the leverage, the higher the value of the company (if it is profitable). We analyse this effect in some detail below.

2. Tax regimes

Current tax regime: interest is deductible from pretax profit.

The current tax system has a CIT rate t which is levied on earnings after the deduction of interest expenses. For the bank these are the interest expenses DI on bank deposits and bond loans. The tax office receives:

$$t(LR - DI).$$

The shareholders are then left with:

$$(1 - t)(LR - DI)$$

Why would the bank's shareholders have an interest in a substantial part of the bank's loans being financed with debt?

We compare what remains available to shareholders and depositors in a hypothetical case where the bank finances all loans with equity (and thus has no depositors, only shareholders) with a case where the bank finances itself at least partly with debt. In the former, the bank pays tLR in corporate tax. While smaller cost items such as personnel costs can be deducted from the amount on which tax is levied, this does not alter the principle that debt finance increases value for shareholders. In the case of full equity finance, $(1-t)LR$ remains available to shareholders after tax.

If the bank finances itself partly with debt, the tax deduction is $t(LR - DI)$. Less tax is paid than with full equity finance. The bank financed with debt saves

$$tLR - t(LR - DI) = tDI$$

in tax payments. If this benefit recurs annually, the total benefit is:

$$\left[1 - 1 + \frac{1}{1+R} + \frac{1}{(1+R)^2} + \frac{1}{(1+R)^3} + \ldots\right] tDI = \left[\frac{1}{1 - \frac{1}{1+R}} - 1\right] tDI = \frac{I}{R} tDI$$

This benefit is known as the tax shield. The tax shield *tD(I/R)* accrues to the shareholders. This means the value of the bank increases by this amount, so the higher the leverage, the less tax is paid and the more remains after tax. The size of this benefit varies with the level of the interest rate *I* and the discount rate *R*, but is always positive so long as the bank is profitable. A higher CIT rate *t* also increases the tax shield. Hence the bank has a strong incentive to finance itself partly with debt. The effect of the tax shield is tempered because income tax is also levied on interest and on shares and dividends. The ultimate effect for individual shareholders is therefore smaller.

Banks have higher debt levels than non-financial corporations. To use giro and electronic payments, it is necessary to have a bank account; when banks issue loans, they create bank deposits. This is one reason why banks have higher leverage than other businesses. The deposit guarantee system and the fact that large (systemically important) banks can count on government support in a crisis are further reasons. Higher capital requirements after the credit crisis are an effort to counter this drive towards high leverage.

What is the effect of corporate tax on leverage? The tax shield varies *tD(I/R)* in proportion to the CIT rate *t*, but a rate change will ultimately also affect the other variables *D*, *I* and *R*. This means empirical research is required to determine the overall effect. Estimates by De Mooij and Keen and the IMF point to an increase of 1.9–3.5% of the debt ratio (i.e. *D/L*), if the CIT rate *t* rises from 25% to 35%.[1] According to this estimate, the full elimination of the preference for debt finance with a CIT rate of 25% would reduce the debt ratio by 4.5–9% of total assets. Groenewegen, Mosch and Wierts estimate that for Dutch banks the net effect of the tax shield due to CIT (less the Dutch bank tax) is around 1% of GDP (approximately €7 billion), which can be seen as the current value of all future tax savings for bank shareholders.[2]

De Mooij, Keen and Orihara show that changing the tax rate affects the debt ratio of smaller banks more than that of larger banks.[3] There are two explanations for this. Large banks are usually close to the upper limit of the legally permitted leverage and thus have little scope to increase leverage. The debt overhang effect applies downward pressure, meaning that once a bank has high leverage, shareholders are unwilling to reduce it.[4] A recent study refers to a ratchet effect.[5] If a bank already has very high leverage, any reduction by attracting more equity will mainly benefit

[1] De Mooij and Keen (2016); IMF (2016b)

[2] Groenewegen et al. (2016)

[3] De Mooij et al. (2014)

[4] See for example Myers (1977)

[5] Admati et al. (2018)

the creditors (the providers of debt finance). Additional capital reduces the likelihood of bankruptcy, so lenders have a greater chance of being repaid in full and – if bankruptcy nevertheless occurs – it is the lenders who benefit from the additional equity. Furthermore, additional equity reduces the tax shield. Since all the benefits of additional equity go to the creditors (depositors and bondholders), the large bank has effectively locked itself into the high leverage level.

De Mooij, Keen and Orihara studied the impact of leverage on the probability of a systemic crisis in the banking sector.[6] With a leverage of 20 (which means the bank's finance comprises 96% bank deposits and bonds, as is roughly the case in the Netherlands) an increase in the CIT rate t from 25% to 26% will make a banking crisis more likely, with estimates ranging from by 0.1% to as much as by 5%. For leverage below 10, the effect is negligible. This shows the importance of constraining debt finance for systemic stability.

Limiting interest deductibility (TCR regime).

The 2017 coalition agreement of the Dutch government included a plan to limit interest deductibility for banks and insurance companies to 92% of total assets. This is known as the 'Thin Capitalization Rule' or TCR for short. The ratio of debt finance to total assets for most Dutch banks is currently around 95–96%, so the proposed measure would be effective for banks.

More generally, let a be the factor that gives the upper limit for interest deductibility. This reduces the size of the tax shield. If there is no limit, the tax shield is tDI/R. If a limit has been set at aL, this will affect the tax shield if debt finance D exceeds it, in which case the tax shield decreases from tDI/R to $taLI/R$. The value of the bank will then decrease by $t(D-aL)I/R$. Over time, the size of debt finance D may adjust, for example to the upper limit aL. This, though, has no impact on the value of the bank.

Plans for this government term also include a reduction in the CIT rate. This will reduce the tax shield and hence the motive for debt finance. Let τ be the new rate, for which $\tau < t$. The tax shield then decreases further from tDI/R via $taLI/R$ to $\tau aLI/R$.

Around 60 countries have a variant of the TCR regime, differing in their objectives (combating tax avoidance or limiting debt finance), affected companies (some differentiate between financial and non-financial companies) and the debts involved (all debts or only debt within the same group). The IMF has found the TCR measure to counter debt financing in companies particularly if it is applied to all debt.[7]

One may wonder why interest deductibility is not simply abolished overnight. Given the current size of the debt mountain, it would cause problems for many companies. Were we to take this route, we would have to do so in small steps to avoid major macroeconomic shocks. For the same reason, in the Netherlands interest deductibility on mortgages is being reduced in small steps. It is a particularly complex process for banks since interest expenses resulting from deposits are an

[6]De Mooij et al. (2014)

[7]IMF (2016b: 22–23)

inherent part of their business model. In business there is also the need to consider arbitrage between different countries. Adjustments to the tax regime may be accompanied by avoidance behaviour through international tax arbitrage.

Equity deductibility (ACE regime).

The Allowance for Corporate Equity regime (ACE for short) seeks to level the playing field between the two types of finance. Instead of limiting interest deductions, it allows tax deductions on equity expenses, using a 'normal' return on equity as a reference rate. If the aim is to reduce leverage in the financial sector, the tax deduction can be introduced exclusively for banks and insurance companies.[8]

Let G be the risk-free interest rate on a government bond which can be used to determine the 'normal' return on equity. ACE then gives a tax exemption of GE, the return on equity capital if it were invested in government bonds. In this regime, the tax office does not receive $t(LR\text{-}DI)$ but

$$t(LR - DI - EG).$$

The shareholders are then left with:

$$(1 - t)(LR - DI) + tEG = (1 - t)(LR - DI) + t(L - D)G.$$

By financing bank loans partly with debt D (bank deposits and bonds), shareholders annually gain

$$t(LR - LG) - t(LR - DI - EG) = t(DI + EG - LG).$$

This gain can also be written using the balance sheet identity

$$L = D + E.$$

For a fixed size of the loan portfolio L the result is

$$t(DI + EG - LG) = t(DI + [L - D]G - LG) = tD(I - G) < tDI.$$

If $I > G$, which means the interest on bank debt exceeds the interest on government bonds, it remains advantageous for the bank to finance itself with bank deposits. The incentive to introduce high leverage into the bank balance sheet is, however, reduced. If $I = G$, it makes no difference what share of the bank balance sheet is financed by deposits. If $I < G$, there is even a preference for equity finance.

The introduction of ACE means that the tax base shrinks due to the deductible item EG, as does tax revenue. On the other hand, the volume of debt will decrease and invested equity will increase as there is less incentive to finance with debt. The

[8]IMF (2016b)

net effect on tax revenue if the tax rate remains unchanged is probably slightly negative.[9] For this reason the CIT rate can be increased slightly so that the introduction of the ACE regime is neutral for tax receipts. But tax arbitrage remains a concern – here as well as in other changes to the tax regime. More complex arrangements could limit the interest deduction combined with a deduction for the return on equity.[10]

The ACE system is used in practice, as seen in countries such as Belgium and Italy. Schepens estimates that its introduction in Belgium has raised the capital ratio (*E/L*) in banks by 13.5% (note that *E/L* is low, so this is a 13.5% rise of a small ratio). Belgium, however, had to amend its laws after introducing ACE to guarantee the free movement of capital in the EU; a partial return to the old CIT system is being considered due to international tax competition. This shows the importance of reaching agreements at the EU level.

3. The tax regime and banks' risk attitude

The relationship between equity and debt in bank balance sheets has decreased over time, partly due to the prevailing tax regime in which interest expenses can be deducted from profit. Empirical evidence supports this hypothesis.[11] Given the risks associated with excessive debt finance, it is desirable to provide a level playing field for debt and equity finance. While the TCR and ACE regimes would bring us closer to this goal, a key question is how such adjustments to the tax regime would affect banks' risk behaviour.

We use a model from the microeconomics of banking that analyses the temptation to adapt behaviour in response to regulatory changes.[12] Deposits are a crucial part of banks' finance. Depositors can easily compare the interest earned on their deposits with offers from other banks; competition means there will be little difference between them. But it is more difficult for depositors to assess the riskiness of a bank's investments as information is asymmetric. Depositors have limited ability to verify banks' financial assets, which gives banks some leeway in their activities.

We assume that the interest I paid on bank deposits is fixed and does not depend on the composition of the loan portfolio. For convenience, we assume that other types of debt finance play no role. We show that if the interest offered to depositors is dissociated from the bank's risk attitude, a bank will be inclined to take more risks when interest rates I are high. We then assess what the levying of CIT does to the bank's risk-taking. Corporate tax curbs risk-taking. We then analyse the effects under the TCR and ACE tax regimes.

Suppose a bank has a portfolio of moderately risky corporate loans worth L. But the bank is considering exchanging these for a riskier portfolio of the same value, with a different return. The moderate-risk portfolio has a success probability of π_M

---

[9] IMF (2016b: 30)

[10] See De Mooij and Devereux (2011)

[11] De Mooij and Keen (2016); IMF (2016b)

[12] See Freixas and Rochet (2008: 33–35)

and generates a return of *LM*, with M being the interest on the moderately risky corporate loans. The high-risk portfolio has a success probability of π_H and a return of *LH*, with H being the interest on these corporate loans. The success probability of the less risky portfolio is greater, which means that $\pi_M > \pi_H > 0$. Also suppose that income from the high-risk loans exceeds that of the less risky loans, so $H > M > 0$; but the risk-weighted revenue or expected revenue is lower, which means that $\pi_H H < \pi_M M$. In the unsuccessful case, a portfolio yields nothing and the bank's capital *E* is lost. The depositors, or the deposit guarantee system, then bears the remaining loss.

The binary results – either success or no revenue at all – are chosen for simplicity, but even with a continuum of possible outcomes and risks the same conclusions follow. If all goes well, the depositors receive the interest *I* on their bank deposits. The shareholders require a return of at least *Q*, the return that can be obtained in the market from alternative projects. We also assume that the equity market lags behind the bank in terms of information – shareholders do not demand different returns in the event of a change in the risk characteristics of the bank's loan portfolio. We also disregard possible changes in capital requirements resulting from a changed risk attitude. At the end of this annex we briefly consider the assumptions in this model.

Revenue from the two possible results of the two portfolios can be represented as follows (see Fig. 2).

Without corporate tax, the expected additional future revenue of the moderate-risk portfolio is[13]:

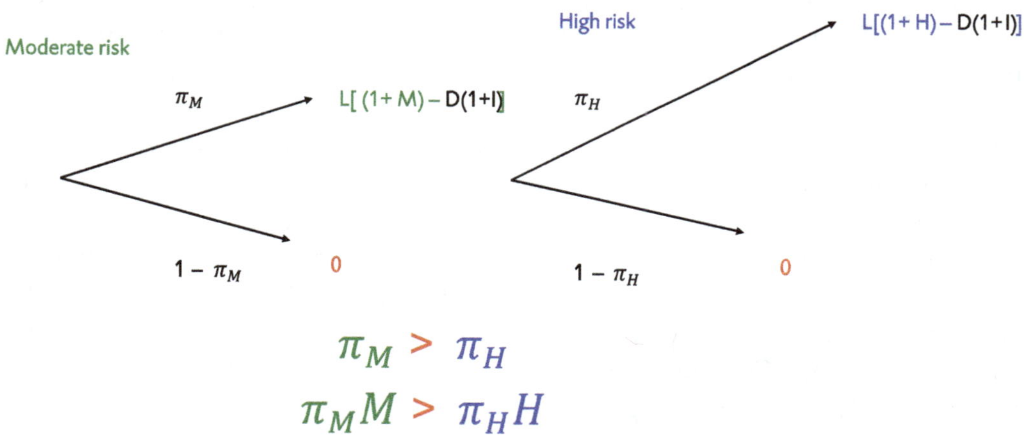

Fig. 2 Two portfolio types

[13]The first expression shows the expected net revenue of the portfolio times the success probability between square brackets. These net revenues are set against the minimum return on equity *E* required by shareholders *(1 + Q)E*. The difference is the additional expected revenue.

$$\pi_M[L(1+M) - D(1+I)] + (1-\pi_M)0 - (1+Q)E$$
$$= \pi_M[LM - DI + (L-D)] - (1+Q)E.$$
$$= \pi_M(LM - DI + E) - (1+Q)E$$

Note that the first part of the above expression is a rewritten form of the expected revenue $L(1+M)$ less the repayment of the debt plus interest $D(1+I)$ in the good scenario, with $L = E + D$ substituted. The expected revenue is $\pi_M(LM - DI + E)$ because the portfolio with the probability $(1-\pi_M)$ yields nothing. This revenue must be set against the amount of equity invested (E) and the amount of the return, QE, which on average can be achieved elsewhere in the market. So long as the difference between the expected revenue $\pi_M(LM - DI + E)$ and the opportunity costs $(1 + Q)E$ is positive, it is sensible for the bank to finance the portfolio with moderately risky loans.

A similar expression applies to the high-risk portfolio:

$$\pi_H(LH - DI + E) - (1+Q)E.$$

We can now analyse the deposit interest rates I at which the bank selects the moderate-risk and high-risk portfolios. The two expressions for the portfolio returns minus the opportunity costs are shown graphically in Fig. 2. There is a particular deposit interest rate at which the bank switches from the low-risk portfolio to the high-risk portfolio, the pivotal interest rate. We use the symbol K to indicate the interest rate I at which the choice of loan type pivots. By equating the two expressions and solving for I, we find that

$$K = \frac{\pi_m M - \pi_H H}{\pi_m - \pi_H} \cdot \frac{L}{D} + \frac{E}{D}$$

Why does the bank prefer to take more risk with a high interest rate I? The reason is as follows. The cost of paying the deposit interest DI has greater impact for the low-risk project because its probability of success is greater: $\pi_M > \pi_H$. This means $\pi_M DI > \pi_H DI$. With low interest rates I the project revenue $\pi_M LM > \pi_H LH$ outweighs the cost, but with high I the cost has greater impact. Fig. 3 shows the costs by means of the slopes of the two projects, while the revenues determine the intercepts along the vertical axis. When the deposit interest I rises, the bank changes its preference for loan portfolios, while the interest I paid to the depositor is unrelated to this choice. This change in behaviour is referred to in the literature as *moral hazard*.

This is precisely what happened in the second phase of the crisis in the US savings banks sector in the early 1980s. To attract sufficient deposits, savings banks had to increase interest rates on deposits although their interest income failed to keep pace. This often led to an 'all or nothing' strategy in which savings banks bet on the recovery by incurring high risks with their investments.[14]

---

[14]Congressional Budget Office (1992)

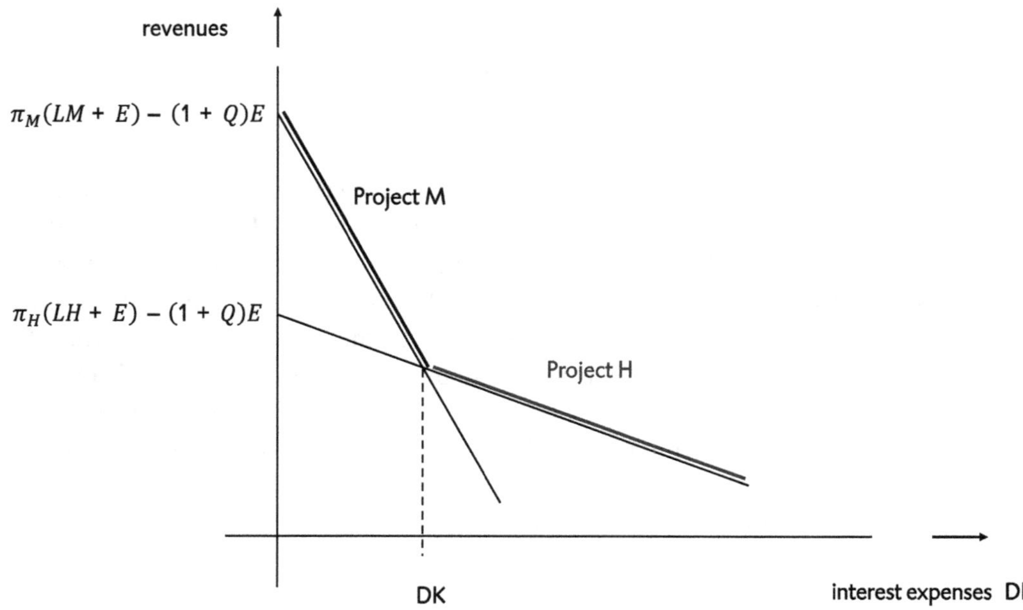

Fig. 3 Project choice of bank without CIT

We then examine the effects of the corporate tax rate on the bank's risk behaviour. With a CIT rate of t, the expected tax payment is $t\pi_M(LM - DI)$ and $t\pi_H(LH - DI)$ respectively. The expected revenue after tax is then

$$(1-t)\pi_M(LM - DI) - (1 + Q - \pi_M)E$$

and

$$(1-t)\pi_H(LH - DI) - (1 + Q - \pi_H)E$$

With these two expressions we can determine the pivotal deposit interest rate I on bank deposits at which the bank is indifferent between the two projects. By equating the two latter expressions and solving for I, we find the pivotal interest rate

$$K = \frac{\pi_m M - \pi_H H}{\pi_m - \pi_H}\frac{L}{D} + \frac{1}{1-t}\frac{E}{D}$$

What does this formula tell us? If the interest I paid on bank deposits is lower than K, the bank chooses the moderate-risk portfolio. If the deposit interest I rises above K, for example because competing banks offer higher returns, the bank chooses the high-risk portfolio.

With the above expression for the pivotal interest rate we can ascertain the effect of a tax rise. We have already shown that a higher CIT rate t increases the tax shield and results in higher leverage. Now we can see what a higher rate does to a bank's risk behaviour. This follows directly from the second term in the expression for the pivotal interest rate K where the denominator has 1-t. The higher the tax rate t, the

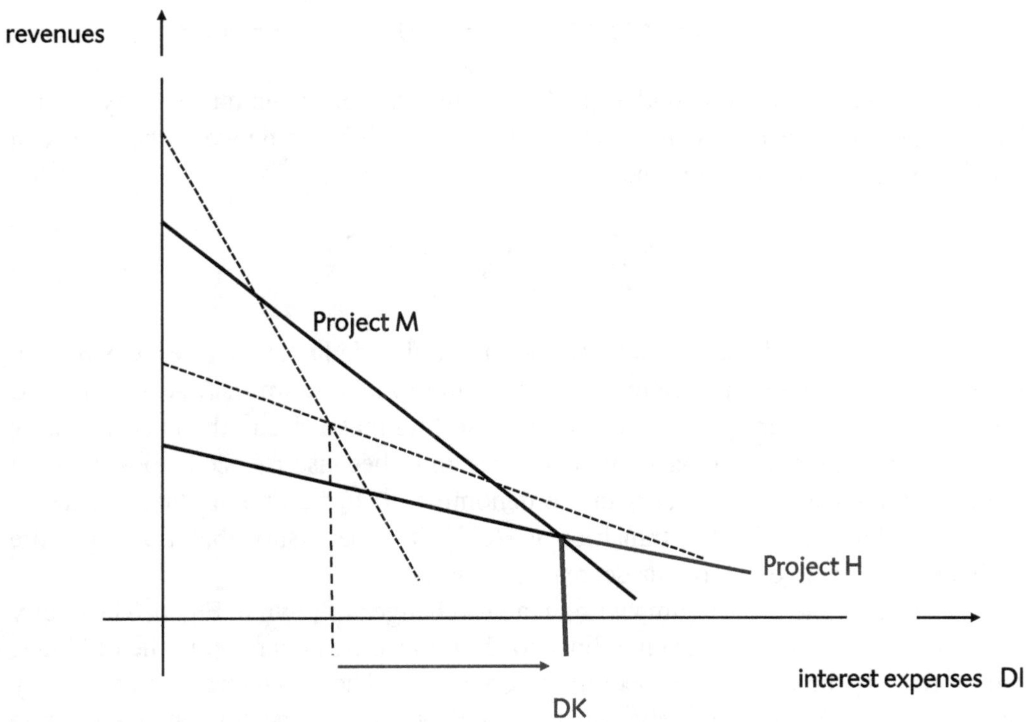

Fig. 4 Project choice of bank with CIT $t > 0$

higher the interest rate K at which the bank will take more risk. If the deposit interest rate is close to the pivotal interest rate, a higher CIT rate will make the bank less inclined to take additional risks. This effect of a higher CIT rate is shown graphically in Fig. 4. As a result of the positive CIT rate, $t > 0$, the lines showing net project revenues (revenues less opportunity costs) shift downwards and become flatter. The pivotal interest rate K consequently shifts to the right.

In addition to this direct 'price effect', the rate change ultimately affects the tax shield. A higher rate t causes the tax shield to grow, implying banks will seek greater leverage. This means the capital-debt ratio E/D decreases. This effect counteracts the direct effect of the rise of $1/(1\text{-}t)$ if t increases; the net effect cannot be precisely determined. How does this work out under the two alternative tax regimes ACE and TCR?

ACE regime

Suppose we introduce the ACE system. What does this do to the bank's risk attitude? Let G be the notional interest rate that can be charged for the equity deduction. This can be the interest rate on 10-year government bonds, for example. If the moderate-risk portfolio is successful, tax is levied on $(LM - DI - EG)$. For the high-risk portfolio the taxable income in the case of success is $(LH - DI - EG)$. The expressions for the expected revenue after tax are then as follows:

$$\pi_M(LM - DI) - \tau\pi_M(LM - DI - EG) - (1 + Q - \pi_M)E$$

and

$$\pi_H(LH - DI) - \tau\pi_H(LH - DI - EG) - (1 + Q - \pi_H)E$$

To designate the tax rate under the ACE regime we once again use the symbol τ. The deposit interest rate K at which the bank is indifferent between the two loan portfolios under the ACE regime is

$$K = \frac{\pi_m M - \pi_H H}{\pi_m - \pi_H} \frac{L}{D} + \frac{1 + \tau G}{1 - \tau} \frac{E}{D}$$

A higher notional interest rate G for the equity deduction causes the pivotal interest rate K to rise, moderating the inclination to take more risk. A higher ACE rate τ also puts upward pressure on K. We also find that a rise in the tax rate τ now has a particularly strong impact on the increase in K, because τG occurs positively in the numerator and $1 - \tau$ occurs in the denominator. For corporate tax revenue to remain unchanged with the transition to ACE, it is necessary that $\tau > t$ and the inclination to change behaviour decreases even more.

The effect of the ACE regime without a rate change is shown in Fig. 5. The equity deduction causes both net revenue lines to shift upwards, in parallel to the old lines, but more so in the case of the medium-risk portfolio. The two intercepts increase by $t\pi_M EG$ and $t\pi_H EG$ respectively, but $t\pi_M EG > t\pi_H EG$, so the pivotal interest rate shifts to the right. The ACE regime is neutral regarding the type of finance and thus has no effect on the angle of inclination of the two lines. Under our assumptions (see below), the introduction of ACE will ultimately not only have a price effect, but will also lead to adjustments in the financing mix.

TCR

In this regime, leverage is limited by an upper limit on the interest deduction. Let a again be the percentage of the total assets to which the deduction is limited. Assume that $D \geq aL$, so the limit is effective for both types of portfolio. We also assume that the CIT rate is reduced from t to τ at the same time as the introduction of the interest rate ceiling, as proposed by the Dutch government. The expressions for expected revenue after tax are then as follows:

$$\pi_M(LM - DI) - \tau\pi_M(LM - aLI) - (1 + Q - \pi_M)E$$

and

$$\pi_H(LH - DI) - \tau\pi_H(LH - aLI) - (1 + Q - \pi_H)E$$

The expression for the pivotal interest rate becomes

$$K = \frac{(\pi_m M - \pi_H H)(1 - \tau)L}{(\pi_m - \pi_H)(D - \tau aL)} + \frac{E}{D - \tau aL}$$

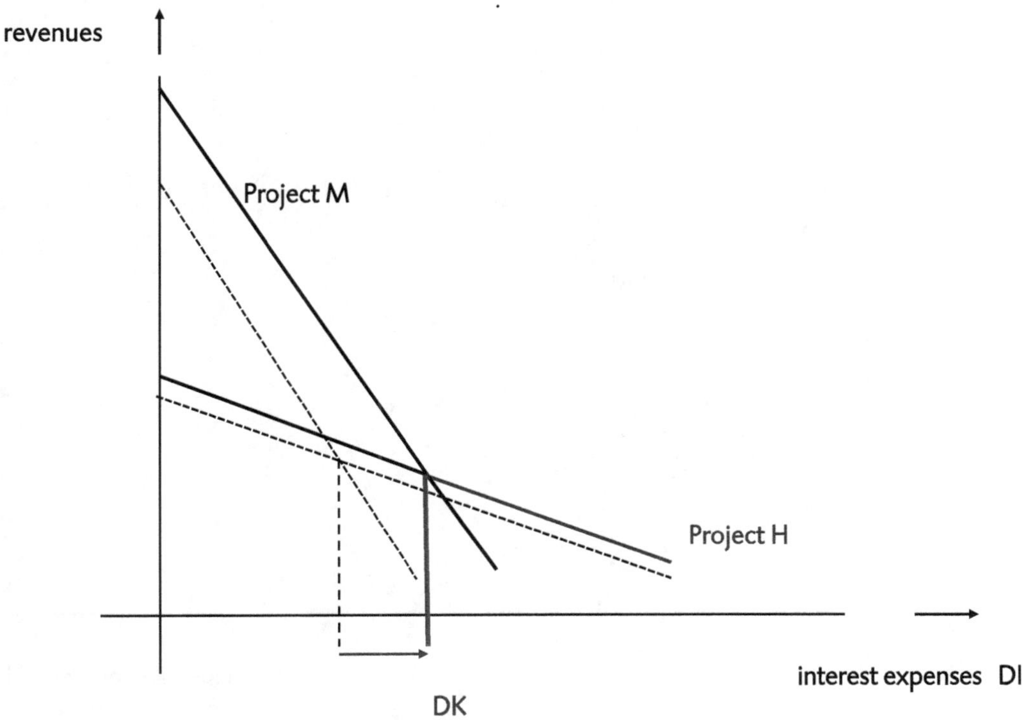

Fig. 5 Project choice of bank with CIT and ACE

We discuss two effects, starting with the price effect without any change in the quantities of debt D and equity E. These will change over time. We then discuss the combined effects of the CIT rate change and adjusted quantities for D and E. Finally we show how combining the TCR and ACE regimes will more effectively moderate risk behaviour.

Price effect

What is the combined effect of a reduction of t to τ, $\tau < t$, and the deduction limiting factor $a < 1$? The TCR rule implies

$$K = \frac{(\pi_m M - \pi_H H)}{\pi_m - \pi_H} \frac{(1-\tau)L}{D - \tau a L} + \frac{E}{D - \tau a L}$$

Previously we had

$$K = \frac{\pi_m M - \pi_H H}{\pi_m - \pi_H} \frac{L}{D} + \frac{1}{1-t} \frac{E}{D}$$

Compare the two parts of both formulas. We assume that the limit is effective, which means that $D > aL$. Under this condition

$$\frac{D}{D - \tau a L} < \frac{1}{1-t}$$

and

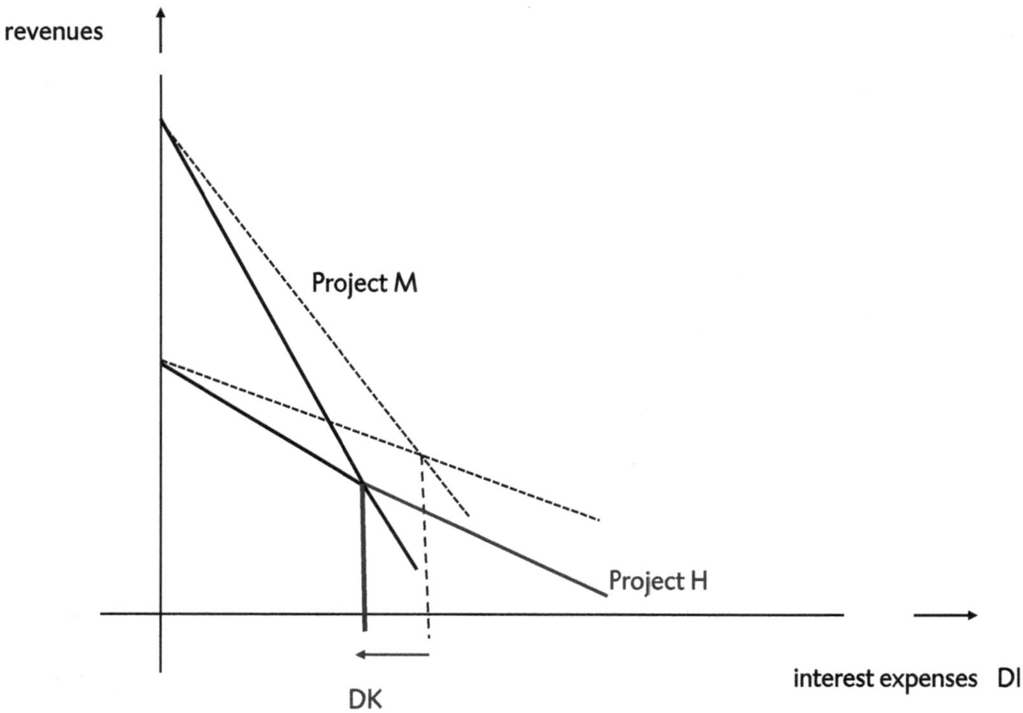

Fig. 6 Project choice of bank with CIT and TCR

$$\frac{(1-\tau)D}{D-\tau aL} < 1$$

This means that the combined reduction in the corporate tax rate and the limiting of the interest rate deduction reduces the pivotal interest rate K. By reducing a in combination with the rate reduction to τ, K initially falls. If there is no change in the leverage, a future rise in the deposit interest rate will likely cause a switch to the financing of riskier loans. Initially this is the opposite of what the ACE system achieves, but ultimately a quantity effect will also apply.

Figure 6 provides a graphic representation of limiting the interest rate deduction when the TCR regime is introduced without a change in the CIT rate. The net revenue lines rotate downwards. This is because the interest deduction is now less effective, accentuating the angle of inclination of the two lines. The pivotal interest rate shifts to the left and the bank will increasingly choose the riskier portfolio if the deposit interest rate I rises. If the tax rate is lowered, the reverse effect applies as in Fig. 3.

Quantity effects

The CIT rate reduction will ultimately lead to a decrease in debt finance as the tax shield decreases.[15] The IMF calculates that – through the reduction of a – the TCR

[15] As shown by estimates in De Mooij et al. (2014) and De Mooij and Keen (2016)

regime also reduces the quantity of deposits.[16] Suppose, for example, that the volume of bank deposits decreases to the deductible margin, i.e. to $D = aL$. This implies that the volume of equity will increase to $(1 - a)L$. This gives a pivotal interest rate of

$$K = \frac{(\pi_m M - \pi_H H)}{(\pi_m - \pi_H)} \frac{1}{a} + \frac{1 - a}{a} \frac{1}{1 - \tau}$$

Compared to the starting point

$$K = \frac{\pi_m M - \pi_H H}{\pi_m - \pi_H} \frac{L}{D} + \frac{E}{D} \frac{1}{1 - t}$$

The result is that the pivotal interest rate K increases due to volume effects if, for example, we enter the parameter values relevant to the Netherlands. These are as follows: in the current situation E/D is approximately 0.04, so L/D is approximately 1.04. The current CIT rate is $t = 0.25$. The 2017 coalition agreement proposes to limit a to 0.92 and the rate decreases in three steps to $\tau = 0.21$. This means that

$$\frac{E}{D} \frac{1}{1 - t} = \frac{0.04}{0.75} = 0.05 < 0.11 = \frac{0.08/0.92}{0.79} = \frac{1 - a}{a} \frac{1}{1 - \tau}$$

The TCR regime proposed by the Dutch government, combined with the CIT rate reduction, therefore ultimately produces an improvement in the risk attitude if the assumed volume of banks' debt finance decreases to 92%. Could it be improved further?

Combining TCR and ACE

The question is whether, given the negative price effects inherent in the TCR regime, a combination of the government's plans and the ACE principle could be more effective. If the government's plans also permit a deduction for equity in addition to the interest deduction, the pivotal interest rate goes from

$$K = \frac{(\pi_m M - \pi_H H)}{(\pi_m - \pi_H)} \frac{1}{a} + \frac{1 - a}{a} \frac{1}{1 - \tau}$$

to

$$K = \frac{(\pi_m M - \pi_H H)}{(\pi_m - \pi_H)} \frac{1}{a} + \frac{1 - a}{a} \frac{1 + \tau G}{1 - \tau}$$

The factor τG in the numerator of the second term applies additional upward pressure to K. But since the additional deduction narrows the tax base, the rate τ must be raised slightly to generate the same revenue if the measure is to be introduced on a

[16] IMF (2016b)

tax-neutral basis. This will also raise the pivotal interest rate and hence curb the inclination for risky behaviour. There could be a separate rate for banks only. The combination of TCR and ACE thus turns out positive in two ways. Ultimately, this combination will probably cause the volume of debt finance to decrease further (below aL).

4. Conclusion

The simple model set out above does not show the tax regime's precise contribution to curbing risk behaviour and bank leverage. The analysis, however, shows that limiting the interest deduction (the interest cap proposed by the government) combined with an equity deduction according to the ACE regime could help to attain a better level playing field between debt and equity finance.

We wish to point out that the model's assumptions simplify reality. We assume, for example, that the banks' debt finance comes entirely from depositors, and that they will not demand higher returns when the bank's risk attitude changes. This is plausible as depositors rarely realize with any precision the risks of what the bank is doing. In practice, however, there will be other lenders who will be better informed and who will demand higher remuneration from banks that take a lot of risk. The model also assumes that shareholders will not respond to changes in the bank's risk attitude. In practice, riskier companies will have higher financing costs. Another simplification is that the analysis does not consider capital requirements that depend on risk in the balance sheet. Including these requirements would not be difficult, but would unnecessarily complicate the calculations. Finally, the model is based on the behaviour of individual banks. It does not indicate whether the findings apply if all Dutch banks were exposed to the new measures.

Empirical studies nevertheless suggest that this approach would help. According to the IMF, the TCR and ACE regimes help reduce the incentives for debt finance. The European Commission has already made a number of proposals for the equal tax treatment of debt and equity.[17] The TCR regime proposed now, possibly combined with equity deduction according to the ACE regime, would help counter excessive debt finance in the banking system. Current circumstances are relatively favourable for introducing the TCR regime, as limiting the deductibility of interest expenses is more palatable when interest rates are low. Circumstances are also favourable for the introduction of the ACE regime, because very low interest rates on government bonds allow a tax-neutral introduction. The equity deduction is relatively limited and could easily be offset by a small increase in the corporate tax rate. If interest rates ultimately rise again, this would result in a gradual adjustment to the equity and interest deductions.

[17] See e.g. European Commission (2016c)

Bibliography

Abdelal, R. (2007). *Capital rules. The construction of global finance*. Cambridge, MA/London: Harvard University Press.

ACM. (2014). *Barrières voor toetreding tot de Nederlandse bancaire retailsector*. Den Haag: ACM.

Adfonso, G., Santos, J. A. C., & Traina, J. (2014). Do "Too-big-to-fail" banks take on more risk? *Federal Reserve Bank of New York Economic Policy Review, 20*(2), 41–58.

Admati, A. R., & Hellwig, M. (2013). *The bankers' new clothes: What's wrong with banking and what to do about it*. Princeton: Princeton University Press.

Admati, A., Allen, F., Brealey, R., et al. (2010, November 9). Healthy banking system is the goal, not profitable banks. *Financial Times*.

Admati, A. R., Demarzo, P. M., Hellwig, M. F., & Pfleiderer, P. (2018). The leverage ratchet effect. *Journal of Finance, 73*(1), 145–198.

Adrian, F. T., & Shin, H. S. (2008). Liquidity and financial contagion. *Financial Stability Review, Special Issue on Liquidity, 11*, 1–7.

Adviescommissie Toekomst Banken. (2009). *Naar herstel van vertrouwen*. Amsterdam: Dutch Banking Association.

Aikman, D., Galesic, M., Gigerenzer, G., Kapadia, S., Katsikopoulos, K. V., Kothiyal, A., Murphy, E., & Neumann, T. (2014). Taking uncertainty seriously: Simplicity versus complexity in financial regulation. *Bank of England Financial Stability Paper, 28*. https://doi.org/10.2139/ssrn.2432137.

Anheier, H. K. (2013). Institutional voids and the role of civil society: The case of global finance. *Global Policy, 5*(1), 23–35.

Arcand, J. L., Berkes, E., & Panizza, U. (2015). Too much finance? *Journal of Economic Growth, 20*(2), 105–148.

Bachetta, P. (2017). The sovereign money initiative in Switzerland: An assessment. *Swiss Finance Institute Research Paper*, 17–25. https://doi.org/10.2139/ssrn.2994926.

Bakker, A. F. P. (1996). *International financial institutions*. London: Longman.

Bakker, A. F. P., & van Lent, M. M. P. (1989). *Pieter Lieftinck, 1902–1989. Een leven in vogelvlucht*. Utrecht: Veen.

Baltensperger, E., & Dermine, J. (1986). *The role of public policy in insuring financial stability: A cross-country, comparative perspective*. Fontainebleau: INSEAD.

Bank of England. (2013). *Quarterly Bulletin 2013 Q3*. Available at: bankofengland.co.uk.

Bank of England. (2015). Cyber risk. *Financial Stability Report, 37*, 31–33.

Bardearr, J., & Kumhof, M. (2016). The macroeconomics of central bank issued digital currencies. Available at: bankofengland.co.uk.

Barendregt, J., & Visser, H. (1997). Towards a new maturity. In M. 't Hart, J. Jonker, & J. L. van Zanden (Eds.), *A financial history of the Netherlands* (pp. 152–194). Cambridge: Cambridge University Press.

BCBS. (2004). *Basel II: International convergence of capital measurement and capital standards a revised framework*. Basel: BIS.

BCBS. (2010, December). *Basel III: A global regulatory framework for more resilient banks and banking systems*. Basel: BIS.

Beck, T. (2011). The role of finance in economic development: Benefits, risks, and politics. *CentER Discussion Paper, 141*.

Beck, T., Büyükkarabacak, B., Rioja, F. K., & Valev, N. T. (2012). Who gets the credit? and Does it matter? Household vs. firm lending across countries. *The B.E. Journal of Macroeconomics, 12* (1) Art. 2.

Benes, J., & Kumhof, M. (2013). The Chicago plan revisited. *IMF Working Paper, 12*, 202.

Benink, H. (2018, October). Banken hebben nog steeds onvoldoende buffers. *ESB, 103*(4766S), 11.

Betlem, R. (2017, July 14). Bitcoin? Is dat een nieuwe betaalkaart? *Het Financieele Dagblad*. https://fd.nl/weekend/1209813/bitcoin-is-dat-een-nieuwe-betaalkaart

Bettendorf, B., & Cnossen, S. (2014). *Bouwstenen voor een moderne btw, CPB Policy Brief 02*. The Hague: CPB Netherlands Bureau for Economic Policy Analysis.

Bezemer, D. (2012). Lessen uit de crisis: Waarom we opnieuw moeten nadenken over geld. *TPEdigitaal, 6*(3/4), 63–73.

Bezemer, D. (2017, March 14). *Oratie Dirk Bezemer: Waarom schuldverschuiving Nederlandse hoogconjunctuur kwetsbaar maakt*.

Bezemer, D. (2018, March 21). Tien jaar later. *De Groene*.https://www.groene.nl/artikel/tien-jaar-later-2018-03-21

Bezemer, D., & Muysken, J. (2015). *Dutch financial fragilities, WRR Working Paper 13*. The Hague: WRR, The Netherlands Scientific Council for Government Policy.

Bijlsma, M. J., & Dubovik, A. (2014). *Banks, financial markets and growth in developed countries – A survey of the empirical literature* (CPB Discussion Paper 266). The Hague: CPB Netherlands Bureau for Economic Policy Analysis.

Bijlsma, M., & Mocking, R. J. M. (2013). *The private value of too-big-to-fail guarantees* (CPB Discussion Paper 240). The Hague: CPB Netherlands Bureau for Economic Policy Analysis.

Bijlsma, M., & van Veldhuizen, S. (2016). Verandert fintech de financiële sector. *ESB*.

Birch, D. (2017). *Before babylon, beyond bitcoin. From money that we understand to money that understands us*. London: London Publishing Partnership.

BIS. (2010). *Basel III: A global regulatory framework for more resilient banks and banking systems*. Basel: Bank for International Settlements.

BIS. (2013). *Basel III: The liquidity coverage ratio and liquidity risk monitoring tools*. Basel: Bank for International Settlements.

BIS. (2014a). *Basel III: The net stable funding ratio*. Basel: Bank for International Settlements.

BIS. (2014b). *Cyber resilience in financial market infrastructures*. Basel: Bank for International Settlements.

BIS. (2015). *85th annual report*. Basel: Bank for International Settlements.

BIS. (2016). *Reducing variation in credit risk-weighted assets – Constraints on the use of internal model approaches*. Basel: Bank for International Settlements.

BIS. (2018). *Central bank digital currencies*. Basel: BIS.

Bjerg, O. (2015). How is bitcoin money? *Theory, Culture & Society, 33*(1), 53–72.

Bjerg, O., McCann, D., Macfarlane, L., Nielsen, R. H., & Ryan-Collins, J. (2017). *Seigniorage in the 21st century: A study of the profits from money creation in the United Kingdom and Denmark*. Available at: https://doi.org/10.2139/ssrn.2921225

Blyth, M. (2002). *Great transformations. Economic ideas and institutional change in the twentieth century*. Cambridge: Cambridge University Press.

Boonstra, W. W. (2015). *Hoe werkt geldschepping?* Utrecht: Rabobank.

Boonstra, W. W. (2018). *Geld; Wat is het, wat doet het, waar komt het vandaag?* Amsterdam: VU University Press.

Boot, A. (2018). Bancaire strategie in tijden van fintech. *ESB, 4766*, 39–43.

Boot, A., & Ratnovski, L. (2016). Banking and trading. *Review of Finance, 20*, 2219–2246.

Bordo, M. D., & Levin, A. T. (2017). *Central bank digital currency and the future of monetary policy* (NBER Working Papers).

Borio, C. (2010). *Implementing a macroprudential framework: Blending boldness and realism.* Basel: Bank for International Settlements.

Borio, C. (2012). *The financial cycle and macroeconomics: What have we learnt?* (BIS Working Paper 395). Basel: Bank for International Settlements.

Borio, C. (2017, September 22). *Through the looking glass.* OMFIF City Lecture.

Borio, C., & Drehmann, M. (2009). *Towards an operational framework for financial stability: 'Fuzzy' measurement and its consequences* (BIS Working Paper 284). Basel: Bank for International Settlements.

Bremmer, D. (2018, October 29). *Minder dan 4 op de 10 betalingen nog contant, DNB is bezorgd,* in AD. https://www.ad.nl/economie/minder-dan-4-op-de-10-betalingen-nog-contant-dnb-is-bezorgd~a7a3fb34/

Broadbent, B. (2016, March 2) *Central banks and digital currencies.* Speech at London School of Economics.

Brunnermeier, M. K., Crocket, A., Goodhart, C., Persaud, A. D., & Shin, H. S. (2009). *The fundamental principles of financial regulation.* Geneva: International Center for Monetary and Banking Studies (ICMB) and Centre for Economic Policy Research (CEPR).

Burgess, S., & Janssen, N. (2007). Proposals to modify the measurement of broad money in the United Kingdom: A user consultation. *Bank of England Quarterly Bulletin Q3.*

Buttiglione, L., Lane, P. R., Reichlin, L., & Reinhart, V. et al. (2014). *Deleveraging? What deleveraging?*

Cannas, G., Cariboni, J., Kazemi Veisari, L., & Pagano, A. (2014). *Updated estimates of EU eligible and covered deposits.* European Commission, Joint Research Centre, Institute for the Protection and Security of the Citizen.

Capie, F., Goodhart, C., & Schnadt, N. (1994). The development of central banking. In S. Fischer, C. Goodhart, & N. Schnadt (Eds.), *The future of central banking: The tercentenary symposium of the Bank of England* (pp. 1–261). Cambridge: Cambridge University Press.

Carmassi, J., & Micossi, S. (2012). *Time to set banking regulation right.* Brussels: Centre for Economic Policy Research.

Carney, M. (2014, September 9). *Speech given at the 146th Annual Trades Union Congress, Liverpool.* Bank of England.

Carruthers, B. G. (2010). The sociology of money and credit. In *The handbook of economic sociology* (pp. 355–378). Princeton: Princeton University Press.

Caruana, J. (2016, November 26). *Monetary policy for financial stability, Keynote speech by Jaime Caruana, General Manager, Bank for International Settlements.* In 52nd SEACEN governors' conference, Naypyidaw, Myanmar.

Cavelaars, P., de Haan, J., Hilbers, P., & Stellinga, B. (2013). Uitdagingen voor financieel toezicht na de crisis. In P. Welp et al. (Eds.), *De staat van toezicht. Sector- en themastudies* (WRR investigations no. 27). Amsterdam: AUP.

CBS. (2001). *Tweehonderd jaar statistiek in tijdreeksen 1800–1999.* The Hague: CBS.

CBS. (2009). *Werkloosheid jaren dertig hoogste ooit.* Available at: https://www.cbs.nl/nl-nl/nieuws/2009/12/werkloosheid-jaren-dertig-hoogste-ooit

CBS. (2017). *Vertrouwen in mensen en in organisaties.* The Hague: CBS.

Cecchetti, S. G., & Kharroubi, E. (2012). *Reassessing the impact of finance on growth* (BIS Working Paper 381). Basel: Bank for International Settlements.

Cecchetti, S. G., & Kharroubi, E. (2015). *Why does financial sector growth crowd out real economic growth?* (BIS Working Paper 490). Basel: Bank for International Settlements.

Chamley, C., Kotlikoff, L. J., & Polemarchakis, H. (2012). Limited-purpose banking – Moving from "Trust me" to "Show me" banking. *American Economic Review, 102*(3), 113–119.

Chiarella, C., Flaschel, P., Hartmann, F., & Proaño, C. (2011). *Stock market booms, endogenous credit creation and the implications of broad and narrow banking for macroeconomic stability* (New School for Social Research, Working Paper 7).

Cohen-Setton, J. (2015). *Blogs review: QE and central bank* (continued). http://bruegel.org/2015/01/blogs-review-qe-and-central-bank-solvency-continued/

Coljé, H. (1988). *Het toezicht op de banken in Nederland*. Amsterdam: NIBE.

Committee on the Global Financial System. (2018). *Structural changes in banking after the crisis* (CGFS Paper 60).

Congressional Budget Office. (1992). *The economic effects of the savings & loan crisis*. CBO study, Congress of the United States.

Constancio, V. (2015, February 13). *Financial stability risks, monetary policy and the need for macro-prudential policy*. Speech by Vítor Constâncio, Vice-President of the ECB, Warwick Economics Summit.

Council for Health and Society. (2014). *De stem van verzekerden* (Advies over de legitimiteit en de governance van zorgverzekeraars). The Hague: Council for Health and Society.

Cournède, B., & Denk, O. (2015). *Finance and economic growth in OECD and G20 countries* (OECD Working Paper 1223).

CPB. (2016). *Risicorapportage Cyberveiligheid Economie*. The Hague: CPB Netherlands Bureau for Economic Policy Analysis.

Danielsson, J., Shin, H. S., & Zigrand, J. -P. (2012). *Endogenous and systemic risk* (NBER chapters, no. 12054).

Danmarks Nationalbank. (2017). *Central bank digital currency in Denmark?* (Analysis no 28).

de Greef, I., Hilbers, P. L. C., & Hoogduin, L. H. (1997). *Moderate Monetarism: A brief survey of Dutch monetary policy in the post-war period* (DNB staff reports, no. 28). Available at: www.dnb.nl

de Jong, A. M. (1967). *Geschiedenis van de Nederlandsche Bank* (Vol. I-III). Haarlem: Joh. Enschedé.

de Larosière, J. (2009). *The high-level group on financial supervision in the EU, Report*. Brussels: European Commission.

De Mooij, R., & Devereux, M. P. (2011). An applied analysis of ACE and CBIT reforms in the EU. *International Tax and Public Finance, 18*, 93–120.

De Mooij, R., & Keen, M. (2016). Debt, taxes and banks. *Journal of Money Credit and Banking, 48*, 5–33.

De Mooij, R., Keen, M., & Orihara, M. (2014). Taxation, bank leverage, and financial crisis. In R. De Mooij & G. Nicodème (Eds.), *Taxation and regulation of the financial sector* (pp. 229–252). Cambridge: MIT Press.

De Ruijter. (2012). *Scenario's Woningmarkt – Risico's voor de woningmarkt en inventarisatie van beleidsopgaven*. Amstelveen: De Ruijter Strategie BV.

De Volksbank. (2017). *Jaarverslag Volksbank NV*. Utrecht: de Volksbank.

de Vré, H. (2014). De bijzondere zorgplicht van financiële dienstverleners onder toezicht. In *Wetenschappelijke Bijdragen, Bundel ter gelegenheid van het 35-jarig bestaan van het wetenschappelijk bureau van de Hoge Raad der Nederlanden*. The Hague: Boom Juridische uitgevers.

de Vries, J. (1989). *Geschiedenis van de Nederlandsche Bank, V, De Nederlandsche Bank van 1914 tot 1948. Visserings tijdvak 1914–1931*. Amsterdam: NIBE.

de Vries, C. G. (2005). The simple economics of bank fragility. *Journal of Banking & Finance, 29*, 803–825.

De Wit Committee. (2010). *Parlementair onderzoek financieel stelsel. Rapport*, Kamerstukken II, 2009–2010, 31980, no. 4.

De Wit Committee II. (2012). *Parlementaire enquête financieel stelsel. Eindrapport*, Kamerstukken II, 2011–2012, 31980, no. 61.

Debelle, G. (2004). *Household debt and the macroeconomy* (BIS Quarterly Review). Basel: Bank for International Settlements.

Demertzis, M. and A. Lehmann (2017) 'Tackling Europe's crisis legacy: a comprehensive strategy for bad loans and debt restructuring', Policy Contribution 11: 1–15, Brussels: Bruegel.

Denk, O. (2015). *Financial sector pay and labour income inequality: Evidence from Europe* (OECD Economics Department Working Papers No. 1225). Paris: OECD Publishing.

Disyatat, P. (2008). *Monetary policy implementation: Misconceptions and their consequences* (BIS working paper 269). Basel: Bank for International Settlements.

DNB. (2001). *Kwartaalbericht December 2001*. Amsterdam: De Nederlandsche Bank.

DNB. (2002). *Tariefstructuren en infrastructuur in het Nederlandse massale betalingsverkeer*. Amsterdam: De Nederlandsche Bank.

DNB. (2010, June). *Een eeuw financiële leverage van Nederlandse banken* (DNB Quarterly Report, 2010).

DNB. (2011). *Overheidssteun aan financiële instellingen*. Available at: https://www.dnb.nl/nieuws/nieuwsoverzicht-en-archief/dnbulletin-2011/index.jsp

DNB. (2015a). *Nederlands depositogarantiestelsel wordt meer risicogebaseerd*. Available at: https://www.dnb.nl/nieuws/nieuwsoverzicht-en-archief/persberichten-2015/dnb334375.jsp.

DNB. (2015b). *Staat van het toezicht 2015*. Amsterdam: De Nederlandsche Bank.

DNB. (2015c). *Visie op de structuur van de Nederlandse bankensector – Stabiliteit en efficiëntie door diversiteit en concurrentie*. Amsterdam: De Nederlandsche Bank.

DNB. (2016a). *De financiële stabiliteitstaak van DNB*. Amsterdam: De Nederlandsche Bank.

DNB. (2016b). *DNBulletin: Achterblijvend vertrouwen onderstreept noodzaak macroprudentieel beleid*. https://www.dnb.nl/nieuws/nieuwsoverzicht-en-archief/dnbulletin-2016/dnb346228.jsp#

DNB. (2016c). *Technische mogelijkheden IBAN-portabiliteit in Nederland*. Amsterdam: De Nederlandsche Bank.

DNB. (2017). *Overzicht Financiële Stabiliteit – Voorjaar 2017*. Amsterdam: De Nederlandsche Bank.

DNB. (2018a). *Beleidsinstrumenten*. Available at: www.dnb.nl

DNB. (2018b). *DNB en resolutie*. Available at: www.dnb.nl

DNB. (2018c, November 7). *DNBulletin: 'Contant of pin? Wie betaalt, bepaalt*.

DNB. (2018d). *Jaarverslag 2017*. Amsterdam: DNB.

DNB. (2018e). *Overzicht Financiële Stabiliteit – Najaar 2018*. Amsterdam: De Nederlandsche Bank.

DNB. (2018f). *Resultaten van de MOB-vergadering 16 mei*. Available at: www.dnb.nl

DNB. (2019). *Banking package main changes of CRD/CRR/BRRD/SRMR review*. Amsterdam: DNB.

Dommerholt, B., & van Tilburg, R. (2016). De voor- en nadelen van publiek geldschepping, *ESB* January 2017.

Dow, S., Johnson, G., & Montagnoli, A. (2015). *A critique of full reserve banking* (Sheffield Economic Research Paper Series). The University of Sheffield.

Drehmann, M., Borio, C., & Tsatsaronis, K. (2011). *Anchoring countercyclical capital buffers: The role of credit aggregates* (BIS Working Paper 355). Basel: Bank for International Settlements.

Dutch Banking Association. (2009). *Code Banken (Banking Code)*. Amsterdam: NVB.

Dyson, B., Hodgson, G., & van Lerven, F. (2016). *Sovereign money. An introduction*. Available at: http://www.positivemoney.org.

ECB. (2004). *The operational target of monetary policy and the rise and fall of reserve position doctrine*. Frankfurt am Main: ECB.

ECB. (2007). *Monthly bulletin February 2007*. Available at: www.ecb.europa.eu

ECB. (2011a). *The monetary policy of the ECB*. Available at: www.ecb.europa.eu

ECB. (2011b). *The implementation of monetary policy in the euro area*. Available at: www.ecb.europa.eu

ECB. (2011c). *Monthly bulletin January 2011*. Available at: www.ecb.europa.eu

ECB. (2015). *The fiscal impact of financial sector support during the crisis* (ECB Economic Bulletin 6). Frankfurt am Main: ECB.

ECB. (2016). *Wat zijn minimumreserveverplichtingen?* Available at: ecb.europa.eu

ECB. (2018). *The definition of price stability*. Available at: https://www.ecb.europa.eu

ECB Task Force on Systemic Liquidity. (2018, October). *Systemic liquidity concept, measurement and macroprudential instruments* (Occasional Paper Series, No. 214).

Eichengreen, B. (1992). *Golden fetters. The gold standard and the great depression 1919–1939*. Oxford: Oxford University Press.

Eichengreen, B. (2011). *Exorbitant privilege. The rise and fall of the dollar and the future of the international monetary system*. Oxford: Oxford University Press.

Eichengreen, B., & Temin, P. (2000). The gold standard and the great depression. *Contemporary European History, 9*(2), 183–207.

Eichengreen, B., El-Erian, M., Fraga, A., et al. (2011). *Rethinking central banking*. Ontario: Committee on International Economic Policy and Reform.

Eijffinger, S. C. W. (1983). *Het monetaire beleid van de Nederlandsche Bank* (Serie Researchmemoranda, no. 19). Amsterdam: Vrije Universiteit.

ESRB. (2014). *Recommendation of the European systemic risk board of 18 June 2014 on guidance for setting countercyclical buffer rates*. Available at: www.esrb.europa.eu

ESRB. (2016). *Confidential transmission of ESRB Warning on medium-term vulnerabilities in the residential real estate sector of the Netherlands*. Available at: www.esrb.europa.eu

ESRB. (2018, September). *EU shadow banking monitor* (No. 3). Frankfurt am Main: ECB.

ESRB ASC. (2014). *Is Europe overbanked?* (Reports of the Advisory Scientific Committee No. 4). European Systemic Risk Board.

European Commission. (2012). *Taxation: The European Commission requests Belgium to amend its rules on the notional interest deduction*. Brussels: European Commission.

European Commission. (2013). *Green paper on long-term financing of the European economy*.

European Commission. (2014). *Economic review of the financial regulation agenda*. Brussels: European Commission.

European Commission. (2016a). *Proposal for a directive of the European Parliament and of the Council amending Directive 2013/36/EU as regards exempted entities, financial holding companies, mixed financial holding companies, remuneration, supervisory measures and powers and capital conservation measures*. Brussels: EC.

European Commission. (2016b). *Proposal for a regulation of the European Parliament and of the Council amending Regulation (EU) No 575/2013 as regards the leverage ratio, the net stable funding ratio, requirements for own funds and eligible liabilities, counterparty credit risk, market risk, exposures to central counterparties, exposures to collective investment undertakings, large exposures, reporting and disclosure requirements and amending Regulation (EU) No 648/2012*. Brussels: EC.

European Commission. (2016c). *Proposal for a Council Directive on a Common Corporate Tax Base*. COM(2016) 685 final.

European Commission. (2017). *Commission Work Programme 2018. An agenda for a more united, stronger and more democratic Europe*. Brussels: European Commission.

European Court of Justice. (2013, July 4). C-350/11 (*Argenta Spaarbank NV vs Belgische Staat*).

European Parliament. (2014). *Consumer protection aspects of financial services*. Available at: www.europarl.europa.eu

Fahr, S., & Fell, J. (2017). Macroprudential policy – Closing the financial stability gap. *Journal of Financial Regulation and Compliance, 25*(4), 334–359.

Federal Public Service Finance. (2018). *Notionele interestaftrek: uniek en innoverend belastingvoordeel in België*. Available at: https://financien.belgium.be/nl/ondernemingen/internationaal/buitenlandse_investeerders/Notionele_interestaftrek/#q1

Feinstein, C., Temin, P., & Toniolo, G. (1997). *The European economy between the wars*. Oxford: Oxford University Press.

Ferguson, N. (2008). *The ascent of money: A financial history of the world*. New York: Penguin Putnam.

Financial Stability Committee. (2015). *Aanbeveling van het Financieel Stabiliteitscomité over de LTV-limiet na 2018*. Amsterdam: Financial Stability Committee.

Finansinspektionen. (2018). *Countercyclical buffer rate*. Available at: www.fi.se

Flaschel, P., Hartmann, F., Malikane, C., & Semmler, W. (2010). Broad banking, financial markets and the return of the narrow banking idea. *Journal of Economic Asymmetries, 7*(2), 105–137.

Fontana, G., & Sawyer, M. (2016). Towards post-Keynesian ecological macroeconomics. *Ecological Economics, 121*(C), 186–195.

Forsyth, D. J., & Notermans, T. (1997). *Regime changes: Macroeconomic policy and financial regulation in Europe from the 1930s to the 1990s*. Oxford: Berghahn Books.

Frederik, J. (2012). *De geschiedenis van het 'banqueroet'*. Follow the Money, https://www.ftm.nl/artikelen/de-geschiedenis-van-het-banqueroet?share=1

Freixas, X., & Rochet, J.-C. (2008). *The microeconomics of banking* (2nd ed.). Cambridge: MIT Press.

Friedman, M. (1948). A monetary and fiscal framework for economic stability. *The American Economic Review, 38*(3), 245–264.

Friedman, M. (1961). The lag in effect of monetary policy. *Journal of Political Economy, 69*(5), 447–466.

FSA. (2009). *The turner review: A regulatory response to the global banking crisis*. London: The Financial Services Authority.

FSB. (2015). *Global shadow banking monitoring report 2015*. Basel: FSB.

FSB, IMF, & BIS. (2009). *Guidance to assess the systemic importance of financial institutions, markets and instruments: Initial considerations*. Report to the G-20 Finance Ministers and Central Bank Governors. Available at: https://www.imf.org/external/np/g20/pdf/100109.pdf

Fung, B. S. C., & Halaburda, H. (2016). *Central bank digital currencies: A framework for assessing why and how* (Bank of Canada staff discussion paper 2016–22). Available at: bankofcanada.ca

Giannini, C. (2011). *The age of central banks*. Cheltenham/Northampton: Edward Elgar.

Goodhart, C. A. E. (2007). *Liquidity Risk Management* (Special Paper 175, LSE Financial Markets Group Paper Series).

Goodhart, C. A. E. (2010). *The changing role of central banks* (BIS Working Paper 326). Basel: Bank for International Settlements.

Goodhart, C. A. E. (2011). Money, credit and bank behaviour: Need for a new approach. *National Institute Economic Review, 214*(1), F73–F82.

Goodhart, C. A. E. (2013). *Goodhart's Law, Le Libellio d' AEGIS*. Vol. 9, n° 4 – Hiver 2013.

Goodhart, C. A. E. (2016). *Determining the quantity of bank deposits* (The Basel Issue, Banking Perspectives).

Goodhart, C. A. E., & Jensen, M. (2015). Currency School versus Banking School: An ongoing confrontation. *Economic Thought, 4*(2), 20–31.

Graeber. (2011). *Debt: The first 5000 years*. Brooklyn: Melville House Publishing.

Gray, S. (2011). *Central bank balances and reserve requirements* (IMF Working Paper).

Groenewegen, J., Mosch, R., & Wierts, P. (2016). *Subsidies and taxes on bank debt: Joint size and incentive effects*. DNB, Mimeo.

Haldane, A. G. (2009, April 28). *Rethinking the financial network*. Speech by Mr Andrew G. Haldane, Executive Director, Financial Stability, Bank of England, at the Financial Student Association, Amsterdam.

Haldane, A. G. (2010, November 20). *Curbing the credit cycle*. Speech presented by Andrew G. Haldane, Executive Director, Financial Stability, Bank of England, at the Columbia University Center on Capitalism and Society Annual Conference, New York.

Haldane, A. G. (2016, May 18). *The great divide*. Speech given by Andrew G. Haldane, Chief Economist, Bank of England, New City Agenda Annual dinner.

Haldane, A. G. (2018). *Climbing the public engagement ladder*. Speech 6 March, Royal Society for the encouragement of Arts, Manufactures and Commerce (RSA).

Haldane, A. G., Brennan, S., & Madouros, V. (2010). What is the contribution of the financial sector: Miracle or mirage? In *The Future of Finance: The LSE Report*. London School of Economics and Political Science.

Handelingen (Proceedings) II, 2015–2016, 65, item 10.

Handelingen (Proceedings) II, 2017/18, 69, item 10, p. 37).

Hart, 't, & du Perron, C. E. (2006). *De geïnformeerde consument*. Deventer: Kluwer.

Hartmann, P., Straetmans, S., & de Vries, C. G. (2004). Bank system stability: A cross-atlantic perspective. In M. Carey & R. M. Stultz (Eds.), *The risks of financial institutions. NBER* (pp. 133–192). Chicago/London: The University of Chicago Press.

He, D., Leckow, R., Haksar, V. et al. (2017). *Fintech and financial services: Initial considerations* (IMF Staff Discussion Note SDN/17/05).

Hebous, S., & Ruf, M. (2017). Evaluating the effects of ACE systems on multinational debt financing and investment. *Journal of Public Economics, Elsevier, 156*(C), 131–149.

Hellwig, M. (2010). Capital regulation after the crisis: Business as usual? *Preprints of the Max Planck Institute for Research on Collective Goods, 31.*

Hilbers, P. (1998). *Financial sector reform and monetary policy in the Netherlands* (IMF Working Papers No. 19).

Huber, J. (2017). *Sovereign money. Beyond reserve banking*. Cham: Palgrave Macmillan.

Humphrey, C. (1985). Barter and economic disintegration. *Man, 20*, 48–72.

IMF. (2012). Chapter 3: Growth resuming, dangers remain. In *Dealing with household debt*. Washington, DC: International Monetary Fund.

IMF. (2015). *From banking to sovereign stress: Implications for public debt* (IMF Policy Papers). Washington, DC: International Monetary Fund.

IMF. (2016a). *Debt, use it wisely, Fiscal monitor October 2015*. International Monetary Fund.

IMF. (2016b, October) *Tax policy, leverage and macroeconomic stability*. Staff Report.

IMF. (2017). *Netherlands financial system stability assessment* (Country Report No. 17/79). Washington, DC: International Monetary Fund.

IMF-FSB-BIS. (2016). *Elements of effective macroprudential policies*. Available at: www.imf.org/external/np/g20/pdf/2016/083116.pdf

Ingham, G. (1996). Money is a social relation. *Review of Social Economy, 54*(4), 507–529.

Ingham, G. (2004). *The nature of money*. Cambridge: Polity Press.

Jak, N. (2014). *Semipublieke instellingen; De juridische positie van instellingen op het snijvlak van overheid en samenleving*. Dissertation.

Jones, R. A. (1976). The origin and development of media of exchange. *Journal of Political Economy, 84*(4, Part 1), 757–775.

Jonker, J. (1997). The alternative road to modernity. Banking and currency, 1814–1914. In M. 't Hart, J. Jonker, & J. L. van Zanden (Eds.), *A financial history of the Netherlands*. Cambridge: Cambridge University Press.

Jonker, J. P. B. (1999). De bakermat van het Nederlandse bankwezen, financiële markten in Nederland vanaf de Franse Tijd tot de opkomst van de handelsbanken, 1813–1870. In *Wereldwijd bankieren, ABN AMRO 1824–1999*. Amsterdam: ABN AMRO.

Jonker, N. (2013). *Social costs of POS payments in the Netherlands 2002–2012: Efficiency gains from increased debit card usage* (DNB Occasional Studies, Vol. 11, No. 2). Amsterdam: DNB.

Jonker, N., Hernandez, L., de Vree, R., & Zwaan, P. (2018). *From cash to cards. How debit card payments overtook cash in the Netherlands* (DNB Occasional Studies, Vol. 16, No. 1). Amsterdam: DNB.

Jordá, O., Schularick, M., & Taylor, A. M. (2014). *The great mortgaging: Housing finance, crises, and business cycles* (Federal Reserve Bank of San Francisco Working Paper Series No. 23).

Kamerstukken (Parliamentary Papers) I, 2013/14, 33362, no. N.

Kamerstukken (Parliamentary Papers) II, 2013–2014, 33362, no. 35.

Kamerstukken (Parliamentary Papers) II, 2015–2016, 34346, no. 19.

Kamerstukken (Parliamentary Papers) II, 2017–2018, 34858, no. 3.

Kamerstukken (Parliamentary Papers) II, 2017–2018, 34971, no. 3.

Kay, J. (2009). *Narrow banking: The reform of banking regulation*. London: Centre for the Study of Financial Innovation.

Keuning, W. (2017, October 6). Rabo-directeur: "Ik heb ook meegewerkt aan overkreditering". *Het Financieele Dagblad.*

Kindleberger, C. P. M. (1978). *Manias, panics, and crashes: A history of financial crises*. London: Palgrave Macmillan.

King, M. (2016). *The end of alchemy: Money, banking and the future of the global economy*. New York: W.W. Norton & Company.

Knafo, S. (2006). The gold standard and the origins of the modern international monetary system. *Review of International Political Economy, 13*(1), 78–102.

Konzelmann, S., Wilkinson, F., Fovargue-Davies, M., & Sankey, D. (2010). Governance, regulation and financial market instability: The implications for policy and reform. *Cambridge Journal of Economics, 34*(5), 929–954.

Kotlikoff, L. J. (2010). *Jimmy Stewart is dead. Ending the world's ongoing financial plague with limited purpose banking*. Hoboken: Wiley.

Kotlikoff, L. J., & Goodman, J. C. (2009). *Solving our nation's financial crisis with limited purpose banking* (Working Paper). Boston: Boston University.

KPMG. (2016). *Money issuance: Alternative money systems*. Report commissioned by the Icelandic Prime Minister's Office. Available at: www.kpmg.com

Kroll, M. (2015). *The monetary system in crisis: Monetary reform proposals, and a simple suggestion for a more effective monetary policy* (World Future Council, Future Finance – Discussion Paper No. 1).

Kumhof, M., & Noone, C. (2018). *Central bank digital currencies — design principles and balance sheet implications* (Bank of England Staff Working Paper 725).

Kymmell, J. (1992). *Geschiedenis van de algemene banken in Nederland 1860–1914, Part I*. Amsterdam: Nederlands Instituut voor het Bank- en Effectenbedrijf.

Kymmell, J. (1996). *Geschiedenis van de algemene banken 1860–1914, Part II-A+B*. Amsterdam.

Lagarde, C. (2017). *Fintech: Capturing the benefits*. Avoiding the Risks, https://blogs.imf.org/2017/06/20/fintech-capturing-the-benefits-avoiding-the-risks/

Laina, P. (2015). Proposals for full-reserve banking: A historical survey from David Ricardo to Martin Wolf. *Economic Thought, 4*(2), 1–19.

Lane, P. R. (2013, April). *Capital flows in the Euro Area* (*European Economy Economic Paper* 497).

Langeveld, H. (2009). Grotendeels buitenspel. Het Nederlandse parlement en de crisis van de jaren dertig van de twintigste eeuw. In C. van Baalen et al. (Eds.), *Jaarboek Parlementaire Geschiedenis* (pp. 37–46).

Lastra, R. M., & Goodhart, C. (2015, September 23). Interaction between monetary policy and bank regulation. In: European Parliament – Directorate General for internal policies – Policy Department A: Economic and scientific policy (ed.), *Interaction between monetary policy and bank regulation* (pp. 37–54). Monetary Dialogue, Brussels: European Parliament.

Lavoie, M. (2003). A fully coherent post Keynesian model of the euro zone. In P. Arestis, M. Baddeley, & J. McCombie (Eds.), *Globalisation, regionalism and economic activity* (pp. 98–126). Cheltenham: Edward Elgar.

Layard, R., Nickell, S., & Jackman, R. (1991). *Unemployment – Macroeconomic performance and the labour market*. Oxford: Oxford University Press.

Lelieveldt. (2017, September 7). Betalingsverkeer: hoe markt en regelgeving elkaar maken en breken. *ESB*.

Levine, R. (1997). Financial development and economic growth: Views and agenda. *Journal of Economic Literature, XXXV*, 688–726.

Liikanen Report. (2012). *High-level expert group on reforming the structure of the EU banking sector*. Brussels: European Commission.

Liu, Y., & Rosenberg, C. B. (2013). *Dealing with private debt distress in the wake of the European financial crisis. A review of the economics and legal toolbox* (IMF Working Paper Series, WP/13/44). Washington, DC: IMF.

Lo, S., & Rogoff, K. (2015). *Secular stagnation, debt overhang and other rationales for sluggish growth, six years on* (BIS Working Paper 482). Basel: Bank for International Settlements.

London Economics, IFF and PaySys. (2013). *Study on the impact of Directive 2007/64/EC on payment services in the internal market and on the application of regulation (EC) No 924/2009 on cross-border payments in the community, final report.* Brussels: European Commission.

Louisse, M. L. (2013). Het wettelijk recht op een betaalrekening is een feit, maar wel een zeer beperkt feit. *Vennootschap & Onderneming*, (1), 11–15.

Lukkezen, J., & Elbourne, A. (2015). *De Nederlandse consumptie – Goede tijden, slechte tijden* (CPB Policy Brief 2015/03). The Hague: CPB Netherlands Bureau for Economic Policy Analysis.

Luyendijk, J. (2015). *Dit kan niet waar zijn: Onder bankiers.*

Maatschappelijk Overleg Betalingsverkeer. (2017a). *Rapportage 2016.* Amsterdam: MOB.

Maatschappelijk Overleg Betalingsverkeer. (2017b). *Pin-only beleid publieksbalies gemeenten – verzoek aan IPO.* Amsterdam: DNB.

Macfarlane, L., Ryan-Collins, J., Bjerg, O., Nielsen, R., & McCann, D. (2017). *Making money from making money. Seigniorage in the Modern Economy.* London: New Economics Foundation.

Mackintosh, S. P. M. (2014). Crises and paradigm shift. *The Political Quarterly, 85*(4), 406–412.

McKinsey & Company. (2006). *Payment services in the Netherlands: An analysis of revenues and costs for banks. Final report.* Amsterdam: McKinsey & Company.

McLeay, M., Radia, A., & Thomas, R. (2014). Money creation in the modern economy. *Bank of England Quarterly Bulletin, Q1*, 14–27.

Menger, C. (1892). *The origins of money.* Auburn: Ludwig von Mises Institute.

Mersch, Y. (2017). *Digital Base Money: An assessment from the ECB's perspective.* Available at: https://www.ecb.europa.eu/press/key/date/2017/html/sp170116.en.html

Mian, A., & Sufi, A. (2010). Household leverage and the recession of 2007–09. *IMF Economic Review, 58*(1), 74–117.

Mian, A., & Sufi, A. (2014). *House of Debt – How they (and you) caused the great recession, and how we can prevent it from happening again.* Chicago: The University of Chicago Books Press.

Ministry of Finance. (2010). *Kabinetsreactie eindrapport Tijdelijke commissie onderzoek financieel stelsel (Commissie-De Wit)*, Kamerstukken II, 2010–2011, 31980, no. 16.

Ministry of Finance. (2014). *Update on recommendations of De Wit Committee, Annex II to Answers to written questions on Government view of the Dutch banking sector*, Kamerstukken II, 2013–2014, 32013, no. 50.

Ministry of Finance. (2016a). *Kamerbrief over Hervormingen en resultaten in de Nederlandse financiële sector*, Kamerstukken II *2015–2016*, 32013, no. 132.

Ministry of Finance. (2016b). *Kamerbrief overzicht verschillende kapitaaleisen*, Kamerstukken II, 32013, no. 119.

Ministry of Finance. (2018a). *Aankondiging afschaffing fiscale aftrek op vergoeding aanvullend tier 1-kapitaalinstrumenten*, Kamerstukken II, 2017–2018, 32013, no. 195.

Ministry of Finance. (2018b). *Kamerbrief over update akkoord Bazelse Comité*, Kamerstukken II, 2017–2018, 32013, no. 169.

Ministry of Social Affairs and Employment. (2018, May 23). *Actieplan brede schuldenaanpak.*

Minsky, H. P. (1986). *Stabilizing an unstable economy.* New Haven: Yale University Press.

Mitchell-Innes, A. (1913, May). What is Money? *The Banking Law Journal*, 377–408.

Moessner, R., & Allen, W. A. (2010). *Central bank co-operation and international liquidity in the financial crisis of 2008–2009* (BIS Working Paper 310). Basel: Bank for International Settlements.

Moggridge, D. (1992). *Maynard Keynes. An economist's biography.* Abingdon: Routledge.

Mujagic, E. (2015). Burgerinitiatief Ons Geld strijdt voor iets dat we feitelijk al sinds 1971 hebben! *Jalta.* Available at: https://jalta.nl/economie/burgerinitiatief-ons-geld-strijdt-voor-iets-dat-we-feitelijk-al-sinds-1971-hebben/

Muns, S., & Bijlsma, M. (2015). Tail dependence: A cross-study comparison. *Journal of Portfolio Management 41, 3*, 109–116.

Murau, S. (2017). Shadow money and the public money supply: The impact of the 2007–9 financial crisis on the monetary system. *Review of International Political Economy*. https://doi.org/10.1080/09692290.2017.1325765.

Musgrave, R. S. (2014). *The solution is full reserve/100% reserve banking* (MPRA Paper No. 57955).

Myers, S. T. (1977). Determinants of corporate borrowing. *Journal of Financial Economics, 5*(2), 147–175.

National Bank of Belgium. (1957). Bijdrage tot de studie van het statuut der buitenlandse munten. *Tijdschrift voor documentatie en voorlichting 32, 2*(4), 257–375.

Nationale Ombudsman. (2017). *Een onderzoek naar pinbetaling als enige mogelijkheid bij betalingen aan de balie van de gemeente*. The Hague.

Netherlands Authority for Consumers and Markets. (2014). *Barrieres voor toetreding tot de Nederlandse bancaire retailsector*. The Hague: ACM.

Netherlands Court of Audit. (2016). *Brief aan de Tweede Kamer over Ontwikkelingen interventies kredietcrisis*. The Hague: Netherlands Court of Audit.

Nooteboom, B. (2017). *Vertrouwen. Opening naar een veranderende wereld*. Utrecht: Klement.

Nouy, D. (2018, September 18). The European banking sector – Towards a single jurisdiction, Speech by Danièle Nouy, Chair of the Supervisory Board of the ECB, ACPR Conference, "Financial supervision and the role of national authorities in Europe", Paris.

NRC. (2018, March 9). *Rutte noemt banken 'semioverheid' en bedankt bij voorbaat voor commissarispost*. https://www.nrc.nl/nieuws/2018/03/09/verkiezingen-rutte-noemt-banken-semioverheid-en-bedankt-bij-voorbaat-voor-commissarispost-a1595156

NVB. (2009). Code Banken, Amsterdam: NVB.

NVB. (2014). The Dutch Mortgage Market, Memorandum of the Dutch Banking Association.

NVB. (2016). *Banking confidence monitor*. Available at: www.nvb.nl.

Obstfeld, M., & Taylor, A. M. (1998). *The great depression as a watershed: International capital mobility over the long run* (NBER working paper w5960).

OECD. (1997). *The OECD report on regulatory reform* (Sectoral Studies) (Vol. 1). Paris: Organisation for Economic Co-operation and Development.

OECD. (2000). *The service economy*. Paris: Organisation for Economic Co-operation and Development.

OECD. (2011). *OECD at 50 – Evolving paradigms in economic policy making*. Paris: Organisation for Economic Co-operation and Development.

OECD. (2012). *Implicit guarantees for bank debt: Where Do we stand?* Paris: Organisation for Economic Co-operation and Development.

OECD. (2015). *Finance and inclusive growth*. Paris: Organisation for Economic Co-operation and Development.

Ons Geld. (2015). *Initiatieftekst Burgerinitiatief Ons Geld*. Available at: http://onsgeld.nu/burgerinitiatief.pdf

Ons Geld. (2016). *Memorandum over het geldstelsel*. Available at: http://onsgeld.nu/kamerdebat-memo-geldstelsel.pdf

Ordoñez, M. F. (2018, February 6). The future of banking. Secure money and deregulation of the financial system, Speech at the Areces Foundation.

Pagliari, E. (Ed.). (2012). *Making good financial regulation – Towards a policy response to regulatory capture, international centre for financial regulation*. Guildford: Grosvenor House Publishing.

Peekel, M., & Veluwenkamp, J. W. (1984). *Het girale betalingsverkeer in Nederland*. Amsterdam: Nederlands Instituut voor het Bank- en Effectenbedrijf.

Pettifor, A. (2017). *The production of money: How to break the power of the banks*. London: Verso.

Philippon, T., & Reshef, A. (2012, November 1). Wages and human capital in the U.S. financial industry: 1909–2006. *The Quarterly Journal of Economics, 127*(4), 1551–1609.

Phillips, R. J. (2015 [1995]). *The Chicago plan and new deal banking reform*. New York: Routledge.

Pontuch, P. (2014). Private sector deleveraging: where do we stand? *Quarterly Report on the Euro Area 13, 3*, 7–19. European Union Publications Office.

Posthuma, J. E. (1955). Tien Jaar Herstelbank. In *Tien jaar economisch leven in Nederland* (pp. 1–45). The Hague.

Rajan, R. G., & Zingales, L. (2004). Making capitalism work for everyone. *Journal of Applied Corporate Finance, 16*, 101–108.

Reid, J., Nicol, G., Burns, N., & Chanda, S. (2017). *Long-term asset return study. The next financial crisis*. London: Deutsche Bank.

Reinhart, C. M., Reinhart, V., & Rogoff, K. (2015). Dealing with debt. *Journal of International Economics, 96*(Supplement 1), S43–S55.

Richter, W. (2017, July 11). *Cryptocurrencies collapsed*. http://wolfstreet.com/2017/07/11/what-is-going-on-with-crypto-currencies-collapse/

Romer, C. D., & Romer, D. H. (2003). *Choosing the federal reserve chair: Lessons from history* (NBER working paper 10161).

Rousseau, P. L., & Wachtel, P. (2011). What is happening to the impact of financial deepening on economic growth? *Economic Inquiry, 49*(1), 276–288.

Ryan-Collins, J. (2015). *Is monetary financing inflationary? A case study of the Canadian economy, 1935–75* (Levy Institute Working Paper, No. 84).

Sanders, M., & Zhang, L. (2018, October 11). Diversiteit in de financiële sector is van groot belang. *ESB*.

Saravelos, G., Brehon, D., & Winkler, R. (2016, April 15). *Helicopters 101: Your guide to monetary financing* (Deutsche Bank Special Report).

Schelkle, W. (2012). In the spotlight of crisis how social policies create, correct, and compensate financial markets. *Politics & Society, 40*, 3–8.

Schepens, G. (2016). Taxes and bank capital structure. *Journal of Financial Economics, 120*(3), 585–600.

Schmiedel, H., Kostova, G., & Ruttenberg, W. (2012). *The social and private costs of retail payment instruments. A European perspective* (ECB-Occasional Paper Series, no. 137). Frankfurt am Main: DNB.

Schoenmaker, D., & Wierts, P. (2015). *Regulating the financial cycle: An integrated approach with a leverage ratio* (Duisenberg school of finance – Tinbergen Institute Discussion Paper). Amsterdam.

Schularick, M., & Taylor, A. M. (2012). Credit booms gone bust: Monetary policy, leverage cycles, and financial crises, 1870–2008. *American Economic Review, 102*(2), 1029–1061.

SER. (2010). *Overheid én markt: Het resultaat telt! Voorbereiding bepalend voor succes, Advies 10/01*. The Hague: Social and Economic Council.

SER. (2013). *Nederlandse economie in stabieler vaarwater*. The Hague: Social and Economic Council.

Sigurjónsson, F. (2015). *Monetary reform. A better monetary system for Iceland*. Reykjavik.

Skingsley, C. (2016, November). Should the Riksbank issue e-krona?, Speech.

Smits, J. P., Horlings, E., & Van Zanden, J. L. (2000). *Dutch GNP and its components, 1800–1913* (Monograph Series no. 5). Groningen: Groningen Growth and Development Centre.

Sobel, J. (2002). Can we trust social capital? *Journal of Economic Literature, 40*(1), 139–154.

Statistics Netherlands. (2001). *Tweehonderd jaar statistiek in tijdreeksen 1800–1999*. Den Haag: CBS.

Statistics Netherlands. (2009). *Werkloosheid jaren dertig hoogste ooit*. Available at: www.cbs.nl/nl-nl/nieuws/2009/12/werkloosheid-jaren-dertig-hoogste-ooit

Stellinga, B. (2015). *Europese financiële regulering voor en na de crisis* (The Netherlands Scientific Council for Government Policy Working Paper 15). The Hague: Sdu Uitgevers.

Stellinga, B. (2018). *The financial valuation crisis. The inherent limits to taming unstable markets (PhD-manuscript)*. Amsterdam: University of Amsterdam.

Stellinga, B. (2019). Why performativity limits credit rating reform. *Finance and Society, 5*(1), 20–41.

Stellinga, B. (2020). The open-endedness of macroprudential policy. Endogenous risks as an obstacle to countercyclical macroprudential policy. *Business and Politics, 22*(1), 224–251.

Stellinga, B. (2021). The rise and stall of EU macro-prudential policy. An empirical analysis of policy conflicts over financial stability, market integration, and national discretion. *JCMS: Journal of Common Market Studies*. https://doi.org/10.1111/jcms.13195

Stellinga, B., & Mügge, D. (2017). The regulator's conundrum. How market reflexivity limits fundamental financial reform. *Review of International Political Economy, 24*(3), 393–423.

Stichting Full Reserve. (2018). *Mission*. Available at: http://www.fullreserve.nl/page/missie

Stoffer, J. (1986). *Het ontstaan van de NMB*. Deventer: Kluwer.

Sustainable Finance Lab. (2015). *De Geldkwestie*. Utrecht: Sustainable Finance Lab.

Sustainable Finance Lab. (2016). *Publieksonderzoek kennis en wensen geldschepping*. Available at: www.sustainablefinancelab.nl/publieksonderzoek-kennis-en-wensen-over-geldscheppping

Sveriges Riksbank. (2017, September). *The Riksbank's e-krona project, report 1*.

Swiss National Bank. (2018). *Arguments of the SNB against the Swiss sovereign money initiative (Vollgeldinitiative)*.

Tarullo, D. (2008). *Banking on Basel. The future of international financial regulation*. Washington, DC: Peterson Institute for International Economics.

Taylor, A. M. (2012). *The great leveraging* (NBER Working Paper Series 18290). Cambridge, MA: National Bureau of Economic Research.

Temin, P. (1993). Transmission of the great depression. *Journal of Economic Perspectives, 7*(2), 87–102.

The Economist. (2017). *American banks have recovered well; many European ones much less so*. London: The Economist.

The Netherlands Scientific Council for Government Policy. (2000). *Safeguarding the public interest* (WRR report no. 56). The Hague: Sdu Uitgevers.

The Netherlands Scientific Council for Government Policy. (2012). *Public interests in a market society* (WRR report no. 87). Amsterdam: Amsterdam University Press.

The Netherlands Scientific Council for Government Policy. (2013). *Supervising public interests. Towards a broader perspective on government supervision* (WRR report no. 89). Amsterdam: Amsterdam University Press.

The Netherlands Scientific Council for Government Policy. (2014). *Policymaking using behavioural expertise* (WRR report no. 92). Amsterdam: Amsterdam University Press.

The Netherlands Scientific Council for Government Policy. (2016). *Finance and society: Restoring the balance* (WRR report no. 96). The Hague: Sdu Uitgevers.

The Netherlands Scientific Council for Government Policy. (2017). *Why knowing what to do is not enough. A realistic perspective on self-reliance* (WRR report no. 97). Amsterdam: Amsterdam University Press.

Tiemeijer, W. (2016). *Eigen schuld? Een gedragswetenschappelijk perspectief op problematische schulden* (WRR Investigation). Amsterdam: Amsterdam University Press.

Tiemeijer, W. L., Thomas, C. A., & Prast, H. M. (Eds.). (2009). *De menselijke beslisser: over de psychologie van keuze en gedrag* (WRR Investigation). Amsterdam: Amsterdam University Press.

Tijdelijke Commissie Huizenprijzen. (2013). *Kosten koper – Een reconstructie van 20 jaar stijgende huizenprijzen*. The Hague: Sdu Uitgevers.

Tobin, J. (1963). *Commercial banks as creators of 'Money'* (Cowles Foundation Discussion Papers 159). Yale University.

Tobin, J. (1985). Neoclassical theory in America: J. B. Clark and Fisher. *The American Economic Review, 75*(6), 28–38.

Tokmetzis, D. (2013, October 2). Niemand weet wie onze staatsschuld bezit. *de Correspondent*.

Turner, A. (2014). *Escaping the debt addiction: Monetary and macro-prudential policy in the post crisis world*. Frankfurt: Centre for Financial Studies.

Turner, A. (2015). *Between debt and the devil – Money, credit, and fixing global finance*. Princeton: Princeton University Press.

Uittenbogaard, R. (2014). *Evolution of central banking. De Nederlandsche Bank 1814–1852.* Dissertation, Utrecht.

Uittenbogaard, R. (2017). Een korte geschiedenis van regulering van retailbetalingsverkeer. *Economisch en Statistische Berichten, 102*(4753S), 55–61.

van Ark, B., & de Jong, H. (1996). Accounting for economic growth in the Netherlands since 1913. *Economic and Social History in the Netherlands, 7*, 199–242.

van Dalen, H., & Klamer, A. (2015). *Geld.* Amsterdam: Amsterdam University Press.

van der Bie, R. (1997). *Een doorlopende groote roes. De economische ontwikkeling van Nederland, 1913–1921.* Dissertation, Vrije Universiteit Amsterdam.

van der Cruijsen, C., de Haan, J., & Jansen, D.-J. (2013). Trust and financial crisis experiences. *SSRN Electronic Journal.*

van der Sangen, G. J. H. (2012). De evolutie van de coöperatie en haar financiering. In *R.C.E. Galle Handboek Cooperatie*. Dordrecht: Convoy.

van der Sluis, M. (2017). *In law we trust: The role of EU constitutional law in European monetary integration*. Florence: European University Institute.

van der Veer, K., Klaaijsen, E., & Roerink, R. (2015). *Scherper licht op financiële stabiliteitsrisico's van het schaduwbankwezen* (DNB Occasional Studies, 13: 7). Amsterdam: DNB.

van Dijk, M., & Voogt, B. (2017, June 6). *Actualisatie economische effecten van een verdere verlaging van de LTV-limiet* (CPB Background Document to the Financial Markets Risk Report 2017).

van Dixhoorn, C. (2013a). *Full Reserve Banking: An analysis of four monetary reform plans.* Utrecht: Sustainable Finance Lab.

van Dixhoorn, C. (2013b). *The 'Nature' of money: Does our current money system hinder sustainable development?* Master thesis Utrecht University.

van Eekelen, L. J. J. (1987). De ontwikkeling van het solvabiliteitstoezicht van De Nederlandsche Bank. *Maandschrift Economie, 51*, 134–149.

van Eerden, L. A. (2001). Structural regulation of the banking industry in the Netherlands: A shift of power, 1980–95. In M. Bovens, P. 't Hart, & B. G. Peters (Eds.), *Success and failure in public governance. A comparative analysis* (pp. 363–382). Cheltenham/Northampton: Edward Elgar.

van Egmond, N. D., & de Vries, B. J. M. (2016). *Monetaire hervorming; de mogelijkheid van een gezond financieel-economisch bestel.* Available at: www.sustainablefinancelab.nl

van Engelen, W. (2009). *Blauw bloed: Opkomst en ondergang van de Postbank.* Amsterdam: Pearson Education NL.

van Goor, H. H. M. (2001). *Banken en industriefinanciering in de 19e eeuw. De relatie tussen Mees en Stork.* Van den Bergh gaat naar Engeland, Dissertation. Amsterdam.

van Renselaar, C., & Stokman, A. C. J. (2001). *Afscheid van de Nederlandse munt: gulden lessen* (WO&E research report no. 667). Amsterdam: De Nederlandsche Bank.

van Riel, A. (2016). *Het financieel stelsel in historisch perspectief.* The Hague: WRR.

van Riel, A. (2018). *Trials of convergence. Prices, markets and industrialization in the Netherlands, 1800–1913.* Dissertation.

van Zanden, J. L. (1997a). *Een klein land in de twintigste eeuw. Economische geschiedenis van Nederland 1914–1995.* Utrecht: Spectrum.

van Zanden, J. L. (1997b). Old rules, new conditions, 1914–1940. In M. 't Hart, J. Jonker, & J. L. van Zanden (Eds.), *A financial history of The Netherlands* (pp. 124–151). Cambridge: Cambridge University Press.

van Zanden, J. L., & van Riel, A. (2004). *The strictures of inheritance: The Dutch economy in the nineteenth century.* Princeton: Princeton University Press.

van Zwet, J. R. (2001). *De ontwikkeling van de Bankwet 1814–1998. Van 's Konings oudste dogter tot integrerend onderdeel van het ESCB* (WO&E research report 649).

Veldhuizen, S., Groot, S., & Van Dijk, M. (2015). *De economische effecten van een verdere verlaging van de LTV-limiet.* The Hague: CPB Netherlands Bureau for Economic Policy Analysis.

Verhoeven, W. H. J., van Essen, C., Folkeringa, M., Ruis, A., & Smit, C. K. (2010). *Het buffervermogen van het mkb. Omvang, achtergronden en een internationale vergelijking*. Zoetermeer: Panteia.

Vickers report. (2011, September). *Independent commission on banking: Final Report Recommendations*.

Visser, H. (2009). *Islamitisch bankieren: financieren met hindernissen*. Available at: http://www.verenigingrimo.nl/wp/wp-content/uploads/Recht-van-de-Islam-23_11-Visser.pdf

Visser. (2015, May 21). *Praktische kant burgerinitiatief ons geld weinig aantrekkelijk*. Me Judice.

Wallace, T. (2017, September 14). Is the Bank of England running out of rhetorical firepower on interest rates? *The Telegraph*.

Warwick Commission. (2009). *The Warwick Commission on international financial reform: In praise of unlevel playing fields*. Warwick: University of Warwick.

White, W. R. (2008, March 3). Past financial crises, the current financial turmoil, and the need for a new macrofinancial stability framework Speech by Mr William R White, Economic Adviser and Head of Monetary and Economic Department of the Bank for International Settlements, at the LSE Financial Markets Group and Deutsche Bank Conference "The structure of regulation: Lessons from the crisis of 2007", London.

Wijffels Committee. (2013). *Commissie-Structuur Nederlandse Banken: Naar een dienstbaar en stabiel bankwezen*.

Williams, D. G. T. (1968). The evolution of the sterling system. In C. Whittlesey (Ed.), *Essays in money and banking*. Oxford: Clarendon.

Wolf, M. (2014, April 24). Strip private banks of their power to create money. *Financial Times*.

Wolf, M. (2017, September 21). Banking remains far too undercapitalised for comfort. *Financial Times*. Available at: www.ft.com/content/9dd43a1a-9d49-11e7-8cd4-932067fbf946

Wortmann, E. (2017). *Deleverage without a crunch* (Working Paper, Stichting Ons Geld).

Wray, L. R. (2004). *The credit money and state money approaches* (CFEPS Working Paper, no. 32). Kansas City: CFEPS.

Wray, L. R. (2014). *From the state theory of money to modern money theory: An alternative to economic orthodoxy* (Working Paper, Levy Economics Institute, No. 792).

WRR. (2000). *Het borgen van publiek belang*, WRR report nr. 56. Den Haag: Sdu Uitgevers.

WRR. (2012). *Publieke zaken in de marktsamenleving*, WRR report nr. 87. Amsterdam: Amsterdam University Press.

WRR. (2013). *Toezien op publieke belangen. Naar een verruimd perspectief op rijkstoezicht*, WRR report nr. 89. Amsterdam: Amsterdam University Press.

WRR. (2014). *Met kennis van gedrag beleid maken*, WRR report nr. 92. Amsterdam: Amsterdam University Press.

WRR. (2016). *Samenleving en financiële sector in evenwicht*, WRR report nr. 96. Den Haag: Sdu Uitgevers.

WRR. (2017). *Weten is nog geen doen. Een realistisch perspectief op redzaamheid*, WRR report nr. 97. Amsterdam: Amsterdam University Press.

Yamaguchi, K. (2011). Workings of a public money system of open macroeconomies. In *Modeling the American monetary act completed. Paper at the 29th international conference of the system dynamics society*. Washington, DC.

Permissions

All chapters in this book were first published in MDTPRB, by Springer; hereby published with permission under the Creative Commons Attribution License or equivalent. Every chapter published in this book has been scrutinized by our experts. Their significance has been extensively debated. The topics covered herein carry significant information for a comprehensive understanding. They may even be implemented as practical applications or may be referred to as a beginning point for further studies.

The contributors of this book come from diverse backgrounds, making this book a truly international effort. We would like to thank all the contributing authors for lending their expertise to make the book truly unique. They have played a crucial role in the development of this book. Without their invaluable contributions this book wouldn't have been possible. They have made vital efforts to compile up to date information on the varied aspects of this subject to make this book a valuable addition to the collection of many professionals and students.

This book was conceptualized with the vision of imparting up-to-date and integrated information in this field. To ensure the same, a matchless editorial board was set up. Every individual on the board went through rigorous rounds of assessment to prove their worth. After which they invested a large part of their time researching and compiling the most relevant data for our readers.

The editorial board has been involved in producing this book since its inception. They have spent rigorous hours researching and exploring the diverse topics which have resulted in the successful publishing of this book. They have passed on their knowledge of decades through this book. To expedite this challenging task, the publisher supported the team at every step. A small team of assistant editors was also appointed to further simplify the editing procedure and attain best results for the readers.

Apart from the editorial board, the designing team has also invested a significant amount of their time in understanding the subject and creating the most relevant covers. They scrutinized every image to scout for the most suitable representation of the subject and create an appropriate cover for the book.

The publishing team has been an ardent support to the editorial, designing and production team. Their endless efforts to recruit the best for this project, has resulted in the accomplishment of this book. They are a veteran in the field of academics and their pool of knowledge is as vast as their experience in printing. Their expertise and guidance has proved useful at every step. Their uncompromising quality standards have made this book an exceptional effort. Their encouragement from time to time has been an inspiration for everyone.

The publisher and the editorial board hope that this book will prove to be a valuable piece of knowledge for students, practitioners and scholars across the globe.

Index

S

T

U

W

www.ingramcontent.com/pod-product-compliance
Lightning Source LLC
LaVergne TN
LVHW080806220926
848485LV00011B/275
9781647266363